The
THEOLOGY
of
WOLFHART PANNENBERG

The THEOLOGY *of* WOLFHART PANNENBERG

Twelve American Critiques, with an Autobiographical Essay and Response

Carl E. Braaten / Philip Clayton
Editors

AUGSBURG Publishing House • Minneapolis

THE THEOLOGY OF WOLFHART PANNENBERG
Twelve American Critiques, with an Autobiographical Essay and Response

Library of Congress Cataloging-in-Publication Data

The Theology of Wolfhart Pannenberg : twelve American critiques, with
an autobiographical essay and response / Carl E. Braaten and Philip
Clayton, editors.
    p.   cm.
  Bibliography: p.
  ISBN 0-8066-2370-5
  1. Pannenberg, Wolfhart, 1928–   . I. Pannenberg, Wolfhart,
1928–   . II. Braaten, Carl E., 1929–   . III. Clayton, Philip,
1956–   .
BX4827.P3T48 1988
230'.044'0924—dc 19   88-26217
                                                                   CIP

The paper used in this publication meets the minimum requirements of American National Standard for Information Sciences—Permanence of Paper for Printed Library Materials, ANSI Z39.48-1984. ∞™

Manufactured in the U.S.A.   APH 10-6294

1   2   3   4   5   6   7   8   9   0   1   2   3   4   5   6   7   8   9

CONTENTS

◆

PART I: PHILOSOPHICAL AND METHODOLOGICAL CRITIQUES

PART II: THEOLOGICAL CRITIQUES

PART III: APPLICATIONS

CONTRIBUTORS

◆

Carl E. Braaten
Professor of Systematic Theology
Lutheran School of Theology at Chicago
Chicago, Illinois

Philip Clayton
Assistant Professor of Philosophy
Williams College
Williamstown, Massachusetts

John B. Cobb Jr.
Ingraham Professor of Theology
Director, Center for Process Studies
Claremont, California

Avery Dulles, s.j.
Professor of Theology
School of Religious Studies
Catholic University of America
Washington, D.C.

Louis Dupré
T. L. Riggs Professor for the Philosphy of Religion
Department of Religious Studies
Yale University
New Haven, Connecticut

Lewis S. Ford
Professor of Philosophy
School of Arts and Sciences
Old Dominion University
Norfolk, Virginia

STANLEY J. GRENZ
Professor of Systematic Theology
North American Baptist Seminary
Sioux Falls, South Dakota

PHILIP HEFNER
Professor of Systematic Theology
Lutheran School of Theology at Chicago
Chicago, Illinois

ROBERT W. JENSON
Professor of Systematic Theology
Lutheran Theological Seminary
Gettysburg, Pennsylvania

RICHARD JOHN NEUHAUS
Director, The Rockford Institute Center on Religion and Society
New York, New York

TED PETERS
Professor of Systematic Theology
Pacific Lutheran Theological Seminary
Berkeley, California

DAVID P. POLK
Associate Professor of Pastoral Ministry
Brite Divinity School
Texas Christian University
Fort Worth, Texas

GEOFFREY WAINWRIGHT
Professor of Systematic Theology
The Divinity School
Duke University
Durham, North Carolina

PREFACE

◆

A new school has been launched," James M. Robinson wrote in 1967 of Wolfhart Pannenberg's early theology.[1] The "working circle" that had published the collection *Revelation as History* in 1961, Robinson continued, was "the first theological school to emerge in Germany within recent years that is not in one form or the other a development of the dialectic theology of the twenties." Pannenberg, the systematic theologian of the group, was receiving increasing attention in the United States after visiting professorships here in 1963 and 1966–1967. Concluding his essay, Robinson wrote of the growing "impetus" behind the discussion of Pannenberg's theology in America and suggested that "the present volume is only a foretaste of significant things to come."

It has now been 25 years since Pannenberg's first visit to the United States and 20 years since Robinson's essay introduced the first collection of American responses to his work. At that time the discussion with Pannenberg focused on the radically historical character of his proposal for theology, the precise point at which his thought was departing from the reigning rival schools of Karl Barth and Rudolf Bultmann. The issues around which the discussion then turned were revelation and resurrection. In the meantime Pannenberg's thought has retained remarkable continuity with the core of his early writings, but has expanded almost encyclopedically into many of the major disciplines studied in a modern university. Without doubt the most comprehensive theologian at work today, his place in the history of 20th-century theology is well assured. By the end of 1988 some 18 of his books will have appeared in English; he has been the subject of at least 32 English-language doctoral dissertations; and a glance at the bibliography in this volume provides a good idea of the extent of the secondary literature on his thought.

It is therefore time to take some soundings. Have Robinson's predictions been fulfilled? Exactly how deep has Pannenberg's influence been on American theology? Which particular ideas or themes from his work have been most persuasive to American thinkers, and

---

1. *Theology as History,* ed. James M. Robinson and John Cobb Jr. (New York: Harper & Row, 1967), 12-13.

which have encountered the greatest resistance? What implications does his position have beyond explicitly theological contexts—e.g., for philosophy, ethics, environmental concerns, political action, and the natural sciences? What new forms have his ideas taken as they have been adapted to fit the very different context of American discussions of theology and religion?

The authors of the 12 critiques that follow represent a broad cross-section of American thought on religion. The essays cover virtually all of the major areas in which Pannenberg has published. In addition, an introductory survey by Stanley Grenz provides a comprehensive overview of the critical literature on Pannenberg from the early 1960s through 1986. Most of the authors are already known for their contributions in the fields of theology, religious studies, or philosophy. Each has been influenced in some manner by Pannenberg's theological project; yet each brings a critical perspective to his work. Together, they represent, we believe, an accurate barometer of the influence Pannenberg has had in America, as well as the sorts of reservations that English-speaking theology brings to his work.

For other reasons also, the timing for a collection such as this seems auspicious. Pannenberg is approaching the summit of his theological career with the publication of his *Systematische Theologie,* the first volume of which is scheduled for publication in 1988. A German *Festschrift* celebrating Pannenberg's 60th birthday will appear this year, appropriately entitled, *Vernunft des Glaubens: Wissenschaftliche Theologie und kirchliche Lehre,* edited by Jan Rohls and Gunther Wenz (Göttingen: Vandenhoeck & Ruprecht, 1988). Rather than undertake a parallel American *Festschrift,* the editors have sought to engage American theologians in a critical appraisal of Pannenberg's thought. To honor him by means of critiques somehow seems more fitting for a thinker who for over three decades has stressed the role of critical reason in theology.

The editors wish to thank Roland Seboldt and Augsburg Fortress, Publishers, for undertaking this venture at a time when market considerations might seem to favor more cautious projects. The editors also wish to acknowledge their gratitude to their good friend Wolfhart Pannenberg for entering into this conversation with American theologians, and thus advancing our mutual interest in exploring the depth and range of the Christian truth in relation to the intellectual challenges of our age.

Philip Clayton

Carl E. Braaten

AN AUTOBIOGRAPHICAL SKETCH

Wolfhart Pannenberg

◆

The city of my birth, Stettin, was located in the heart of what once was Germany, less than two hours east of Berlin. This place is no longer German, but part of Poland, and it is never without sadness that I remember the place of my birth, which seems so far away now. I spent no more than the first seven years of my life there. After that, my family moved a few hundred miles further to the east, to Schneidemuhl, close to what was then the national border between Germany and Poland. There my father served as customs officer for two years, until we had to move to Aachen, near the western border of Germany, for another four years. During those years, between 1936 and 1942, I read my first historical novels, and my imagination was immersed for many hours in medieval and early modern history. At the age of seven I began piano lessons and during the years at Aachen music became the most important concern in my life, so much so that my father was afraid I might neglect my work at school. I received additional lessons in composition and wrote little pieces of music for myself. I also went as often as I could to listen to the still unknown Herbert von Karajan conducting the Aachen symphony orchestra, which was his regular job during those years. It was also the time, however, when the war started. German troops were moving through the city in May 1940. A few weeks later I stood with my father on the roof of the apartment house where we lived and looked at the city of Aachen in flames all over as a result of an early British air raid.

In 1942 my family moved to Berlin. The next winter, the schools were sent out of the city to the country; I spent the winter with my class in the Silesian mountains, where I learned to ski, and the following summer at the Baltic Sea in eastern Pomerania. During the next winter in Berlin the city increasingly suffered from the air attacks, and on one day in early March 1944 my family lost their home in a western suburb of Berlin, where in one of the first daytime air attacks American planes laid a bomb carpet. We barely escaped and spent the next couple of months with relatives in Pomerania. It was there that I chanced upon my first philosophical book, while searching the public library for some reading in music. The intriguing title of a hitherto unknown author—unknown to me, of course—ran: "The Birth of Tragedy from the Spirit of Music." During the following months I devoured everything written by Nietzsche that I could get hold of. Meanwhile, we had a new home in a small town in that part of the country. My father was finally drafted into the army. In another nearby town I continued my music lessons, went to school, dated my first girl friend. It was a quiet winter until early January 1945. On the sixth of January, while I was walking back home from school (instead of using the train)—a somewhat lengthy walk of several hours—an extraordinary event occurred in which I found myself absorbed into the light of the setting sun and for one eternal moment dissolved in the light surrounding me. When I became aware again of my finite existence, I did not know what had happened but certainly knew that it was the most important event of my life; I spent many years afterwards to find out what it meant to me. But first, a few weeks later, my mother with my three considerably younger sisters had to leave that part of the country in a hurry, together with so many other German civilians, in order to take refuge far away from the rapidly advancing Russian army, west of the Oder river at the town of Wolgast. I went to be a soldier at the age of 16, was trained but saved by scabies from being kept for combat where the comrades of my unit were going to die a few days later, after the Russians had crossed the Oder river. Instead, I was sent with a hospital to Northern Germany, where I was taken prisoner by the British and spent the spring of 1945. Released in early summer, I returned to the East in the early fall, retrieved my family and went to school again for two more years, while we with all the people in that part of the Russian Zone almost starved.

It was only during those two years that I became more attentive at school, but also started reading Kant and writing down my own immature ideas. For the first time in my life—my parents had left the church in the early 1930s—I became interested in studying Christianity, because our teacher in German literature, though a Christian, did not fit the picture of Christian mentality which I had received from Nietzsche. Contrary to my expectations, this teacher obviously enjoyed and appreciated the fullness of human life in all its forms, which he was not supposed to do, according to Nietzsche's description of the Christian mind. I decided that I had to find out about this, still worrying at the meaning of that extraordinary experience of January 6, 1945. Thus, in the spring of 1947 I resolved to enroll at the Humboldt University in East Berlin, not only in philosophy but also in theology. Before long, the exploration of Christianity fascinated me to the degree that I knew I was to be a theologian for the rest of my life, although I continued philosophical studies with at least equal intensity.

I was a student at Berlin for one and one-half years, and there it happened that I was induced by teachers and friends and, most importantly, by an aunt of mine, whom I genuinely admired, to concern myself seriously with Marxism. I tried to read everything from the young Marx to *Das Kapital,* but also Lenin and Stalin. The humanism of Marx's early writings did not fail to impress me deeply. In spite of the first-hand evidence around me, I was fascinated by the intellectual brilliance of a system that offered an explanation for all the facts of life. It took a number of years for me to begin to feel the weight of critical arguments against the economic theories of Marxism. Only then did I become more aware of the ideological function of Marxism as it serves to legitimate an oppressive system of government. At that point, after I had liberated myself from the fascination of Marxist ideas, I did not suspect that my extensive reading in Marxist literature would prove useful in later years of my life—during the student revolution of the late 1960s and, afterwards, with the rising tide of liberation theology.

In the fall of 1948, I went to Göttingen for a year. There I learned from Friedrich Gogarten and from Nicolai Hartmann, the most learned German philosopher of the time. By pure chance, a paper assigned to me in a seminar of Hans Joachim Iwand on Luther introduced me to

13

medieval Scholasticism, which was to become the field of my doctoral work as well as of my Habilitationsschrift. After that year at Göttingen, a scholarship from the World Council of Churches enabled me to spend a term at Basel. Before going to Basel, I had read through all the volumes of Karl Barth's *Church Dogmatics* that had been published up to then. I greatly admired Barth and I never ceased to do so, but at Basel already I was dissatisfied by the lack of philosophical rigor in his thought. My teacher in philosophy at Basel, Karl Jaspers, did not excel in philosophical rigor either, but there was more intuitive evidence and no less breadth of vision.

When I continued my studies at Heidelberg in the fall of 1950, it was my fourth year of theological studies. But I had not yet succeeded, in spite of several attempts, really to involve myself in biblical exegesis in addition to systematics, philosophy, and church history. After attending a few lectures of Gerhard von Rad, however, the dime dropped. I discovered a new world, the traditions and history of ancient Israel, because von Rad was unique in communicating to his audience its exotic charm: the mind of ancient Israel was presented as exotic, but at the same time as more real than the world of our modern experience. In this way the Old Testament, through the aesthetic skill of von Rad's exegesis, came alive in the hearts of innumerable students. On the basis of this experience, finally the New Testament also began to make sense to me. *History* was the code word of biblical exegesis at Heidelberg in those years, and to my ears it was echoed by the lectures of Karl Löwith on philosophy of history. It was a pity, or so it appeared to us students, that systematic theology at Heidelberg was not yet quite up to that new agenda. Thus a group of students tried to find out for themselves what a systematic theology would look like on the basis of von Rad's exegetical vision. This was how the so-called Heidelberg Circle started to work. But it took 10 years of discussions before our new approach to theology in terms of "Revelation as History" was published in 1961. We thought it was one of the less provocative issues we had discussed.

Meanwhile, most of us had left Heidelberg. I had finished my doctoral work on Duns Scotus in 1953, and Edmund Schlink encouraged me to go on with academic work. In order to teach systematics, I had to submit another dissertation, a Habilitationsschrift. Its focus was again in the area of medieval studies, but the subject, the doctrine of analogy, had become important to me since my early attempts to come to grips with the thought of Karl Barth. In 1955 a first draft of a critical history of the concept of analogy—the subject Schlink had advised me to investigate and describe—was accepted by the faculty. I became a docent and continued to work on that project in connection with some of the first lecture courses I offered at Heidelberg. The history of the concept of analogy both in philosophy and theology continued to be the main focus of my research until the early 1960s, when the modest proposal of the Heidelberg Circle to revise the concept of revelation met with unexpected resistance and polemics from all sides so that I decided to rearrange my priorities for publication plans. The history of the analogy concept was never published, but the work in preparation for it has been invaluable in the course of my academic education, because it made me familiar with the history of thought from the pre-Socratics to the modern period.

Also in 1955, I became an ordained minister at the university chapel of Heidelberg, where the members of the faculty took turns in preaching. The year before, I married a student of English and French language and literature whom I had met during my first winter at Heidelberg. Through all the following years my wife devoted her life and energies completely to create the context and style of life that enabled me to concentrate on the development of my work. Without her, I would have never obtained the emotional stability and the discipline that is indispensable in working out the details of an intellectual vision, especially since that vision itself takes shape only in the course of detailed studies.

Among my academic teachers at Heidelberg, I owe abiding gratitude in the first place to Gerhard von Rad, but also to Hans von Campenhausen, who kindled my enthusiasm and admiration for Christian patristic theology, a theology that did not bifurcate faith and reason, and to Edmund Schlink, who advised me in the final phase of my doctoral work and encouraged me to continue in systematic theology. Although I could never persuade myself to conceive of the task of theology in what appeared to me the somewhat narrow limits of confessional Lutheranism, Schlink influenced my thought in important ways, especially by introducing me to ecumenical dialogue and to dialogue with other disciplines, particularly natural science.

My lecture courses at Heidelberg were repeatedly devoted to the history of medieval theology and I could easily have continued in that particular field for the rest of my life. But I also had to teach courses concerned with the Lutheran Reformation and, especially, with the modern history of Protestant theology. It was in this connection that I came to appreciate the importance of Hegel's thought in the development of modern theology, but mainly as a challenge to theology. I never became a Hegelian, but I decided that theology has to be developed on at least the same level of sophistication as Hegel's philosophy and for that purpose I studied his writings carefully and repeatedly. Because my publications also gave evidence of this, the tenacious prejudice of my alleged Hegelianism developed, and it effectively concealed the more important philosophical roots of my thought.

In 1958, I became a professor of systematic theology at the seminary of Wuppertal, where I taught for three years together with Jürgen Moltmann. It was during those years that I started to work on my first strictly systematic projects, anthropology and Christology. But it was only after I was called to the University of Mainz in 1961 that I had to face the task of treating the whole of Christian dogmatics and also ethics. It was an extremely demanding task and it took many years before the whole range of topics began to fit into a systematic scheme. In my experience, the most difficult subject to deal with was the doctrine of God. I soon became persuaded that one first has to acquire a systematic account of every other field, not only theology, but also philosophy and the dialogue with the natural and social sciences before with sufficient confidence one can dare to develop the doctrine of God. In fact, not until the early 1980s did I begin to feel solid ground under my feet in this area. To be sure, I published reflections on the idea of God much earlier, especially in 1967 on God as the power of the future. But that was done in terms of daring extrapolation from other fields of reflection, from Jesus' proclamation of the kingdom and from Wilhelm Dilthey's analysis of the historicity of experience. It is only in a little book on metaphysics and in the first volume of my systematic theology, both forthcoming in the spring of 1988, that I have published an argument which deals with the idea of God in its own right. Everything else, however, remains insecure in theology, before one has made up one's mind on the doctrine of God.

It is not necessary in this introduction to deal extensively with my published work. Nor is there much need to explain why I focused on Christology, anthropology, and theological method as topics of three voluminous books. In my mind, they were necessary stages before I could produce a systematic theology. There are, of course, many other subjects that would have deserved more extensive treatment, but these I considered absolutely indispensable. The same is true, in principle, with metaphysics. Some of my American friends have urged me for many years to work out in more detail the metaphysical implications of my theological approach. A first effort in this direction was presented in 1965, in a lecture course on "Ontology and Eschatology." The encounter with process philosophy during my first trip to America in 1963 as a visiting professor at the University of Chicago was an important incitement to such a venture. But not before I came to terms with the question of how the relevance of Kant's critique of the metaphysical tradition is to be assessed and, especially, what the limitations are of that critique, did I feel it possible seriously to reconsider the metaphysical question. In my view, Whitehead did not take Kant seriously enough. It is only since the early 1980s that the limitations of Kant's critique became clear in my understanding. At the same time, while writing my anthropology book, I became more confident that the principle of self-conscious subjectivity need not be accepted as the final basis for every discussion of metaphysics, as was the case in the entire tradition of German idealism.

The experience of American theology and culture, an experience that was deepened and broadened when I taught as a visiting professor at Harvard in 1966 and at Claremont in early 1967 and again in 1975, but also through lecture tours that brought me to the United States nearly every other year, was important not only in contributing to my philosophical ideas but in many other ways, especially in my understanding of the ecumenical situation of Christianity in terms of cultural heritage and tradition as well as in the interaction of churches. The impact of my American experience, together with my participation in the World Council of Churches, helped me to see my work as a theologian related to the entire Christian community, not just to my own confessional tradition. I am aware, of course, of the Lutheran confessional roots of my thought as well as of the deep connections with the history of German Protestant theology. But I also feel free to criticize what seems too narrow in both. Sometimes I have been accused of continuing to do theology in the Western academic style. I have no qualms to confess to such a sin, if it is considered to be one. In doing theology, each theologian of our time should have in mind the global Christian community. But each of us must do it within his or her own context, while seeking not to be caught in the particularity of that context but to express what can claim universal truth. In the history of the church, each culture that was conquered by the gospel has been turned into an element of the cumulative process of the Christian tradition. In that way contemporary Christians inherited the cultural glories of Greek and Roman antiquity, and our Christian culture was decisive in keeping their memory alive. In a similar way, the Christian culture of the West will remain part of the heritage of Christian churches everywhere.

THE APPRAISAL OF PANNENBERG: A SURVEY OF THE LITERATURE

Stanley J. Grenz

◆

For two and one-half decades the program of Wolfhart Pannenberg has been the subject of debate in theological circles, not only in his own country of Germany, but also in the English-speaking world. Aspects of his theology have been the focal point of some 200 articles in scholarly journals, and his name is mentioned in nearly every book on theology published in recent years.

In his published works Pannenberg has devoted himself primarily to questions of theological method and only secondarily to an explication of his own systematic theology.[1] Despite the fact that in his published works Pannenberg has not yet delineated fully the theological system that arises out of his methodology, its basic direction can be discerned even in his early writings. He is seeking to provide a new direction in theological understanding to combat what he perceives to be a widespread privatization of theology. For him theology is a public discipline, subject to the same critical canons as are the other sciences.

---

1. Some might claim that Pannenberg's Christology, *Jesus—God and Man*, is an exception to this statement. But, given the methodological proposal outlined in the book and the central significance of Christology for Pannenberg, this work may more correctly be seen as a major statement of theological method.

Pannenberg's reception during the last 25 years has been mixed. On the one hand, he has been acclaimed by all as one of the major seminal thinkers of our day. Certain of his proposals have gained adherents among theologians of various persuasions. On the other hand, his work has been the subject of intense debate and criticism. In part because he defies categorization into the traditional schools of theological thought, Pannenberg has been both lauded and criticized by persons from across the theological spectrum. Carl Braaten aptly summarized this phenomenon more than 20 years ago:

> The neo-fundamentalists would enjoy his position on the historical verifiability of the resurrection as a datable event of past history. The orthodox would like the sound of *notitia, assensus,* and *fiducia* but wouldn't know what to do about his antisupernaturalism. *Heilsgeschichte* theologians would endorse his stress on history but would generally not approve of eliminating the prophetic word from the definition of revelation. Historians would applaud his devotion to the facts, but few would succeed in reading revelation right off the facts of history. Those who see Pannenberg's theology as a revival of conservatism need only to meet his doctrine of scripture and of the confessions to be disabused of any illusions. Pannenberg's theology obviously escapes ready-made labels.[2]

Braaten's appraisal, written in 1965, remains appropriate even after more than 20 years of further development in Pannenberg's thought. The one profound change that the intervening time has brought is the changed status of Pannenberg himself. When Braaten wrote these words Pannenberg was seen as a new, young voice from Germany. In the intervening years he has consistently established his reputation, so that today he is a respected theological giant.

The purpose of this article is to survey the reception that Pannenberg has gained in the English-speaking world, especially in the United States, during the last two and one-half decades. More specifically, the criticisms that his work has called forth between 1960 and 1986 will be summarized. This survey of the literature will look almost exclusively at English-language publications, noting the discussions carried out in other languages only insofar as major works have been

---

2. Carl Braaten, "The Current Controversy in Revelation: Pannenberg and His Critics," *Journal of Religion* 45 (1965): 233-234.

translated into English. No attempt will be made to appraise the validity of the criticisms found in the secondary literature nor the extent to which Pannenberg's critics have correctly understood him. This task, while important, is simply too involved for a survey article.

A thematic rather than a chronological approach will be followed. The varied criticisms of Pannenberg's theological program will be discussed under three general headings. The first two sections will focus on the questions surrounding two central aspects of his work: issues of method and foundation and issues of systematic theology. The third section will briefly touch on several additional topics.

I. ISSUES OF METHOD AND FOUNDATION

Because most of Pannenberg's published works have focused primarily on questions of theological method, not systematic theology as such, it is quite natural that the greater number of critical responses to his program have thus far centered on issues of method. Two major subdivisions form a helpful categorization of the various criticisms of Pannenberg's methodology: *(a)* faith and reason and *(b)* hermeneutics and history.

A. *Faith and Reason*

A central foundational issue to theology throughout its history has been the question of the relation between faith and reason. In Pannenberg's view, 20th-century existentialist theologies have tended to compartmentalize reason and faith into separate spheres, thereby shielding faith from the potentially critical findings of reason (i.e., scientific discovery). Pannenberg decries this compartmentalization as an illegitimate privatization of theology. For him faith is not a separate way of knowing truth not open to the scientific method but rather is a personal commitment to the God who can be indirectly seen in history and therefore whose acts are open to scientific confirmation. Quite expectedly, this proposal has been met with opposition.

A first focal point of criticism of Pannenberg's understanding of faith and reason centers on his proposed solution to the problem of "Lessing's ditch," that is, the question posed by Lessing as to how a particular historical event in the past can be of significance for a person living in the present. Pannenberg's solution to this problem centers on his concept of the history of the transmission of traditions. For him there is an inner connectedness in all of history which binds the present to the past, and this because all events are a part of a universal whole, the one process of universal history.

Critics have assailed this solution to the problem of historical connectedness. Pailin, for example, declares that universal history cannot bridge this gulf, because history is not yet complete. It is a story that twists and turns so that, contrary to Pannenberg's assertion, the character of universal history is unknown. Further, he suggests that Pannenberg in effect begs the question, because in actuality universal history lies beyond the concern of the historian.[3] Holwerda criticizes Pannenberg at this point as well, declaring this to be a chief difficulty in his proposal. In Holwerda's estimation Pannenberg has not overcome the problem of the transition from the probabilities of historical reason to the certainty of faith.[4]

Related to this criticism is the question of faith stance and historical research. In this connection Apczynski notes that the final verification of theological truth claims is eschatological. Yet particular religious truth claims are judged in the present by means of human experience. This, however, presupposes the ability to understand the truth claims of a religious tradition provided by the experience of faith.[5] Similarly Obitts suggests that some faith stance is presupposed in Pannenberg's contention that event and meaning are united.[6] Obayashi accuses Pannenberg of making faith a cognitive substitute, because in his system a person hopes his or her knowledge will be justified in the future.[7]

---

3. David Pailin, "Lessing's Ditch Revised: The Problem of Faith and History," in *Theology and Change*, ed. R. Preston (London: SCM, 1975), 97-98. See also Daniel Fuller, *Easter Faith and History* (Grand Rapids: Eerdmans, 1965), 184-187.

4. David Holwerda, "Faith, Reason and the Resurrection in the Theology of Wolfhart Pannenberg," in *Faith and Rationality,* ed. Alvin Plantinga and Nicholas Wolterstorff (Notre Dame: University of Notre Dame Press, 1983), 306.

5. John V. Apczynski, "Integrative Theology: A Polanyian Proposal for Theological Foundations," *Theological Studies* 40/1 (March 1979): 34-35.

6. Stanley Obitts, "Apostolic Eyewitnesses and Proleptically Historical Revelation," in *The Living and Active Word of God,* ed. M. Inch and R. Youngblood (Winona Lake, Ind.: Eisenbrauns, 1983), 137-149.

7. H. Obayashi, "Pannenberg and Troeltsch: History and Religion," *Journal of the American Academy of Religion* 38 (1970): 191-203.

In the early discussion between Pannenberg and several American theologians, this point was raised by Grobel. He claims that the way in which an individual understands and assimilates a "brute fact" does not arise from the fact, as is the case in Pannenberg's view as understood by Grobel, but is brought to it. Grobel terms this process of understanding "faith."[8]

Central to Pannenberg's methodology is the resurrection of Jesus, which for Pannenberg is the prolepsis of the eschatological revelation of the meaning of universal history. The various criticisms of this point will be addressed at length later. In the present context, however, it is significant to note that even this event has been seen by his critics as an illustration of the bringing of faith to an event. Thus, Scaer declares Pannenberg's claim that the Christ event is the appearance of the future in history is in actuality not a historical but a theological assertion.[9] In short, Pannenberg is charged with imposing faith on reason,[10] while not seeing clearly that faith is in actuality an aid to the assimilation of history.[11]

Pannenberg has repeatedly been described as a rationalist. Several conservative critics have found aspects of his rationalistic approach problematic for the relation between faith and reason. For them Pannenberg has failed to see that the human problem of spiritual blindness goes deeper than merely a lack of historical evidence. Rather, there is in humans a moral bias toward evil that interferes with the rational process and makes the task of reading revelation in history difficult.[12] Thus he has been accused of holding a deficient view of the fall, which fails to take seriously its noetic effect[13]—spiritual blindness.[14]

---

8. Kendrick Grobel, "Revelation and Resurrection," in *Theology as History*, ed. James M. Robinson and John B. Cobb Jr., volume 3 of New Frontiers in Theology (New York: Harper & Row, 1967), 161. See also H. Harder and W. T. Stevenson, "The Continuity of History and Faith in the Theology of W. Pannenberg: Toward an Erotics of History," *Journal of Religion* 51 (1971): 51-53.

9. David P. Scaer, "Theology of Hope," in *Tensions in Contemporary Theology*, ed. Stanley Gundry and Alan F. Johnson (Chicago: Moody, 1976), 225.

10. Holwerda, "Faith, Reason and the Resurrection in the Theology of Wolfhart Pannenberg," 287-292.

11. Laurence W. Wood, "History and Hermeneutics: A Pannenbergian Perspective," *Wesley Theological Journal* 16 (Spring 1981): 19.

12. J. Robert Ross, "Historical Knowledge as a Basis for Faith," *Zygon* 13 (Spring 1978): 209-224.

13. Fred H. Klooster, "Aspects of Historical Method in Pannenberg's Theology," in *Septuagesimo Anno: G. C. Berkouwer*, ed. J. T. Bakker et al. (Kampen, 1973), 126.

14. Scaer, "Theology of Hope," 219.

In addition to criticisms related to Pannenberg's understanding of the problem of faith and reason, concern has been expressed over Pannenberg's understanding of revelation. Evangelical scholars have repeatedly faulted him for minimizing the Bible as divine revelation.[15] Certain criticisms relate to his hesitancy to use the concept of revelatory word.[16] Although the main target of Pannenberg's hesitancy is the "new hermeneutic" of Ebeling and Fuchs, evangelicals have seen therein a deprecation of the prophetic word as divine communication.[17] For these theologians revelation is not simply found in events which convey their own significance. Rather, the events must be interpreted by competent spokespersons (prophets) to whom the significance of events has been given by God.[18] Bloesch goes even so far as to assert, contra Pannenberg, that according to historical evangelical theology revelation is not open to general reasonableness but is disclosed only to the ears and eyes of faith.[19]

Critics suggest that this slighting of the prophetic word results in additional problems. Henry claims dogmatics is thereby made totally dependent on historiography.[20] In Scaer's estimation the Reformation position, which links law and gospel to revelation, is undercut.[21] Pannenberg's view constitutes a one-sided emphasis on historical event as revelation, according to Wood, who declares that not all knowledge is historical.[22] Dulles maintains that Pannenberg's position dooms humanity to being deprived of revelation. He proposes that Pannenberg give more attention to a theology of signs, testimony, and faith. And against what he perceives to be the thrust of Pannenberg's enterprise, he suggests that the divine communication in events is best interpreted

---

15. E.g., Klooster, "Aspects of Historical Method in Pannenberg's Theology," 116, 122.

16. See also Carl Braaten, "The Current Controversy on Revelation," *Journal of Religion* 45 (1965): 234-235.

17. Wood, "History and Hermeneutics: A Pannenberg Perspective," 17; Clark H. Pinnock, "Pannenberg's Theology: Reasonable Happenings in History," part 1, *Christianity Today* 21 (November 5, 1976): 22.

18. Carl F. H. Henry, *Frontiers in Modern Theology* (Chicago: Moody, 1964, 1965), 73.

19. Donald Bloesch, *Essentials of Evangelical Theology* (San Francisco: Harper & Row, 1978), I: 54; II: 267.

20. Carl F. H. Henry, *God, Revelation and Authority* II (Waco: Word, 1976), 304.

21. Scaer, "Theology of Hope," 220.

22. Wood, "History and Hermeneutics: A Pannenbergian Perspective," 18.

by persons who are qualified by grace, rather than by the technical historian.[23]

Pannenberg's emphasis on the universal character of revelation leaves little room for the traditional category of special revelation. Some critics have questioned how this view is compatible with the divine working with Israel. Scaer, for example, claims that the Bible underscores God's sovereign election of Israel apart from any human ability possessed by the nation. In fact, the Scriptures suggest that Israel was characterized by spiritual ignorance. But Scaer finds in Pannenberg indication that Israel was able to acquire a special consciousness of history.[24] Fuller suggests that the way out of this problem—how the totality of history reveals God but only to a select few— would be resolved by the inclusion into Pannenberg's system of the concept of two-story history.[25]

Related to this is the problem of the nature of illumination. Pannenberg has repeatedly been criticized for minimizing the role of the Holy Spirit in the epistemological process of grasping the revelation of God in history. This criticism has come from a wide variety of scholars, including evangelicals (Fuller, Holwerda, Wood, Beegle), Roman Catholics (McDermott), and mainline Protestants (Hamilton). Fuller, for example, points to Paul's speech in Athens as the place where Pannenberg's system would most expect a response of faith. Yet Paul's words fell on deaf ears. The working of the Spirit was the missing element, Fuller maintains against Pannenberg, in whose system no such supernatural element must be added to the historical event carrying its own inherent meaning.[26] In a similar assessment Hamilton charges Pannenberg with substituting proper methodology for the Spirit.[27]

McDermott, moving beyond mere negative criticism, offers a theological reason for the need of the Spirit in the knowing process. Pannenberg, he maintains, has underestimated the obscurity of faith's object, thereby neglecting the dimension of divine mystery. God is

---

23. Avery Dulles, *Models of Revelation* (Garden City, N.Y.: Doubleday, 1983), 64-66.
24. Scaer, "Theology of Hope," 221.
25. Daniel Fuller, *Easter Faith and History*, 252.
26. Ibid., 186.
27. William Hamilton, "The Character of Pannenberg's Theology," *Theology as History*, 188.

mystery to humans not only because of sin, but also because of God's infinite nature. Thus, the Spirit is needed not only to overcome sin but also to attune the human person to the things of God.[28]

Related but somewhat different approaches are suggested by other critics. Parker is an example of those who would give more emphasis to the role of the church in the process of illumination. He awaits in Pannenberg's future writings a delineation of the place of the church in theologizing about faith and history.[29] Thomsen, following a more existentialist approach, finds Pannenberg's historical methodology simply erroneous. He sees in Jesus' life a self-authenticating claim of grace. Once this grace is experienced the believer is able to agree with the conclusions of Pannenberg's historical research.[30]

It is precisely this existential aspect of faith which many critics find absent in Pannenberg.[31] Yet others indicate that this dimension is not totally lacking. Parker, for example, suggests that the German theologian, rather than being unaware of the faith dimension, is in actuality attempting only to caution against the view that sees faith as bringing some kind of additional knowledge.[32]

Perhaps the major difference between Pannenberg and his critics concerning faith and reason has been disclosed in Holwerda's criticism. Pannenberg, he maintains, erroneously presupposes the autonomy of reason, which leads to an internal dilemma. In the end he must either assume an epistemology which is contrary to his dominant thesis that faith is not an avenue of knowledge or he must acknowledge that he has not fully escaped subjectivism.[33]

B. History and Hermeneutics

Since the reopening of the discussion in the 19th century, the question of hermeneutic(s) has gained increasing importance in theology.

---

28. B. McDermott, "The Personal Unity of Jesus and God according to W. Pannenberg" (dissertation, Nijmegen, 1973), 277-278.

29. Thomas D. Parker, "Faith and History: A Review of Wolfhart Pannenberg's *Jesus— God and Man," McCormick Quarterly* 22 (1968): 74-75.

30. M. Thomsen, "Lordship of Jesus and Theological Pluralism," *Dialog* 11 (1972): 125-132.

31. E.g., H. Obayashi, "Future and Responsibility: A Critique of Pannenberg's Eschatology," *Studies in Religion* 1 (1971): 191-203. See also P. G. Hodgson, "Pannenberg on Jesus," *Journal of the American Academy of Religion* 36 (1968): 374-375.

32. Parker, "Faith and History," 72-73.

33. Holwerda, "Faith, Reason and the Resurrection in the Theology of Wolfhart Pannenberg," 306-309.

Through his early articles and more recently in his book *Theology and the Philosophy of Science* Pannenberg has shown himself to be an important party to the more recent debate. In fact, one important aspect of his overall program is the historical hermeneutic he advocates.

Several writers have discussed Pannenberg's relation to the leading figures in the hermeneutical discussion. For example, he has been portrayed as seeking a third way between the position of Barth on the one hand and Heidegger and Gadamer[34] on the other, and this by means of the category of universal history.

Halsey offers a lengthy interaction with this topic. He maintains that Pannenberg has failed in this task, because the German theologian sees the strengths and weaknesses in each of the other two alternatives.[35] Halsey suggests that in Pannenberg's concept of universal history the interpreter stands over against the text as one outside of history because the interpretation of the revelation found in history is eschatological and thereby lies outside of history. In this way Pannenberg has not eliminated the dualism he finds in Barth, for the subject–object schema remains. The Barthian position is likewise not overcome by Pannenberg in that the latter's instrumental philosophy of knowledge continues Barth's dualism between scientific and theological language. At the same time, Pannenberg's view approaches the concept of the non-objectifying character of language present in Gadamer by maintaining that statements about God are doxological. But Halsey asks how such statements can objectify. This point is raised likewise by Henry, who suggests that the concept of doxological statements scuttles the universal validity and cognitive truth status of statements about God.[36]

Pannenberg's relation to the 19th-century philosophers of history has sparked the interest of several critics. His use of Hegel, for example, has been the subject of debate. On the one hand, some critics

---

34. Pannenberg's relationship to Gadamer has been delineated by Ted Peters, "Truth in History: Gadamer's Hermeneutics and Pannenberg's Apologetic Method," *Journal of Religion* 55 (January 1975): 36-56.

35. Jim S. Halsey, "History, Language and Hermeneutics: The Synthesis of Wolfhart Pannenberg," *Westminster Theological Journal* 41 (Spring 1979): 284-289.

36. Henry, *God, Revelation and Authority*, III: 294.

have sought to point out the presence of Hegelian themes in Pannenberg's work.[37] Pasquariello sees Pannenberg's emphasis on prolepsis as a development from his acceptance of Hegel's contention that "truth is the whole."[38] Similarly, Olson finds Hegelian elements in Pannenberg's Christology.[39] On the other hand, Westphal calls Pannenberg "the most articulate anti-Hegelian since Kierkegaard."[40]

Likewise, critics have discussed Pannenberg's relation to the English philosopher of history, Collingwood. Hogan, for example, finds in Pannenberg occasional misunderstandings in the application of Collingwood's program.[41] Nicol interacts with five principles he discovers in Pannenberg's use of the historical critical method to develop a theology of history. Two of these, openness to the world as an anthropological given and apocalyptic as having permanent validity, entail an unacknowledged, concealed a priori understanding of faith in Pannenberg's position, Nicol suggests. According to Nicol, openness to the world may mean that new events could transpire which would have the power to shatter the apocalyptic tradition, a threat which Pannenberg, in his judgment, seems to deny.[42]

Both of the principles discussed by Nicol have been questioned by others. Murdock develops a radical critique of Pannenberg's understanding of apocalypticism.[43] The end of history anticipated in apocalypticism did not entail the goal *(telos)* of history, as in Pannenberg's

---

37. Galloway finds points of comparison and of contrast between Pannenberg and Hegel. Allan D. Galloway, *Wolfhart Pannenberg,* Contemporary Religious Thinkers Series, H. D. Lewis, ed. (London: George Allen & Unwin Ltd., 1973), esp. 25ff., 37, 113ff. See also Allan D. Galloway, "The New Hegelians," *Religious Studies* 8 (1972): 367-371.

38. Ronald D. Pasquariello, "Pannenberg's Philosophical Foundations," *Journal of Religion* 56 (1976): 338-347. See also Cornelius P. Venema, "History, Human Freedom and the Idea of God in the Theology of Wolfhart Pannenberg," *Calvin Theological Journal* 17 (April 1982), and W. Hill, *The Three Personed God* (Washington, D.C.: Catholic University of America Press, 1982), 155-157.

39. Roger E. Olson, "The Human Self-Realization of God: Hegelian Elements in Pannenberg's Christology," *Perspectives in Religious Studies* 13 (1986): 207-223.

40. Merold Westphal, "Hegel, Pannenberg, and Hermeneutics," *Man and World* 4 (1971): 276-293.

41. John P. Hogan, "The Historical Imagination and the New Hermeneutic: Collingwood and Pannenberg," in *The Pedagogy of God's Image,* ed. R. Masson (Chico, Calif.: Scholars Press, 1982), 9-30, esp. 23-25.

42. Ian G. Nicol, "Facts and Meanings: Wolfhart Pannenberg's Theology as History and the Role of the Historical-Critical Method," *Religious Studies* 12 (June 1976): 129-139.

43. William R. Murdock, "History and Revelation in Jewish Apocalypticism," *Interpretation* 21 (1967), esp. 176-187.

understanding, but rather the judgment of individuals and the destruction of the present aeon (i.e., the destruction of history). Likewise, Pannenberg's proposal does not accurately reflect the apocalyptic view, Murdock maintains, in that the concept of revelation in apocalypticism was not the indirect divine revelation in history, but a divine wisdom of the mysteries and secrets of God, and this because of the discontinuity between the ages. The apocalypticists located present revelation in word and sign, which would be fulfilled by an eschatological revelation in deeds and wonders. Murdock concludes that Pannenberg's concept is a modified idealism that reflects neither the Old Testament nor the apocalyptic understanding of history and revelation.

Pannenberg's concept of universal history, which lies at the center of his proposal, has been criticized from various quarters. Narrative theologian Stroup builds on the evaluation of James Barr, who finds three weaknesses in Pannenberg's concept of revelation in history, when viewed from the perspective of the Old Testament. Barr claims that this is neither the only nor the normative theme of Scripture. In fact, some biblical speeches are seen as the preconditions of divine acts. And even the category of history is not applicable to all narrative in the Old Testament.[44] For Stroup universal history is not the sphere in which God's word is heard. Rather this occurs in a particular narrative history.[45]

Song, speaking from a third-world perspective, claims that Pannenberg's concept of history is Western, thereby raising the question as to its value for the third world.[46] This criticism is voiced in a different manner by Henry, who suggests that Pannenberg does not expound the implication of universal history for the history of the nations. He also wonders why Pannenberg has chosen the particular history of Israel, as opposed to exposing the revelation found in some other national history.[47]

The implications of the concept of history for both the present and the future have been the subjects of scrutiny by critics. Bloesch

---

44. As summarized in George W. Stroup, *The Promise of Narrative Theology* (Atlanta: John Knox, 1981), 57.
45. Ibid., 243.
46. C. S. Song, *The Compassionate God* (Maryknoll, N.Y.: Orbis, 1982), 60-62.
47. Henry, *God, Revelation and Authority*, II: 300.

sees a nonsupernatural event in Pannenberg's concept of the kingdom of God as the meaning of universal history. For Pannenberg, he maintains, the kingdom is not the supernatural intervention of God into history, but merely the destiny of present society.[48] According to Burhenn, Pannenberg is not engaged in theology of history at all, for in his estimation the German theologian does not indicate the direct value of Christ as prolepsis for the writing of history today.[49]

American process theologians have been outspoken critics of Pannenberg's concept of universal history, especially his insistence that there is an absolute end to the historical process. This understanding and the related theme of the retroactive power of the future on the past are seen by Ford as contradicting Pannenberg's assertion of the radically open-ended nature of history.[50] Likewise, Pannenberg's claim that the kingdom of God becomes a present reality, Ford maintains, contradicts the concept of God as the power of an absolute inexhaustible future. James finds unconvincing the assertion that a particular event consummates the history of creation, when viewed from the perspective of the universe in its entirety.[51] In an unexpected turn Williams declares untenable Pannenberg's expectation of a final event, based on the biblical image of lostness and on the ethical notion of love as the acceptance of risk. He suggests that Pannenberg's position requires that one embrace universalism, a move Williams is hesitant to make.[52]

Several theologians have found the resurrection of humanity as the symbol of the end of universal history to be problematic. Cobb sees therein a deprecation of history and a contradiction to the contemporary sense that human history may end in an explosion whereas

---

48. Bloesch, *Essentials of Evangelical Theology*, II: 176; *The Evangelical Renaissance* (Grand Rapids: Eerdmans, 1973), 36.

49. Herbert Burhenn, "Pannenberg's Doctrine of God," *Scottish Journal of Theology* 28 (1975): 546.

50. Lewis S. Ford, "Whiteheadian Basis for Pannenberg's Theology," *Encounter* 38 (Autumn 1977): 313. A similar criticism is raised by Robert Jenson, *The Triune Identity* (Philadelphia: Fortress, 1982), 172.

51. Ralph E. James Jr., "Process Cosmology and Theological Particularity," in *Process Philosophy and Christian Thought*, ed. D. Brown (Indianapolis: Bobbs-Merrill,1971), 403. See also R. P. Roth, *The Theater of God* (Philadelphia: Fortress, 1985), 7.

52. Daniel Day Williams, "Response to Pannenberg," in *Hope and the Future of Man*, ed. Ewert H. Cousins (Philadelphia: Fortress, 1972), 86-87.

the cosmos may continue forever. The bodiliness of Pannenberg's symbol likewise promotes a private individuality which Cobb finds untenable.[53] Clark calls the symbol "frustrating" rather than healing.[54] For him, if there is an eschaton which includes a general resurrection, then the distinction between humanity and God is imperceptible.

Finally, Gilkey calls into question the entire approach that looks to history for the basis for a theological system. Pannenberg, he maintains, sees nature as "secular" and history as theological. But this approach is for Gilkey an optical illusion. The jump from humanist to theological categories is as difficult in historical inquiry as it is in science.[55]

II. ISSUES OF SYSTEMATIC THEOLOGY

Prior to the appearance in print of Pannenberg's projected dogmatics, discussions of his doctrinal formulations are somewhat premature. Although his writings to date have touched on certain aspects of systematic theology, his statements do not constitute a delineation of his full understanding of Christian doctrine. Foundational to Pannenberg's thought, however, are several interrelated theological propositions, including the following: God is defined as the power that determines everything. The human person is seen as a naturally religious being. The focal point of God's self-revelation is the historical process. Although God's self-disclosure is found at the end of history, it is proleptically present in Jesus' resurrection. These (and all) theological statements are not known merely by an act of faith apart from the explorations of reason, but rather are subject to critical inquiry.

As would be expected, one finds in the critical literature relatively little interaction with Pannenberg's views on the major topics of dogmatics. There are, however, two significant exceptions, (a) the doctrine of God and (b) Christology. Pannenberg's writings, even the primarily methodological works, repeatedly touch on, and at times even focus on these subjects. For this reason critical appraisal is more abundant.

---

53. John B. Cobb Jr., *Christ in a Pluralistic Age* (Philadelphia: Westminster, 1975), 250.
54. W. Royce Clark, "Christian Images of Fulfillment: Healing within Anticipation," *Religion in Life* 46 (Summer 1977): 186-197.
55. Langdon Gilkey, *Reaping the Whirlwind* (New York: Seabury, 1976), 336, n. 4.

It must be kept in mind, however, that even here Pannenberg's purpose seems to be directed more to questions of methodology than to the explication of doctrine.[56]

A. The Doctrine of God

Although Pannenberg has not produced a full-length treatise on the doctrine of God, his writings interact with issues in this area, revealing to some extent his positions. Pannenberg's critics have centered on four aspects of this doctrine.

1. In keeping with his revision of traditional ontology, Pannenberg describes God as the power of the future and as the reality that determines everything. Some critics, however, question the clarity of the concept.[57] They point out that Pannenberg has yet to offer a clear delineation of the "ontological priority of the future." Others question the necessity of this radical revision in ontology to achieve the theological progress Pannenberg desires.[58]

Frequently the question is raised as to whether Pannenberg seeks to speak only epistemologically (God does not yet exist in human knowledge) or also ontologically (God does not yet exist in fact).[59] Scharlemann probes even further, however, questioning the legitimacy of what he views as Pannenberg's proposal of a specific definition of God. He finds "the power that determines everything" to be an arbitrary definition.[60] Koenig chides Pannenberg for not writing more "personalistically" about God,[61] and proposes that a more biblical formulation would speak of God as "having" power over the future

---

56. To date the closest to a doctrinal work is his *Apostles' Creed in the Light of Today's Questions,* which is actually directed to a lay audience.

57. Philip Clayton, "The God of History and the Presence of the Future," *Journal of Religion* 65 (January 1985): 105-106; David McKenzie, "Pannenberg on God and Freedom," *Journal of Religion* 60/3 (July 1980): 307-329. See also Elizabeth Johnson, "Resurrection and Reality in the Thought of Wolfhart Pannenberg," *Heythrop Journal* 24 (1983): 15-17.

58. Clayton, "The God of History and the Presence of the Future," 106-107.

59. Cornelius P. Venema, "History, Human Freedom and the Idea of God in the Theology of Wolfhart Pannenberg," 75-76; Burhenn, "Pannenberg's Doctrine of God," 539.

60. R. Scharlemann, *The Being of God* (New York: Seabury, 1981), 108-109.

61. A. Konig, *Here Am I* (Grand Rapids: Eerdmans, 1982), 197.

or as "keeping his promises." Liberation theologians, following Moltmann, see in Pannenberg's focus on futurity as God's mode of being
a lack of emphasis on God as the one who suffers.[62]

Pannenberg's concept of the future as God's mode of existence
has brought negative responses from opposite ends of the theological
spectrum. Bloesch maintains against modern theology in general and
Pannenberg in particular that God is an existing being.[63] Gilkey declares
that the trend to move God to the future divests present experience of
any relation to the divine and provides no theological ground for political action.[64]

A softer criticism is offered by Jenson, who faults the German
theologian's "contortion of time," which, however, moves in the right
direction, he agrees.[65] McKenzie, in contrast, is more radical in his
criticism. He virtually dismisses Pannenberg's entire concept of God
as the reality that determines everything, suggesting that process theology provides a more conducive setting for the crucial ideas in his
work.[66]

2. Pannenberg's emphasis on God as the power of the future has
evoked a repeated questioning of the value of this understanding for
the problem of causality. Burhenn sees Pannenberg's concept as unable
to reconcile the general and special providence of God. He also asks
concerning the implications of the concept for God's ability to act
positively in the world.[67] Kaiser calls the system a "Calvinism in reverse,"[68] and Hefner declares that in such an understanding God's
power leaves no role for human will.[69] Hill raises two questions of

---

62. Jon Sobrino, *Christology at the Crossroads* (Maryknoll, N.Y.: Orbis, 1978), 78, n. 28;
Jürgen Moltmann, *On Human Dignity* (Philadelphia: Fortress, 1984), 112, n. 6.

63. Bloesch, *Essentials of Evangelical Theology,* 1:31.

64. Gilkey, *Reaping the Whirlwind,* 234-236. For Pannenberg's understanding of the relationship of past and future to the present, see also John B. Cobb Jr., "Past, Present, and Future,"
Theology as History, 219.

65. Robert W. Jenson, *The Triune Identity,* 177.

66. David McKenzie, "Pannenberg on God and Freedom," 307-329.

67. Burhenn, "Pannenberg's Doctrine of God," 539-542.

68. C. Kaiser, *The Doctrine of God,* (Westchester, Ill.: Crossway, 1982), 123.

69. P. Hefner, "The Concreteness of God's Kingdom: A Problem for the Christian Life,"
Journal of Religion 51/3 (July 1971): 195-199.

internal consistency: Is this not a covert endowing of God with actuality? And why does God not thereby become the Lord of the present in both its achievements and its failures?[70]

The discussion of the causality concept in Pannenberg's doctrine of God has led some to conclude that he has not solved the problem of evil nor of human freedom.[71] The relationship of God as the power of the future to the concept of freedom has likewise been the subject of scrutiny. Jentz, for example, finds Pannenberg's view as not so much a reasoned argument showing God to be the highest form of personal freedom as simply defining God in this way.[72] Others concentrate on Pannenberg's concept of human freedom. McKenzie finds Pannenberg denying human free will in the form of freedom of "indifference," a denial which he claims results in a loss of attractiveness for Pannenberg's concepts of "openness to the world" and the future determinative power of God.[73]

3. Pannenberg's doctrine of God has been criticized in terms of its implications for the divine attributes. He links God and human history much more closely than is the case in traditional theology. Venema questions how Pannenberg can avoid Hegel's view which sees universal history as necessary for the being of God.[74] Hill finds Pannenberg equating God with history, insofar as history is the unfolding of the being of God.[75] Process theologian Cobb declares that Pannenberg's concept is nontheistic, in that God becomes but another name for the end of history itself which is the general resurrection.[76] This is evident, Cobb declares, in Pannenberg's equating of God's deity with

70. William J. Hill, *The Three Personed God* (Washington, D.C.: Catholic University of America Press, 1982), 161.

71. Gilkey, *Reaping the Whirlwind*, 234-236. C. Kaiser, *The Doctrine of God*, 123.

72. Arthur H. Jentz Jr., "Personal Freedom and the Futurity of God: Some Reflections on Pannenberg's 'God of Hope,' " *Reformed Review* 31 (1978): 151.

73. McKenzie, "Pannenberg on God and Freedom," 325-326. See also Roger E. Olson, "Pannenberg's Theological Anthropology: A Review Article," *Perspectives in Religious Studies* 13 (1986): 164.

74. Venema, "History, Human Freedom and the Idea of God in the Theology of Wolfhart Pannenberg," 75.

75. Hill, *The Three Personed God*, 157.

76. J. B. Cobb Jr., "Wolfhart Pannenberg's *Jesus—God and Man*," *Journal of Religion 49* (1969): 200-201.

God's rule over creation, which rule is eschatological. Pinnock concludes that Pannenberg's choice of words in speaking about the being of God is "unwise."[77]

Some critics maintain that Pannenberg's program results in a misunderstanding of God's eternality. For Hill, Pannenberg's virtual identification of God with history no longer conceives of God as eternal in the sense of being timeless,[78] a view which in turn undermines history.[79] Hill further suggests that Pannenberg can only speak of God "for me"; of God as he is in himself nothing can be said.[80]

Pannenberg's view is judged as incapable of doing justice to other aspects of the divine being as well. God's "otherness from creation" is left unclear, according to Clayton.[81] The biblical concept of God's absence is not taken into account in Pannenberg's proposal, Koenig declares.[82] Burhenn echoes this by asking to what degree God is now absent.[83]

4. Finally, Pannenberg's conception of the doctrine of the Trinity has been the subject of criticism. Hanson characterizes it as an extreme form of the Latin or relational view.[84] Olson, in contrast, emphasizes the eschatological nature of Pannenberg's understanding of the immanent Trinity; the unity of the trinitarian persons is based on their self-differentiation in the work of the kingdom of God.[85]

A most penetrating interaction with Pannenberg's doctrine is offered by Hill. He maintains that the German theologian's trinitarianism is neither doctrine nor kerygma, but rather doxology.[86] Further, he sees Pannenberg's view as ultimately nontrinitarian. The Spirit is not understandable as a distinct person in the Godhead, but rather as the Word embracing the believer. In fact, for Pannenberg God is, in the final

---

77. Clark H. Pinnock, "Pannenberg's Theology," Part 2: "No-Nonsense Theology," *Christianity Today* 21 (November 19, 1976): 16. See also Konig, *Here Am I*, 195-196.
78. William J. Hill, "The Historicity of God," *Theological Studies* 45 (June 1984): 323. See also Hill, *The Three Personed God*, 159.
79. Hill, "The Historicity of God," 324.
80. Hill, *The Three Personed God*, 157.
81. Clayton, "The God of History and the Presense of the Future," 105.
82. Konig, *Here Am I*, 195-196.
83. Burhenn, "Pannenberg's Doctrine of God," 547.
84. Anthony T. Hanson, *Grace and Truth* (London: SPCK, 1975), 87.
85. Roger E. Olson, "Trinity and Eschatology: The Historical Being of God in Jürgen Moltmann and Wolfhart Pannenberg," *Scottish Journal of Theology* 36 (1983): 213-227.
86. Hill, *The Three Personed God*, 162-166.

analysis, not three persons, but one person, according to Hill. Mc-Dermott concludes that at this stage Pannenberg's trinitarian theology is "sorely underdeveloped,"[87] at least in his published works.

B. Christology

By far the most controversial and most discussed aspect of Pannenberg's proposal is his Christology. Two major and several minor aspects have been the subject of debate in recent years.

1. A first area of controversy has been Pannenberg's Christological method, specifically his defense of Christology "from below." In his book, *Jesus—God and Man,* Pannenberg charts for himself a methodology which seeks to begin with the historical man Jesus and then move to the concept of incarnation. Although this proposal has been widely acclaimed, there have been certain criticisms raised concerning it. Pannenberg begins the book by stating three reasons why the opposite approach ("from above") is not viable. These are criticized point by point by the English theologian Lash.[88] Tracy pursues the point at a deeper level by declaring the distinction itself to be theologically incorrect.[89] Dawe maintains that all theology is in the final analysis "from above," in that faith selects a particular event as the key to all history.[90] Segundo calls into question the radicality of Pannenberg's proposal, accusing him of returning in the end to the old Christology, for he begins with the question of the relationship of the historical Jesus to God, a question for which Jesus himself had no answer.[91]

Colin Brown voices very different reservations with this method. For him the approach "from below" appears to suspend all judgment concerning God's activity in Jesus until after the resurrection, at which time an approach "from above" is allowed to take over. But, he adds, nothing can be apprehended from a point of absolute neutrality. In fact,

---

87. B. McDermott, "Pannenberg's Resurrection Christology: A Critique," *Theological Studies* 35 (1974): 719.

88. Nicholas Lash, "Up and Down in Christology," in *New Studies in Theology* 1, ed. S. Sykes (London: Duckworth, 1980), 31-45.

89. David Tracy, *Analogical Imagination* (New York: Crossroad, 1981), 243, n. 5.

90. Donald G. Dawe, "Christology in Contemporary Systematic Theology," *Interpretation* 26 (1972): 272.

91. Jon Segundo, *The Historical Jesus of the Synoptics* (Maryknoll, N.Y.: Orbis, 1985), 30.

judgments about Jesus did not begin with the resurrection. Rather, this event is to be seen as confirming the identity of God's personal presence in Jesus. It is a vindication of Jesus and of the faith of his followers.[92]

Concerning Pannenberg's Christological method as a whole several criticisms have been expressed. Hanson finds Pannenberg building his entire Christology on Jesus' filial self-consciousness.[93] Some conservative critics see in this a somewhat truncated methodology. According to Henry, for example, Pannenberg denies that the teaching and deeds of Jesus disclose his divine being.[94] From the other end of the theological spectrum, liberation theologians such as Sobrino accuse Pannenberg of taking seriously only the first, the Kantian phase of the Enlightenment challenge, ignoring the second phase, that of Marx.[95]

A widespread concern voiced by evangelicals, liberationists, and Roman Catholics is that Pannenberg's Christology fails to do justice to present experiences of Christ. Gunton claims that Pannenberg confuses the significance of Jesus within the context of interpretation and the significance of Jesus now.[96]

According to Cone, Pannenberg employs the historical Jesus as the sole criterion for Christology. The witness of the black church tradition, however, is that the meaning of Christ for today is found in the encounter with the historical Jesus as the crucified and risen Lord who is present in the struggle for freedom.[97] Cone claims Pannenberg overreacts to earlier theologies. In contrast to a strict theology from below, Cone maintains that contemporary interest in Jesus' past cannot be separated from an encounter with his presence in contemporary existence. Therefore, against Pannenberg, Cone refuses to choose between a Christology "from below" and one "from above."

In a similar way Van Beeck complains that Pannenberg's construct leaves too little room for the actuality of Jesus present in the Spirit now. He also finds Pannenberg's definition of Christology too narrow,

---

92. Colin Brown, *Miracles and the Critical Mind* (Grand Rapids: Eerdmans; Exeter, Devon: Paternoster Press, 1984), 289-290.
93. Anthony T. Hanson, "Alan Richardson and His Critics in the Area of Hermeneutics," in *Theology and Change*, ed. R. Preston (London: SCM, 1975), 28-30.
94. Henry, *God, Revelation and Authority*, II: 302, 308.
95. Sobrino, *Christology at the Crossroads*, 26-28.
96. C. Gunton, *Yesterday and Today* (Grand Rapids: Eerdmans, 1983), 24.
97. James H. Cone, *God of the Oppressed* (New York: Seabury, 1975), 121-122.

for it leaves out reflection on the Christological a priori (i.e., the actualization of a priori Jesus present in the Spirit), and it omits the performative function of Christology.[98]

Pannenberg has not been insensitive to such criticisms. Recently Johnson described the shift in emphasis which is occurring in Pannenberg's Christology. His earlier strict methodology "from below" is being moderated by a shift to anthropology which is resulting also in a new and more fully developed doctrine of God.[99] The need for development in this direction is voiced by McDermott. After a sympathetic summary of *Jesus—God and Man*, he notes that Pannenberg's seminal concept of the Father as the only divine "Thou" in Jesus' earthly life is one direction in which fruitful development could lie.[100]

2. The subject which has received the greatest amount of attention is the resurrection of Jesus. Critics have perceived that this doctrine constitutes a linchpin for Pannenberg's entire enterprise. The great amount of critical comments in this area can be viewed under four headings.

a. First, the exact nature of the resurrection of Jesus in Pannenberg's understanding has been discussed. Many note that he defends the resurrection as an event in history. DeYong is not convinced, however. In his estimation, Pannenberg does not see supernatural intervention by God in Jesus' death and resurrection.[101] He questions whether Pannenberg holds to "a literal bodily" resurrection of Jesus.[102] While others have not been so harsh in their evaluation of Pannenberg's position, a certain lack of clarity in his descriptions has been claimed by several.[103] Clark, who thinks that Pannenberg's image of the resurrection is frustrating rather than healing, suggests the presence of several problems and contradictions. The German theologian, he claims, views the resurrection as both substantial and unsubstantial. Further, Clark

---

98. F. J. Van Beeck, *Christ Proclaimed* (New York: Paulist, 1979), 312-324.
99. Elizabeth A. Johnson, "The Ongoing Christology of Wolfhart Pannenberg," *Horizons* 9/2 (1982): 245-250.
100. McDermott, "Pannenberg's Resurrection Christology: A Critique," 720.
101. James C. DeYoung, "Event and Interpretation of the Resurrection," *Interpreting God's Word Today*, ed. S. Kistemaker (Grand Rapids: Baker, 1970), 140.
102. Ibid., 149.
103. E.g., John Macquarrie, "A Generation of Demythologizing," in *Theolinguistics*, ed. J. Van Noppen (1981).

does not find the Pauline concept of the "spiritual body," employed by Pannenberg, to be a symbol with an obvious meaning.[104] For Pailin a primary problem is that of establishing the nature and significance of the Easter experience.[105]

Michalson finds Pannenberg's view of the resurrection as a metaphor to be an unexpected move. For him Pannenberg's attack on the historicist's principle of analogy would lead one to expect a defense of the idea of the resuscitation of a corpse. The shift to metaphor at this point leads basically to the Bultmannian position, Michalson claims.[106] The limitations Pannenberg places on the concept of resurrection by viewing it as a metaphor leads to a "death by qualification," according to Clayton.[107]

The discussion of the metaphorical nature of Jesus' resurrection has led some critics to conclude that, contrary to his intent, Pannenberg has actually placed the resurrection into a type of "metahistory." In North's estimation Pannenberg's relegation of the resurrection of Jesus to the status of metaphor indicates that this event has a special historicity.[108] Dillenberger agrees, for he terms the resurrection in Pannenberg "special history," in that it functions as the clue to the meaning of all history.[109] Reginald Fuller, however, welcomes this move as wholly in keeping with the nature of the event.[110]

Some critics find Pannenberg's metaphorical understanding of the resurrection problematic on other grounds. Clark takes issue with Pannenberg's contention that Jesus' resurrection ought to be seen as unique, compared to other resurrections in the New Testament.[111] The distinction between resurrection (i.e., of Jesus) and resuscitation (all others) is not in keeping with the view of the Fourth Gospel. While admitting

---

104. W. Royce Clark, "Christian Images of Fulfillment: Healing within Anticipation," 188, 192.

105. Pailin, "Lessing's Ditch Revised: The Problem of Faith and History," 94-95.

106. Gordon E. Michalson, "Pannenberg on the Resurrection and Historical Method," *Scottish Journal of Theology* 33/4 (1980): 355-359.

107. Clayton, "The God of History and the Presence of the Future," 102-103.

108. R. North, "Pannenberg's Historicizing Exegesis," *The Heythrop Journal* 12 (1971): 396.

109. John Dillenberger, *Contours of Faith* (Nashville: Abingdon, 1969), 123.

110. Reginald Fuller, *The Formation of the Resurrection Narratives* (New York: Macmillan, 1971), 22-23.

111. W. Royce Clark, "Jesus, Lazarus and Others: Resuscitation or Resurrection," *Religion in Life* 49 (Summer 1980): 230-241.

a difference between these events, Clark declares that this difference is not sufficiently significant to constitute a basis for Christology. For him Pannenberg is too dependent on the Pauline, as opposed to the Johannine view. Pannenberg's contention that the resurrection not only *proved* who Jesus previously was, but *made* Jesus who he was, is not in agreement with John. Clark also suggests that Pannenberg is mistaken in insisting that the second generation Christian authors held to a concept of the solitary nature of the resurrection of Jesus.

Cobb raises a related problem, that of the present location of the resurrected body of Jesus:[112] If Pannenberg locates the body in the future, then the future must be seen as in some sense already extant, producing the very dualism Pannenberg is seeking to avoid. Hodgson likewise finds Pannenberg's concept confusing. In looking at Pannenberg's treatment of the evidences for the resurrection as a historical event, he notes the acceptance of the empty tomb tradition, which tradition, Hodgson maintains, suggests revivication. This raises the question as to why Pannenberg defends the tradition, while maintaining that the resurrection has nothing to do with the resuscitation of a corpse.[113]

b. A second area of discussion has been the relation of the resurrection of Jesus to that of humanity in general. Abraham disagrees with Pannenberg's understanding of the relation between these two, and this for two reasons. First, Pannenberg is wrong in claiming that the future general resurrection is an obvious philosophical truth. Second, he is mistaken in maintaining that the concept of a general resurrection provides warrant for the claim that a particular person has been raised.[114]

Clark finds the concept of resurrection in Pannenberg's thought self-contradictory. The German theologian maintains that human life cannot be fulfilled individually. But if this is the case, Clark asks, how did Jesus find his true fate in resurrection so as to be the guarantor of

---

112. J. B. Cobb Jr., "Wolfhart Pannenberg's *Jesus—God and Man*," 197.

113. Peter G. Hodgson, "Pannenberg on Jesus: A Review Article," *Journal of the American Academy of Religion* 36 (1968): 378.

114. William Abraham, *Divine Revelation and the Limits of Historical Criticism* (New York: Oxford University Press, 1982), 212, n. 62.

ours?[115] Van Buren objects to Pannenberg's claim that with the resurrection of Jesus the end of history has come.[116] This in effect sweeps all following history "into the bin of insignificance," he states.

c. A problem has been raised concerning the retroactive significance of the resurrection as seen by Pannenberg. McDermott asks whether for Pannenberg the resurrection was a contingent or necessary event in Jesus' life. If contingent, which seems to be the preferred response, then in what sense can it be said that Jesus was the presence of God in history during his earthly life?[117] Similarly, Olson finds Pannenberg's concept of retroactivity to be closer to adoptionism than to classical incarnational Christology.[118]

d. The most debated aspect of Pannenberg's concept of the resurrection of Jesus is his attempt to defend it as a historical event. The discussion of his apologetic for the historicity of the resurrection may be viewed under four categories.

(1) First, critics have assailed Pannenberg's historical methodology. Pailin perceives here an illegitimate attempt to use the resurrection to solve the problem of Lessing's ditch.[119] He describes this as a proof from miracle revisited, and claims that such an appeal to the process of history is doomed to failure.

Herzog responds to Pannenberg with the use of biblical counterexample. There is no evidence in the New Testament that the resurrection of Jesus was felt to have been less puzzling to the disciples than the cross, he suggests. And this is to be expected, he maintains, because the meaning of the resurrection simply cannot be read off the bare events of history by means of the right methodology.[120] Herzog cites the story of the appearance of the risen Lord to the disciples on the Emmaus road as an illustration of his contention, contra Pannenberg, that on purely historical grounds a resurrection need yield no more information about God than a cross provides.

---

115. W. Royce Clark, "Christian Images of Fulfillment: Healing within Anticipation," 194.

116. P. M. Van Buren, *Discerning the Way: Theology of the Jewish-Christian Reality* (New York: Seabury, 1980), 43.

117. B. McDermott, "The Personal Unity of Jesus and God according to W. Pannenberg," 292-294.

118. Olson, "The Human Self-Realization of God," 221.

119. Pailin, "Lessing's Ditch Revised: The Problem of Faith and History," 93-103.

120. Frederick Herzog, *Understanding God* (New York: Scribner's, 1966), 62-63.

Burhenn's criticism is more involved. He finds that Pannenberg's argument comes in two phases, the first historical (i.e., relating to the data of history) and the second methodological. But this argument, he maintains, presupposes that the historian must opt for what is believed to be the best account of the event. This is a misreading of the logic of the historian's enterprise. Further, Burhenn adds, the historian simply cannot opt for Pannenberg's explanation of the resurrection. The historian cannot use the concepts Pannenberg employs in his explanation of the event, for they do not belong to the commonsense body of knowledge of contemporary society, which forms the source of the historian's concepts.[121]

Even as sympathetic an interpreter as Braaten finds methodological difficulty at this point. He maintains that Pannenberg's argument should be seen as removing false objections to belief. The historical method cannot go beyond establishing that the earliest Christians believed Jesus had been resurrected, Braaten claims.[122] Evans adds that Pannenberg leans heavily on Paul as one for whom the resurrection of Jesus did not need to be interpreted. But even this move, Evans maintains, is exegetically questionable.[123]

(2) Pannenberg's argument for the historicity of the resurrection is based on two major traditions that arose in the early church—the appearances tradition and the empty tomb tradition. His use of each of these has been assailed. Placher finds the appeal to appearances unconvincing.[124] Paul's experience of the risen Lord, he maintains, does not require that Christ be objectively raised. In the face of this Pannenberg appeals to a cumulative case of independent experiences. In this, however, social psychology does not support Pannenberg's understanding, according to Placher.

Wood questions whether Pannenberg's account of the appearances

---

121. H. Burhenn, "Pannenberg's Argument for the Historicity of the Resurrection," *Journal of the American Academy of Religion* 40 (1972): 368-379.

122. Carl Braaten, "The Current Controversy on Revelation: Pannenberg and his Critics," 233.

123. C. F. Evans, *Resurrection and the New Testament* (Naperville, Ill.: A. R. Allenson, 1970), 181.

124. William C. Placher, "The Present Absence of Christ: Some Thoughts on Pannenberg and Moltmann," *Encounter* 40 (1979): 173-174.

has proved the resurrection, or merely that Paul's contemporaries remembered certain "appearances." If Collingwood's sense of history is utilized, Wood concludes, then Pannenberg's account is not scientific history but "a scissors-and-paste history."[125] Ladd refuses to lump all the postresurrection appearances together. Pannenberg is mistaken, he maintains, in claiming that all the appearances were of the order of Paul's encounter.[126]

Cobb questions the validity of Pannenberg's use of this tradition for his claim that the resurrection is a historical event. Pannenberg's argument from the appearances, Cobb declares, would not favor the symbol of the resurrection of the body.[127] Hodgson claims that the appearances are better interpreted as experiences of the presence of the living Lord than as belonging to the past event of resurrection.[128] These, in other words, do not constitute proofs for the resurrection. In fact Hodgson finds Pannenberg's distinction between the resurrection reality and the resurrection event unwarranted.

(3) Many critics find even more problematic Pannenberg's employing of the empty tomb tradition. Placher, for example, claims against Pannenberg that talk of a resurrection in first-century Judaism need not have implied an empty tomb.[129] In support of this he appeals to the apocalyptic literature and to Paul, who never speaks of the empty tomb of Jesus.

(4) Closely tied to Pannenberg's use of traditions to argue for the historicity of the resurrection is his claim that apocalypticism forms the context for the understanding of this event. Four important questions have been raised by critics.

(a) Some, including Ladd, claim that Pannenberg is simply wrong in grounding the Pauline concept of the glorified body on Jewish apocalyptic. Ladd finds its source in Paul's theology of glory and in Paul's own experience of the risen Jesus.[130]

---

125. Wood, "History and Hermeneutics: A Pannenbergian Perspective," 12.
126. George E. Ladd, *I Believe in the Resurrection of Jesus* (Grand Rapids: Eerdmans, 1975), 127, 138.
127. J. B. Cobb Jr., "Wolfhart Pannenberg's *Jesus—God and Man*," 199-200.
128. Hodgson, "Pannenberg on Jesus: A Review Article," 376-378.
129. Placher, "The Present Absence of Christ: Some Thoughts on Pannenberg and Moltmann," 172-173.
130. Ladd, *I Believe in the Resurrection of Jesus*, 124-125.

(b) Others, such as Selby, suggest that apocalyptic was not the only understanding of the resurrection in the New Testament nor in church history.[131]

(c) Pannenberg's understanding of the apocalyptic view of history and the world has been criticized by many scholars. Basically these criticisms maintain that the apocalypticists were not concerned with history as the sphere of God's revelatory activity, but with the eschaton, when the present evil world would be done away with.[132] Torrance claims that Pannenberg runs together "historical, logical, and epistemological priorities," and does not take adequate account that Judaism did not anticipate the resurrection as the decisive event of history nor that Jesus transformed the entire concept of resurrection.[133] Brown points out that not all scholars agree that the resurrection is an indispensable element in the apocalyptic outlook.[134]

Travis provides a summary of the criticisms of Pannenberg's understanding of apocalyptic: The understanding of universal history in the apocalyptic movement is different from Pannenberg's, for the apocalypticists saw history not merely as positive, but also as constituting God's great no.[135] Likewise there were no universal hopes in apocalypticism, as is definitely the case in Pannenberg's understanding. Beyond these two, Travis offers an additional criticism. Pannenberg, he declares, pays no attention to hopes for life after death in the intertestamental literature and overlooks the fact that Judaism did not expect the resurrection as the decisive event of history. This last argument is echoed by Evans, who says that it is doubtful whether the general resurrection was a sufficiently fixed theologumenon in Jewish tradition.[136]

(d) Several critics question whether the apocalyptic outlook

---

131. P. Selby, *Look for the Living* (Philadelphia: Fortress, 1976), 144, 149-150.

132. Wood, "History and Hermeneutics: A Pannenbergian Perspective," 10. See also the previous discussion of apocalyptic.

133. Thomas Torrance, *Space, Time and Resurrection* (Grand Rapids: Eerdmans, 1976), 34, n. 10.

134. Delwin Brown, *The Divine Trinity* (LaSalle, Ill.: Open Court, 1985), 129.

135. Stephen Travis, *Christian Hope and the Future* (Downers Grove, Ill.: InterVarsity, 1980), 53-55.

136. Evans, *Resurrection and the New Testament,* 180.

is relevant for contemporary humanity, even if Pannenberg's under-standing of the first-century thought world is accurate.[137] In this "prob-lem of transformation," declares Scharlemann, Pannenberg slights what he acknowledges otherwise, namely, that the conception of res-urrection, which is unproblematic for the apocalyptic context, is prob-lematic for us.[138]

Burhenn's criticism at this point is the most significant: Pannen-berg asks readers to step out of the shared 20th-century knowledge into Jewish apocalyptic. He defends this move philosophically, by appeal to anthropology, and not historically. But this defense is not convincing. His doctrine of humanity is but one of many, is shared by very few philosophers today, and is clearly not that of the majority of histori-ans.[139]

C. Other Issues of Christology

In addition to these major topics of discussion (methodology and the resurrection), two other areas have been noted by a few critics, the concept of Jesus' death and the virgin birth. Pannenberg's explication of Jesus' death has been criticized in terms of the methodology that underlies it. Moltmann and the liberation theologians have taken the lead in this issue. Sobrino sums up the critique by suggesting that Pannenberg's philosophical presuppositions result in almost no role given to the cross. Pannenberg overlooks the revelatory meaning of the cross, and this because he makes use only of apocalyptic traditions to the exclusion of the Servant of Yahweh Christology.[140]

A similar criticism is noted by Gunton, who claims that Pannen-berg has limited soteriology to matters of meaning at the expense of matters associated with the cross.[141] Pinnock is troubled by Pannen-berg's characterization of the cross as a fate which befell Jesus. He

---

137. P. Selby, *Look for the Living*, 150-151; D. Brown, *The Divine Trinity*, 129; C. B. M. McCullagh, "Possibility of an Historical Basis for Christian Theology," *Theology* 74 (1971): 513-522.
138. R. P. Scharlemann, Review of *Jesus—God and Man*, *Dialog* 8 (1969): 75.
139. Burhenn. "Pannenberg's Argument for the Historicity of the Resurrection," 368-379.
140. Sobrino, *Christology at the Crossroads*, 26-28.
141. Gunton, *Yesterday and Today*, 29.

takes exception to Pannenberg's insistence that Jesus had no clear perception of the significance of his coming death and that Jesus was not an active agent in it.[142]

Pannenberg's unwillingness to classify the virgin birth as a historical event is generally passed over in silence. However, a few critics have offered counterarguments to it. Heinitz claims that Pannenberg takes the virgin birth out of its theological context.[143] Delwin Brown is displeased by Pannenberg's handling of the historical evidence. He also maintains the German theologian has made a conceptual mistake. Even if Matthew and Luke intended to mark Jesus' birth as the beginning of the existence of the Son of God by means of the virgin birth story, as Pannenberg suggests, it does not follow, Brown argues, that the one who accepts the virgin birth must make the same intention.[144]

Another criticism is found in a footnote in a book by Raymond Brown. Against Pannenberg's contention that the virgin birth opposes the concept of preexistence, he claims that natural generation results in a new person, whereas the virgin birth involved a preexistent person. He notes further that the denial of the virgin birth more often has favored an adoptionist than a preexistence Christology.[145]

III. OTHER ISSUES

Critics of Pannenberg have tended to center on the two areas already discussed, basic theological methodology, especially the relation between faith and reason and questions of hermeneutics and history, and theological formulation, especially in the doctrine of God and Christology. However, Pannenberg's program extends to other issues as well. Therefore, it is not surprising that critical response is found in several other areas.

---

142. Pinnock, "Pannenberg's Theology," Part 2: "No-Nonsense Theology," 14.
143. Kenneth Heinitz, "Pannenberg: Theology 'From Below' and the Virgin Birth," *Lutheran Quarterly* 28 (May 1976): 181.
144. Brown, *The Divine Trinity,* 122-123.
145. Raymond Brown, *The Virginal Conception and Bodily Resurrection of Jesus* (New York: Paulist, 1973), 43, n. 58.

A. Anthropology

Pannenberg wrote on the subject of anthropology quite early in his career. Yet, critical response to this specific topic, which actually is fundamental to his theological program, has been relatively meager. This situation will be changing, however, now that his newer volume on the subject has been translated. Reviews of this work are beginning to appear.[146]

In a lengthy review Walsh claims that Pannenberg's *Anthropology* suffers from three related problems. First, he is never precise about the content of human destiny, Walsh claims. Second, by making fallenness constitutive of creatureliness, Pannenberg is unable to affirm the goodness of all being. And, third, his position suffers from a one-dimensional understanding of both sin and redemption.[147]

Olson's review is largely applauding. Yet, several criticisms are offered. Pannenberg's conception of sin is faulted for seeming to be as unfair and arbitrary as the Augustinian view he rejects. Further, the attempt to ground the image of God and sin in general anthropological studies rather than special revelation is seen as unjustifiable. Olson then faults Pannenberg for blurring the distinction between nature and grace. Finally, the author of the review would have expected a more Christocentric approach to anthropology than Pannenberg offers.[148]

B. Theology and Science

Pannenberg's attempt to carry on a dialogue with science is readily seen in several of his writings. The *Anthropology,* for example, interacts specifically with the human sciences. And his fundamental outlook toward the relationship between theology and the sciences in general is given in *Theology and the Philosophy of Science.*

The latter book has been the subject of many reviews since its publication. One reviewer, White, is highly critical of Pannenberg's program, detecting four problems therein: the problem of evil, the third

---

146. In addition to the articles noted below, see the author's review in the *Reformed Journal* 36/9 (September 1986).

147. Brian J. Walsh, "A Critical Review of Pannenberg's *Anthropology in Theological Perspective," Christian Scholars Review* 15/3 (1986): 258-259.

148. Olson, "Pannenberg's Theological Anthropology: A Review Article," 161-169.

order nature of theological hypotheses, the problem of religious pluralism, and the testing of hypotheses. These problems lead him to conclude that in the final analysis Pannenberg's program does not constitute scientific testing.[149] Another writer evaluates Pannenberg's proposal for a scientific and theological cosmology as being too strong.[150]

C. Christianity and World Religions

Pannenberg's ecumenical interests are given expression through his continuing involvement in the Faith and Order Commission of the World Council of Churches. But in his writings he occasionally moves beyond Christian ecumenicity to address the wider issue of the relation between Christianity and the religions of the world. The implications of his theological program for this issue have been discussed by several critics.

Peters describes Pannenberg's thought as making no arbitrary claim for Christianity. Rather, this religion is one set of phenomena within the wider study of the history of religions. Further, the historical nature of reality in Pannenberg's understanding is shared by both the secular and the religious, Peters concludes.[151]

Not all critics accept this positive evaluation, however. Knitter suggests that in Pannenberg's system the religions of the world cannot move beyond the question stage.[152] Bollinger cites Buddhism as a counterexample to what he calls Pannenberg's "religious essentialism."[153] Against Pannenberg he suggests that not all religions find their true meaning and being in the same ultimate, for Buddhism looks to Emptiness, not to God. This basic argument is advanced by Cobb as

---

149. Harvey W. White, "A Critique of [Wolfhart] Pannenberg's Theology and the Philosophy of Science," *Studies in Religion* 11/4 (1982): 419-436.

150. Ernan McMullin, "How Shall Cosmology Relate to Theology?" in *The Sciences and Theology in the Twentieth Century*, ed. Arthur R. Peacocke (Notre Dame: University of Notre Dame Press, 1981), 50-52.

151. Ted Peters, "Truth in History," 55.

152. P. Knitter, "What Is German Protestant Theology Saying about the Non-Christian Religions?" *Neue Zeitschrift für Systematische Theologie* 15 (1973): 48-54.

153. Gary Bollinger, "Pannenberg's Theology of the Religions and the Claim to Christian Superiority," *Encounter* 43 (Summer 1982): 273-285.

well. He faults Pannenberg for deriving his understanding of all religions by generalizing from Western forms. Although voicing confidence that Pannenberg does not intend to continue "the Western tradition of intellectual imperialism," he anticipates that a genuine encounter with the East would both enrich and complicate Pannenberg's program.[154]

In another article Cobb expresses his displeasure with Pannenberg's expectation that Christianity will supersede the other world religions. This expectation fails to see other religions as complex wholes which lose something of their importance for the history of salvation when they are reduced to the status of contributions.[155] Cobb himself sees no reason to assume that the history of salvation is bound up with the history of religions, as is the case in Pannenberg's outlook. His own preference is a secularized history of salvation.[156]

D. Ethics

Pannenberg has not yet published a definitive work in ethics. Nevertheless, certain ethical implications of his theological program have been tested by critics. Hauerwas and Sherwindt, for example, find Pannenberg's ethic somewhat incomplete. They suggest that the German theologian nowhere explains why justice and love are the defining marks of the kingdom of God. The problem they note therein is that of abstracting the kingdom ideal from the concrete community which it presupposes.[157]

Political theologians on both sides of the Atlantic have assailed what they see as a conservative political ethic in Pannenberg's proposal. Pannenberg's fellow German, Jürgen Moltmann, suggests that this ethic follows from his emphasis on the anticipatory character of the message and resurrection of Jesus and from his neglect of the contradictory character of Jesus' message and cross.[158]

---

154. John B. Cobb Jr., Review of *Theology and the Philosophy of Science, Religious Studies Review* 3 (1977): 213-215.

155. John B. Cobb Jr., "The Meaning of Pluralism for Christian Self-Understanding," in *Religious Pluralism,* ed. L. Rouner (Notre Dame: University of Notre Dame Press, 1984), 175.

156. Ibid., 170.

157. Stanley Hauerwas and Mark Sherwindt, "The Kingdom of God: An Ecclesial Space for Peace," *Word and World* 2 (Spring 1982): 130-131.

158. Jürgen Moltmann, *On Human Dignity,* 112, n. 6.

Just as Moltmann finds Pannenberg's Christological method leading to a faulty ethic, so Hefner finds in his concept of God certain unfortunate ethical implications. He sees Pannenberg's proposal as weak in its understanding of the place of human beings in shaping events.[159] The historical realm is so filled with God's power that the human will plays no actual role. This in turn results in no concrete ethical guidance offered to persons in the present, he claims.[160]

E. Relevance

Several critics have questioned the contemporary relevance of Pannenberg's program. In the early discussion published as *New Frontiers in Theology,* volume 3, Hamilton claims that Pannenberg's program presupposes the natural religiousness of humanity and thereby fails to take seriously the world of modern unbelief.[161] A similar evaluation of Pannenberg's eschatological program is voiced by Young, who states that it does not speak to the current intellectual climate.[162]

Walsh claims that Pannenberg's "geneticism," as he characterizes this system, does not provide an adequate alternative to structuralism. However, from his study of Pannenberg he finds insight into the task of evangelical theology in the contemporary theological world.[163]

F. General Theological Approach

Pannenberg's general approach to the theological task has called forth comments of a general nature from various theologians. Fuller claims the addition of a place for the supernatural in Pannenberg's proposal, allowing what is contingent in history to be viewed as supernatural, would clear up certain outstanding problems without sacrificing the gains he has made.[164]

---

159. Hefner, "The Concreteness of God's Kingdom," 195.
160. Ibid., 198. See also H. Harder and W. T. Stevenson, "The Continuity of History and Faith in the Theology of W. Pannenberg: Toward an Erotics of History," 53-54.
161. Hamilton, "The Character of Pannenberg's Theology," 178-179.
162. Francis Young, "The Finality of Christ," in *Incarnation and Myth: The Debate Continued,* ed. M. Goulder (Grand Rapids: Eerdmans, 1979), 185.
163. Brian J. Walsh, "Pannenberg's Eschatological Ontology," *Christian Scholars Review* 11/3 (1982): 248-249.
164. Daniel Fuller, "New German Theological Movement," *Scottish Journal of Theology* 19 (1966): 175.

Harder and Stevenson offer three other suggestions.[165] (1) They find in Pannenberg's system a fundamental ambiguity, the description of the transition from historical fact to faith. Pannenberg, they suggest, should recognize more clearly that faith is operative in the perception of fact, which from the beginning is a perception of reality by means of faith. (2) Pannenberg's treatment of the "present" should be less equivocal, they maintain, allowing for a more adequate recognition of the dimension of historical experience. Such a move would soften Pannenberg's opposition to the theology of existential encounter.[166] (3) They contend with various other critics, including Hefner, that in Pannenberg's proposal humanity's role in history is unfortunately overshadowed by God.

Macquarrie senses four problems in Pannenberg's program: remythologizing, a speculative idea of history, an obsession with the future resulting in a loss of the presence of God in the present, and an insufficient distinction between Christian hope and mere optimism.[167] Johnson cites three unresolved problems in Pannenberg's project: a fragmentary treatment of ontological issues, a lack of precise relation of the future to the present with respect to causality, and the clarification of the existence of evil in the present.[168]

The sustained interest process theologians have in Pannenberg's work is expressed by John Cobb's ongoing interaction with his writings. In 1977 a somewhat general response to the German theologian appeared.[169] Elsewhere he raises a problem similar to one seen by Johnson and Macquarrie. Cobb claims Pannenberg subordinates the present too much to the future and the past, although he admits that in another respect he is keenly interested in the present.[170]

In 1965 Carl Braaten wrote an insightful preliminary analysis of Pannenberg's program, pointing out that the German theologian defies

---

165. H. Harder and W. T. Stevenson, "The Continuity of History and Faith in the Theology of W. Pannenberg: Toward an Erotics of History," 51-55.

166. See also P. G. Hodgson, "Pannenberg on Jesus," 374-375.

167. John Macquarrie, "Theologies of Hope: a Critical Examination," *Expository Times* 82 (1971): 100-105. See also Macquarrie, *Thinking about God* (New York: Harper & Row, 1975), 228-231.

168. Johnson, "Resurrection and Reality in the Thought of Wolfhart Pannenberg," 15-17.

169. John Cobb Jr., "Response to Pannenberg," in *John Cobb's Theology in Process,* ed. David R. Griffin and Thomas J. J. Altizer (Philadelphia: Westminster, 1977), 185-192.

170. John B. Cobb Jr., "Past, Present, and Future," *Theology as History,* 219.

ready-made labels. But Braaten finds Pannenberg's attempt to set himself apart from all other theological schools to be detrimental for establishing a true theological synthesis. Further, he faults Pannenberg for offering an evaluation of the theology of the Word that is too negative, and suggests that his diminishing stress on the kerygmatic dimension constitutes an oversimplification. Based on this, Braaten challenges Pannenberg to a reevaluation of, and a more accurate reading of Martin Kähler.[171]

Pannenberg has not been totally insensitive to the comments of his critics. Nor have his critics always interpreted him accurately or offered helpful insights. Over the years there has been development in Pannenberg's own thought as well, although its central features have remained basically unchanged. Perhaps it could be concluded that the critical discussion of the last 25 years has reached something of a standstill. Pannenberg's methodological proposal and the insights into his understanding of Christian doctrine offered by his writings to date have been discussed and debated. This discussion now awaits the appearance of the final form of his dogmatics. The publication of the projected three-volume Systematic Theology could serve to rekindle the debate over Pannenberg's theology and raise it to a new level, as focus shifts to the actual theology that this controversial methodology produces.

---

171. Braaten, "The Current Controversy on Revelation," 234-235.

PART I

◆

PHILOSOPHICAL
and
METHODOLOGICAL
CRITIQUES

1

PANNENBERG AND
PROCESS THEOLOGY

John B. Cobb Jr.

◆

Pannenberg was the first German theologian to take a serious
interest in process theology. As he explains,[1] he found himself
pressured to do so by encountering a group of process theologians when teaching at the Divinity School of the University of Chicago. However, something else was at work, for other German theologians had visited Chicago without being drawn into this discussion.
Pannenberg was unusual among German theologians in that he shared
with process theology the desire to relate theological discussion inter-
nally to the natural and social sciences. It was the contribution of Alfred
North Whitehead's thought to this task that sustained his interest.

Process thought has certainly not preoccupied Pannenberg. Nevertheless, he has gained a profound understanding of its strengths and
weaknesses. Process theology has no more perceptive or better informed critic than he.

One cannot say reciprocally that Pannenberg is the first German
theologian seriously studied by process theologians. The German he-
gemony in theology has been such that process theologians in the United
States, like all theologians here, have cut their teeth on German theology. The influence of Rudolf Bultmann on process theologians has

---

1. Wolfhart Pannenberg, "Atom, Duration, Form: Difficulties with Process Philosophy,"
trans. John C. Robertson Jr. and Gerard Vallee, *Process Studies* 14/1 (Spring 1984): 21.

been quite important.[2] Even so, one can say that a number of process theologians, among whom I am one, have felt peculiarly drawn to Pannenberg as a conversation partner and influence. He alone among 20th-century German theologians has dealt with the full range of issues important to Whiteheadian process theology, and on many points his treatments are congenial. On others there are subtle differences that turn out to have considerable importance.

The most striking difference between Pannenberg and process theologians, perhaps, is that Pannenberg undertakes to accomplish as an individual thinker what among process thinkers has required a whole school. First, Pannenberg is his own philosopher, whereas process theologians have depended on process philosophers. In addition, within the theological fields, Pannenberg is his own biblical scholar and his own historian, whereas no single process theologian encompasses so much with comparable thoroughness and originality.[3] Finally, Pannenberg is engaged dialogically with a whole array of physical and social sciences, whereas no process theologian has been able to engage so wide a range. Indeed, it is doubtful that there is another thinker alive today who is as comprehensive in the command of wide-ranging disciplines as Wolfhart Pannenberg. On the process side, only Whitehead himself can compare with him, and Whitehead is not of this generation!

For these and other reasons, when Pannenberg explicitly critiques process theology, we who work in that stream must take his objections with great seriousness. He understands us all too well. And he views us from that inclusive perspective toward which we aspire. If in the end we do not change course markedly in response to his criticisms, we are bound to say why.

Pannenberg has written one essay directly critical of my theology[4]

---

2. In particular, Schubert Ogden's theological program has integrated Bultmann's kerygmatic theology with a Hartshornian theism. In less focused ways Bultmann's influence among process theologians of Ogden's generation was pervasive.

3. In his early years he associated closely with scholars from other theological disciplines, and some spoke of the Pannenberg circle. But this group no longer appears as a unified school, and all along Pannenberg has been able to take stands on biblical, historical, and exegetical matters based on his own scholarship. Among process theologians Schubert Ogden is unusual in his ability to engage biblical scholars on their own turf. Daniel Day Williams and Norman Pittenger have combined historical scholarship with systematic theological work.

4. Wolfhart Pannenberg, "A Liberal Logos Christology: The Christology of John Cobb," in *John Cobb's Theology in Process*, ed. David Ray Griffin and Thomas J. J. Altizer (Philadelphia: Westminster, 1977), 133-149.

and another critique of process theology[5] that applies to me more directly than to such other process theologians and philosophers of religion as Henry Nelson Wieman, Bernard Meland, Bernard Loomer, Charles Hartshorne, or Schubert Ogden. Hence in responding as a process theologian I will speak primarily of my own form of process theology. Section I is a defense of my approach and of the feature of Whitehead's thought I follow and Pannenberg rejects. Section II critiques Pannenberg's systematic position from the point of view I defend in Section I. Section III comments on the opposing relations to liberationist modes of theology that have come to characterize Pannenberg on the one side and most process theologians on the other.

I

One of Pannenberg's criticisms of my form of process theology is that it ties itself too closely to a single thinker, namely, Whitehead. It is this critique that cannot reasonably be directed at any of the process thinkers listed above[6] but that does have significant relevance to my own program and that of some of my colleagues. Whether process theology should follow Whitehead in some detail or should locate itself more fluidly in a larger tradition of process thought, as Pannenberg recommends, is an issue within process theology itself.

In the long run the critics of the narrower focus are correct, even from my more narrowly Whiteheadian point of view. Whitehead's own understanding of the life of the mind precludes so attaching oneself to one thinker as to neglect others and to fail to engage the task of fresh creative thought in the broadest context of interchange with other traditions. A Whiteheadian scholasticism would be inherently un-Whiteheadian. Hence, to whatever extent my theology is of this sort, as Pannenberg and others sometimes charge, I am caught in a contradiction.

---

5. "Atom, Duration, Form."
6. At the time Pannenberg was at Chicago, Bernard Loomer was teaching *Process and Reality* with a devotion to its details not characteristic of his work either earlier or later. This may have colored Pannenberg's perception of a wider segment of the process theology movement. In his later years Loomer would have strongly supported Pannenberg's critique, even though their respective quarrels with Whitehead were quite different.

Further, I would regard it as quite unhealthy if the theological community as a whole became as closely bound to Whitehead's thought as is my own work. The most dynamic movements of theology in our time, such as the various liberation theologies, would then not have developed. Those who have paid close attention to the experience of the economically oppressed or of women or of ethnics treated by whites as inferior have been more faithful to Whitehead's own spirit than have those, like myself, who have paid close attention to Whitehead.

But I see no danger that the theological community in general will devote excessive attention to the texts of Whitehead. It still devotes far more attention to the texts of Thomas and Luther and Hegel and Barth, to mention only a few. Since it is my judgment that Christians today have more to gain from Whitehead than from continuing preoccupation with any of these classic figures, I do not apologize for my focus. However, defending a careful study of Whitehead's texts is not really a response to Pannenberg's criticism. He does not object to a few people specializing in the study of Whitehead. His objection is to theologians binding themselves to particular philosophers when, in the service of the faith, they should look for help wherever it is available and judge potential contributions by theological norms. This is the way he works with Hegel and with the many philosophers and other thinkers from whose work he draws. His method and the brilliant use he makes of it are admirable. Nevertheless, at this point in history I see good reasons for focusing—even as a theologian—on Whitehead's thought.

The justification of my theological program is bound up with my perception of our situation. I see us as living in the decay of the modern world, by which I mean the world of the Enlightenment. The great triumphs of Newtonian physics have been paradigmatic and normative for this world, and the resultant worldview has had massive religious implications. During the 18th and 19th centuries Protestant theology was largely an adaptation and response to these.

One Christian response to the decay of the modern worldview has been to cut Christian faith loose from questions of worldview. Immanuel Kant showed how to do this in relation to the natural sciences, but he bound faith closely to modern ethical sensibility. It was Karl Barth who realized the full meaning of this project, grounding Christian thinking entirely in revelation.

Barth's program has been the greatest achievement of 20th-century theology, but since World War II it has lost much of its convincing power. More and more would-be Barthians have found it impossible to separate the grounds of faith so fully from history. There has been a reexploration of the 19th-century project, adapting it to the decay of modernity. The single most sustained and thoroughgoing embodiment of this theological response to the decay of modernity is that of Pannenberg. Pannenberg has rethought the relation of Christianity and the Enlightenment profoundly and brilliantly.

Others have found that the decay of the modern world amounts to a collapse. For them this collapse requires the rejection of all the positive or constructive programs of the 19th century. Only the critical work of that century can be appropriated. Typically in this movement the collapse of the modern worldview is the end of all efforts to construct worldviews. The category of the "whole," so important to Pannenberg,[7] is meaningless for them. The human mind must accept a very limited compass of legitimate activity. This dominant strand of post-modern thinking abandons all efforts to put the pieces together in a coherent way. Theologians who accept this context find "meaning" only in the end of the quest for meaning.

I agree with these postmodernists that the decay of modernity is in fact a collapse. But I do not agree that the collapse of the modern worldview means the impossibility or undesirability of any worldview at all. On the contrary, I see it as a reason for rethinking the world radically with a different model of reality. I believe that in the process of such rethinking Christian faith has an important role to play and that faith will be able to express itself more convincingly in this kind of post-modern context than it could in the modern world. The reason I believe such a new beginning to be possible is that I find it accomplished already in Whitehead's work.[8]

---

7. Cf., e.g., "The Significance of the Categories 'Part' and 'Whole' for the Epistemology of Theology," trans. Philip Clayton, *The Journal of Religion* 66 (1986): 369-385.

8. Whitehead himself gave to William James the honor of providing the new beginning (*Science and the Modern World* [Toronto: Collier-MacMillan Canada, Ltd., 1967], 143). Whitehead could then be viewed as having systematized and extended the key insights of a post-modern philosophy: the rejection of the Cartesian ego and of scientific materialism. However, in this case, the systematization and extension are essential to the demonstration that a new worldview or cosmology is possible on the basis of these negations.

My perception of Whitehead's potential contribution is such, therefore, that an eclectic use of Whitehead along with other process thinkers would not suffice to realize it. Much of process thought has not broken sufficiently with modernity or has not gone deep enough to provide an alternative basis for rethinking. This is true especially of those process thinkers most favored by Pannenberg, namely, those who have retained the view of the process as a continuum.

That Whitehead, and Whitehead alone, has undertaken the needed restructuring of thought with sufficient radicality, scope, and depth to constitute a viable new beginning does not mean that he is inerrant or incorrigible! That would be absurd. He himself changed and developed over a period of many years. At the end as at the beginning, his work had the character of being "in process." To absolutize it in any of the forms he gave it would be arbitrary and would falsify its spirit. The proper tribute to Whitehead would be to go beyond him. To claim his work as a new beginning entails this.

But to pursue the new directions and opportunities he opened up is quite different from rejecting or moderating the revolutionary new approach he offered. Thus far, as is to be expected, most interpreters and critics have viewed him within the context of issues and alternatives already familiar within the tradition. Though helpful to a certain extent, these interpretations do not do justice to the radical change implied in Whitehead's proposal. By moderating his ideas, interpreters bring him back within the modern world and view his thought as an interesting alternative within it. In trying to improve upon his formulations, most of us—and I include myself—have fallen back into, or toward, established modes of thought. The time will come when we can go beyond, but for the present the main task is still to catch up and assimilate. My vocation is this quite pedestrian one along with the effort to think through the meaning of Whitehead's new beginnings in a variety of areas in which he had little to say. Traditional theological topics, of course, have played a far larger role in my thinking than in his, along with the more fundamental question as to what it means to be a believer.

The feature of Whitehead's thought most objectionable to Pannenberg is the open-endedness of an infinite future. He has found in much of the tradition, and especially in 19th-century thinking, a testimony to a whole that is temporal. Meaning is found only in anticipation of an end. What things are is progressively determined by the course of events and is not determinate except in the final consummation. The process is determinate only in the end and gains such determination as it now has from its anticipation of the end. The end is the cause of this anticipation. Thus the decisive causality is of the present by the future. The power of the future is God.

Whitehead's analysis agrees with Pannenberg that the present is never simply the outcome of the past. It agrees also that what provides the present with transcendence over the past is the working of God in the present. But for Whitehead the God who introduces this transcendence is not the power of a temporally remote future but the everlasting companion through whom relevant aspects of eternal possibilities become effective in each moment.

Whitehead's lack of need for final temporal closure is closely related to his doctrine that there is closure in every moment. There is in every momentary occasion of experience a becoming of something definite. Further, this definiteness, once attained, is unalterable. Whitehead speaks of it as "objectively immortal." This definiteness is a definite relation to all possibilities and to all events or occasions that for it are actual, namely, all occasions in its past. In human occasions this relation includes interpretation. The human occasion of experience is in itself a definite value and meaning. This meaning is affected by its anticipation of how it may affect the future, and this anticipation may be relatively accurate or relatively inaccurate. But the present meaning to which anticipation of the future contributes is forever definite.

To this objective immortality of every occasion must be contrasted the contingency of the role it will in fact play in the future. That it will play some role in constituting future occasions is inevitable, but exactly what role it will play, how it will be valued and interpreted—that is unsettled in advance and settled only as new occasions arise that value and interpret it. Since there will be no end to the arising of new occasions, there will be no final definitive meaning of the occasion, although, in another sense, God's valuing of the occasion does give it an ultimate and everlasting meaning.

The doctrine underlying this indeterminacy of the future is that God's role in shaping each occasion is to offer it multiple possibilities for supplementing what is given to it by the past world. The occasion itself decides among these possibilities. That decision is the element of self-determination in each occasion that supplements both the innumerable decisions of past occasions and the decision of God for the occasion.

Pannenberg rightly sees that Whitehead's position is based on what Whitehead sometimes calls a "cellular" or "atomic" view of reality. Whitehead's view is that human experience comes in "droplets," to use the language of William James, or in quanta or event particles, to relate this position to contemporary physics. This is a crucial break with antecedent ways of Western thinking, although it was anticipated in some ancient Buddhist writers.

The argument is that what gives itself to consciousness as continuous is actually composed of discrete units. The continuous surface of a desk, when analyzed with sufficient care, turns out to be composed of discrete molecules, atoms, and subatomic entities. The Greek atomists already saw that this must be. But they supposed that the final spatial units, necessarily indivisible, and therefore "atoms," exist continuously through time. They did not anticipate the vibratory or wave-like character of "atoms." Today these "atoms" are best viewed as trains of "atomic" waves, each of which is an event. That means that the units of nature are four-dimensional happenings or "actual occasions." If human experience is truly a part of nature, as Whitehead believes, the independent analysis of James is strengthened. Both human experience and physical energy can be analyzed into a series of "actual occasions" or "occasions of experience."

Since it is this "atomic" view of reality that provides an alternative to the view of the world as a single process requiring completion for its definiteness, Pannenberg rightly centers his critique upon it. In doing so he can unquestionably find obscurities and problems in the interpretation of Whitehead along with disarray among his followers. Since the notion of temporal atomicity is new, Whitehead had to construct his doctrine of the becoming or "concrescence" of each occasion out of whole cloth. His work, though brilliant, remains in process. His several formulations are not entirely consistent with one another. And they involve ways of thinking so new to the West that they have to struggle against both ordinary and philosophical language. In some respects they are profoundly counterintuitive.

Pannenberg states the problem well. "When Whitehead, in *Process and Reality*, presents a genetic analysis with its differentiation of various phases in the self-constitution of the event (cf., e.g., PR26f./ 40, 248f./380f.), he becomes liable to the suspicion of confusing the abstract and concrete, thereby committing the 'fallacy of misplaced concreteness,' which he has often astutely criticized in other thinkers. If we cannot, in fact, really divide the actual occasion further but can only abstractly differentiate the relationships which constitute its identity, then we cannot, by the same token, characterize the actual occasion as being the result of a process in which these aspects which can only be distinguished in the abstract are actually integrated. This is even more difficult since these relations themselves are said to be constituted only by the actual occasion."[9]

With unerring insight Pannenberg has stated the heart of the problem for Whiteheadians. As he sees, the radical novelty of Whitehead consists in viewing the world as made up of events each of which is itself a process of becoming, so that in addition to the macrocosmic process which is temporal there are microcosmic processes that constitute the units of this macrocosmic process and whose own becoming is not temporal. This becoming is not divisible into earlier and later units of becoming. From a temporal point of view it happens all at once.

While the notion of a process that occurs all at once is inherently puzzling, not fitting with any precast modes of thought, Pannenberg astutely goes beyond this puzzle to ask about its elements. He poses the challenge that the parts of this process are abstractions. But for Whitehead it would be disastrous to acknowledge this. If "prehensions" are abstractions, and if concrescence is a process of integration of these abstractions, and if these abstractions are abstracted from the completed occasion, we have a hopeless muddle!

My judgment is that standard Whitehead interpretation is highly vulnerable to this critique, but that Whitehead himself is much less so. Much Whitehead interpretation has viewed what concresces as aspects of the concrescing occasion and has agreed with Pannenberg that the prehensions are constituted only by this occasion. Close attention to

---

9. Pannenberg, "Atom, Duration, Form," 25.

the text of Whitehead offers a different picture. For him every occasion is an instantiation of creativity. Creativity is best understood as the many becoming one and being increased by one.[10] The new occasion is the "superject" of this many which exercise "causal efficacy" by participating in the constitution of the new one. Thus the agents active in constituting the new occasion's "conformal phase" are the past occasions. These are not abstractions.

In addition each occasion in some measure, however slight, supplements this conformation to the past world. This is made possible by the participation of God in the constitution of the occasion. It is God's agency that introduces a lure to the realization of possibilities relevant to, but not offered by, the past world. Just how some aspect of these possibilities is integrated with the physical contribution of the past world is decided by the concrescing occasion itself. This new occasion does not exist apart from this decision as the preexisting decider. Instead, it constitutes itself as the subject it becomes in and through the decision.

There is much more to the story, and the description of this more introduces puzzles and perplexities. Pannenberg's concern about abstractions is not to be wholly rejected. But the basic picture of the concrescence is that of the many actual occasions together with God becoming one actual occasion. It is not a picture of abstractions jointly constituting a concrete occasion. Wherever Whitehead's formulations seem to fall victim to the charge of misplaced concreteness, they need to be viewed in light of this basic picture and be reformulated so as to avoid that impression. The concrescence is explained by decisions, those of past occasions, of God, and of the concrescing occasion itself. That the latter plays a role justifies the assertion that the occasion is *causa sui*. But that the former play the dominant roles indicates that the element of self-determination is always within narrow limits and deals only with how the consequences of past temporal decisions are to be supplemented, not with how the causal efficacy of the past, or of God, acts.[11]

---

10. Cf. Alfred North Whitehead, *Process and Reality,* corrected edition, ed. David Ray Griffin and Donald W. Sherburne (New York: The Free Press, 1978), 21.

11. Whitehead's strong emphasis both on determination of each occasion by others and on

II

Section I has offered a defense in response to two very astute criticisms by Pannenberg, one methodological and one material. No criticism of his own work is entailed in these defenses. Of course, the defense of one way of seeing the situation in which we work may be an implicit critique of work resulting from another perception. In this case, I have presented Pannenberg as seeing more continuity between the 19th-century responses to the historical situation and our own than I find warranted. But such perceptions are highly relative. I do not consider my perception "true." On such matters there can be discussion but no proof. I regard it as desirable and appropriate that some theologians pursue the option that commends itself to Pannenberg. The extent to which I thus relativize all our theological projects may be objectionable to him, but it provides me a basis for deep appreciation of his accomplishment.

Nevertheless, there are three features of Pannenberg's theology that have troubled me over the years. In some of his writings they have been sharply and polemically formulated. More recently they are generally muted. Indeed, I have thought at times that his most careful expositions removed from them what I have found objectionable, but other statements indicate that our differences remain. I have studied his most recent major work, *Anthropology in Theological Perspective*,[12] with these issues in mind, and in this section I shall report my findings.

The concerns are as follows. First, to what extent does Pannenberg retain his claim that theology can and should be an objective rather than a confessional way of thinking? Second, does he insist upon a temporally future consummation of history? And third, does he do justice to human freedom?

---

the element of self-determination is carefully stated in the category of freedom and determination. He writes, "This category can be condensed into the formula, that in each concrescence whatever is determinable is determined, but that there is always a remainder for the decision of the subject–superject of that concrescence. This subject–superject is the universe in that synthesis, and beyond it there is nonentity. This final decision is the reaction of the unity of the whole to its own internal determination. This reaction is the final modification of emotion, appreciation, and purpose. But the decision of the whole arises out of the determination of the parts, so as to be strictly relevant to it" (ibid., 27-28).

12. Wolfhart Pannenberg, *Anthropology in Theological Perspective*, trans. Matthew J. O'Connell (Philadelphia: Westminster, 1985).

(1) Pannenberg has seemed to hold that theologians can and should formulate their case in a way that is fully objective—not affected by their particular concerns, commitments, and interests. I have not believed that any purely dispassionate inquiry is possible. To me this has never meant that one should avoid the public arena or appeal to criteria or norms that are protected from public scrutiny. But it has meant that one should acknowledge that what one investigates, what appears to be the appropriate method of investigation, and what counts as adequate evidence are all affected by one's perspective. For Christians who do not bracket their faith when they think, this means that it is appropriate to acknowledge the Christian perspective that shapes their thinking.

How Pannenberg now sees these matters is not entirely clear in this book. Certainly the claim for pure objectivity is muted, while the insistence on thinking in the public domain remains. The Christian understanding of human existence is presented as the fuller implication of what social scientists are saying on the basis of their examination of the evidence. This is admirable.

On the other hand, Pannenberg does clearly affirm that the work of social scientists is itself historically and culturally conditioned. He writes: "Modern anthropology has been historically characterized by a certain tendency and will not allow theologians to claim it as a neutral basis for theological reflections making use of its results."[13] Indeed, it is for just this reason that the theologian is to make a "critical appropriation."[14]

Some of Pannenberg's earlier writings would suggest that this critical appropriation is purely rational and therefore neutrally available for all honest thinkers. The relevant passages in this book could be read in that way. By presenting quite objectively the history out of which modern anthropology comes, it could be argued, one is able to overcome the tendencies that prevent it from being objective and draw the needed neutral conclusions.

On the other hand, in addressing theologians, Pannenberg does appeal to particularities of the theological point of view. "Theologians, moreover, must expect that a critical appropriation of these findings

13. Ibid., 18.
14. Ibid.

65

for theological use is also possible, if the God of the Bible is indeed the creator of all reality." [15] This could be interpreted as meaning that the critical appropriation by theology is motivated and guided by the Christian conviction that the world is the creation of God. The implication might be that others, not believing this, would be led by their different critical appropriation to somewhat divergent conclusions. This would be my own judgment. But Pannenberg seems not to draw this conclusion. Instead, he follows this sentence with a warning: "It is not possible, on the other hand, to decree a priori that the expectation will actually be fulfilled." I am left unsure whether theology, too, is inherently shaped by "certain tendencies" or whether the goal of pure neutrality and objectivity remains intact. Certainly, I have no interest in a priori decrees. As Pannenberg says, "We must wait upon the anthropological phenomenon itself." But does the rejection of a priori decrees entail the denial that as Christians we bring a certain angle of vision, and certain concerns, that differentiate us from most other inquirers into the anthropological phenomenon itself and cause us to see in the phenomena something distinctive?

It may be that Pannenberg intends to affirm that the belief in God the creator does shape theological inquiry, but without predetermining results. As the book proceeds, I would argue that in fact this happens. But it may be that Pannenberg also holds that in other contexts what is presupposed here is rationally demonstrated. That could mean that no acknowledgment of a conditioned perspective is required. This would leave his bolder claims for the demonstrability of Christian faith intact while recognizing that in dealing with one topic—anthropology— in some separation from the rest of the theological system certain Christian beliefs do provide the requisite angle of vision. This is how I am now reading this book. It is a result that justifies the method actually employed in the book on grounds different from that by which I would justify it. But it also removes the debate from the content of the book itself. The method in this book is critical appropriation from a Christian point of view of what has been learned by modern anthropology. This method seems to me sound, and Pannenberg's ability to work with his method is indeed impressive.

---

15. Ibid., 19.

(2) Pannenberg has always emphasized the importance of the future. Human behavior is shaped as much by anticipation as by the weight of the past. The possibility of novelty lies in the power of the not-yet to shape what happens now. On this I am in appreciative agreement. And Pannenberg is on strong ground in showing the importance of expectation of the resurrection of the dead in the early church.

He moves from there, at least in some of his writings, to an affirmation that what is anticipated in the future *is* the resurrection of the dead, and that this, as a temporally future event, is what is shaping the present. He reads human history as a movement toward this final consummation, which he identifies as the kingdom of God and sometimes even as God. The implication is that we are collectively destined for this outcome, that although it is not yet extant, it does already exercise determinative efficacy in drawing the world process to itself.

This way of interpreting openness to the future has never seemed plausible to me. I associate openness to the future with the openness of the future. To me the danger of human self-destruction seems very real. That does not mean that God can be destroyed, and I do believe that in God we too will survive in some perfected way analogous to what Pannenberg calls resurrection. But I cannot connect this with an assured consummation of history or locate this resurrection of all at a single, temporally future time.

Some of Pannenberg's comments have indicated that for him, too, the consummation of history need not be conceived as located at the end of a linear temporal sequence, and I have hoped to find increasing convergence in our eschatological thinking. Hence, I approach his book on anthropology with keen interest. But given the importance of eschatology for Pannenberg's program as a whole, the topic is remarkably muted here. It is not, of course, absent. It appears chiefly in considering personal identity. Pannenberg insists that our individual identity is constituted only by our entire lives and thus exists only in the future and as our destiny. We live now in anticipation of who we are to be, and thus the future shapes the present.

His account of the Spirit as the divine presence is connected with this. This "is the operative presence of a sphere of meaning that precedes individuals and both constitutes and transcends their concrete existence." [16] All life expresses the presence of Spirit, and human self-transcendence embodies it with particular fullness. "The presence of the eschatological future in the life of the church is in a special way the work of the spirit." [17]

With all this, if I am free to understand it in my own way, I am in agreement. The disagreement comes at another level, in "our understanding of reality as such." [18] And Pannenberg says that a book on anthropology is not the place to deal with that topic. Nevertheless, it is clear that his formulations *are* connected with views about reality that do lead, even in this book, to positions with which I disagree.

(3) The best place to articulate a direct disagreement is with respect to human freedom. If human beings are free—in my understanding of freedom—then the historical future is open. What will be is not yet determined. Pannenberg, on the other hand, holds that our historical destiny is assured. Of course, he, like all theologians, speaks emphatically of freedom, and his discussion in this book does much to clarify this murky topic.

Pannenberg opposes all traditional forms of causal determinism. They picture the present as the direct outgrowth of the past and the future as the direct outgrowth of the present. This excludes the possibility of any real novelty and makes a mockery of purpose and hope. His alternative is to stress the power of the future. In other books he has used strong language about the determination of the present by the future. Although that language is not prominent here, his exposition shows that he is thinking in this way. Thus, the alternative to a determinism based on the causal efficacy of the past is a determinism based on the causal efficacy of the future.

Pannenberg is correct that this avoids many of the problems of a determinism of the past. He is also correct that the freedom emphasized and prized in the Bible is not the formal freedom to choose between good and evil, the freedom he denies. It is the freedom to do good, a freedom for which he can account.

On the other hand, although formal freedom is not what is prized

---

16. Ibid., 520.
17. Ibid., 532.
18. Ibid., 521.

in the Bible, it seems clearly presupposed. The call to choose, to repent, and to believe assumes an ability in the hearer that may or may not be exercised. Moral condemnations assume that the one condemned *could* have acted otherwise.

Pannenberg no doubt disagrees. He knows, of course, that people make choices. But in his view the choice is made according to what seems best at the moment of decision. It is not arbitrary.

At times Pannenberg equates formal freedom with the freedom of indifference. That equation arises in the philosophical literature in reflection that follows Pannenberg's line. If we assume that we always act as seems good to us, then the action is determined by the appearance which is in turn determined for that occasion by past forces or anticipation of the future. This determination would break down only when two options are equally attractive, that is, when one is indifferent between them. It is obvious that if this is the only locus of formal freedom, it is of trivial theological interest. It is then easy to understand why for Pannenberg the important questions of freedom lie elsewhere.

But there are other ways of thinking of the act of choosing or deciding. Instead of focusing on conscious choices between two clearly defined alternatives, we can attend instead to the much subtler decisions that characterize life from moment to moment. Pannenberg's own account can be read as providing illustrations of this freedom. For example, he writes: "The call of freedom is always to a harmonization of one's behavior with one's own destiny." [19] I find that a persuasive formulation. But if there is a constant call to such harmonization affecting us moment by moment throughout life, can we not think of more and less responsiveness to that call? Pannenberg would probably agree, but he would interpret imperfect responsiveness as resulting from misperception of our own good. He even acknowledges that we are culpable for misperceiving our good, at least sometimes, but this does not mean for him that in fact, given exactly the situation in which we found ourselves, a different response was possible.

Pannenberg is right that given both the past and the call, much is determined for the responder. But is the response totally determined? There is no evidence for that. And the sense of moral effort supports

_____
19. Ibid., 116.

the view that something is being decided in the response itself. To decide means to cut off, and to cut off implies that there were real possibilities subtly different from those actualized in the moment.

The rationalist will still want to know why the chosen option was in fact decided upon. Did that not imply that it appeared best at the moment? In my opinion, not necessarily, unless one defines "appeared best" in a circular fashion in terms of what was chosen. On any other definition, it seems to me that my decisions often express a tension with what appears best to me.

I have suggested that in each moment the response to the call may be largely determined by the combined effects of the inherited world and the call itself, that what is left over to decide in the decision is quite subtle. But, whereas clearly self-conscious choices of the sort philosophers like to analyze are rare in the course of life, subtle resistance to the call is not. Indeed, decision in this sense is a continuous activity, and however narrow the range of choice in each moment, it is cumulatively very important. Decisions become habitual, and what is habitual forms character. Character is in part, therefore, the product of the exercise of what Pannenberg calls "formal freedom," although it is certainly not much influenced by the freedom of indifference.

III

In addition to these concerns about theological method and content, I wish to conclude by voicing another more general one. Not out of ignorance, but out of choice, Pannenberg has closed himself in writing his anthropology to the voices coming from the third world and from women. He has worked entirely out of the academic North Atlantic heritage. The richness of that academic tradition, mastery of which Pannenberg displays, and the originality and power of his conclusions are beyond question. But in our time, how can we avoid asking whether the *anthropos* so brilliantly discussed is not the male of the species and whether it is not North Atlantic "man" who is in view in the North Atlantic discussion?

Process theology also has its roots in the North Atlantic tradition. They are shallower and more limited than those of Pannenberg, but that is not the reason, I think, for its more open response to the new voices. Since this greater receptivity has characterized almost all process theologians, I doubt that it is purely temperamental. Hence, I have tried to understand how the structures of the two ways of thinking lead to these divergent responses. I will consider first why process theologians think it important to listen to new voices and to allow themselves to be affected in their thinking by what they hear. I will then discuss how Pannenberg's divergent views lead to lack of openness to these voices.

For process theologians, thinking is a part of an experience that is at base "feeling." Indeed, thinking is a form of feeling. What is felt physically is the specific world that flows into an occasion of experience—its past. What is felt mentally must be relevant to what is felt physically even though it can transcend it in some measure. This means that all thinking, including process theological thinking, is conditioned by bodily, social, and historical factors, even though it is not a mere product of its conditions. Determination of the social location of thinkers is always relevant to understanding them, although this does not justify treating their thought reductively.

Knowing that one's own thought is conditioned through and through, one seeks to interact with others who are conditioned by different factors. This enhances the possibility of transcending one's own conditioning. Creative novelty arises through efforts to integrate familiar insights with alien ones. The thinker is always "in process." There can be no completed system.

Process theology grew up in conversation with a variety of older theological traditions as well as through reflection on other fields of inquiry. To some degree it long ago incorporated elements from these. Further encounter is always desirable, but its fruitfulness can decline except as these traditions and fields themselves take on new forms. On the other hand, when new voices give expression to profoundly different experience, the opportunity grows for creative novelty and relative transcending of heretofore limiting conditions.

Obviously, process theologians are humanly just as defensive as others, and just as likely to cling to old ideas in face of new challenges. But when the old ideas themselves call for openness to new ones, the general tendency toward closure is countered by another toward openness. Ideas *do* have consequences.

Pannenberg's theology, despite parallel features, has different effects. In it, the general openness to new stimuli is replaced by the power of the future. This future is a determinate end. Its effectiveness in the past can be traced through a particular history, and Pannenberg can discern in the present the movements that carry that history forward. Other strands of history can make contributions, but only as these feed into the mainstream.

The mainstream of history is traced through the Bible and through Christendom. In recent centuries the Enlightenment and the institutions it produced have played an important role. Today movements toward Christian unity can enable the church to represent the unity of all humanity.

The movement toward ultimate consummation advances through objective knowledge. Theology needs to appropriate the truth of all the sciences. Hence, the academic disciplines developed during the Enlightenment play a major and positive role. Theology accepts the Enlightenment goal of objectivity.

Viewing the situation in this way, Pannenberg is not favorably disposed toward those who turn away from the disciplined methodologies of modern scholarship by which objectivity is approached to emphasize the importance of their diverse experiences. Since academic disciplines have developed ways of checking the excesses of subjectivity of their participants, Pannenberg is not sympathetic with the view that they merely express what is seen from one social location among others. He listens respectfully only to those who accept the disciplines honed over generations of scholarship and contribute to their advance. It is evident that one who interprets God's work in history in this way will not be attuned to liberationist voices.

Ignoring the voices of the oppressed can appear harsh and seem to indicate insensitivity to suffering and injustice. Of course, individuals differ in the degree of their sensitivity, but this is not the issue here. Those who see the only solution to the evil of history in a radical future change almost inevitably regard too much attention to the amelioration of present evils as a distraction. It is important to keep the eye on the goal and pay the necessary price now for advance toward it. This stance characterizes Pannenberg.

An opposite position holds that life should be lived in present immediacy responding to the needs of the moment with no overarching view of where it is leading. Advocates of this position point out how much suffering is engendered by those who are committed to causes and who see them in light of a final consummation.

Process theology takes an intermediate position. It anticipates no final consummation of history and it denies our capacity at any point in the process to foresee even a more proximate future and to engineer its realization. Nevertheless, it does hold that what we now do constitutes conditions which will deeply affect the limitations and the possibilities faced by our descendants. To fail to consider these relatively remote consequences of our actions is irresponsible. And sometimes this means that some present sacrifice on the part of people now alive is needed. For example, to forestall ecological disasters 20 to 50 years from now, we need to change aspects of our economic system now even if that means some lowering of material standards of living on the part of the affluent.

For process theologians, however, this does not reduce the importance of listening to many voices. Whatever the economic changes we need to make now for the sake of our children, we should make them with as much sensitivity as possible to how they will affect those other peoples with whom we share this planet. Also, these others will have much to teach us about ways to order our economy other than those our Western society has generated. Sensitivity to the suffering of others now and in the future and openness to hearing the voices of the oppressed are, for process theology, mutually supportive and supplementary.

Pannenberg, on the other hand, sees the primary importance of "staying the course," confident that the end toward which we are drawn is the only solution to the world's problems. To pay too much attention to those who demand justice now, when the implementation of such supposed justice would distract from those steps that genuinely move toward fundamental fulfillment of all, would not express genuine concern for human beings. It would express instead weakness and sentimentality.

Whether Pannenberg will accept in detail my explanation of his position is for him to say. My point in concluding with these comments is to argue that there is a close connection between our respective theological commitments and our divergent views on matters of this kind. Becoming aware of the divergence of practice in these regards has made me less sanguine about the possibility of overcoming the theoretical issues that separate my position from Pannenberg's. With sadness I acknowledge that my vocation differs from his.

2

THE NATURE OF THE
POWER OF THE FUTURE

Lewis S. Ford

◆

Pannenberg has made us aware of the significance of the future
as few others have done. "From the standpoint of [the God of
the Bible], all reality is referred to the future and is experienced
as eschatologically oriented. . . . [This God is experienced] as the God
of the promises, as the God who leads history into a new future, and
as the God of the coming kingdom."[1] In Jesus' message "the conviction
about the nearness of the kingdom so intensified concentration upon
God's future that alongside this everything transmitted from the past
and all present reality lost any independent meaning, and God's future
itself became determinative of the present."[2] Even though Johannes
Weiss and Albert Schweitzer rediscovered Jesus' eschatological understanding of reality, this has still not been fully appreciated even now.

The real problem in appropriating this biblical orientation lies in
the difficulty of understanding how the future can exert power upon
the present. As Pannenberg observes, "the idea of the future as a mode
of God's being is still undeveloped in theology despite the intimate
connection between God and the coming reign in the eschatological

---

1. Wolfhart Pannenberg, "The God of Hope," in *Basic Questions in Theology,* 2 vols.,
trans. G. Kehm (Philadelphia: Fortress, 1971), 2:237.
2. Ibid.

message of Jesus."[3] It will be our task to consider various ways in which the future might influence present activity.

I

If we bracket God for the time being, the only future beings that can affect us are possibilities. Actualities are too determinately concrete to be future, while subjects are generally not regarded as transcending the present. Possibilities, the humblest sort of beings, however, may have such a future status. Note, however, that the future possibilities that affect the present refer to what might be, not to what in the actual course of things will be actualized. Thus in seeking to interpret Pannenberg's claim that the "future has an imperative claim on the present," Philip Hefner takes as his example the decision to marry or not to marry the next day.[4] Our decisions concern such unactualized alternatives. They concern what might be, for what will be is the determined outcome in some subsequent time, not the alternatives which now impinge upon us from the future.

Yet in many accounts of causation, possibilities have no effective role to play whatsoever. Prior efficient causes are considered to produce their effects jointly. In the ideal case this results in causal determinism, leaving no room for any choice between alternative possibilities. Freedom has been crowded out.

Freedom is included in our analysis only if made central and essential, as Pannenberg does: "Freedom itself presupposes openness to the future. Man is free only because he has a future, because he can go beyond what is presently extant. And so freedom is in general the power that transforms the present."[5] We freely determine our future, however, because we freely appropriate our past. Past conditions do not determine our present situation willy-nilly, for it is only the way we organize and unify them that gives them their present status. Efficient causes actively constitute our being, but only insofar as they have been taken up into our present activity, and are ingredients in the final unification we achieve.

---

3. Ibid., 242.
4. "Questions for Moltmann and Pannenberg," *Una Sancta* 25/3 (1968): 45f.
5. "The God of Hope," 245.

Now if this process of appropriation were only free *from* causal determinism, it would just blindly proceed. The activity of the occasion necessary for organizing the past and freeing it from its domination would be aimless without goals to seek. It is not free unless it is free *to* respond to some possibility of future actualization.[6] On the other hand, it is this intrinsic activity that enables it to respond to possibilities.

Possibilities often appear as mere human projections upon a passive and largely unknown future. But this is never the character of the genuinely novel. As Henry Nelson Wieman has observed, the really novel is that which is capable of transforming our imaginations, that which transcends our projections. Pannenberg criticizes Ernst Bloch for not sufficiently appreciating the power of the novel. "Bloch's appeal to the potencies and latent aspects of the process are difficult to reconcile with his emphasis on the factor of novelty in the coming future. . . .The primacy of the future and its novelty are guaranteed only when the coming kingdom is ontologically grounded in itself and does not owe its future merely to the present wishes and strivings of man."[7]

If the future is ontologically grounded in itself, we shall find that it must be grounded in God as future. If so, God would be thereby the ultimate source of the possibilities for actualities. Also, freedom must be intrinsic to these actualities in order to enable them to respond to such possibilities.

Thus far we have restricted ourselves to the domain of being. In that domain the past seems to have the most power, the future the least, merely what is resident in possibility. In the domain of becoming, we shall see this relationship reversed. At least the past has no power with respect to becoming, since it has already become whatever it is.

II

The one philosopher who has most developed the view that God provides the world with its novel possibilities is Alfred North Whitehead. We need to sketch some pertinent features of this system.

---

6. David McKenzie questions Pannenberg's designation of the "indeterminist theory of the will" as a "false, one-sided representation of the reality of human freedom" (*Jesus—God and Man,* 352), but perhaps it is one-sided because the element of valued possibilities from the future is omitted in favor of human projections from the present; cf. "Pannenberg on God and Freedom," *Journal of Religion* 60/3 (July 1980): 325f.

7. "The God of Hope," 239f.

"Actual occasions" are for Whitehead spatiotemporal instances of concrescence (processes of achieving concreteness), whereby objective beings come into being. Since every being depends upon an antecedent act of becoming, it is possible to reformulate Whitehead's ontological principle as "being is dependent upon becoming for its existence." This inverts the usual order, which designates being as that which has primary existence, with becoming as derivative existence.

This can be very misleading, since in many philosophies being by definition is whatever has primary existence. For Whitehead, however, the secondary contrast between being and becoming takes precedence. This is the contrast between that which already exists, whether as persisting or as acting or as changing, and the creative act which brought it into existence. Normally, philosophy simply brackets the creative act as part of theology, but in Whitehead's philosophy it is brought into the very heart of things. To be sure, there is no transcendent creator who creates everything, usually in a single primordial act, but there are many finite, temporal, self-creative acts (the actual occasions) bringing themselves into being out of the past conditions they inherit. Because the contrast between creative act and created being (or, in Whitehead's terms, between becoming and being) is so basic, the status of primary existence must be specified with respect to them so that becoming is primary, being derivative.

If being were that which had primary existence, then God should be a being or being-itself. But if, as we have argued, becoming is primary, then God should be the supreme instance of becoming, if not becoming itself.

The notion of God in process *(der werdende Gott)* is often dismissed out of hand because of the ideas some have devised in its name. Thus F. W. J. von Schelling, for example, in the various drafts of *Die Weltalter* sought to trace a necessary development from pure absolute indifference to a self-conscious creator of the universe. Development here is the troublesome notion. Thus in a later context Pannenberg can accept divine temporality, but only by distinguishing this sharply from development: "We cannot agree when Whitehead suggests that the futurity of God's kingdom implies a development in God."[8]

---

8. *Theology and the Kingdom of God*, ed. Richard John Neuhaus (Philadelphia: Westminster, 1969), 62.

For Whitehead, however, just because some features are in process does not mean that all are. The metaphysical principles God exemplifies are invariant, and therefore exempt from all development. What is novel for God are the particular concrete contingent achievements of the world. Without this contingency, there would be no divine process. Yet even so, there is no development imposed upon God, since God determines the way in which the concrete being of the past is to be incorporated within the divine experience.

Whitehead's God is personal, subjectively responding to each even as it arises. Because framed in terms of becoming, this concept can resolve a difficulty first formulated with force by J. G. Fichte in 1798: How can a being be both personal and infinite? To be personal it must have something over against itself to experience, while that which is infinite must have all things already within itself. For infinite being this may be impossible; not so, however, for infinite becoming. That which becomes continually incorporates whatever emergent beings there are into itself. What is incorporated is that which is over against it, but it never remains so isolated.

III

Pannenberg, however, has some major reservations about Whitehead's approach, both with respect to its basic coherence as a philosophy[9] and with respect to its application to theology. "Theologically it must be noted that Whitehead conceives of God as only one factor among others within the system of the universe, and not as the creator of the world."[10] Here there is a clear opposition, for Whitehead does conceive of God as the highest being, i.e., as the chief actual entity.[11] Moreover, he strongly opposes the claim that God is creator. In order to have created the world *ex nihilo,* God would require unilateral power, which if it

---

9. See the appendix.

10. "Gott und die Natur," *Theologie und Philosophie* 58 (1983): 491.

11. Paul Tillich strongly opposed this notion: "The being of God is being-itself. The being of God cannot be understood as the existence of a being alongside others or above others. If God is *a* being, he is subject to the categories of finitude, especially to space and substance. Even if he is called the 'highest being' in the sense of the 'most perfect' and the 'most powerful' being, this situation is not changed. When applied to God, superlatives become diminutives. They place him on the level of other beings while elevating him above all of them" (*Systematic Theology,* vol. 1 [Chicago: University of Chicago Press, 1951], 235).

does not determine all beings (preempting any freedom for us) must always be available to intervene at will to prevent evil or suffering. But if God could prevent evil and yet does not, then God is not good. Whitehead was an atheist from about 1898 until 1925 when he discovered a workable concept of God which did *not* entail that such a God was also creator.[12]

There may well be irreconcilable differences between Whitehead's thought and Pannenberg's, although we shall see below that the latter's eschatological understanding of creation may differ from the sort of creation Whitehead opposes. Yet it may be possible to modify Whitehead's philosophy in ways which can enter into more fruitful dialog with Pannenberg's approach.

While pioneering a radicalized notion of becoming, Whitehead did not apply it in any thoroughgoing way to God, who is conceived both in terms of being and becoming. The modification I propose is that we reconceive God solely in terms of becoming. This means, within the Whiteheadian framework, that God cannot be "prehended" or objectively encountered, since only beings are objective. Instead of being prehended, God empowers each actual occasion to prehend its past. For Whitehead, it is the creativity intrinsic within each occasion which enables it to act, but no source for this creativity is ever given.[13] If God is identified with the creativity of the future, considered as the whole continuous field (the extensive continuum) lying in the future of the creative advance, then this creativity becomes pluralized as the many independently active occasions of the present.[14]

By the ontological principle, the extensive continuum, insofar as present, only exists insofar as exemplified by the actual occasions. Pannenberg finds it "unsatisfactory that space and time for Whitehead appear merely as functions of the eventful actual entities. Whitehead recognizes no concept of an ontologically primordial totality, somewhat in the form of a field, which would have reality prior to particles and

---

12. See my study *The Emergence of Whitehead's Metaphysics* (Albany: State University of New York Press, 1984), 101-107.

13. That is, in his major work, *Process and Reality* (New York: Macmillan, 1929). In *Adventures of Ideas* (New York: Macmillan, 1933), it is derived from the past, taken as a whole.

14. These ideas are developed in "The Divine Activity of the Future," *Process Studies* 11/3 (Fall 1981): 169-79, and "Creativity in a Future Key," in *New Essays in Metaphysics,* ed. Robert C. Neville (Albany: State University Press of New York, 1986), 179-198.

events, and should be understood moreover thus as the ground for their reality."[15] This difficulty is resolved if God is identified with future creativity.

The way that God empowers each occasion by means of communicating to it its creativity has important affinities with a central feature of Aquinas' thought: the way in which God as *esse ipsum,* the infinite act of being, communicates *esse* to each creature.

On the other hand, Aquinas, along with many others, holds God to be immutable and infinite. If God is perfect, it is argued, God must have perfect unity, i.e., simplicity, lacking parts. But becoming involves at least temporal parts, the before and after of achieved being. To be simple, God must be immutable, impassible, existent only as being. This is a very influential argument, yet it must be carefully noted that it assumes that God is being, which therefore as perfect unity must be simple. If, on the other hand, God is becoming, then God must be perfect becoming, i.e., the perfect ongoing unification of all things.[16]

Classical theists often charge that Whitehead's God is finite. He does hold "that all actualization is finite,"[17] for "every occasion of actuality is in its own nature finite. There is no totality which is the harmony of all perfections. Whatever is realized in any one occasion of experience necessarily excludes the unbounded welter of contrary possibilities. There are always 'others,' which might have been and are not."[18] From this it would seem possible to infer that if God were an actual being, God would have to be finite, but we can more appropriately infer that God, since infinite,[19] cannot be a being, or even

---

15. Pannenberg, "Gott und die Natur," 491. Elsewhere Pannenberg questions Whitehead's claim that every unity is a unification of some multiplicity (just as every being is the outcome of some becoming). Pannenberg rightly points out that every multiplicity requires unity, for the members of that multiplicity must be many ones. If each were not one, together they would not make many. Then, of course, there would be an infinite regress, with each many requiring prior ones, each one presupposing some many. Such an infinite regress in time, however, poses no problems if there is no beginning to the world process.

16. This argument is examined in greater detail in my essay on "Process and Thomist Views Concerning Divine Perfection," in *The Universe as Journey: Conversations with W. Norris Clarke,* S.J., ed. Gerald A. McCool, S.J. (New York: Fordham University Press, 1988), pp. 115-29.

17. Whitehead, *Adventures of Ideas,* 333.

18. Ibid., 356.

19. I have argued for "The Infinite God of Process Theism" in the *Proceedings of the American Catholic Philosophical Association* 55 (1981): 84-90.

being, but becoming. As Whitehead observes, this intrinsic incompatibility among possibilities with respect to their realization "has never been applied to ideals in the Divine realization [nor to the way God experiences the world]. We must conceive the Divine Eros as the active entertainment of all ideals, with the urge to their finite realizations, each in its due season. Thus a process must be inherent in God's nature whereby his infinity is acquiring realization [in the actual world, and in God's experience of that world]." [20]

As long as we restrict ourselves to the domain of being, certain problems for Pannenberg's approach seem insuperable. Philip Hefner observes that when he speaks about the future determining the present, "he seems to be saying that the future as cause is subsequent to its effects in the present. He seems to be asking us to reverse our prevailing notions of causality, so that the customary earlier/later relationship between cause and effect which we presume can be overturned. Conceptually, I find this to be a very difficult thing to accomplish." [21]

Here we see the clash of two fundamental intuitions: the scientific claim that the earlier always affects the later, not vice versa, and the idealist claim that the part is conceptually dependent upon the whole. [22] As long as individual sequences of efficient causation alone are considered, or the part/whole relationship is entertained apart from time, no conflict need arise. But Pannenberg conceives of the future as the whole in terms of which present and past parts are shaped. Then it

---

20. *Adventures of Ideas*, 357.
21. Philip Hefner, "Questions for Moltmann and Pannenberg," 45.
22. Whitehead sought to acknowledge the idealistic claim within the context of science in his notion of "organic mechanism": the "organic whole" influences the parts, while the mechanically conceived parts affect the whole (*The Emergence of Whitehead's Metaphysics*, 31-37). See *Science and the Modern World* (New York: Free Press, 1967), 79f., 103f., 106-109, 149f. Yet this resolution is achieved by ignoring time. Later, in *Process and Reality*, he sought first to conceive of an individual concrescence as a whole influencing its component feelings by means of the mutual sensitivity of feelings (*Process and Reality* [New York: The Free Press, 1978], 222f.; cf. *The Emergence of Whitehead's Metaphysics*, 216f.). Still the difficulty persists, for then the later outcome (which alone is the whole) influences the earlier components.

Once he had established the conceptuality of the subjective aim which directed the activity of the concrescing occasion towards the establishment of its final determination, however, mutual sensitivity was carefully restricted. The aim is progressively modified during the course of the concrescence, and each of these modifications is designated a "subjective end" (*Process and Reality*, 224). Each feeling is affected by all subjective ends which precede it, and each end influences whatever feelings succeed it. By this principle the part/whole relationship, while reciprocal, does not conflict with the before/after rule.

does seem that the later affects the earlier, contrary to the asymmetries of time.

While it is true that only the earlier can affect the later, it need not be true that the future must always be conceived as later than the present. This is certainly true for beings, for what will be first occurs when it becomes present, and this is always later than that which had then been present. It is not true for becoming, however, for this concerns (processes of) determination, not the succession of determinate events. What is least determinate is earliest in the process of determination; what is most determinate is latest. Yet the most determinate is that which is fully concrete, like the concreteness of the past, while the least determinate is most like future possibility. For a process of becoming, the future can affect us because in that order the future is earlier, not later.

The future is the whole, to be sure, but the future I envisage is not the future of being, that which will be, but rather the future of becoming, that which now might be, only gradually becoming what will be as contingencies are freely realized in the course of time. It is as what might be that the future can influence us, for what will be is not yet. God is the dynamic source of such novelty, but God has both necessary and contingent features, and these contingent features, such as the divine experience of the world, dependent upon the course of the world, are not yet determined. Only God's invariant features must influence us now.[23]

---

23. Hartshorne here appeals to God's abstract nature, while Whitehead introduces the metaphysical principles that even God exemplifies. Yet I sometimes wonder whether *any* metaphysical principle is invariant over all worlds that might come into existence. Perhaps the goodness of God is invariant over all worlds, even though the particular form of goodness could vary. Does God seek the welfare of every world? Yet what about worlds so inherently evil that they do not deserve to persist? Would divine goodness then mean something like: "seeking the welfare of every possibly redeemable world?"

Pannenberg seconds Paul Tillich's objection that God does not exemplify metaphysical categories (*Systematic Theology*, vol. 1, 235). Tillich's reason for so objecting is that God is not a being, a view I have come to be sympathetic with, since God for me is not being but becoming: "Notes toward a Reconciliation of Whitehead and Tillich," *Union Seminary Quarterly Review* 39/1-2 (1984): 41-46. Yet the categories of being could be transformed into the categories of becoming. Pannenberg's objection may apply to both: "The idea of God is destroyed when he is conceived as an application instance (even though it be the highest instance) of some general structure that in its generality is distinct from God [since predicated of other entities as well] . . ." ("The Significance of the Categories 'Part' and 'Whole' for the Epistemology of Theology,"

Other modifications of Whitehead's philosophy may also be needed to enter into dialogue with Pannenberg's theology. Whitehead's own position has no way to address the future in terms of possibility, since possibility is interpreted in terms of timeless eternal objects. These are pure possibilities applicable to all situations, not real possibilities specifying what is actualizable under those conditions in the relevant future. Pure possibilities by themselves are neither good nor evil, for that depends on the particular situations within which they are to be actualized. In a sparse agrarian society a large family was a boon in earlier times, not so in the crowded slums of Latin America. Values attach to the real possibilities lying in the relevant future. If God creates himself by creating such real possibilities, then God is active futurally and not timelessly in terms of some primordial nature.[24]

On this view God creates our future by creating the novel possibilities we seek to actualize. In Pannenberg's words, God "touches every present concretely as its future in the possibilities of its transformation."[25] In so doing, God is personal. "Personality expresses itself in freedom," and "freedom is in general the power that transforms the present."[26] Personality is essential to humanity, which is not something that is merely existent as something past: "a person is the opposite of an existent being. Human beings are persons by the very fact that they are not wholly and completely existent for us in their reality, but are characterized by freedom. . . ."[27] "Man is free only because he has a future, because he can go beyond what is presently extant. And

---

Journal of Religion 66 [October 1986]: 380).

These are not alien structures for Whitehead, who argues that God's "conceptual actuality at once exemplifies and establishes the categorial conditions" (*Process and Reality,* 344, cf. 40). If we interpret "establishing" in terms of creating, and construe creating as inherently temporal, it seems that none of the principles God exemplifies has any status apart from God nor is even capable of being invariant throughout the whole of the temporal process. But these two conditions have yet to be adequately established.

24. The uncreated eternal objects constituting the primordial nature form the reason why God is thought of as a being as well as becoming. Yet if uncreated, there is no reason in actualization why they are as they are, which restricts arbitrarily the scope of the ontological principle (*Process and Reality,* 24f.). If God creates real possibilities in God's self-creation, then we might see eternal objects as pure possibilities abstracting from these real possibilities. If viewed in abstraction from their emergence, such objects will *appear* as timeless.

25. "The God of Hope," 246.

26. Ibid., 245.

27. "Speaking about God in the Face of Atheist Criticism," *The Idea of God and Human Freedom* (Philadelphia: Westminster, 1973), 112.

so freedom is in general the power that transforms the present."[28] Couched in terms of my modification of Whitehead, freedom is the human expression of creativity, and that creativity is the present appropriation of the future creativity which is God.

IV

Yet while Pannenberg conceives God as the power of the future who grants us our freedom, there is also a strain in his thought which is apparently at odds with this: the identification of God with the reality which determines everything ("die alles bestimmende Wirklichkeit"). Pannenberg agrees that this would generate a conflict if God and humankind were present realities, but not if God is future: "A being presently at hand, and equipped with omnipotence, would destroy such freedom by virtue of his overpowering might. But the power of the future is distinguished by the fact that it frees man from his ties to what presently exists in order to liberate him for his future, to give him his freedom."[29] Indeed, it gives him his freedom from the past, but does it give him his freedom from God?

As future, "it is necessary to say that, in a restricted but important sense, God does not yet exist."[30] Insofar as God does not yet exist, God places no limitations upon creaturely freedom, to be sure, but at the same time no real connectedness is established as well. This could be a kind of futuristic deism. Everything depends upon the character of this connection. Does present human freedom constitute its character, or does the future being of God? Pannenberg recognizes that "God's being is still in the process of coming to be,"[31] but not that there is any development. If there is no development, it is difficult to see how our actions can constitute God's inner nature, since our actions are radically contingent and might not have been. If God's nature comes into being as that which it is, without any inner change, then that nature is the constitutive and all-determining factor of our activity in the present.

---

28. "The God of Hope," 245.
29. Ibid., 242f.
30. *Theology and the Kingdom of God*, 56.
31. Ibid.

To be sure, "what turns out to be true in the future will then be evident as having been true all along."[32] It will be true all along, whatever the final nature of God is, but the key question then becomes: Is the divine nature constituted by our free acts, or are our present acts somehow retroactively constituted by that final nature?

The same issue is posed by the question of creation. Pannenberg does not understand by creation simply some past or primordial act, but has reinterpreted it creatively in terms of the future. God creates the whole of reality as the future determiner of all things. This is justified by an appeal to the New Testament: "But the God of the coming kingdom had to become the occasion for an eschatological reversal of the idea of creation as soon as he was recognized—as happened in the message of Jesus—as the one who by the future of his lordship is alone powerful over the present world and decisive for its meaning, its essence."[33]

There is a perfectly analogous sense in which God could be said to create the world for Whitehead, although Whitehead would not use the term *create* in this sense. Terms such as *self* and *world* are indexical, made with reference to the particular actual situation at hand. Thus each occasion has its own world, and there is no single privileged event which could be described as the end of the world or the end of history. Each occasion is the end of its world as the final summation and appropriation of all its conditions. Likewise, God at every phase of the divine concrescence experiences the world in terms of everything that has happened up to then. Moreover, God supplements God's direct experience with whatever additional imaginative supplement that may be needed in order to overcome the evil of its conflicts and suffering, thereby determining its ultimate significance in the scheme of things.[34] In this sense Whitehead's God is the ultimate determiner of all things, not as determining each act individually, but as determining its role and significance in the unity of the final whole.

But if *world* is understood relatively, there is no absolute end of

---

32. Ibid., 63.

33. "The God of Hope," 2:243.

34. This theme has been explored in my essay on the "Divine Persuasion and the Triumph of the Good," 287-304, in *Process Philosophy and Christian Thought*, ed. Delwin Brown, Ralph E. James Jr., and Gene Reeves (Indianapolis: Bobbs-Merrill, 1971).

the world or of history. Even though each occasion consummates the whole of the world prior to itself, there are always occasions succeeding it. The problem with any absolute, whether of time or the world or history, is that nothing temporal succeeds it, and the temporal modalities are radically altered. When the end of history becomes realized, or when the kingdom comes, the divine activity of the future becomes present, and overpowers our freedom. Our freedom can be respected only if it is not subject to divine control. Yet how then can God be the present all-determining reality in that future day?

Whitehead's solution, as we have seen, is to reconceive the eschaton in terms of divine experience, whereby our (present) free acts are included in the (future) divine experience. We might think of this as the continual creation of the whole to which the multiplicity of the world contributes. This is possible only if God is in becoming, capable of being enriched, rather than in being, whether present or future.

The end of history is usually taken to be a public event in eschatological speculation. Those alive on that day will witness it; in fact, those who have died will be resurrected to share in that event.[35] This is what would make it a present event with its attendant difficulties for the freedom of those participants. The present is the domain of a plurality of free subjectivities. If the future belongs solely to God, however, it is the domain of one cosmic subjectivity, capable of experiencing the whole. Insofar as the end is conceived to be the whole of history, the whole of reality, it must needs be a private event. Subjects, not objects, are the more inclusive. A subject can experience an object, but not vice versa. A plurality of subjects can only be finally included in one cosmic experience, a final private event.

This need not mean that, if a Whiteheadian perspective were true, we would have no personal participation in the eschaton. For even though there should not be survival of disembodied souls, and there would be no multiplicity of separate personal beings on that day, our subjectivity might be sustained by its participation in God. Then God's experience becomes the bodily support we would need to experience

---

35. The original notion of resurrection did not consider the end of all temporal ages, but only the end of this age. We are resurrected to enjoy life in another temporal age, the age to come.

with God (in our own limited way) God's experience of the totality of the world-process "whole and perfect in a single moment."[36] If so, the eschaton could be an ongoing process whereby God would always be experiencing the world anew. The eschaton is still the end of the world, but that end is relative to God's state at that particular time.

Pannenberg finds that there is an absolute end to time, however, citing this argument: "But Kant himself, in his transcendental aesthetics, characterized time (like space) as conceived primarily as a *whole* because all identification of partial spaces and times already presupposes the whole of space and the whole of time (A 39-40; B 47-48). In reference to the concept of time, this seems to entail that any awareness of time already implies the idea of an end of time, because a *whole* of time is conceivable only if an end of the temporal sequence is assumed. However, if such an end is conceived as the end of time and not as [the] end of a temporal process within time, then it would be contradictory to ask what will happen *after* that end."[37]

The first sentence of this argument points to an undoubted feature of time: all temporal entities (events) occupy portions of time, and hence belong to a wider temporal whole. But it is left an open question whether the temporal whole is infinite or finite. A similar line of reasoning leads Whitehead from the spatiotemporal properties of events to the extensive continuum in which they are embedded, this continuum thought of as infinite. The key claim lies rather in the second sentence, that "a whole of time is conceivable only if an end of the temporal sequence is assumed." This is surely true for all finite temporal wholes, but is it true for an infinite one? If it be argued that only finite wholes are conceivable, I see no difficulties with the conceivability of an infinite temporal whole, particularly as every event, no matter how large, seems to have events which were before and events coming after it.

---

36. Whiteheadians have developed a diversity of viewpoints concerning the hereafter, but this viewpoint has been developed by Marjorie Suchocki in "The Question of Immortality," *Journal of Religion* 57 (July 1977), and *God—Christ—Church* (New York: Crossroad, 1982), chap. 17. See also Lewis S. Ford and Marjorie Suchocki, "A Whiteheadian Reflection on Subjective Immortality," *Process Studies* 7/1 (Spring 1977): 1-13.

37. "Constructive and Critical Functions of Christian Eschatology" (Ingersoll Lecture 1983), *Harvard Theological Review* 77/2 (1984): 137. The citation of Kant refers to his *Critique of Pure Reason.*

Pannenberg on the basis of his argument, however, concludes: "The end of time does not border on some other time, but the notion of an end of time expresses the finite character of time as such. The end of time borders on eternity where the finitude of time, the separation of its succeeding instants from its predessors and successors will be removed." [38] If the end of time is conceived dynamically as the end of all present and past time, it would be the future divine experience of all that has become actual. This experience is both immediately future to our present, and also eternal in the Boethian sense of the summation of temporal succession in a single simultaneous whole. For all pasts, no matter how distant, are components of this single experience. [39]

There are differences here whether the final eschaton is public or private, and whether it is to be conceived as absolute and fixed, or as relative and dynamic. Yet when we consider what the divine experience at the eschaton might be, there is possible agreement. Thus for each of us God determines the organization and meaning (significance) of the whole. If placing God in the future of each free act is to allow that act to constitute God's experience (and not vice versa), then God as future comes into being by being constituted by the actualization of all temporal acts, then there would seem to be very little difference as to how the power of the future actualizes itself. If so, however, what is the point of the opposition to "development" in God? If these issues are agreed to, we might just drop the term, which plays no role in working out the Whiteheadian conception of God anyway.

God as future exists for the world as its lure and creative empowerment. But on our Whiteheadian perspective, God cannot be simply identified with the absolute future of the world. God is forever future, no matter what the present might be.

APPENDIX: PANNENBERG'S CRITIQUE OF WHITEHEAD

Pannenberg's reluctance to use more of Whitehead's categories in articulating his own theology reflects his own reservations about this

---

38. Ibid.
39. See my essay on "Boethius and Whitehead and Time and Eternity," *International Philosophical Quarterly* 8/1 (March 1968): 38-67.

philosophy. Fortunately, he has spelled out in some detail these reservations in his essay "Atom, Duration, Form: Difficulties with Process Philosophy."[40] This is a very perceptive critique deserving of careful response. We shall consider some of his many objections.

Pannenberg is surely correct that "process philosophy," if construed broadly as dismissing "the thought of a timeless, identical substance" (21), certainly includes other thinkers such as Bergson and Alexander. Process can certainly be conceived more monistically than Whitehead conceives it. The key question is rather whether Whitehead's own particular intensification of "process" as the coming into being of actualities[41] requires Whitehead's specific hypotheses about atomic occasions or eternal objects.

Objection 1: Pannenberg challenges Whitehead's contention that only the possible is continuous, while the actual is always atomic. Yet the past (which alone has concrete being) is also continuous, and so is the future;[42] it is only the present which is atomic.

The present must be discrete and atomic for Whitehead because of the dynamics of becoming, which is effected by the unification of the many into one. Were the process not to terminate in unity, no being would emerge. If it does terminate, there is a discrete boundary between that occasion and its successor, since the successor as yet lacks any determinate unity. If there were only a continuous process of determination, no determinateness would ever be achieved. Such a continuous process, never having any result that has being, would be objectively indistinguishable from sheer nothing.

Objection 2: In contrast to Whitehead's (apparent?) emphasis on

---

40. *Process Studies* 14/1 (Spring 1984): 21-30. All page references in this appendix shall be to pages of this essay.

The German original, "Atom, Dauer, Gestalt. Schwierigkeiten mit der Prozess philosophie," appears in *Whiteheads Metaphysik der Kreativitäet,* ed. Friedrich Rapp and Reiner Wiehl (Freiburg: Verlag Karl Alber, 1986), 185-195, including an important final note on Cobb, Gilkey, and creation not in the English translation.

41. Much confusion over this point stems from the fact that Whitehead had a rather conventional understanding of "process" in *Science and the Modern World,* but intensified it in *Process and Reality;* see my essay on "The Concept of 'Process': From 'Transition' to 'Concrescence,' " in *Whitehead and the Idea of Process,* ed. H. Holz and E. Wolf-Gazo (Freiburg: Verlag Karl Alber, 1984).

42. If we adopt my modification reconceiving the future as the activity of God, then it is both active and continuous, and the continuity of process is prior to its discontinuity.

the many, Pannenberg counters that "without the One the others can be neither one nor many and there would be absolutely nothing" (23).

The issue of the many and the one is faced by Whitehead within a dynamic context. The many must be many ones, namely, the many past occasions constituting the initial phase of the inner process or concrescence of an occasion. In turn each one is derived from, and constituted by, its particular many, for in concrescence the many become one. Neither many nor one has the ultimate priority, for each one comes from a many, and each many is formed from many ones. This constitutes an infinite regress, to be sure, but it is a nonvicious regress of a temporal series which has no absolute beginning. Yet this borders on questions concerning creation *ex nihilo*.

Objection 3: "The idea of the radical self-creation of each actual occasion is the reason why Whitehead's metaphysics cannot be reconciled with the Biblical idea of creation nor, therefore, with the Biblical idea of God" (28). It cannot be reconciled with creation *ex nihilo,* but could make sense of the divine creative words in Genesis 1 if these are understood as imperatives. For commands are simply the authoritative form of persuasion. The difficulty with the traditional account of creation is that it requires classical omnipotence, in which God is either the all-determiner, precluding any causal determination from the past and thereby undercutting all scientific investigation of the world (as in the theories of al-Ghazzahi or Nicholas of Autrecourt), as well as any nondivine self-determination, or God's power recedes into the background as the source of the being but not of the determinate structure of things. Pannenberg's own reconceptualization of God's activity as the power of the future effectively contrasts with past efficient causation and present creaturely freedom, provided these other kinds of determination are affirmed in the process.[43]

---

43. The relation between the present self and the future power of God may be understood in terms of anticipation. Here I find myself in fundamental agreement with Pannenberg's observation that "Whitehead does not go so far as to describe the significance of anticipation for the formation of the subject, as constituting its subjectivity out of a future which already [partially?] determines the present by way of anticipation" (28). Whitehead (like most others) treats the future as purely passive, upon which the present lays down conditions.

Whitehead so distinguished God and creativity that he does not conceive God as creator in the sense of being the source of the being, or even of the becoming, of an occasion. If, however, we reconceive God as the creativity or activity of the future, then the pluralization of that creativity into the present is the way in which God gives finite occasions their power of becoming whereby they are capable of determining themselves.

Objection 4: There is no real counterbalance to the atomicity of occasions "because the whole of the universe or of the spatiotemporal continuum, on his account, has no ontological independence over against the monad-like events" (24). Yet should there be any such counterbalance? The world, in itself, is simply the multiplicity of past events. Should it have a unity by itself, apart from the actual concrescenses which unify it? Even the unity which God establishes for it is context-dependent and fleeting, requiring a new unity to incorporate each day as it occurs.

Objection 5: "On the one hand, the actual occasion or entity ought to be the ultimate constituent of the physical universe. On the other hand, these final constituents of the universe are taken to be still further analyzable into the relations or 'prehensions' which constitute them" (25). If we say that the actual entities are the final concrete actualities, and the divisions into prehensions are merely hypothetical, then "how is it possible to continue to interpret the actual occasion itself as a process with different phases, in which it generates itself [*Process and Reality,* p. 26], while asserting that the end phase of this process, on the other hand, ought to be identical with the complete duration of the event? [*Process and Reality,* p. 283]" (25).

In order to untangle the many issues these questions raise, I think it important to insist on the distinction between "being" and "becoming." Most human inquiries and all empirical sciences concern themselves with the things which are. This is also true for most philosophy, though we expect theology to concern itself with creation as well. Whitehead, at least in the later parts of *Process and Reality,* was concerned primarily with "becoming," how that which is comes to be.

Now if we adopt the standpoint of "being," only it is concretely actual. Any divisions are hypothetical and abstract, though individual coordinate divisions, which indicate sections of the final determinate beings, are themselves determinate. Genetic division, which distinguishes the various phases of the process whereby it came to be what it is, is doubly abstract, for its divisions (the phases) are all indeterminate, except for the final one. From the perspective of "being," we have only a bloodless dance of abstractions.

From the standpoint of the "becoming" of the occasion, however, there is a real coming into being, whereby an initial indeterminacy is transformed into a concrete outcome. Such a process takes time. Since it is a self-creation, the occasion in becoming (in the present) occupies the same spatiotemporal region which the event has as it emerges (in the immediate past). The region is the same, having the same spatio-temporal coordinates, but the creative advance has moved on. "Becoming" and "being" do not occupy the same region simultaneously, but successively, for the "becoming" is that which produces the "being."

Objection 6: How can the process take time, if concrescence "implies the paradoxical assumption of a nontemporal process"? It should be carefully noted that Whitehead reserves the term "nontemporal" to refer exclusively to God's primordial envisagement of the eternal (time-less, atemporal) objects, although since the mental pole is out of time, we may think of conceptual realization, when divorced from physical interaction with actuality, as nontemporal by extension. Thus if we say that ordinary concrescence is nontemporal, we are apt to confuse physical and conceptual realization, while if we say that it is atemporal, then we confuse the dynamics of concrescence with the static structure of eternal objects. Yet we have no other good word for that which is not temporal. Concrescence seems to be some *tertium quid,* which is neither temporal nor not temporal.

The idea of concrescence need not be at fault here so much as the way of referring to it in temporal terms. Here I find Whitehead's specification of time unduly narrow. He insists that "the genetic process is not the temporal succession" (*Process and Reality,* p. 283), but specifies in the preceding paragraph that "this genetic passage from phase to phase is not in physical time," i.e., in the time we objectively experience, and which is investigated by physics and the other sciences. This is the B-series McTaggart has isolated. In order to prevent the difficulties that arise from talking of concrescence as not temporal, I propose we broaden our understanding of time to include the subjective experience of time (McTaggart's A-series). Generally, time is the order of real succession. According to physical time, it is the succession of determinate beings. According to genetic time, it is the succession of phases of increasing determination, with the earlier the least deter-minate.

In the order of being, the past simply refers to what is earlier than the present. As being it is completely determinate. In the order of becoming, what is earlier than the present is even less determinate than the present, and hence can only be the future, while what is later than the present must be more determinate, and hence more like the past. Thus with respect to being and becoming, the two orders are reversed. This apparent paradox may have led Whitehead to avoid the term "time" with respect to becoming. But in any case, concrescence takes place in an order of real succession, even though this is not the physical time of being.[44]

Objection 7: "If we cannot, in fact, really divide the actual occasion further but can only abstractly differentiate the relationships which constitute its identity, then we cannot, by the same token, characterize the actual occasion as being the result of a process in which these aspects which can only be distinguished in the abstract are actually integrated" (25).

Concrescence is not a process of being where each stage has its own being. In becoming, nothing exists until that which is to become appears, which is only in the final phase. That is, nothing objective exists. Nevertheless, just because nothing exists during becoming is not to say becoming is not dynamic. Since the result finally exists, when nothing did before, the process itself was dynamic.

Objection 8: "The fact that the emergence of form [or perhaps more appropriately, *Gestalt*] cannot be derived from the actual occasions of which [it] might consist shows once again that the unity of the field cannot be reduced to [the] elementary momentary events which [are present] in it" (27). Whitehead agrees that every occasion is a new *Gestalt,* which cannot be wholly constituted out of the occasions of its past. But he looks to God as the instrument of novelty for the world, providing for the individual in terms of a particular novel possibility for it, whereby it can integrate just that past in its own appropriate way. The actual occasions of the past are an inadequate resource for explaining emergent *Gestalten,* but fortunately there are other resources at Whitehead's disposal.

---

44. For a fuller account on this point, see my essay "Creativity in a Future Key," in *New Essays in Metaphysics,* esp. 189-192.

3

THE DISSOLUTION OF THE UNION OF NATURE AND GRACE AT THE DAWN OF THE MODERN AGE

Louis Dupré

◆

F
ew theologians have kept their reflection more in tune with the intellectual currents of our age than Wolfhart Pannenberg. He has persistently searched for the (often hidden) presence of a transcendent dimension in the thought of those who have defined the shape of modern culture. Among his sources Herder, Kant, Hegel, and Popper occupy a position at least equal to that of Barth, Bultmann, and Rahner. Still, Pannenberg's enterprise stands at the opposite side of the so-called secular theologies of our time. Instead of simply redefining the fundamental issues of Christian theology, he succeeds in detecting a real continuity of the major thinkers of our age with the earlier tradition. In a well-known critique of Hans Blumenberg's thesis about modern culture, he has denied that the theological concerns of the past have ceased to play a role in the present.[1] But neither does Pannenberg embrace Löwith's position according to which the philosophies of the modern age are no more than laicized theologies. Rather, they present totally new ways of thinking *traditional problems*.

---

1. "The modern age did not come about through an act of humanist self-assertion against the absolutism of grace in the Christian idea of God. It is true that its origins were characterized by a break with medieval thought. But the issue here was not the omnipotence of God and the freedom of his grace, but the positivism of the ecclesiastical system of salvation, the ecclesiastical authority which for the late Middle Ages was incapable of rational justification" (*The Idea of God and Human Freedom* [Philadelphia: Westminster, 1973], 188).

In the relation between the old and the new I can think of no intellectual factor that has played a more decisive role than the transformation of the concept of *nature*. While this concept in the Christian as well as in the classical tradition had an intrinsically religious content, a certain interpretation of transcendence formulated at the end of the Middle Ages, as well as a methodological separation of the respective domains of theology and philosophy, eventually resulted in two orders of reality. Thus grace, which earlier had penetrated the order of nature, at the beginning of the modern age came to be reduced to an addition to nature, an imputed justification of it, or a supernature beside it. The following essay investigates the origins of this process. It assumes throughout that this dualism is directly connected with, and greatly responsible for, the desacralization of modern culture.

Once the order of grace had become marginal to nature, however much it might claim to remain its ultimate goal, its potential for intrinsically affecting culture vanished. Theology thereby lost much of its original role. Instead of shaping the very substance of culture, as it had done in the past, it became reduced to a science among others with a method and an object exclusively its own. Because of its remoteness other sciences could freely ignore it and, where it continued to retain a modicum of (mostly political) authority, went out of their way to avoid any contact with it. Incapable of remedying a condition inherent in the modern concept of culture yet still controlling the consciences of the majority of its members, theology had little choice but to move forward on its self-made path. To many it remained a respectable, to some a venerable science, but few considered it indispensable for understanding either themselves or their culture. By the end of the last century this marginalization had reached the proportions of a major crisis. Systematic theology, both the Catholic scholastic and the Protestant orthodox or liberal, had become an esoteric enterprise reserved to a few cognoscenti and foisted off on an either reluctant or resigned clergy in training. Even today it remains possible to protract a theological game which has lost no internal coherence but all vital interest for believers as well as unbelievers. Toward the middle of this century powerful voices for change were heard. Bultmann, Barth, and Tillich were among the first of their generation to defend a reunion with culture. Pannenberg stands in the present generation of that integralist movement. To them, a theology that has nothing to say to its culture has lost its very raison d'être. To succeed in this new task all had to bridge the cultural gap between the two worlds, and that meant, in some way, reuniting with theology the nature which an earlier tradition had severed from it.

Pannenberg has written little on nature as such, but he is clearly aware of the baneful impact of the modern separation of nature and grace and constantly concerned to overcome it. The very fact that anthropology and theory of science occupy such a significant position in his theological thinking witnesses to his conviction that "the two orders" of reality need not remain separate. The very possibility of a theological anthropology and cosmology fully integrated with modern science, psychology, and philosophy presupposes the existence of a fundamental unity. It also assumes, if I am not mistaken, that the modern worldview which has gradually overcome that theological dualism in a secular homogeneity of its own offers once again an unexpected opportunity for retrieving the human being's existential relation to the transcendent from a Christian perspective in a new nondualist theological model.

Not before the 13th century do we perceive any signs of an opposition between nature and grace. The Aristotelian scholastics considered the order of nature the formal object of a rational investigation in its own right. While Albert and Aquinas clearly subordinated this semi-independent realm to that of theology, the Averroist Aristotelians in various degrees detached the study of nature from that of revelation. With the condemnation of the theory of "double truth" the powers of Averroism were roundly defeated. Yet the most serious problem facing the attempt to incorporate Aristotle's philosophy into Christian theology remained its different concept of nature. In Latin theology *nature* had referred to human nature in the concrete context of grace. Thus St. Augustine calls the original state of justice "natural"—an expression that would be seriously misunderstood by Baius and Jansenius. Even as late as Duns Scotus did *nature* include a "natural" desire toward a "supernatural" vision. Aristotle's concept, obviously different, had a teleology of its own. Here the end would have to be strictly proportionate to the available (human) means. Aquinas, immediately perceiving the restrictions of this Aristotelian concept of nature for the interpretation of life in grace, conceded nature also contained a narrowly human teleology—the life of virtue and contemplation in the good city, which Aristotle had described. Yet this beatitude was only a partial fulfillment of human destiny and had to be subordinated to the transcendent, Christian end.[2] His 16th-century followers were less cautious. Accepting Aristotle's principle concerning the proportion of ends to means they denied *nature* was capable of any "supernatural" desire or end at all. De Lubac has shown how this idea of *pure nature* was an innovation formed in the wake of late-medieval nominalism and 16th-century personalism.[3] Once it gained entrance in Thomist theology it would avail itself of Aristotle's philosophy to justify itself.

In Aquinas there was no question of a supernatural order "added" to nature. "Supernatural" referred to the *means* for attaining our one, final end, an end for which our natural powers no longer suffice.[4] God himself is called *agens supernaturale,* not to separate the order of grace from that of nature, but rather to distinguish the order of the creator from that of creation (in which nature and grace appear together). Nature thereby becomes the effect of a "supernatural" agent. The term *supernatural* would not begin to refer to an order of grace separate from the order of nature until in the 16th century the "natural" end of a human came to be conceived as distinct from his revealed destiny. Still, one feature of St. Thomas's theological construction could, and eventually would, threaten the marvelous balance of its complex unity. It had nothing to do with the acceptance of the Aristotelian apparatus, but everything with the too exclusively medicinal interpretation of grace in the Latin tradition. Rather than considering the incarnation a decisive but by no means discontinuous moment of a divine self-communication that had begun with creation, as Scotus was to do, Aquinas saw it essentially as a divine response to remedy the effects of the fall. To this postlapsarian nature, grace was no longer a supernatural means enabling a human being to attain his "natural" end in the order of God's vocation. The fall had given nature itself some sort of distorted

---

2. *Summa contra Gentes* I, 2, c. 4; *Summa Theologiae* Ia,q.3, art. 2 and 4.

3. Henri de Lubac, *Surnaturel* (Paris: Aubier, 1946), chap. 5.

4. The crucial text (cited by de Lubac) reads: "Opportet quod homini superaddatur aliqua supernaturalis forma et perfectio, per quam convenienter ordinetur in finem . . . . Homini, ad consequendum ultimum finem, additur aliqua perfectio super propriam naturam, scilicet gratia" (*Summa contra Gentes* III, c. 150 and c. 153.)

independence which redemption could redress only by setting up a *new* end that would initiate an order of grace next to that of nature.

Yet another idea of 13th-century Scholasticism would, at a later stage, become instrumental in separating nature from the divine altogether. I am referring to a particular causal interpretation of the relation between God and creation. The idea of causality had always played a part in linking the world to God, for the ancients as well as for Jews and Christians. Yet comparing the nature of this causal relation in modern thought with that of the classical and medieval one, we note a major difference in the degree of immanence of the cause in the effect. In Plato's *Parmenides* the psychic cause of motion remains entirely within the effect. So do the combined causes (the *synaitiai*) of the cosmos in *Timaeus*. To them Plato adds the efficient causality of the Demiurge. But this mythical unification of all other causes ought not to be understood as containing the primary meaning of Plato's idea of causality. Indeed, all the important functions which later philosophy assigns to efficient causality Plato ascribes to *participation*. Aristotle's notion of causality in its fourfold aspect continues to reflect a similar immanence. Natural substances contain the source of motion and change within themselves and the concept of *nature (physis)* itself refers to the *intrinsic* principles of substantial motion and rest. Yet, significantly, the causal relation between God and all lower beings appears no longer as intimate as it had been in Plato's theory of participation.

Misunderstanding Plato's metaphysical principles as physical entities out of which the Demiurge fashioned the world, early Christian theologians anxious to stress the *creatio ex nihilo* had almost exclusively emphasized the efficient causality in God's creative act. Aristotle's theory of the prime mover had seemed to confirm their position. But never had they claimed exhaustively to explain thereby the intimate, permanent presence of God to the finite being. Only after Aristotle's philosophy had become accepted for the articulation of Christian theology did the more extrinsic conception of efficient causality come to determine the relation between God and humankind altogether. St. Thomas continued to hesitate between Plato's participation and Aristotle's efficient causality for expressing the relation between God and the creature.[5] In the *Summa Theologiae* we read:

Being is innermost in each thing and most fundamentally present within

---

5. Cf. Cornelio Fabro, *La nozione metafisica di partecipazione secondo S. Tomasso d'Aquino* (Brescia, 1939) and L. B. Geiger, *La participation dans la philosophie de St. Thomas* (Paris, 1942).

all things, since it is formal in respect of everything found in a thing. . . . Hence it must be that God is in all things, and innermostly.[6]

Nonetheless, when it comes to defining the nature of this divine immanence, Thomas concludes that it must consist in a relation of causal dependency. This explication by means of Aristotelian categories somehow appears to give less than what the "innermost presence" promised. How much Aquinas here sacrifices to the Aristotelian conception becomes evident in the rest of the passage:

> An agent must be joined to that wherein it acts immediately, and touch it by its power; hence it is proved in the *Physics* (VII, 2) that the thing moved and the mover must be together. Now since God is Being itself by his own essence, created being must be his proper effect; just as to ignite is the proper effect of fire.

Here the Aristotelian category of efficient causality proves inadequate for describing God's presence to his creation. Nevertheless, participation in Thomas's thought continues to balance efficient causality. Moreover, Aristotle's efficient causality essentially differs, precisely on the immanence of the cause in the effect, from the later mechanistic conception.[7]

Despite these tensions, the Thomist concept of nature still continues to receive its definitive interpretation from the order of grace. Independently of grace it is an abstraction—or, as Rahner called it, a residual concept *(ein Restbegriff)*[8]—that must be understood through its dialectical counterpart. Being thus tightly linked to the order of grace, the question what human nature by itself would be able to accomplish becomes unanswerable in Aquinas's theological perspective. To be sure, as a follower of Aristotle St. Thomas also uses a purely philosophical concept of nature. But this object of rational reflection unsupported by revelation, has nothing in common with the *natura pura* which 16th-century theologians abstracted from the concrete reality of fall and redemption. Aquinas's philosophical *nature* is

---

6. *Summa Theologiae* I, q.8, art. 1.

7. *If* God was to remain truly immanent in all reality, as religious thinkers had always held, in a mechanistic system of reality, this could mean only, as Spinoza perceived, that God had to be a *part* of the system, or, since this would conflict with the definition of an infinite being, the *totality itself* in its originating aspect—*Deus, sive natura,* that is, *natura naturans.*

8. Karl Rahner: *Theological Investigations,* vol. 1 (London: Barton, Longman, Todd, 1968), 302.

not a nature without grace, but human nature as we concretely find it, when considered independently of what revelation teaches about grace. It possesses a transcendent openness to grace and, some Thomists would claim, a *desiderium naturale* toward a fulfillment in grace.

> Certainly the philosopher has his own well-grounded concept of the nature of man: the irreducible substance of human being, established by recourse to human experience independently of verbal revelation. This concept may largely coincide with the theological concept of man's nature, insofar as without Revelation the greater part of what goes beyond this theological "nature" is not experienced, and at any rate is not recognized *as* supernatural without the help of Revelation to interpret it.[9]

These words written by a modern Thomist show how coherent the relation of nature and grace remains even after the formal object of philosophy has become distinguished from that of theology.

The solidity of the Thomist synthesis appears in the vision of the cosmos—both natural and transparent of grace—that continued to inspire poets and artists throughout the 13th century. The majestic construction of nature and grace, of cosmology and theology, of politics and philosophy, which Dante erects in *De Monarchia* and assumes throughout the *Comedia* shows the creative and enduring power of that Christian Aristotelianism which Aquinas had first conceived. If the synthesis showed any weakness as compared with that of the Greek fathers and Augustine, it consisted in what its authors must have considered its strength, namely, the distinctness of its various components. Precisely because of its neat conceptual separation this distinctness would, at the slightest imbalance in emphasis, harden into a base-superstructure dualism. This is of course what happened once the distinction between nature and the supernatural developed into one between two separate orders. Aquinas's genius had kept this separatist tendency in check. But it appeared almost from the start among less moderate proponents of the Aristotelian synthesis, such as Siger of Brabant, or Boethius of Dacia. In them the synthesis of Christian revelation with Aristotelian philosophy became reduced to a mere juxtaposition of two orders of being without even a proper concern for their compatibility. Aquinas correctly regarded those extreme Aristotelians whose sources were so close to his own, the greatest threat to

---

9. Ibid.

his synthesis. He emerged victorious from the battle with these antagonists. But the very belief in the viability of his project had been shaken. In 1277 Michel Tempier, the archbishop of Paris, condemned some of the crucial Aristotelian theses. The resistance against Aristotle's philosophy concentrated on the *Physics* and the *Metaphysics*—the Logic and *Ethics* had been accepted without major problems—because these treatises provided the basis for philosophy to separate from theology. Precisely in this separation we detect one of the decisive factors that contributed to the distinctness of the modern age.

Even so, Aristotle's philosophy was neither the immediate nor the sufficient cause of the separation of grace and nature into two orders. As Thomas had proven, they could be kept in perfect harmony within an Aristotelian synthesis. The real separation merely foreshadowed by a few Averroist philosophers, was essentially achieved by those who had led the resistance against Aristotelianism—the nominalists. The nominalist theologies of God's omnipotence that made their entrance in the following period destroyed the intelligible continuity between creator and creature. The idea of an absolute divine power unrelated to any known laws or principles definitively separated the order of nature from that of grace. Such a nature created by an unpredictable God has lost its intrinsic intelligibility in favor of the mere observation of actual fact. Nor does creation itself teach us anything of God beyond what this divine omnipotence has revealed in Scripture. Grace itself became a matter of divine decree unmeasured by human standards and randomly dispensed to an unprepared human nature. Detached from its transcendent moorings, nature was left to chart its own course. The rise of the supernatural signaled the loss of an intrinsically transcendent dimension in nature and the emergence of a profound distrust of that nature on the part of theology. The delicate balance was permanently disturbed.

We may well regard the early period of modern thought—from the 15th through the 17th centuries—as a prolonged attempt to recover the lost unity. This took different forms. The Reformation marked a return to the earlier, pre-"Aristotelian" Christian synthesis with, however, a hazardous emphasis on the late Augustine's conception of a thoroughly corrupted nature. The humanist movement, driven by a new confidence in nature, went in the opposite direction. Yet the naturalism of the early humanists had been inspired by a Platonic-Christian theology, still apparent in the later Michelangelo. The sympathies of important figures of the Reformation for classical humanism (Melanchthon, Budé, Lefèvre d'Étaples), as well as the Protestant leanings of many humanists (Marguerite de Valois and much of the French court under Francis I, Justus Lipsius, the early Erasmus) shows the early compatibility of two movements which, despite a different inspiration, presented in fact parallel quests for a lost synthesis. As we know, both failed. Reformed theology expressed an awareness of *total* human involvement in the drama of sin and redemption far more profound than the late medieval theologies with their dual vision of a supernatural order "added" to nature. Yet Protestant theologians soon returned, for different motives, to the kind of nominalist thinking of which they had fled the philosophical consequences. The very seriousness with which they stressed the impact of sin—the *corruptio totalis*—resulted in a concept of fallen nature which grace itself would no longer be able to transform intrinsically. The "imputed" righteousness, while expressing a change in God's attitude, left nature right where it found it. Thus a separation not unlike the earlier one between nature and a supernatural order here emerged at a later stage. The gap between nature and what once had been its *own* transcendence remained as wide as it had been before.

The Anglican divine William Law attributed much of the secularism of the 18th century to the extrinsic character of a forensic justification. In a few memorable pages of *The Spirit of Love*, he rejects outright the notion of an "imputed" righteousness as well as the distinction between a natural and a supernatural order. Divine righteousness intrinsically transforms human nature. Yet since it had been first *received* at creation and then *restored* by a divine redemption, he is willing to call it *God's* righteousness, as long as we remember that God "calls us to own the power, presence, and operation of God in all that we feel and find in our own inward state."[10] Whenever it affects human nature it is *eo ipso* "natural."

> There is nothing that is supernatural but God alone; everything besides Him is form and subject to the state of nature . . . . There is nothing supernatural in it [redemption] or belonging to it but that supernatural

---

10. William Law, *The Spirit of Love,* Dialogue III, in The Classics of Western Spirituality (New York: Paulist, 1980), 439.

love and wisdom which brought it forth, presides over it and will direct it till Christ. . . .[11]

Law correctly perceived that to reduce righteousness to an imputed quality had provided Deism with grounds for setting up a *natural* religion next to one so severely separated from nature. For Law, Christianity itself, basically founded in the nature of things, following the powers of nature, and responding to nature's demands, is the "one true, real, and only religion of nature. For a religion is not to be deemed natural because it has nothing to do with revelation; but then is it the one, true religion of nature when it has everything in it that our natural state stands in need of?"[12]

I have referred to Law because he saw the problems created by a forensic theory after they had had occasion to grow up and contribute to the religious crisis of the 18th century, but also because he appreciated the more fundamental drive of the Reformation to restore the unity of nature and grace lost by the distinction between the orders of nature and the supernatural. Reformed theology had attempted to overcome the separation between nature and grace. Yet in its theory of forensic justification that attempt failed and indirectly contributed to the destructive separation.

A comparable, even more sustained effort to overcome the extrinsic aspect of the forensic relation between nature and grace from within the theology of the Reformation was made by Hamann. He regarded the redemption in Christ as the key to the understanding of human nature, even though that key had reached us from a transcendent source.[13] Holy Scripture serves as "our dictionary" of nature.[14] Nature in turn sheds light on revelation and provides a commentary on God's Word. All creation physically manifests God's glorious presence, and it does so as he revealed himself in Scripture, that is, as glorious while emptying himself, as manifest in hiddenness. In its incarnated expression of language, the mind partakes in that primary divine revelation which was completed in God's Word. But if nature, especially human

---

11. Ibid., 444.

12. Ibid., 453.

13. Johann-Georg Hamann, *Biblische Betrachtungen,* ed. H. Joseph Nadler (Vienna, 1949–1957), 1:28.

14. Ibid., 243.

nature, has thus been endowed with the power to reveal, then all religion, even outside the gospel, must be able to do so. Hamann finds prophets of Christ among the heathens as well as among the Jews. Socrates, even Apollo's oracle, must count as hidden manifestations of the God to be openly revealed.[15]

The idea of a universal, natural religion brings us to the other movement which long preceded Hamann and from which he may, indirectly, have borrowed it—classical humanism. Humanist theology seldom receives the attention it deserves. Past interpretations tended to dismiss the whole movement as a return to paganism with a few halfhearted compromises between an undogmatic Christianity and a Neoplatonic philosophy. Partly responsible for this negative evaluation is an equation of humanism with the Renaissance understood through its most pagan representatives. This interpretation started with Michelet, who regarded the "Renaissance" as an antireligious anticipation of 18th-century French rationalism. A similar assumption underlies Burckhardt's classic, *The Civilization of the Renaissance*. Wernle, explicating and radicalizing Burckhardt's position, speaks of a total failure of Christian values and a total absence of every moral and religious ideal—"die volle Diesseitigkeit." If one collapses early Italian humanism with the later Renaissance and focuses on such places as the Pontifical court, then one may indeed agree with Valla's famous evaluation: "Nulla itaque religio, nulla sanctitas, nullus Dei timor . . . ."[16] These simplistic conceptions have since greatly been corrected by recent studies.[17]

What we find instead is an attempt to overcome the separation between nature, particularly human nature, and its transcendent source. Clearly, theological concerns are present from the beginning. Already by the end of the 14th century we notice, underneath an aversion for the late scholastic theologies of distinction, a desire to forge a tighter bond between Christian revelation and nature. Humanists pursued this

---

15. *Sokratische Denkwürdigkeiten* (Nadler II), 70ff.

16. *Opera* (Basel, 1540), 794.

17. A pioneer in them was G. Toffanin in his *Il secolo senza Roma* and *Storia del Umanesimo*, who emphasized the distinction between the humanist movement and the civilization of the Renaissance: the former he interprets as a theologically inspired attack upon the naturalism unleashed by the Averroistic philosophy of the 13th century. This position, equally extreme, has been abandoned as well and so has Croce's reading of humanism as a pantheistically inclined "immanentization" of the Christian faith.

unity in two different ways. One took the form of a search for a universal religion, an attempt to bridge the theological chasm between revelation and nature which itself must already be religious. The other consisted in showing how the Christian faith responded to, and fulfilled, the expectations aroused by ancient thought. The former addressed the scandal of a polytheism that appeared to conflict with the superiority of the ancient mind. Thus Coluccio Salutati argued that the ancient mythology presented in fact a rigorous monotheism barely hidden under a functional polytheism.

> For as they [the Greeks] called one and the same divinity in the heavens Luna, in the forests Diana, and in the underworld Prosperina, they also presupposed this whole complex of gods as a single essence of them all and named it according to the plurality of its possibilities and with the different names of their activities.[18]

Ancient poetry constituted a "natural" theology before revelation, one which retains its meaning after its fulfillment by Christ.

The search for a universal religion took less orthodox forms in later writers. Thus the neo-Aristotelian Pomponazzi advances an evolutionary theory of religion which subjects Christianity itself to the law of generation and corruption. The Christian faith, like other religions before it, is growing frigid, scarce in miracles, and seems to be approaching its end.[19] The idea of one natural religion for the whole human race appears in Campanella and receives its most radical expression from the man who may be said to conclude Italian humanism, Giordano Bruno (d. 1600). Resuming Salutati's interpretation of the ancient gods he writes: "The Greeks did not adore Jupiter as if he were the deity; they adored the deity as if it were Jupiter."[20] What they adored was the name and representation of God who in a particular mode had manifested himself.

---

18. Coluccio Salutati: *De laboribus Herculis*, II 2.12. Cf. Ernesto Grassi, *Heidegger and the Question of Renaissance Humanism* (Binghamton, N.Y.: Center for Medieval and Early Renaissance Studies, 1983), 57ff.

19. *De effectuum causis*, chap. 12.

20. Giordano Bruno, *Lo spaccio della bestia trionfante: Dialoghi italiani*, ed. Giovanni Gentile (Firenze Sansoni, n.d.), 779.

As for the *praeparatio evangelica* of the ancient writers, the significant point here is that *nature* is taken to be continuous from its pre-Christian aspirations to its Christian fulfillment. Indeed, Marsilio Ficino saw in Plato's philosophy the means to stem the Averroist tide of dualism between philosophy and theology. Plato's *eros* as presented in the middle dialogues, *Phaedrus, Phaedo,* and *Symposium,* laid the basis for a transcending thought completed by Christian revelation. One might object to such an easy identification of Plato's *eros* with Christian *agapē*. But the point of the *Theologia platonica* is precisely that it refuses to accept the absolute separation between "natural" aspiration and "supernatural" reality. Instead Ficino transforms the notion of *eros* itself, directing it, beyond any sensuous satisfaction, to the contemplation of divine harmony. This total rethinking of love places the Florentine Platonist closer to the Greek fathers than to Plato or Plotinus.[21] He supports this religious naturalism by reinterpreting the concept of *form* in an aesthetic sense which may be applied to God himself. "In the highest Being to be is to be 'formosus' and bright, indeed to be form and light."[22] God includes all forms without being restricted by any *formaque fons formarum*. Thus Ficino converts Plato's theory of participation into a basis for a Christian aesthetics. He supports his innovation of transcendent form by the more traditional one of light which the Greek fathers had attributed to God himself. The divine light which causes seeing—*In lumine tuo videbimus lumen*—is also the object of seeing, the sublime element in which form reaches perfection.[23] God, the fullness of light, is also the perfection of form. Ficino avoids the all too physical implications of identifying God with light and formal perfection by asserting the invisible quality of both this transcendent light and form. *Deus ob nimiam lucem est incognitus.* The all too abundant light renders the divine form unknowable. But, though unknown to the intellect, the warmth of this light makes itself

21. In distinguishing love from *libido* Ficino places himself in the medieval tradition of courtly love in Italy represented by Brunetto Latini, Guido Cavalcanti, and Dante. Festugière suggests a direct acquaintance with the theoretical *Flos Amoris* which circulated under Boccaccio's name.

22. "Argumentum in Platonicam Theologiam ad Laurentium Medicem," in *Opera* (Basel, 1576), 1:709.

23. "Lumen quod cumque videtur, nihil est aliud quam purae efficacisque formae spiritalis quaedam amplificatio," "Argumentum. . . ," *Opera* 1:694 (Garin, 314).

all the more felt in the will.[24] Pico della Mirandola likewise asserts the priority of love. "As long as we dwell in this world, imprisoned in the life of the senses, it is through love more than through reason that we are able to grasp God."[25]

Pico and Ficino went far beyond the traditional "expropriating the spoils of the pagans." Rather than using the classical philosophers for spare parts in an exclusively Christian theology, they placed Plato and Plotinus on equal footing with the prophets. The assumption here is a fundamental continuity from creation to elevation. Since the Christian revelation is true, it must be universally accessible, and that requires a full compatibility with the great teachers of antiquity. Revelation, far from being a restrictive norm, is an ever-expanding truth continuously acquiring new depth and meaning. This Platonic theory of form as a transcendental quality of Being would provide religious artists of the Renaissance with a justification fully to display the natural world which contained, in its very essence, an upward movement surpassing its own finitude. As Cassirer wrote, the Renaissance artist "must constantly unite what is separated and opposed: in the visible he seeks the invisible."[26] No one pursued this religious naturalism more consistently than Michelangelo who, though coming at the end of the Renaissance, perhaps most perfectly realized its ideals.[27]

And yet the religious impetus of early humanism failed. In the end it did not succeed in fully integrating the disparate elements of which it built its synthesis. It was not only that pagan antiquity and Christian revelation intrinsically differed. They did, and any synthesis would have to be an accommodation constantly in need of reexamination. But, more fundamentally, the new source of meaning upon which the Renaissance drew, the priority of the human subject, implied an idea of *nature* that could not be made continuous with the order of grace. It was new, independent of ancient sources, and not directly

24. "Deus ergo in summa intellectus cognitione quodammodo nox quaedam est intellectui. In summo voluntatis amore certe dies est voluntati," *Opera* 1:710.

25. *Opera* (Basel, 1576), 250.

26. Cassirer, *Individuum und Kosmos in der Renaissance* (Darmstadt [1927], 1963), 142.

27. Having in his adolescence often been admitted to the Medici Academy where Pico and Ficino exposed their theories, he had over the years deepened a Neoplatonic aestheticism of form into a religious vision. In the light of this vision the artist had become ever more dissatisfied with the purely finite form. He had increasingly turned away from the too individual, personalized expression of sculpture and painting. On the religious quality of Michelangelo's work, cf. Rolf Schott, *Michelangelo* (New York: Harry Abrams, 1965).

assimilable. The change appears first in a different moral attitude. The concept of *virtus (virtù)* already present in Salutati becomes a vehicle for new moral and aesthetic ideals. The person is given a greater autonomy than Christianity had ever allowed. Freedom becomes a unified, dynamic center of unlimited potential destined to shape itself and its world. Such a conception constitutes a conscious effort to surpass the dualism of the natural and the supernatural. The new assertiveness had a vertical dimension as well as a horizontal. Its authors praised the contemplative life—from Petrarch to Salutati to Landino, Pico, and indeed to Lorenzo de Medici himself.[28] Yet the dynamic center was not the transcendent source; it was the self in its own right. The delicate balance between transcendence and immanence would soon be broken in favor of an ever-increasing immanentism. The new orientation which used the ancients as it needed them for its own self-expression would have required a synthesis as complex as the one St. Thomas elaborated at the arrival of Aristotle's philosophy. For this neither was the time propitious nor the genius available.[29]

Thus the later humanism of the Renaissance, whether Aristotelian or Platonic, lost its Christian orientation altogether. Pomponazzi's treatise on immortality can no longer count as an Averroist exercise in the theory of double truth. That theory is still professed but no longer believed. Even if we assume Pomponazzi's personal acceptance of Christian faith to have been sincere, his thorough naturalism leaves the reader no doubt about the logical conclusion in which his argument must result. That naturalism also underlies his theory on the universal fate (and presumed equality) of all religions. Since nature is *one,* the diversity of its expressions, even regarding its relation to the transcendent, must ultimately be reducible to a common denominator.[30] The more Platonic humanists (e.g., Machiavelli) end up with a similar naturalism. The only distinction left in the later part of the Renaissance

---

28. "Ottima parte elesse Maddalena,
poich'una delle due e necessaria,
quella di Marta e d'inquiete piena . . . ."
(*Altercazione* III, 103-105 [Bari: Simione, 1914]).

29. In that sense Blumenberg's thesis of the essentially nonreligious orientation of the modern epoch *became* true, even though it needed not to have been true. The crisis leading to modern culture *because of the failure to accomplish the new synthesis* both announced and initiated in early humanism, resulted in a "break."

30. *De incantationibus,* Bk. 12.

between Aristotelians (who dominated the University of Padua) and "humanists" is that the latter placed the emphasis directly on man while the former's focus remained on the "natural processes." But in the end *naturalism* triumphed in both. If Ficino, Pico, Erasmus, and so many other men of genius and sincere Christian concern failed to achieve a lasting synthesis, it was because their work remained at the surface of the modern problem. One could hardly hope to reunite by means of Plato's theory of participation what a strong tradition of Aristotelian (especially the Averroist variety) and nominalist theology had separated. A philosophy that had originated before the modern problem existed was clearly inadequate for bridging a theological chasm between an anthropocentric view of reality and a theocentric one.

A third attempt to restore the lost unity of grace and nature resulted in one of the most complex systems Western thought has ever designed. It was also one of the most elusive. Though attacked, criticized, and theologically condemned, it was never definitively refuted. The condition for its existence was created by the nominalist theology of God's *potentia absoluta*. This included the possibility of a *pure nature,* that is, a human nature without supernatural gifts, grace, or participation in divine life. Until the 16th century this fiction appears to have remained a mere working hypothesis for developing theories of grace. In the 16th century some theologians began to assume it to be a reality in its own right. It immediately gained great popularity and, when the leading Thomists as well as the most prominent Jesuit theologians (especially Molina and Suarez) embraced it, came to be almost universally accepted outside the Augustinian camp. No previous theory had more overtly asserted the dualism of nature and grace which had been prepared for centuries but had never clearly surfaced.

Two Louvain theologians, Baius and Jansenius, clearly perceived how much the new conception deviated from a tradition established since Augustine. Baius attempted to consolidate that tradition by including the modern views of nature. His efforts to rebuild the lost synthesis ended in a peculiar mixture of a most untraditional "naturalism" and an equally new, antinatural determinism. Jansen, his admiring student and successor at the Louvain faculty, elaborated these insights into an enormously complex, yet coherent system that he presented as St. Augustine's theology of grace.

On the basis of a well-known passage in Augustine, Baius denied that human nature had been fully formed until it received the *forma filiorum Dei*—the original state of justice which later Scholasticism in order to stress its gratuitousness had come to call "supernatural." Grace is a *demand* of nature and God's image in grace is the natural image of the soul. In that original condition of nature "actual" grace is required only for acting, not for "elevating." Adam by his natural powers attains his divine destination. Thus Baius with one bold stroke unites what centuries had sundered. But the problems return with his description of the fall. Once the fall deprives humans of original justice, nature itself breaks down to a truncated reality. Since nature itself was essentially justified, the loss of that original justice affects its essence, rendering it intrinsically incapable of natural goodness. Even a habit of accomplishing one's duty becomes vitiated by a general orientation toward concupiscence rather than toward charity. The virtues of this fallen nature intrinsically committed to sin are but *splendida vitia*. Here we begin to feel the failure of Baius's attempt. The opposition between a nature that is either "naturally" justified or "naturally" sinful introduces a discontinuity that must inevitably result in a new dualism of nature and grace even more pronounced than the one it replaces. Whatever restoration grace will achieve cannot but result in a new reality diametrically opposed to the fallen nature.

Ironically, Baius's theory, based upon the anti-Pelagian writings of Augustine, came under fire for Pelagianism. In the state of original justice, humans by nature alone elicit salvific acts. The charge, directly opposed to Baius's own intentions, nevertheless shows up an unresolved ambiguity in his thought. The basic assumption about the original condition of the human race secretly shares an axiom of Renaissance Stoicism, namely, that nature *must be perfect* in all respects. This optimistic principle is no more Christian in origin than Ficino's Platonism: it rests on a clear misreading of Augustine's text. The pessimistic description of lapsed nature directly follows from the disappearance of this "natural" justification. Despite the reversal of original sin, the general tone of Baius's theology remains basically within the optimistic Renaissance mood.

Jansenius's mood was different. Temperamentally tending towards emotional gravity and subject to the influence of the dour abbé de Saint-Cyran, Jansenius gave a pessimistic twist as well as a greater consistency to his mentor's theses. Adam's state, he explains in his

Augustinus, could not be called a state of *grace,* even though he did not *merit* its orientation toward a divine beatitude. God morally *owed* it to an intellectual creature to call it to the highest form of spiritual life. In its original state, nature itself was grace. Adam needed no "grace" (symptomatically defined as what is *added* to nature) to be properly disposed for *willing (velle)* this end, only divine assistance for *being able (posse)* to act rightly toward its attainment. We, after the fall, require grace both for the *velle* (disposition) and the *posse* (the ability to act).[31]

Combining Baius's rigorous logic about a nature wounded in its very essence by the fall with a pessimism of his own, Jansenius concluded to a determinism of damnation and, for the few elect, of salvation, in the present state of mankind. Since nature had been crippled, grace, rather than assisting it, had to substitute for it. Once the will has turned to *cupiditas* it can be transformed only by losing its *liberum arbitrium,* that means, by ceasing to function naturally. De Lubac dramatically expresses this conversion: "C'est sur les ruines de la nature, autrefois maîtresse d'elle-même, que règne aujourd'hui la grâce de Dieu."[32] Instead of a dualism of complementarity, we have now a full-dressed battle between nature and grace. A destructive opposition in time has replaced their gentler coexistence in space. Jansenius overcomes the dualism he is combatting by successively eliminating either one of the two elements of the synthesis: first nature exists without grace, then grace without nature. "Tantôt instrument aux mains souveraines de l'homme, tantôt force envahissante qui supplée toute activité naturelle et réduit celui qu'elle libère en un nouvel esclavage . . . ."[33]

Jansenism remains hard to refute on its own terms, even though we may clearly perceive its failure, because more than any other theological system it has consistently drawn the conclusion from the modern premises. To be sure, one can hardly fault Jansenius for denying any neutral ground between *cupiditas* and *caritas.* Yet the opposition between the two has become more rigid than when St. Augustine first

---

31. Jansenius supported this naturalist interpretation of Adam's condition by an amazing interpretation of Augustine's expression of wonder at the even *greater abundance* of grace granted to the elect after the fall for keeping the path of righteousness. Cf. Henri de Lubac, *Surnaturel,* 56-63.

32. Ibid., 69.

33. Ibid.

formulated it. It is difficult to criticize the foundations of Jansenius's thought without in some way implicating Augustine himself. The tradition initiated by the Latin father moved, from the start, in a hazardous direction. The medicinal concept of grace so exclusively emphasized in Western Christianity carries within itself the seeds of a dualism that, mixed with the right ingredient, would become explosive. Yet only the modern equation of the real with what is actually present to consciousness provided that ingredient. Without that equation Augustinism would never have become Jansenism. In the medieval synthesis grace, being primarily a *habitus,* inserted into nature a mode of being. Reduced to a conscious intention—the *motivum caritatis*—it comes to stand independent of nature and exists as in a *vacuum.* A state that must be thus *actualized* at each moment becomes totally detached from the nature it is supposed to "heal" and turns into a substitute for it. The problem we encounter here anticipates in the theological order that of Kant's moral theory. The same insistence on actual intention and the same absence of context appear in both cases. The primacy of the subject found its way into theology before philosophy had fully formulated it.

Comparing the Jansenist attempt to regain the lost unity with the two others, we may consider it a "heroic failure," because even its instigators knew that it would require a tragic sacrifice of those humanist values which had come to grace the new culture of the Renaissance. The moral grandeur involved in thus abandoning the familiar security of nature in order to confront alone a distant God may not have resolved the religious predicament of the age, but it inspired some of its greatest minds. Pascal, Racine, indirectly also Corneille, detected in this heroic antinaturalism the new stand of Christianity. Their new Christian humanism lost out to the divisive forces which had helped to create it. After Jansenism came 18th-century rationalism. Much earlier, that other, less tragic humanism, introduced by Ficino, Pico, More, and Erasmus, had been defeated. Its synthesis had been submersed by the very "spoils of the pagans" they had so proudly conquered. But here also it was the modern factor rather than the nature of the synthesis that had caused it to fail. If a typically modern self-assertion of the human subject had not taken over the synthesis, it might have resulted in yet another of those Christian–classical Renaissances, as the Carolingian epoch, or the 12th century, or even the early Italian humanism of Dante, Petrarch, and Boccaccio had been. Still, Christian humanism did not disappear without leaving a trace. To this "beautiful failure" the Christian 17th century owes one of the most attractive schools of piety—the *humanisme dévot* of Francis de Sales, Camus, and much of 17th-century spirituality in France. In Italy it continued to flower in a number of diverse devotional movements. Much of its final energy went into that sadly misunderstood mystical current which we derogatorily call "Quietism."

About the Reformation we cannot say that it failed in achieving a synthesis that would last. The movement resulted in a powerful branch of Christianity that drew theology back to its early sources. The success of this synthesis, which continues to inspire believers, may well be due to its radically religious and Christian character. As Clemens-Maria Hofbauer, a canonized Catholic, once claimed, the Reformation succeeded because there were some Christians left to take their faith seriously. Yet who would dare to claim that it succeeded in rebuilding the lost harmony of nature and grace? If we must speak of failure in this uniquely religious movement, it should be of a "religious failure." Here more than in the other two cases the question assumes a particular urgency: Why should what was so exclusively inspired by ancient Christian sources not have succeeded in restoring the ancient Christian harmony? The cause lies once again, I believe, in the intervention of a modern factor.

In his *Anthropology* Pannenberg points out what decisively distinguishes the image of God in reformed theology from the ancient and medieval one. While the latter had located it in a structural quality of the human essence itself, which grounds and precedes all actual relatedness to God (the so-called *similitudo* or *homoiosis*), the former ascribes it exclusively to the *actual relation*.[34] Hence Adam's original justice consists in the actual union of his will with God's will. After the fall, since the state of concupiscence is identified with actual sin (as also in Jansenius), the image of God vanishes from humans. Pannenberg points out that this interpretation, purportedly based on Augustine, in its "one-sidedness" fails to do justice to the complexity of

---

34. Pannenberg, *Anthropologie in theologischer Perspective* (Göttingen: Vandenhoeck & Ruprecht, 1983), 47, 45, 72. (Eng. trans., *Anthropology in Theological Perspective* [Philadelphia: Westmister, 1985]).

his thought.[35] Clearly the "novel" element here consists in the total "actualization" of the states of grace and sin. We find some of the same equation of reality and consciousness, characteristic of modern thought, that defined Jansenius's theory. Still, the opposition between state and act appears to be drawn less rigidly. To be sure, the theology of imputed justice assumes a state of actual sinfulness incompatible with the ancient Christian theology of the image.

But other elements point in a different direction. Both Lutheranism and Calvinism at their origin display a humanist streak not always consistent with their theological presuppositions. It appears most clearly in a theologian such as Melanchthon, himself a "humanist." But it also shows in the hesitations wherein the sacramental symbolism is interpreted and in a continuing ambiguity concerning the human capacity to be an image of God. If that image consisted exclusively in the *actual* relationship of love of God, then it should vanish when that act becomes perverted by concupiscence. Yet not all reformers were willing to draw such a radical conclusion. The issue, somewhat submerged in the early years of the Reformation, resurfaced with all desirable clarity in the exchange between Barth and Brunner. Here the issue was whether the image of God in humankind had *totally* disappeared after the fall, or whether there remained some "remnant" of it that would enable humans to understand God's address in the revelation. Brunner claimed there was, and claimed Luther's authority to support his position. Others before him had already gone much further: he himself had attacked Schleiermacher for his naturalist evolutionism.[36] Pannenberg has shown how much of this initial humanism of the Reformation survived and, after having been transformed, inspired Herder's *Humanitätsideal* as an image of God to be achieved in the future. Unfortunately, the neoclassical movement that joined the Protestant Enlightenment would soon become disconnected from its Christian sources and lead to Goethe's and Schiller's naturalist humanism. A similar development would lead to Shelley and Keats in England.

---

35. Ibid., 84.
36. Indeed, in his *Christian Faith* Schleiermacher had written: "In the knowledge of the elements of this original perfection present in everyone we find a justification for the original demand that the God-consciousness should exist continuously and universally (*Christian Faith*, trans. H. R. Mackintosh and J. S. Stewart [New York: Harper Torchbooks, 1963]), 1:247. On this entire controversy see Pannenberg, *Anthropologie*, 52.

At the end of this reflection on the concept of nature in modern theology, we must raise the question: Could theology have returned to the harmony of a nature elevated in grace *without* having to erase centuries of its own history? At least one man, educated in late medieval theology and at the same time acutely aware of the emerging currents of modern thought, succeeded in achieving a new unity from the dual strands of grace and nature. One can only speculate about the direction modern Christian thought might have taken if Nicholas of Cusa had exercised the influence which he, the greatest speculative thinker at the dawn of the modern age, deserved to exercise. But somehow his expression proved too demanding, possibly also too personal and too fragmentary, to command the attention of his epoch.

Cusanus developed a new synthesis with traditional components. A lifelong student of Eckhart and of Denys, he conceived a system that culminated in a confession of ignorance of the *Deus absconditus.* The manner in which he developed this negative theology, however, reveals a mind that belongs to the modern age. The cosmos no longer holds that central position wherein the power of the prime mover transmitted via the astral bodies retains it in continuous causal contact with God. As totally other, God stands infinitely distant from the world. At the same time, the cosmos *explicates* the divine reality itself which it "contracts." Cusanus's daring theses—one Being existing unified *(complicatio)* in God and diversified *(explicatio)* in creation, an infinite universe reflecting an infinite God, the hypothesis of a plurality of worlds—anticipated some to be formulated by Telesio, Bruno, and Campanella. But while the Renaissance philosophers had nothing but contempt for the medieval past, the cardinal was constantly concerned to show the continuity of the old with the new. The modern quality of Cusanus's thought appears even more clearly in his unqualified profession of the human mind's power. Human knowledge is as autonomous as God's own creative act.[37] Even as God creates real beings and material forms, the human being creates rational entities and artificial forms that reflect his intellect in the same manner in which creatures reflect the divine mind. The human being does not imitate an inimitable

---

37. "Nam sicut Deus est creator entium realium et materialium formarum, ita homo rationalium et formarum artificialium, quae non sunt nisi sui intellectus similitudines, sicut creaturae Dei divini intellectus similitudines. Ideo homo habet intellectum, qui est similitudo divini intellectus in creando" (*De beryllo* VI, 268).

divine "model" but, in his own way, creatively reshapes the indeterminate mass of experience into intelligible form.[38] Participating in the divine process of *explication,* he imitates God's own creativity. Among all creatures the human mind alone displays a genuine *likeness (similitudo)* with God in that it recognizes that which it reflects. Cusanus boldly asserts: "Man is God, but not absolutely, for he is man."[39] The projective synthesis of human knowledge imitates the divine unity (the *complicatio*) of all things. Cusa's theory of the synthesis of judgment anticipates not only Kant's productive power of the imagination, but even the creative one of German idealism. Truth essentially consists in the immanent unfolding of a system of assertions that imitates the divine *complicatio* in a finite mode.[40]

In building a new synthesis of nature and grace, Cusanus had to circumvent the nominalist problems caused by the concept of God's *potentia absoluta,* and this required rethinking the idea of *possibility.* Nominalist theologians had taken it out of reality and placed it as a wedge between human intelligibility and divine omnipotence. An unlimited realm of possibility separated the entire rational structure of the existing cosmos and its laws from the divine nature. Not only did it render those laws contingent and reversible, but, even while they prevailed, it dispensed God's redemptive activity from conforming to what he had once created. God could save the sinner without justifying him, if he chose to do so, for divine justice was nothing but what he regarded as such. The intrinsic law of things thereby lost its resistance to randomness. At first glance Cusanus seems to accept the nominalist position when declaring possibility as much a creation of God as actuality. Yet in fact he *reunites* this possibility with the order of actual reality, regarding both as constitutive elements of one divine act. Possibility, for him, is not an independent vacuum that "existed" before creation and, indeed, would have existed without creation. Independent of created actuality there is no possibility: it originates simultaneously with reality. The question of the best possible world could never occur.

38. Cf. Maurice de Gandillac, *Nikolaus von Kues. Studien zu seiner philosophischen Weltanschauung* (Dusseldorf: Schwarm, 1953), 147.

39. *De coniecturis,* sec. II, 14.

40. Hans Blumenberg, *The Legitimacy of the Modern Age,* trans. Robert M. Wallace (Boston: MIT Press, 1983), 527.

Whatever God creates expresses his perfection and allows no room for alternatives. Whatever *is*, is *eo ipso* the best possible.[41]

Still, the elimination of an independent realm of possibility alone does not suffice to reunite nature and grace. For God could have created nature in one way and redeemed it in another. This discrepancy, I believe, Cusanus excludes by his unified concept of creation. God's self-expression definitively defines the structure of the real. To introduce inconsistency militates with the entire concept of creation as *explicatio* of God's own Being. This whole argument rests upon the intimate unity in which Cusanus conceives of the relation between God and creation. Following Eckhart he posits in *De non-aliud* that with respect to creation God is totally other as well as totally same. The negation resulting from divine transcendence concludes in an affirmation of total immanence. In its dispersion the created cosmos removes itself from divine unity. Yet God remains that unity, without which it could not continue to exist. "Deus ergo est omnia complicans in hoc, quod omnia in eo. Est omnia explicans in hoc, quod ipse in omnibus."[42] Without God there would be nothing left of creation. Beyond difference lies a more fundamental unity. *Unitas alteritatem praecedit.* The creature's *Being* is not another, but God's own Being in a contracted mode *(cuius esse est ab-esse)*. The absolutely *one* tolerates no total otherness: it must include all otherness in itself. Hence what appears most other to the finite is, in fact, what is most identical.

But if God remains so intimately present to creation, then that creation must, despite its unlikeness, in some way also reflect the hidden presence—not as a likeness but as a cipher. To detect God's reflection in what is "unlike" God requires the intellectual powers of the human being, the only creature made into "the image and likeness"

---

41. *De possest.* It is true that in his last great work, *De venatione sapientiae* (1463) Cusanus claims that God could have created any other world than the present one (chap. XXVII). Is this discrepancy caused by "a certain resignation regarding his own attempt at disposing of this problem" (as Blumenberg claims, op. cit., 521), or, as I think, by a decision to emphasize more radically the total dependence (and hence total contingency) of the world on God? In the latter case it would mean, not a return to nominalist voluntarism, but rather a stronger affirmation of God's transcendence and of that of divine rationality. Cusanus has no intention of letting his whole cosmic construction collapse by allowing an inscrutable divine decree to reverse all principles of rationality. Not divine freedom escapes the mind, but divine nature, that is, for Cusanus, divine reason (*De venatione sapientiae*, chap. XXVI and XXVII).

42. *De docta ignorantia*, 107.

of God. Other finite realities display *traces (vestigia)* of the infinite: they possess no resemblance, but merely signal the trail the hunting mind has to follow in order to reach the divine game. They *direct,* but do not *represent* in the sense of manifesting a presence. Even as mathematical ciphers and figures bear no resemblance to the realities to which they refer, yet precisely as nonintuitive symbols are able to assist the mind in its pursuit of the real without misleading it by the illusion of resemblance, so creation, if studied in its formal aspect (as a cipher), serves as the stepping stone for the ascent toward the infinite. Cusanus describes this symbolic process as follows:

> All mathematical objects are finite and cannot be imagined otherwise. If we desire to use the finite as an example by which to ascend to the absolutely greatest, we must consider finite mathematical figures with their characteristics and relations, and then transfer those relations correspondingly to similar infinite figures. Next, on a still higher level, we must transfer the relation of the infinite figures to the infinitely simple totally free of any figure. Only then will our ignorance be taught in an incomprehensible mode, while we still labor in the enigma, how we have to think more correctly and truly about the Highest.[43]

Precisely in performing this kind of intellectual operation the mind turns into an *image* of God, for in projecting symbols of itself the mind directly imitates God's creative act. It *projects* itself outside itself only in order to return to itself. That is precisely what God does in his creative act.

But it is in the theology of the hypostatic union, presented in the third, often neglected part of the *Learned Ignorance,* that Cusanus fully transcends the nominalist dualism between a divine and a human order. The concrete order of salvation elevates human nature as such and in its model sets the final goal for the entire species. The hypostatic union intrinsically transforms human nature as a whole. Indeed, because of the central position of the human being on the scale of created being, it raises the *entire* creation to a divine level.

> Human nature is that [nature] which, though created a little lower than the angels, is elevated above all the [other] works of God; it enfolds

---

43. *Nicholas of Cusa on Learned Ignorance,* trans. Jasper Hopkins (Minneapolis: The Arthur Banning Press [1981], 1985), 33. In this one instance I have slightly simplified the translation for practical reasons.

intellectual and sensible nature and encloses all things within itself, so that the ancients were right in calling it a microcosm, or a small world."[44]

This union, Cusanus insists, must not be conceived as a "composite" of God and human nature, "since a composition of God and creature is impossible." It must be "Creator and creature without confusion and without composition."[45]

Nor must the hypostatic union be considered an "addition" in time, the result of an afterthought provoked by human failure through sin. "Divinity does not exist in different ways according to an earlier and a later time."[46] The incarnation is not posterior to God in time: the God-man, insofar as he is God himself, stands above time and is ontologically "prior to all things."[47] He mediates all temporal events as their ultimate goal and reason. The participation of created nature in Christ's perfect humanity implies that God is in all things and all things are in God.[48] Human nature is divinized to a point where it no longer exists in itself, but "in oneness with Infinite Power."[49] In it God achieves his most perfect work—that which enables him personally to inhabit creation. Even the distinction between philosophy and theology vanishes. Natural knowledge leads to a *docta ignorantia,* an awareness beyond strict reasoning, which allows the receptive attitude of faith to unite with the active one of "conjectures." Because Cusanus regards the mind as a copy of the divine original, philosophical and revealed faith coincide for him. There are not two *sources* of that unified divine knowledge, but only one—the one constituted in the incarnation and revealed in Christ.[50]

Cusanus succeeds in combining an amazing diversity of cosmo-logical, anthropological, and epistemological elements in a theological synthesis, because at the heart of his thought lies a contemplative vision. His unifying synthesis rests upon spiritual writings and sermons (e.g., *On the Vision of God, On the Hidden God)* of which the Christology of *Learned Ignorance,* Bk. III, reveals the full significance.

44. Ibid., 198.
45. Ibid., 194.
46. Ibid., 193.
47. Ibid., 202.
48. Ibid., 204.
49. Ibid., 202.
50. Karl Jaspers, *Anselm and Nicholas of Cusa,* The Great Philosophers 2, trans. Ralph Manheim (New York: Harcourt, Brace, Jovanovich, 1974), 53-59.

Precisely for that reason he appropriately concludes our investigation of the split at the beginning of the modern age that separated the "order of grace" from nature, and of efforts to restore the lost unity. Those attempts failed to recapture the unity in theology at large. Yet that unity survived in mystical and devotional movements. In different forms—some of them continuing the earlier Augustinian–Franciscan tradition, others feeding on the new syntheses here discussed—mystical theology steadfastly upheld the union of nature and grace. Here, however, the failure of modern theology in recapturing the lost terrain stands most clearly revealed. For mystical thought itself becomes marginalized, if not expelled altogether, from the main currents of Christian thought. Even when various warring branches of late scholastic theology rallied around the idea of *pure nature* as if it were a point of Catholic dogma as well as the only possible defense against Jansenism and Calvinism, "mystical theology," now a separate branch, was left alone—because, as de Lubac observes, no one cared about it. Perhaps a lesson waits there to be learned. If the union of nature and grace, vital to the survival of the Christian message, was maintained only as long as theology retained a contemplative, practico-spiritual dimension, then the future success of that theology in influencing a now largely dechristianized culture may well depend on its ability to reincorporate the contemplative aspect that once belonged to its very essence.

4

ANTICIPATION
and
THEOLOGICAL METHOD

Philip Clayton

◆

U nder Pannenberg's construal of theological method theologians and their secular colleagues work at close quarters. Salvation history gives way to universal history *(Revelation as History)*, dogmatic Christology relies upon Christology "from below" *(Jesus— God and Man)*, and theology itself becomes an unabashed "science of God" as the "all-determining reality," a science accountable to philosophy, the history of religion, and natural science *(Theology and the Philosophy of Science)*. The 27 articles in his *Grundfragen systematischer Theologie*[1] and dozens of others continue to deal with traditional dogmatic topics; but even a cursory reading reveals the pervasive concern with philosophical themes and styles of argumentation.

All this is well known. It is not the fact or extent but the precise nature and the ultimate success of his opening up of theology that I would like to consider here. It is no secret that the concept of antici-

---

1. Volume 1 is translated as *Basic Questions in Theology*, 2 vols., trans. George H. Kehm (Philadelphia: Fortress, 1971) and *The Idea of God and Human Freedom*, trans. R. A. Wilson (Philadelphia: Westminster, 1973); the translation by David Polk of the second German volume will be published by Westminster Press as volumes 4 and 5.

pation lies at the heart of Pannenberg's theological project. This notion supplies his answer to a perennial issue facing theologians: How is Christ's universal significance to be combined with the particularity of his person and work? If the notion of anticipation, despite its strengths, does not settle the question, then one is left with several options: One might claim to possess an alternative solution to the problem of Christ's particularity and absoluteness; one might dismiss one or the other of the two poles; or one might defend the inevitability of the dilemma while expressing skepticism regarding our current (or future) possession of any adequate solution. This broader debate will provide the context for the discussion of anticipation in the following pages.

Five questions will guide our examination of this problem: (1) Does Pannenberg's construal of theological method provide an adequate framework for approaching the question? (2) What does anticipation or prolepsis mean and whence does he derive it? (3) What conceptual framework aids him in appropriating anticipation for theology? (4) Is his theory of anticipation adequate as it stands? (5) If it is not, can one pole of the tension between particular and universal be discarded, or can the two be otherwise reconciled?

I

Pervasive criticizability is perhaps the central tenet of Pannenberg's theological method. Readers often find it difficult to believe that his theology does not separate theology and criticism at some point. Yet Pannenberg insists that there is no separate prolegomena to decide the truth question, no natural theology to serve as foundation for a "science of faith." Instead, theology is a science *(Wissenschaft)* and "a scientific investigation can admit assertions only to the extent of treating them as problematic and trying to test their claims."[2] Since the theme of theology is the reality of God,[3] even within theology statements about God retain their problematic status *(Strittigkeit)*.

2. *Theology and the Philosophy of Science,* trans. Francis McDonagh (London: Darton, Longman & Todd, 1976), 364.
3. *Anthropology in Theological Perspective,* trans. Matthew J. O'Connell (Philadelphia: Westminster, 1985), 21; cf. *Theology and the Philosophy of Science,* chap. 5.

I regard this methodological commitment to interaction with other disciplines as one of Pannenberg's most significant contributions to theology. But it is important to note that it does not entail (as many have supposed) an entire "theology from below." If Pannenberg insists that theology be criticizable from below, he equally insists that its content not be limited to anthropological or historical statements. Beginning with the 1975 "Afterword" to *Jesus—God and Man,* he began to work out "from above" *(von oben)* the logic of the being of God.[4] We might say that the evidential project of the early Christology has been supplemented by a systematic theological project: How is this God, for whose existence we have various evidences, to be conceived? Addressing this task has led him to a series of articles on the Trinity and to straightforwardly metaphysical speculation.[5] Pannenberg correctly argues that theology "from above" is still consistent with his "hypothetical" approach, for the Christian hypothesis has to be fully elaborated and made coherent before serious testing can take place.

At one point Pannenberg was viewed as a Renaissance theologian, heralded by liberals and conservatives alike. His role as an anti-Barthian who battled theological "immunization strategies" with the appeal to "universal history" led to an early celebrity status on the American theological circuit. His Christology seemed to demonstrate an openness to reevaluation of the Christian tradition that pleased many liberals, while providing a defense of the historicity of the resurrection and a commitment to evangelical essentials that pleased conservatives. When *Theology and the Kingdom of God* appeared in 1969, with its suggestive statements about the God who "in a restricted but important sense. . .does not yet exist" (p. 56), there seemed the possibility of rapprochement with process theologians as well.

But obviously the role of theologian for all readers could not last.

---

4. See my essay "The God of History and the Presence of the Future," *Journal of Religion* 65 (1985): 98-108. For Pannenberg's own criticism of his Christology and his new use of the term "from above," see *Grundfragen systematischer Theologie Gesammelte Aufsätze,* vol. 2 (Göttingen: Vandenhoeck & Ruprecht, 1980), 131.

5. See *Grundfragen systematischer Theologie,* vol. 2, chaps. 3-5; "Problems of a Trinitarian Doctrine of God," trans. P. Clayton, *Dialog* 26 (1987): 250-257; and Wolfhart Pannenberg, "The Significance of the Categories 'Part' and 'Whole' for the Epistemology of Theology," trans. P. Clayton, *Journal of Religion* 66 (1986): 369-385.

The subsequent mixed reaction to Pannenberg in the secondary literature is somewhat ironic: he has been criticized both for not doing theology in the traditional mode, for not contributing to dogmatics, and for being *too* traditional, too preoccupied with traditional dogmatic issues that the contemporary theologian really ought to move beyond. On the one side, some allege that books such as *Theology and the Philosophy of Science* and the recent *Anthropology* are not really contributions to dogmatics or traditional theology at all. For example, Hermann Fischer has recently criticized the latter book for being insufficiently theological. It dwells on the difficulties of philosophical anthropology and contemporary social science at the expense of the distinctively theological, even Christian, content of traditional theological anthropology:

> It amazes one in the new anthropology, viewed as a whole, how little Pannenberg argues theologically. The reader receives the impression that the theological voice is increasingly muffled for the sake of the project of mediating to the modern consciousness. As a result the contours of the field of inquiry, which is being mediated at such great expense, become unclear.[6]

Fischer worries that Pannenberg's approach to anthropology "awakens the impression that dogmatic theology itself may have become impossible in light of modern consciousness" (p. 45).

By contrast, others have found Pannenberg too traditional and conservative. He remains arbitrarily bound to a trinitarian notion of God, to belief in a final eschaton, to the normativity of Jesus and his worldview for contemporary theologizing. An adequate theology for today must undertake more extensive revisions than Pannenberg seems willing to consider. Think, for instance, of the question of other religions.[7] It may be important to engage in dialogue with the Western

---

6. Hermann Fischer, "Fundamentaltheologische Prolegomena zur theologischen Anthropologie. Anfragen an W. Pannenbergs Anthropologie," *Theologische Rundschau* 50 (1985): 41-61, quote on p. 60.

7. This is a point that was raised already by John Cobb Jr. in his first published response to *Theology and the Philosophy of Science*, in *Religious Studies Review* 3 (1977): 213-215.

philosophical tradition, with the methods and worldview of contemporary natural science, and with data from the social sciences concerning human nature. Indeed, theologians should demonstrate that religion is still relevant to contemporary experience, that secularism clashes with the nature of human existence. But—critics continue—Pannenberg's position commits him to research in the comparative study of religions as well, since he holds that the history of religions is the place where God's revelation is most likely to be found.[8] His own methodology thus entails a comparative theology that forays beyond the borders of the Christian tradition. Yet his work does not reflect extensive examination of other major world religions.[9]

Why this dissatisfaction on both sides? The answer, I think, lies in Pannenberg's different "voices," his effort to mediate the demands of the theological tradition with the demands for its reformulation. I will argue below that this synthetic aim is exactly correct, both as a position on theological method and with regard to the particularity and universality of Christian claims. Against conservatives like Fischer, it seems inevitable that a thinker who speaks to contemporary questions will deviate, at least in form, from traditional answers; central foci will be altered, earlier debates left behind. Fischer recognizes that Pannenberg's vocation is to "bring Christian truth into relation with the general consciousness [of contemporary thought]" (p. 44). Yet this *must* involve thematizing Christian claims from the perspective of contemporary consciousness, in which a different set of distinctions is operative than formerly. Without the use of nonbiblical philosophical categories, theological revision in light of the contemporary horizon becomes impossible. Such rethinking forms a central tenet of what I will defend as revisionist theology or "revisionism."

Nevertheless, if Pannenberg is a revisionist, he is a moderate one. The champion of criticizability within theology has not become the new German prophet of thoroughgoing revisionism, whether it be in

---

8. Cf. *Theology and the Philosophy of Science,* chap. 5.

9. In the contemporary academic set-up, this examination would proceed in dialogue with researchers in the study of religion. But we find a surprising underemphasis on the results of this discipline in Pannenberg's corpus. Even the treatment of *Religionswissenschaft* in *Theology and the Philosophy of Science* does not adequately represent the blossoming of this discipline, especially in the United States, in the last 20 or so years.

the direction of "theology in a revolutionary situation" (Bonino) or "theology for a nuclear age" (Gordon Kaufman). This fact helps account for a certain estrangement between Pannenberg and many American liberals. Perhaps there has been general disappointment that the German theologians of hope have returned to the doctrine of the Trinity and other classical theological loci, rather than writing "theology in a new key." And certainly, all methodological issues aside, Pannenberg's political conservativism has detracted from his appeal during a period influenced by feminist, black, and Latin American liberation theologies.

The amount of revising and reformulating countenanced by differing theological methods varies greatly; the lines between positions are often fuzzy and difficult to draw. For instance, I will criticize Pannenberg in Section V for not going far enough, based on the status and function he ascribes to the biblical horizon. On the other hand, I have elsewhere defended his resistance to a thoroughgoing revisionism that too quickly dismisses the normative claims of Christianity.[10] Pannenberg's method is thoroughly steeped in the history of theology, its questions and loci. Although he has let the present horizon weigh heavily in testing the truth and meaningfulness of Christianity, his theology continues to wrestle with the normative claim posed by the Christ event. Excursuses into anthropology, philosophy of science, or metaphysics belong to the "from below" component of theology as a science; yet they never take the place of systematic theology. Significantly, Pannenberg will culminate his career with a multivolume dogmatics.

In summary, Pannenberg's theological method involves the quest for points of contact in all religions and all academic disciplines. Where revisions are called for, he is committed to making them. In fact, however, he believes that these revisions will be moderate rather than extreme; we will still be able to preserve the fundamental conceptual structure of the Christ event. What is this structure, and is it indeed a sufficient foundation upon which to build a theology for today?

---

10. See my *Explanation from Physics to Theology: An Essay in Rationality and Religion* (New Haven: Yale University Press, 1989), esp. chap. 6.

127

II

That Pannenberg strives to find a mean between the past as determinative and the past as irrelevant does not set him apart from other Christian theologians; most try in some way to mediate between the past and present horizons of Christianity. The crux of the matter lies in one's particular balance between the two horizons, and in the conceptual means one employs in the process. How then has Pannenberg conceptualized the Christ event such that it remains normative but not absolutely determining?

The heart of his answer is anticipation. I need not argue for the centrality of his appeal to anticipation or prolepsis, for virtually every author to write on his theology has drawn attention to the use of this concept. Little reflection is required to compile an impressive list of Pannenbergian positions that depend crucially on anticipation: his theory of truth, being, rationality, religion; his doctrine of God, the Trinity, Christ, the church, the eschaton; his views on revelation, resurrection, the kingdom of God, hope, the politics of Christianity; his solution to the problems of faith and reason, change in God, God's relation to the world; his understanding of dogmatic assertions, theological method, apologetics, ecumenical dialogue; his philosophy of time, history, personhood, meaning, hermeneutics—the reader can extend the list at will. In his seminars Pannenberg often worked to get his students to grasp the systematic impulse or principle that underlies every systematic theology. Without a doubt, his is the insight into the structure of anticipation.

Religion is not alone in its concern with human contexts of meaning, anticipation, or totality. In religion, however, "this anticipatory wholeness of meaning, be it obscure or pellucid, is to be found in the experience of the significant particular." [11] For Christianity, if there is a normative particular, it can only be Jesus. The thesis of *Jesus—God and Man* is that Jesus is the historical particular in whom the whole of reality is anticipated. Christ is not just the model for how Christians think things will work out in the end; he is the proleptic inbreaking of the end into the ongoing course of human history. The proof of his

---

11. *The Idea of God and Human Freedom,* 133.

apocalyptic significance is the resurrection: the resurrection is the sign that Jesus' message and self-understanding ought to be heeded, namely, his self-proclamation as the unique Son of God and divine revelation.

Pannenberg did not come to a theory of anticipation by reading Hegel or Heidegger. Rather, his pivotal systematic principle is meant to express the fundamental structure of the central event of Christianity, the resurrection. Moreover, he intends this direction of proceeding to be normative for theology. It amounts to a demanding criterion: *any* adequate systematic theology, however dependent it may be on philosophy for its conceptual framework, must derive its content and structure from the Christ event. Since the Christ event presupposes apocalypticism, all theologians must develop their epistemologies or their ethics out of this perspective. Let us call Pannenberg's standard for theology the "apocalyptic horizon" criterion; we return to it below.

What then is the underlying theory of anticipation in *Jesus—God and Man?* Nowhere in the text, to my knowledge, does Pannenberg explicitly discuss his choice of the term *prolepsis* or elaborate on its meanings. Moreover, the critical reaction to Pannenberg has been surprisingly silent regarding this notion, perhaps because of a certain mystique surrounding it: commentators apparently assume that it conveys some esoteric theological or philosophical logic with which one is not quite familiar. Yet traditionally the word has connoted little more than the sense of *anticipation* or, according to the *Oxford English Dictionary,* "the representation or taking of something future as already done or existing." The root is the Greek *prolepsis,* from *prolambanein,* "to take beforehand" (sometimes translated simply "to anticipate"). The term was often used for the rhetorical device of anticipating objections before they are stated, for the artistic device of representing an effect to be produced as already produced (a soldier being killed is depicted in the same picture as being eaten by dogs), or simply for any preassumed notion or presupposition. *Proleptic* as adjective most often means merely "anticipatory," i.e., something future is referred to as being present. As far as I can tell, none of these antecedents supplies the robust ontological doctrine Pannenberg is seeking.[12]

---

12. Theology does establish a precedent for (though not a full conceptual outworking of) Pannenberg's usage. Johannes Weiss spoke of Jesus' "proleptic sayings" and Albert Schweitzer

However, the term takes on a wealth of meanings in *Jesus—God and Man*. In its first occurrences *proleptic* characterizes Jesus' claim; it means "an anticipation of a confirmation that is to be expected only from the future," the "anticipation of the future verdict" (pp. 58, 60). Often, as in the discussion of the delay of the parousia (pp. 106–108), it serves as a shorthand for the "already and not yet" structure of the resurrection as expounded by Conzelmann and others. The resurrection, we are told, is essentially an eschatological event. As such, it is both truly past (the resurrection occurred at a moment in human history) and essentially future (the essence of this event lies at the end of time). The paradigmatic status for Pannenberg of this one event, which belongs both to human history and to a time beyond time, cannot be overemphasized.

Against weaker interpretations of anticipation in his theology, the word *proleptic* is used in *Jesus—God and Man* in contexts that refer to the eschaton as having "already begun" or "already happened" (pp. 391, 397) in Jesus. With the resurrection the eschaton is no longer fully future. Occasionally the word also connotes the problematic character of this state of affairs, as in "the prolepsis of the eschaton is itself paradoxical" (p. 157) or in the discussion of doxological language about God, in which "the conceptual clarity of the ideas used disappears" and "contradictory conceptions inescapably result" (p. 185). At these times the recourse to prolepsis—that the resurrection constituted Christ as the preexistent Son of God—is not altogether happy; it is a case where "theology really does find itself forced to make contradictory assertions that once more give cause for further reflection" (p. 158n). But, we are reminded, paradox as a challenge for further thought is something quite different from out-and-out contradiction in which reflection meets final defeat.

---

of the "proleptic messianic consciousness of Jesus." See Weiss, *Die Predigt Jesu vom Reiche Gottes*, 2d ed. (1900), 71, ET *Jesus' Proclamation of the Kingdom of God*, trans. and ed. Richard H. Hiers and David L. Holland (Philadelphia: Fortress, 1971); and Schweitzer, *Von Reimarus zu Wrede* (1906), 282, ET *The Quest of the Historical Jesus: A Critical Study of Its Progress from Reimarus to Wrede*, trans. W. Montgomery (London: A. & C. Black, 1911). Prolepsis is usually negative in Barth: with regard to human attempts, "there is no becoming one of God and man, no elimination of the line of death, no proleptic appropriation of the fullness of God (kein proleptisches Ansichreissen der Fülle Gottes). . . ." See Barth's *Römerbrief*, 129f.; ET *The Epistle to the Romans*, trans. Edwyn C. Hoskyns (London: Oxford University Press, 1933).

The key notions seem to be: (1) Jesus can only be understood as combining the already of the resurrection and the not yet of the eschaton. (2) The eschaton has in some sense begun in Jesus' resurrection. The final state of affairs is thus "anticipated" in an ontological and not just metaphorical sense in Jesus' life. Admittedly, the mode of its presence must be specified: Is it present partially or sacramentally (or just proleptically)? (3) If the "already" has any force, it must convey that the eschatological rule of God has *already been decided* in Jesus' resurrection, though "what really happened in Jesus' resurrection" will only be *fully disclosed* at the eschaton (p. 397). I can only interpret this as meaning that any further change will be epistemological but not ontological: the gist of the final outcome has been decided (ontologically) in Jesus' resurrection, though we still have more to learn about its nature. Consequently, I will define the term *prolepsis* as "strong anticipation," i.e., as that particular theory of anticipation according to which what is anticipated in the present has already been determined (in some sense) in the future. (4) Prolepsis therefore involves for Pannenberg the assertion of retroactive causation: the resurrection retroactively establishes Jesus' unity with God throughout his earthly existence; indeed, it even establishes it from that moment in time *back through all eternity* (p. 321).

This is not an easy teaching. Whether it represents the necessary or even the most satisfactory framework for comprehending Jesus' life has been extensively debated and will not be my focus here. I merely note that it is no coincidence that Pannenberg's first monograph was a Christology. It was thinking through the logic of Jesus' resurrection, along with the resultant authority of his message and divinity of his person, that led Pannenberg to the central systematic principle of his theology, the concept of anticipation. As the apocalyptic horizon criterion suggests, *the anticipatory structure that characterizes most of what Pannenberg has written is generalized directly from the conclusions of his Christology.*

Granting (for the purposes of this essay) the proleptic structure of the Jesus story, and Pannenberg's understanding of theological method as outlined in Section I, the Christian theologian has no other recourse but to turn to philosophy with prolepsis in hand. At best, she will be able to show the philosophical inevitability of such a notion as a necessary condition for all meaning whatsoever; at worst, Pannenberg hopes, his philosophical efforts will reduce any contradiction to a paradox, an affront to (but not an out-and-out rejection of) reason. Let us examine the philosophical framework which Pannenberg has employed in conceptualizing this structure of already and not yet.

III

Pannenberg early extended anticipation to the nature of a dogmatic assertion[13] and only later began to defend it as central to the theories of meaning, hermeneutics, truth, and others. Thus the various philosophers who contribute to his conceptual framework as described in this section serve an ancillary role. If Pannenberg is successful, he will have found in them not a natural theology but a nontheological exposition of his central theological tenet, anticipation. Consequently, we cannot agree with claims such as Obayashi's that Pannenberg's understanding of history *"takes off from* the classical ontological question [sc., of essence] as the motivating principle of his work."[14]

Whatever borrowings there may have been from recent philosophy, Pannenberg's work remains faithful to the breadth and systematicity of classical metaphysics. His recently translated "Part and Whole" (note 5 above) is fully at home in that tradition; its concern may be with the "epistemology [*Wissenschaftlichkeit*] of theology," but the question is posed by Aristotle and concluded in conversation with Hegel. Likewise, a major treatment of God's proleptic actions in the present, "Appearance as the Arrival of the Future,"[15] is couched in terms of (though in contradistinction to) Aristotle's final causality.

Critics have long argued that Pannenberg's philosophical allegiance is, in the final analysis, to Hegel. One German introduction to theology, for instance, includes a chart of modern theologians, with a straight line linking Pannenberg to Hegel as the only influence! Further,

---

13. *Basic Questions in Theology,* 1:182-210.
14. See H. Obayashi, "Pannenberg and Troeltsch: History and Religion," *Journal of the American Academy of Religion* 38 (1970): 405, emphasis mine.
15. *Theology and the Kingdom of God,* chap. 4.

in a recent, insightful article, Roger Olson has effectively underscored the Hegelian elements in Pannenberg's Christology.[16] There are certainly close ties. For instance, the recent *Anthropology* appears to be a sort of theological retelling of Hegel's *Phenomenology of Spirit*, combining the various phenomena of human existence into a coherent worldview not through the necessary self-development of Absolute Spirit but through the proleptically self-revealing actions of the Christian God. The parallels include the holism of the appeals to totality, the repeated conceptual unions *(Aufhebungen)* as the argument progresses, the triadic structure within each part, and even the book's overall dialectical movement from "the person in nature" through "the person as social being" into "the shared world" of culture and history.[17]

But Pannenberg has rejected enough of Hegel and incorporated enough of others that the label "Hegelian" will not stick. "The Significance of Christianity in the Philosophy of Hegel"[18] castigates Hegel for a notion of the Absolute that is pantheistic and nonpersonalistic and for a view of history that is deterministic and too early brought to an end (namely, in Hegel). "Part and Whole" (note 5 above) defends a reworking of Hegel's system in which the whole or totality becomes the "category of categories" and God's distinction from the world is preserved. "Hermeneutic and Universal History"[19] does defend "a philosophy or theology of world history" (p. 135), but only in the face of the complete failure of Hegel's attempt. I well recall stressing the Hegelian influence on Pannenberg during my first meeting with him in Munich, an unfortunate opening comment which he paused to refute in some detail. Given the far-reaching disagreements and modifications, there is more than a little truth to Westphal's comment, "Pannenberg may well be the most articulate anti-Hegelian since Kierkegaard."[20]

---

16. Roger E. Olson, "The Human Self-Realization of God: Hegelian Elements in Pannenberg's Christology," *Perspectives in Religious Studies* 13 (1986): 207-223.

17. Of course, there are disanalogies. Especially important is Pannenberg's stress on sin and finitude as opposed to what he views as the "justification by works" presupposed in many modern anthropologies, including Hegel's. See also Roger E. Olson, "Pannenberg's Theological Anthropology: A Review Article," *Perspectives in Religious Studies* 13 (1986): 161-169.

18. In *The Idea of God and Human Freedom*, 144-177.

19. In *Basic Questions in Theology*, 1:96-136.

20. See Merold Westphal, "Hegel, Pannenberg, and Hermeneutics," *Man and World* 4 (1971): 276-293. The discrepancies are nicely described in Allan D. Galloway, *Wolfhart Pannenberg* (London: George Allen & Unwin Ltd., 1973).

Once the myth of Pannenberg the Hegelian has been laid to rest, I believe his actual philosophical allegiances can be fairly briefly outlined.[21] Hegel had correctly introduced a historicized notion of being, albeit one that remained imprisoned to rational necessity rather than the vicissitudes of actual human history. More helpful was the work of Wilhelm Dilthey, who adopted the pervasively historical framework of Hegel's thought and the insistence on truth and reality as the final whole of experience. But the appeal to final coherence works better as a semantics than as a logic. The development of meaning—call it a hermeneutics of totality—moves from individual to the whole; in Dilthey's crucial phrase from the *Gesammelte Schriften:*

> One would have to wait for the end of a life and, in the hour of death, survey the whole and ascertain the relation between the whole and its parts. One would have to wait for the end of history to have all the material necessary to determine its meaning (7:233).[22]

Each part of human existence, down to each individual term or assertion, is meaningful only in terms of some broader context; moreover, the movement to ever-broader frameworks admits of no arbitrary breaking-off until one has attained the most comprehensive horizon, that of history as a whole. It is my belief that this "idealist" (or "totalist") insight provided (if retroactively) the philosophical foundation for the appeal to universal history in *Revelation as History,* and later guided Pannenberg's difficult treatment of hermeneutic theory at the heart of his theological methodology.[23]

Yet it was not Hegel or Dilthey but rather Heidegger who first saw the major consequence of a hermeneutics of totality: the primacy

---

21. Key passages for gaining insight into Pannenberg's use of modern philosophers occur in "Faith and Reason" (in *Basic Questions in Theology*, 2:59-62) and "On Historical and Theological Hermeneutic" (ibid., 1:161-174). See also his "Meaning, Religion and the Question of God," trans. P. Clayton, in *Knowing Religiously*, ed. Leroy Rouner (University of Notre Dame Press, 1985), and my "Being and One Theologian," *The Thomist* 50 (October 1988).

22. Wilhelm Dilthey, *Gesammelte Schriften*, ed. Bernhard Groethuysen (Leipzig: B. G. Tuebner, 1927); translated in *Dilthey: Selected Writings*, ed. and trans. H. P. Rickman (Cambridge: At the University Press, 1976), 236.

23. *Theology and the Philosophy of Science*, chap. 3.

of the future.[24] In *Being and Time* Heidegger describes the individual's present existence as combining and constituted by his or her past and future. But now the future plays the crucial role. It is the locus of possibility, specifically the possibility of *Dasein's* wholeness or completion. Existing means projecting oneself onto the future, anticipating one's possible wholeness in the future. For Heidegger this possible wholeness comes at the moment of death; we exist authentically through the anticipation of our own death *(das Vorlaufen zum Tode)*.[25]

But *is* death the final horizon that allows us to speak of the identity of a person as complete? What of reinterpretations of a person's life *after* her or his death? Here Pannenberg relies on the detailed criticisms of Heideggerian anticipation first raised by Jean-Paul Sartre.[26] One's life is never complete at its end, for it continues to be reinterpreted by others after one's death. But if the framework of interpretation transcends the individual, where does one reach a sufficiently broad horizon? For Pannenberg the final totality of meaning must encompass the whole of history, as Dilthey insisted. Only a final future, a place beyond history (say, an eschaton) could provide a totality which is truly total and unsurpassable by any further history. In short, philosophical considerations themselves lead to a concept of universal history which can only be fully grasped from a theological—more specifically, an eschatological—perspective.

With philosophical arguments such as these, Pannenberg has sought a conceptual anchor for his position, specified its basic parameters, linked it to contemporary philosophical developments, and sketched the outlines of a research program that unfolds into his works in epistemology, anthropology, and other areas. As the apocalyptic

---

24. In fact, Heidegger has contributed more to Pannenberg's thought than a philosophical justification of the priority of the future. His analysis of individual human existence in terms of modes of being-in-the-world, everydayness, thrownness, and projection has played a central role in Pannenberg's anthropological writings, perhaps less noticeably in *What Is Man?* but certainly very clearly in the recent anthropology. The index lists discussions of Heidegger on 37 different pages; although his thought hardly serves as a philosophical foundation for the book, clearly it is seen as a project parallel to Pannenberg's own.

25. See Karl Rahner, *On the Theology of Death,* trans. Charles H. Henkey (New York: Herder and Herder, 1961) for an interesting theological appropriation of this Heideggerian framework.

26. See Sartre, *Being and Nothingness,* trans. Hazel Barnes (New York: Philosophical Library, 1956), 531-553.

horizon criterion should make clear, neither these three thinkers, nor any of the other philosophers from Parmenides to Ernst Bloch whom Pannenberg treats, form the starting point for his theology. Nonetheless, they provide the core of the conceptual framework that supports his theological use of anticipation. Only now that the general background has been exposed can we turn to the crucial question: How are we to evaluate Pannenberg's *apologia* for anticipation as the systematic principle for his theology?

IV

To review: we have noted that Pannenberg eschews any merely subjective theory of anticipation in favor of a strong, ontological interpretation. We do not merely hope in a possible future outcome; rather, the future is in some sense present in the present, in such a way that it proleptically determines and gives meaning to that present. Anticipation is thus not merely a "regulative idea of the unity of the whole content of experience"[27] nor a "theoretical fiction."[28] Instead, Christians can have "rational confidence of future success, a confidence inspiring the attitude of the present moment."[29] Likewise, given Pannenberg's understanding of theology (Section I), we know that one must be able to abstract this strong doctrine of anticipation from the Jesus story and test it as a general philosophical position. It must ground an ontology, as well as a philosophy of history and of time, according to which the end of time is present *in* time as the essence and truth of all temporal things. I would like to raise five difficulties with the notion of anticipation as so far developed.

1. *The need for a systematic outworking.* Pannenberg's position suggests rather than presents a complete theory of reality. It is not impossible that an ontology of anticipation can be developed. If it can, it would be ideal for formulating a general theory of reality while remaining faithful to the structure of the Christ event. But the task

---

27. *The Idea of God and Human Freedom,* 132.
28. Ibid., 139.
29. Ibid.

requires an explicit and systematic treatment. Many passages in Pannenberg discuss Aristotle, Hegel, Dilthey, Bloch, Whitehead, and others, expressing disagreement and suggesting an anticipation-based alternative; yet the outcome is usually more criticism than appropriation. Until such a time as a full "eschatological ontology" is written, prolepsis remains a paradox (in Pannenberg's sense), i.e., a call to further reflection. Pannenberg granted this point in *Jesus—God and Man;* I am unsure whether he takes his intervening publications to have sufficiently resolved the matter.

2. *The two senses of anticipation.* The paradoxical nature of the Christ event stems from the tension between its two constitutive moments, the already and the not yet. The passages discussed above that refer to the resurrection as an event in which the eschaton has "already begun" or "happened" suggest an ontologically determinate view of history. On the other hand, Pannenberg counts on the "not yet" to allow for the openness of human history and a progressive view of God for whose being events subsequent to Christ are genuinely constitutive.[30]

I believe there are two notions of anticipation at work here, corresponding roughly to these two moments; we might call them anticipation$_1$ and anticipation$_2$. *(a)* Some passages speak of the eschatological future as having broken into human history in Christ's resurrection. Anticipation$_1$ is thus the inbreaking of God at a given moment in history, at which point the end of history is decided. This is the notion of anticipation that must underlie denials of development in God[31] and assertions that Christ always was who he "became" in Jesus. *(b)* At other times Pannenberg stresses the openness of history. In these contexts anticipation$_2$ implies that the outcome of history and the nature of God depend on the contingent course of history. This is the basis for speaking, e.g., of "the God of history" who is essentially dependent on the outcome of history, whose Godhood is genuinely at stake in the course of human affairs. Further, anticipation$_2$ must be what Pannenberg has in mind when he speaks of every meaningful

---

30. This theme is worked out nicely in "The God of History" ("Der Gott der Geschichte"), in *Grundfragen systematischer Theologie,* vol. 2, chap. 5.
31. *Theology and the Kingdom of God,* 64.

assertion as a guess about how the end will be. If there is indeed this conceptual distinction between the two anticipations, then some adequate way of resolving the tension must be found lest equivocation arise. Pannenberg would presumably say that the Christ event implies both, that there is a dialectical relationship between the two moments. But how is this dialectic to be understood?

3. *The idealist framework.* Anticipation involves some strong idealist presuppositions which may be difficult to swallow for those not sympathetic to the idealist tradition. The anticipatory doctrines of truth and of meaning state that any particular statement is true (meaningful) only in terms of the whole of reality, which for Pannenberg means the completion of history. This claim demands the supposition of an intimate link between thought and being, whereby history is the process of the gradual unification of thought and being, of anticipation and the anticipated. Thought strives continually to formulate truly, i.e., in light of the whole of what will be, always necessarily falling short when compared with the future totality, always propelled thereby to ever-new anticipations. Future being (God's kingdom), for its part, is already present now as what will be, effecting the relativization of all current anticipations while itself being in some sense constituted by these efforts.[32] Ronald Pasquariello has nicely expressed the organic link of thought and being that is here implied:

> It is only on the basis of an understanding that truth is the whole that thought and being can become equatable—when, that is, they are grasped as reciprocally implicated in a dialectical process of development that aims at total comprehensiveness. . . . Being, because it is knowable, calls forth thought. Thought, because it can know, anticipates the call. It takes up the knowable, but is driven beyond it because finite being itself is only provisionally true.[33]

But why should what is be *constituted* by its being thought? Why think that the future is really present in the present rather than present

---

32. This is the framework implied in "On Historical and Theological Hermeneutic," which presents the correct understanding of "thought" as a hermeneutical one; see, e.g., *Basic Questions in Theology*, 1:158ff.

33. See Ronald D. Pasquariello, "Pannenberg's Philosophical Foundations," *Journal of Religion* 56 (1976): 338-347, esp. 343-344.

only as illusion, hope, ideal, construct? In what way is the whole of history really required to account for the truth of "this is a dog"[34] or, say, "2 + 2 = 4"? One might be equally drawn to a theory of truth that grants the relative independence of such statements. For example, if we work "upward" from contemporary natural and social science, we might be less inclined to an idealist theory of meaning than those who approach the philosophy of science from a metaphysical or idealist background. It is almost a condition of the possibility of modern science to declare its independence from any final horizon; doing so is the only way to make scientific explanation and research possible in practice.

Likewise, why should we expect the real to be thinkable, even in its entirety, rather than opaque to reason? Why posit, that is, a dialectical interplay of reason and reality leading to their final fusion rather than, say, an inherent limitedness of reason which closes it off forever from what really is? Thinkers from Kant to W. Sellars have stressed the possibility that our conceptual schemes do not correspond to the way things actually are—or that any correspondence there might be is inherently unknowable. At least, there is cause to hesitate before espousing a robust rationalism of future thought-being identity—especially if one is critical of previous efforts toward an idealistic metaphysics (e.g., Hegel, Bradley). At worst, unanswered skeptical worries provide sufficient reason to eschew an idealist theory of meaning, being, and truth.

4. *Theory of time.*   Prolepsis also employs a problematic dialectic regarding the theory of time. How can the future be both present and future at the same time? Think again of anticipation$_1$ and anticipation$_2$ as outlined above. We might interpret them as assuming Augustinian and process views of time, respectively. Under anticipation$_1$ we could have a history that was open until a certain time, at which time timeless divine reality broke into the contingent flow of history from the end of time and determined its subsequent outcome. At points Pannenberg seems to hold such a two-tier, Augustinian view of reality: there is real development and change in human history but none in God, who will

---

34. *Basic Questions in Theology,* 2:62.

always have been the One who he turns out to be at the end of history.[35] This eternally self-identical One is dependent on history's outcome without as a consequence developing through the course of history. On the other hand, anticipation$_2$ could allow for a process God caught up in the flow of history and working to direct it toward particular goals.

Pannenberg clearly maintains that these two notions of God and anticipation can be combined into one, hence that at the eschaton time will not cease but will be transcended-*and*-preserved *(aufgehoben)* into eternity. But if one rejects the Hegelian dialectic and its *Aufhebungen,* one must insist that time is either transcended or preserved. Anticipation$_1$ militates for the former. Drawing on Plato, Augustine held that time was less than really real. Eternity is the eternal present of God above and beyond the limited reality of human time. Anticipation$_2$, I think—and process views generally—make it difficult to posit a final completion. This is Lewis Ford's main cause for disagreement with Pannenberg.[36] If time is not to be eliminated, it must continue; thus locutions such as "the end of time" must be avoided. In short, it is not the coherence of anticipation$_1$ or anticipation$_2$ alone, but rather the seeming incoherence of their combination that should give us pause.

5. *Doctrine of freedom.* Several thinkers have argued that anticipation is unsatisfactory for solving the problem of freedom.[37] Pannenberg has linked human freedom to the fact that theology deals with a reality that is not yet complete.[38] The reasoning seems to be that, if reality *were* complete, there could only be one correct way to interpret it; all the data would be in, and one would only have to establish which

---

35. For example, "what turns out to be true in the future will then be evident as having been true all along" (*Theology and the Kingdom of God,* 63); "although the essence of God is from everlasting to everlasting the same, it does have a history in time" (*Revelation as History,* 133-134). For Pannenberg's sympathy with the Augustinian view of God, see his "Christentum und Platonismus. Die kritische Platonrezeption Augustins in ihrer Bedeutung für das gegenwärtige christliche Denken," *Zeitschrift für Kirchengeschichte* 96 (1985): 147-161. Of course, history plays a more crucial role for Pannenberg's God than for Augustine's.

36. On Ford's view see, e.g., his essays "God as the Subjectivity of the Future," *Encounter* 41 (1980): 287-292; "Creativity in a Future Key," in *New Essays in Metaphysics,* ed. Robert C. Neville (Albany: State University of New York Press, 1987), 179-197; and his contribution to this volume.

37. See the detailed treatment in David McKenzie, "Pannenberg on God and Freedom," *Journal of Theology* 60 (1980): 307-329; cf. also the articles by Cobb and Ford in this volume.

38. *The Idea of God and Human Freedom,* chap. 4.

interpretation is most justified given the totality of facts. By contrast, the meaning that concerns theology "transcends what merely is."[39] It anticipates the final completion of reality when the meaning of everything will be clear; yet, because history has not yet decided the outcome, it remains indeterminate and humans can be said to be free.

But either determinism is the case or it is not. If Christ was the proleptic inauguration of God's rule (anticipation₁), then the end is in some sense set, and it is only epistemologically "in question" *(strittig)*, i.e., it is *our* knowledge that is inadequate. At best, our freedom could be that of not knowing that the course of history is in fact determined by the "all-determining reality." On the other hand, if Christ was the revelation of a *possible* outcome or possible mode of being-in-the-world,[40] but the final actuality is undetermined (anticipation₂), then history is genuinely open and we are free. But in this case Christ cannot be said to have predetermined the outcome. Pannenberg has argued that freedom can be otherwise specified than as the merely formal freedom of libertarianism.[41] But I am not convinced that "the presence of the being, destiny, and selfhood of the human being"[42] still merits the name freedom, even if it is compatible with some notion of moral responsibility.[43]

These five criticisms do not prove that nothing can be made of the doctrine of anticipation. The Pannenbergian presuppositions explored in (3) and (4), for instance, could never be falsified; hence Pannenberg's position cannot be "refuted." My thesis has been that anticipation in the strong, "ontological" sense—Pannenberg's prolepsis—invokes a number of notions that are philosophically problematic, enough to cause one to hesitate before basing a system upon it. By contrast, a weaker, "epistemological" reading of anticipation may well have important things to contribute to the philosophies of history and

---

39. Ibid., 133.

40. As suggested, e.g., by Paul Ricoeur, "Biblical Hermeneutics," in *Paul Ricoeur on Biblical Hermeneutics,* Semeia 4 (Chico: Scholar's Press, 1975), 27-148, and David Tracy, *The Analogical Imagination: Christian Theology and the Culture of Pluralism* (London: SCM, 1981).

41. *Anthropology in Theological Perspective,* 104-119.

42. Ibid., 114.

43. It still seems inevitable that an agent is free only as he or she has the possibility of doing *or not doing* some action. Redefinitions of freedom without real choice stretch the term *freedom* to the breaking point. In such cases, why not argue for a theory of soft determinism or compatibilism that preserves human responsibility without recourse to human freedom at all?

of meaning. Specifically, I propose that the end of history can be defended not as a given but as "a regulative idea in the service of faith." Positing an ultimate end of history and a judgment of God makes faith possible now; it expresses what faith hopes for and what is as yet unseen (Heb. 11:1). An anticipation limited to hope gives the future a constitutive function for the present; it is sufficient for faith, while preserving human freedom and the contingency of history.

Consequently, I would like to turn to the question, what portions of theological method and practice will be altered if one proceeds without prolepsis (deterministic anticipation) while retaining Pannenberg's commitment to "theology from below" and to the intimate link between theology and external criticism? What revisions will need to be made, and what different conclusions might one reach?

V

Pannenberg takes the task of theology to include formulating "a Biblically grounded understanding of being and truth."[44] This is the apocalyptic horizon criterion discussed above: the Christ event must be interpreted in terms of its original horizon of understanding. If one does not use the framework of apocalyptic, then one must bring a "foreign" framework to the origins of Christianity. The decision between frameworks, he believes, then becomes merely arbitrary:

> The knowledge of Jesus . . . cannot be established from the perspective of these other patterns of thought [such as Gnosticism]. Where such a new basis has been sought, Jesus again and again has become merely the example of a Gnostic or a philosophical idea whose truth is ultimately independent of the history of Jesus. The basis of the knowledge of Jesus' significance remains bound to the original apocalyptic horizon of Jesus' history. . . . If this horizon is eliminated, the basis of faith is lost; then Christology becomes mythology. . . .[45]

---

44. "The Revelation of God in Jesus of Nazareth," in *Theology as History*, ed. James M. Robinson and John B. Cobb Jr. (New York: Harper & Row, 1967), 132, note. See also *Theology and the Kingdom of God*, 63, and passages such as those in *Basic Questions in Theology*, 1:8-14, 74-80.

45. *Jesus—God and Man*, 83.

Why arbitrary? According to Pannenberg, if we must choose between frameworks, our present understanding of Christ will lack continuity with the original horizon of understanding:

> If the apocalyptic expectation should be totally excluded from the realm of possibility for us, then the early Christian faith in Christ is also excluded. This would, however, also destroy the continuity of that which might still remain as Christianity after such a reduction with Jesus and the primitive Christian proclamation through Paul's time.[46]

Obviously, if we could accept both the historicity of the resurrection and the continued viability of an apocalyptic worldview without alteration, the difficulties of justifying our choice of interpretive scheme would be avoided. There would be no problem (1) establishing the continuity of our faith with theirs, nor (2) preserving the historical particularity of Christian belief, nor (3) holding on to claims of the universal significance of the Christ event. In fact, continuity, particularity, and universality seem to summarize the three central tasks (and hence criteria) for any theological account of Christianity. Think of a parallel example: if we could accept the theoretical framework underlying the biblical writers' views on science or miracles or the male–female hierarchy, the continuity of our position with theirs would be easier to establish. For many of us, though, their positions on these issues are no longer live options, and some difficult revisions are called for. Similarly, what if apocalypticism is no longer a meaningful worldview for many 20th-century persons?[47] In this case also, we are forced to revise our conceptual framework. We remain liable to the same three criteria; but now the reformulations will be more radical and more extensive. Nevertheless, need it follow that such a de-apocalypticized theology can have no significant relation to Jesus? Must we conclude that all nonapocalyptic attempts at explicating the meaning of the Christ event are subjective and arbitrary?

I think not. Consider, for instance, the Hegelian reading of Christianity. Is Hegel guilty of reducing theology to nothing more than "the

---

46. Ibid., 82, translation modified.
47. Pannenberg stresses the criterion of continued meaningfulness; cf. *Theology and the Philosophy of Science*, chap. 5, and his article, "Meaning, Religion and the Question of God" (see note 21 above).

art of using the biblical materials to express the spirit of the times," as Westphal has argued?[48] What bothers Westphal about Hegel is what we might call his "externalism," which Westphal argues leads to "arbitrariness and subjectivism." First, Hegel brings philosophical criteria to the biblical witness which then "stand as the norm of [its] meaning and truth"; but using an "extra-biblical norm" amounts to a capitulation to Feuerbach, for "God is being created in the image of man."[49] Second, even a weak version of externalism, one which allows an extrabiblical set of questions or preunderstandings to guide our search for theological answers (Bultmann, Tillich), is inadequate: "it is not clear that this distinction between questions and answers is very significant in any case, for if an extrabiblical framework of thought is given veto power over what questions the biblical materials may answer (for us), its control over the content is not exactly minimal."[50]

The first thing to note is that, if these are the sins of externalism, Pannenberg is guilty of both of them. Like Hegel, he views theology as entering of necessity into philosophical debate; its concepts, though derived originally from Christian contexts, must stand the test of philosophical analysis. This is externalism of precisely the sort that theologians like Hans Frei and George Lindbeck so heartily oppose.[51] Moreover, he often makes use of something very much like Tillich's method of correlation.[52] Now, granting Pannenberg's divergence from Westphal here, suppose that a somewhat stronger dose of externalism is called for? Suppose, as the criticisms of the last section imply, that prolepsis fails to combine "the finitude of human experience and thereby the openness of the future" with "the intrinsic claim of the particular" (e.g., Jesus)—a task Pannenberg admits "might seem like that of squaring the circle, since the totality of history could only come into view

---

48. Merold Westphal, "Hegel, Pannenberg, and Hermeneutics."
49. Ibid., 287.
50. Ibid.
51. See Hans Frei, *The Eclipse of Biblical Narrative* (New Haven: Yale University Press, 1974), and George Lindbeck, *The Nature of Doctrine: Religion and Theology in a Post-Liberal Age* (Philadelphia: Westminster, 1984). Westphal's article "Hegel, Pannenberg, and Hermeneutics" seems to be an attempt to read Pannenberg as compatible with Frei's position. Though the need for mediating between these two theologians is urgent, I do not think his attempt provides it.
52. See esp. "The Question of God," in *Basic Questions in Theology*, 2:201-233. It could be said that *Anthropology in Theological Perspective* is a venture in precisely this exercise.

from the perspective of its end. . . ."⁵³ I am not convinced that theology must then become either arbitrary or impossible. The three criteria for theological reformulations are still operative, even if meeting them should remain an unfulfilled challenge.

Of course, given the difficulties of satisfying the criteria I have proposed, one could question the need for retaining them at all. Let us pause, then, to consider two other routes available to theologians who are willing to discard one or the other of these requirements.⁵⁴ Either they can base claims for Christ's universal significance on a nonbiblical framework (philosophical, political, ethical), which would reveal the true essence of Christianity freed from its historical sources, thereby justifying it as the highest religion, or they can continue to ascribe an important role within the Christian religion to the individual man Jesus while forgoing claims to the absoluteness of his person or teaching. Does either approach represent a viable alternative to Pannenberg's methodological stipulations for theology?

(1) *Christianity dehistoricized.* This option takes the biblical teachings and Christian tradition as a context for discovering certain more fundamental truths. As in Kant's *Religion within the Limits of Reason Alone,* one unapologetically derives this more essential structure according to criteria other than intrabiblical criteria. One's concern may be with the highest ethical ideals or with liberating political action or with the most adequate philosophy. In any case, the original horizon of the Christ event is de-essentialized; its role becomes heuristic (it happens to point us to certain other truths that we hold to be important) or aesthetic or symbolic (the form these truths took in the Christian story is a particularly attractive or appealing one). Under this position, the person of Christ is not constitutive for the truths in question; he plays no *causal role* in bringing them about or making them true. Instead, his importance is derived from the truths or actions to which he points (or is believed to point).⁵⁵

---

53. *Basic Questions in Theology,* 1:135.

54. These options bear obvious affinities to the Jesus of history/Christ of faith debate.

55. This option is nicely described (though not endorsed) by Stephen Knapp in "Collective Memory and the Actual Past," forthcoming in *Representations.* One might defend Hegel's treatment of Christianity as somewhat of an exception to this position, since each moment in the development of Absolute Spirit (hence also the Christ event) is ontologically constitutive of what

(2) *Christianity relativized.* The other option dispenses with claims of universal significance on behalf of Christianity, perhaps in view of other religious traditions, perhaps due to a pervasive historicism. The first move, for example, opens up the sort of dialogue with other religions advocated by thinkers like Cobb and Hick. It brings Christian theology into closer de facto conformity to the study of religions. The truth question may still be thematized, but the discussion must remain without a final answer until the end of history. Any theology of religions that is attempted must preserve the particularity and validity of the various religions and avoid demanding a privileged status for Christianity.

Pannenberg's answer to the relativizing move involves the appeal to prolepsis. His history of religions article castigates dialectical theology for not taking seriously the "facts of the sciences of religion." [56] Appeal to a subjective faith-stance, or even to a phenomenology of religious experience, is not adequate to answer criticisms of religion based on a general anthropology (Feuerbach, Marx, Freud). For this task, according to Pannenberg, we need to show that "a mysterious ground of all reality" that transcends finite existence is implied in the very structure of finite experience.[57] This effort requires an anthropology (thus Pannenberg's recent monograph in this genre); once one has been established, we need only discover which religion and which God or gods best do justice to this structure, i.e., which religion can be said to describe the all-determining reality in a way that is meaningful to our contemporary experience. Yet this judgment is not merely subjective, since only one religion can correctly anticipate the final outcome.

Pannenberg is indeed right that the battle against the critics of religion can only be fought on their turf, i.e., in terms of a general philosophical anthropology. This sort of a project is already far removed

---

it finally becomes. But, as has often been pointed out, the moments of Hegel's system are, finally, logical rather than temporal: Hegel's logic is not in the first place a description of empirical history; it is preeminently a chronicle of the steps by which "thought comes to itself" that in fact coincides with history. As the imposition of an extrabiblical ontology, Hegel's work is different only in degree from that of Lessing or Kant.

56. See "Toward a Theology of the History of Religion," in *Basic Questions in Theology,* 2:65-118.

57. Ibid., 102.

from a positivistic science of religion that claims to proceed purely descriptively and to eschew any normative judgments. The study of religion necessarily finds itself engaged in the task of explaining the multitude of religious phenomena with which it deals. Its work includes the evaluation of the truth content of the religions in question—assuming that false propositions in a religion do not "falsify" that religion in any simplistic sense.[58] Pannenberg is also right to focus on religions in their concrete historicality, on the historical particulars rather than (or at least before) universal judgments are made. His aim is to steer a course between a science of religion that never proceeds beyond descriptions of the particularities of each given religion, and a natural theology that attempts to leave historical specifics behind.

But without prolepsis the *status* of one's results must be interpreted differently. Instead of speaking of "the definitive appearance" of the divine reality[59] *via* prolepsis, one is tempted to view the competing truth claims as equally lacking in epistemic warrant: the historian of religions does not have but rather seeks a defense of the universality of the historically concrete. I find much to condone in this more skeptical approach. In its strongly relativist or subjectivist form, however, it is often bolstered by problematic appeals to the doctrine of historicism. One often begins, like Ernst Troeltsch, by claiming to know that our historical perspective can provide only transitory insights: "real history recognizes only individual and temporary structures that are related to their goal strictly in terms of a tendency toward the absolute."[60] This would mean, as Dyson has written of Troeltsch, "that theology can no longer take as its subject-matter certain normative, absolute, unique events of a supposed objective salvation-history."[61] On the other hand, a particular religious tradition could still be preferred

---

58. This assumption is defended in Donald Wiebe, *Religion and Truth: Towards an Alternative Paradigm for the Study of Religion* (The Hague: Mouton, 1981), esp. chaps. 2, 10, and 12.

59. *Basic Questions in Theology*, 2:110.

60. See Ernst Troeltsch, *The Absoluteness of Christianity and the History of Religions*, trans. David Reid (Richmond: John Knox, 1971), 158.

61. A. O. Dyson, "Ernst Troeltsch and the Possibility of a Systematic Theology," in *Ernst Troeltsch and the Future of Theology*, ed. John Powell Clayton (Cambridge: At the University Press, 1976), 86.

147

or practiced for subjective (ethical, cultural, ideological) reasons. Appeal is often made to Troeltsch's slogan:

> The Christian religion is in every moment of its history a purely historical phenomenon, subject to all the limitations to which any individual historical phenomenon is exposed, just like the other great religions.[62]

Perhaps this sort of theologian *cum* student of religion is spared the difficulties of making universal epistemic claims on the part of one religion. Yet I believe some nonrelative claims inevitably remain, be they objective historical claims or beliefs about the universal truth of a religion or religion in general. Troeltsch is a paradigm case of this dilemma facing the historicist position. In his late "The Place of Christianity among the World Religions" (1923), Troeltsch still wished to assert that "each of the faiths may experience its contact with the divine life." J. L. Adams summarizes Troeltsch's point using Nicholas of Cusa's metaphor of an omnivoyant human portrait that faces directly the various people who simultaneously confront it, each of them experiencing the directness of its gaze.[63] A similar tendency toward an absolute amidst the relative characterizes Paul Tillich's late *The Future of Religions,* in which he compared the different religions to different styles in art. Recall Tillich's manifesto:

> Let us not look at history in the sense of progress which will be going on and finally come to an end which is wonderful and fulfilling. There is no such thing in history, because man is free, free to contradict *his own essential nature* and his own fulfillment.[64]

---

62. Troeltsch, *Absoluteness,* 85.

63. See Adams' introduction to *Absoluteness,* 17.

64. See Paul Tillich, "The Significance of the History of Religions for the Systematic Theologian," in *The Future of Religions,* ed. Jerald Bauer (New York: Harper & Row, 1966), 80-94, quote on p. 79, emphasis mine. In this late lecture, Tillich outlines a program of theology as the history of religions, insofar as "there are revealing and saving powers in all religions" (81). Tillich's position here is so close to Pannenberg's, yet so different: "There may be—and I stress this, there *may* be—a central event in the history of religions which unites the positive results of those critical developments in the history of religion in and under which revelatory experiences are going on—an event which, therefore, makes possible a concrete theology that has universalistic significance" (ibid.). But, given the openness of history, we must be satisfied with studying the *kairoi* or great symbolic moments in all religions. Admittedly, there are difficulties with Tillich's "religion of the Concrete Spirit" and with his "dynamic-typological" approach, which may not do full justice to the variety of religious phenomena.

Such an approach is certainly congenial to those writers on religion who are seeking dialogue rather than judgment between religions. As Gerrish notes in his concluding comment on Troeltsch's position, "the relativising of all historical forms implies a relative truth in them all."[65]

Nonetheless, I am not satisfied that either of these two alternate routes—Christianity dehistoricized or Christianity relativized—provides an adequate methodological framework for Christian theology. The former option subsumes Christianity without embarrassment under (or "sublates" it into) philosophy or a related discipline, and thereby leads to its abandonment as a historical religion. The latter is more complicated, for it claims to preserve precisely what is historically particular to Christianity, abandoning only universal claims on its behalf. Still, problems arise. If universalist claims are endemic to this particular religion, then of course it will turn out to be intrinsically incompatible with a relativist framework. Further, the tendency to self-refutation in assertions of relativism is notorious. Historicism is not least among the offenders: it has too often relied on an ahistorical theory to support the belief that all theories are historically relative. A final problem is of historical origin and thus contingent. In practice, in cases where the first-century source has been relativized to just another historical event, another framework inevitably begins to play the normative role for Christian thinkers. In natural theology, Enlightenment thought, arguably in the history of Unitarianism, the Jesus event became a story or metaphor valued only in that it encouraged believers in their ethical or political efforts or pointed them toward belief in a universal religion. If I am right about this connection, the relativization of Christianity has tended historically to lead to the dehistorization of Christianity, and hence to its replacement by philosophy, ethics, or a theology of world religions.

I have taken Pannenberg's methodology of theology as the framework for this paper. He correctly makes theology radically dependent on the philosophical analysis of theological concepts. Other disciplines are allowed to contribute to the clarification of theological questions, and no "immunization strategies" are allowed to protect it from the

---

65. Brian Gerrish, "The Possibility of a Historical Theology," in *Ernst Troeltsch and the Future of Theology*, 135.

difficulties that may arise. I have also argued that Pannenberg has not been successful in using prolepsis to unify the two poles of particularity and universality. Of course, the difficulties discussed may be temporary, awaiting a fuller philosophical defense of prolepsis, the completion of his systematic theology, or only his comments at the end of this volume. We may hope that he will address these issues further. In the meantime, though, how are we to live with, and within, this tension?

When two demands can neither be unified conceptually nor rejected, one is constrained to maintain both in tension. *Pace* Hegel, I do not believe that this tension can be *aufgehoben,* transcended-yet-preserved. It is not an answer but a continuing problem. Pannenberg's methodology makes theology accountable both to the history of religions and to philosophy. Theology will consequently have solved its task only when it has unified the study of the particular context of Jesus Christ with a universal, philosophically adequate framework in such a way that the particular plays an indispensable role in the universal.

At this point, I have argued, this task remains an ideal for theology. If the task is as fundamental as I think it is, we may even consider it a guiding or regulative ideal for the discipline as a whole. That is, if Christian theology is essentially the task of bringing a particular historical fate under the aegis of a universal conceptual framework that is satisfying to reason, then this project—whether or not we can or do ever complete it—may define or constitute theology as a discipline. I believe that Pannenberg has specified and contributed to this task as impressively as any theologian this century. He has given a philosophical explication of theology which strives for universality and rational acceptability at every point. If theology cannot live without the particularity *and* the universality of its foundational story, then we will find ourselves pursuing the same path that Pannenberg has traversed, though perhaps with different conceptual means.[66]

---

66. I am grateful to Stanley Obitts and Kevin Vanhoozer for helpful criticisms of an earlier draft of this paper, and to Steven Knapp for extensive discussions which have influenced my formulations of the issues here.

PART II

THEOLOGICAL
CRITIQUES

5

THE ALL-DETERMINING GOD
and
THE PERIL OF DETERMINISM

David P. Polk

◆

Wolfhart Pannenberg has dared to claim boldly the defensibility of the Christian theistic enterprise in the face of modern atheistic critique, with a passion and a brilliance of mind which are genuinely impressive. Rather than deny their cogency, he applauds Fichte's atheism of empty transcendence, Feuerbach's atheism of the science of religion, and Nietzsche's atheism of human freedom for having "shattered the shells of inappropriate concepts of God" and thereby "freed the kernel which can provide the opportunity for some other kind of talk about God."[1] Pannenberg presents his exploration into the science of God as that one who is the all-determining power of the future as the next crucial step in the development of this theological conversation.

The focus of this essay is on the internal structure of Pannenberg's alternative proposal for how we are rightly to conceive of God. My intent is to demonstrate that unresolved problems in his conceptualizing of divine power and of the relation between God and temporality di-

---

1. "The God of Hope," in *Basic Questions in Theology*, 2 vols., trans. George H. Kehm (Philadelphia: Fortress, 1971), 2:235. See also his essay in the same volume concerning "Types of Atheism."

minish the persuasiveness of this remarkable tour de force and invite further refinement. Specifically, the key issue to be investigated here is whether God as the all-determining power of the future can be interpreted nondeterministically, and, if so, whether the temporal progression of the creative order must not be understood to contribute in some way to the ultimate being of God. The critique moves from an overview of Pannenberg's notion of God as the power of the future to a consideration of how he identifies "future" in relation to eternity and temporality, and then examines his defining of this powerful future in terms of an "all-determining reality." This is followed by an assessment of "hard" and "soft" determinism as alternative possibilities for understanding Pannenberg's resulting position, leading finally to a recognition of the unintended and possibly untenable consequences deriving from either perspective.

I

A trio of overlapping concerns seems to have pointed Pannenberg toward his creative resolution of the being of God as essentially futural, namely: (1) If God is indeed the guarantor of the unity of universal history, can one properly speak of the full reality of God *within* the context of ongoing, unfinished, nonunified history? (2) If Jesus' teaching and activity are oriented toward an essentially *futural* reign of God, in what sense can one refer to God in the present? Would not a God whose power is not yet consummated be less than God? (3) Since it is the case that in our human questioning we are open beyond everything extant *(vorfindlich)* in our world, must God not be conceived somehow in a manner that transcends everything presently real?

From an earlier period of talking simply about "the future of God" and "the power of God's future,"[2] Pannenberg moved to an affirmation of the ontological primacy of the future itself as the actual locus of the fullness of divine being. The occasion for this crucial shift was his

---

2. See, for example, "On the Theology of Law," in *Ethics,* trans. Keith Crim (Philadelphia: Westminster, 1981), 52, 54, 56; *Jesus—God and Man,* trans. Lewis L. Wilkins and Duane A. Priebe, 2d ed. (Philadelphia: Westminster, 1977), 366.

dialogue with the future-oriented philosophy of Ernst Bloch.[3] The question of the degree of influence of this neo-Marxian thinker on Pannenberg's work is open to debate. One can certainly see the justification for his own contention that it is very minimal, insofar as the window through which he looks in on Bloch's work is an extremely narrow one,[4] and no substantial indebtedness to the basic philosophical notions developed by Bloch is discernible in his theology. What appears to be the case is that he was already moving in the direction of his ideas of God's futurity on the basis of the implications arising within his own work, independently of any influence from Bloch's eschatological philosophy, so that what emerged was a confluence of similar modes of reflection. Even so, reading Bloch appears to have opened him up to what he was searching for: a notion of the ontological primacy of the future in terms of which he could bring to verbal expression and provisional completion his insights into the futurity of God. From "The God of Hope" onward, and specifically from then, Pannenberg has consistently pursued a "thoroughgoing eschatological" transformation of the doctrine of God.

The heart of his justification for affirming the futural character of God's being can be set forth in a very simple syllogism: *the kingdom/power of God is future; the being of God is God's power; therefore the being of God is future.* The basis for the first premise is found in his interpretation of the message and activity of Jesus of Nazareth, who proclaimed and proleptically embodied the reign of God as irreducibly futural. The key component is the other premise: that—as he expresses the matter at one point—"a God without power would be a God without reality."[5]

The extent to which Pannenberg endeavors to defend this understanding is scanty indeed. For the most part, he tends to regard the matter as self-evident—even, perhaps, tautological. The closest thing to argumentation, other than the suggestion that Jesus' concentration

---

3. "The God of Hope," in *Basic Questions in Theology*, vol. 2, originally appeared in *Ernst Bloch zu ehren*, ed. Siegfried Unsel (Frankfurt am Main: Suhrkamp Verlag, 1965), 209-225.

4. All but three of his citations of Bloch in the article relate to but two short sections of *Das Prinzip Hoffnung*, viz., to 1405-1417 and 1524-1534.

5. "Can Christianity Do without an Eschatology?" in *The Christian Hope*, ed. G. B. Caird et al. (London: SPCK, 1970), 31.

on the coming kingdom implied a unity of God and God's rule, is an appeal to the study of religious ideas: "In the language of the philosophy of religion, the being of the gods is their power. To believe in one god means to believe that one power dominates all."[6] There are, nevertheless, two other factors that also undergird the necessity for the legitimacy of understanding God as having to do essentially with future. First, the realization that God will ultimately be *revealed* as God only in the eschatological arrival of God's universal lordship carries with it the implication that God's own being is inseparable from that futural disclosure.[7] Second, power and *unity* go together. Insofar as the unity of all contingent reality remains within history an anticipation, not a present attainment, therefore the *power* that unifies all is equally futural. God is unimaginable as an *extant* "unifying unity of the world," since that unity is nowhere presently forthcoming. Therefore God's being is futural.[8]

All of this comes to pregnant expression in Pannenberg's explicit identifying of the revealed God of cosmic and human history as *die Macht der Zukunft*, the power of the future. The primacy of the future of God is explicitly a corollary of the primacy of the *power* of the future, which is none other than God in the manifestation of God's reign. It is therefore less appropriate to say that "God is not yet, but is yet to be," than to realize that God *is*, God exists, "only in the way in which the future is powerful over the present." Remaining always ahead of all speech about God, and outdistancing every concept of God, God is "no thing, no object presently at hand," nor does God appear as one being among others or as timeless being underlying all that is real; rather, God has being explicitly as "the power of the future."[9]

II

What is at stake here, in coming to terms with this fascinating notion, is to be found in an unpacking of the meaning that Pannenberg invests

---

6. *Theology and the Kingdom of God,* ed. Richard John Neuhaus (Philadelphia: Westminster, 1969), 55.

7. "The God of Hope," 2:242.

8. The summary is derived from *Theology and the Kingdom of God,* 60, and "Christian Theology and Philosophical Criticism," in *The Idea of God and Human Freedom,* trans. R. A. Wilson (Philadelphia: Westminster, 1973), 131. The quoted phrase is my translation from the original of the latter.

9. All quotations in this paragraph are from "The God of Hope," 2:242.

in each of the key words in this pivotal phrase. This and the following section offer such an unpacking, beginning with an examination of what is meant by *Zukunft,* future.

We are accustomed to thinking of the future in terms of the not-yet-present, in comparison with the past as the no-longer-present. In relation to the present as the temporal moment in which contingent occurrences are concretely becoming, the past would seem to comprise the totality of events already constituted, already decided, and the future accordingly would be seen as the realm of pure potentiality, having no being of its own. The future, on this understanding, is that which has not been decided yet, has not yet entered into the concreteness of becoming. But this is not Pannenberg's perspective at all. The notion of the past as already decided is alien to his understanding: past events are open to their own futural determination of meaning. *All* of history— past, present, and the contingent future not yet emergent—is perceived as a sort of moving front on its way to its destiny in an *ultimate* future which is God *as* the kingdom of God.

Therefore it appears that an important distinction between two different modes of being ''future'' must be recognized. For one can speak, on the one hand, of the future of history as that which has not yet transpired but one day will, within the historical process itself. Thus viewed, all that has become within history shares this quality of once having been futural. But, on the other hand, one can speak of the future of history as *that which is futural to the whole of history.* It is precisely in this latter sense that Pannenberg wishes to develop the thesis that God is futural: God is named as the *ultimate* future, the future even of all that yet remains *historically* futural to our present perspective.[10] And this ultimate future, as particularly represented in Jesus' concentration on the radical nearness of the kingdom, is immediately at hand to every becoming moment. It is not to be thought of as separated from the now by the length of time remaining to the end, as Jewish apocalyptic tradition had reflected.[11]

---

10. In English one can readily identify this distinction by using upper case and lower case, ''Future'' and ''future.'' Though Pannenberg has acknowledged to me that he has no objection to this procedure, he himself has not chosen to do so in his own English-language essays and addresses, so I will resist doing so here—even though much confusion might possibly be avoided by employing that convention.

11. *Theology and the Kingdom of God,* 54, 133.

In "The God of Hope" Pannenberg first made explicit a precise correlation between God's essential futurity and the notion of eternity, which is not to be understood as timelessness or "the endless endurance of something that existed since the beginning of time," but rather as "the power of the future over every present."[12] Subsequently he presented the thesis that "the *eschaton* is eternity in the fullest sense," insofar as that "is the mode of God's being in the coming of his Kingdom."[13] This notion, then, of God's eternity as a "final future" which comes to be comprehended as the "totally comprehensive present" opens the way to overcoming "the differences of past, present, and [historical] future" precisely *in the eschaton*.[14] From that vantage point, it becomes possible to discern that it is *as the powerful future* that God is understandable as "contemporaneous [*gleichzeitig*] to every time."[15] And this represents a terminological conceptual shift of crucial importance, from the *Gleichzeitigkeit* of eternity to all historical time to the *Gleichzeitigkeit of God's future as mode of the eternal* to all time.

This provides the basic breakthrough for encompassing the insights, emerging earlier in the Christology, into Jesus' new understanding of time as characterized by the power of the future (kingdom) in the present. Jesus' message is understood to reflect a sense "that future and present are inextricably interwoven,"[16] which leads Pannenberg to the general conclusion that one is justified in speaking of a "remarkable entwining" or "interweaving" *(Verschränkung)* precisely of *eternity and time*.[17]

This key notion of *Verschränkung* is developed in an essay on "Time and Eternity in the Religious Experience of Israel and of Christianity," where he champions the apocalyptic worldview in its presupposition that what is hidden on earth is already disclosable in advance

---

12. "The God of Hope," 2:244.
13. *Theology and the Kingdom of God,* 64. Cf. also "Future and Unity," in *Hope and the Future of Man,* ed. Ewert H. Cousins (Philadelphia: Fortress, 1972), 72, where eschatological future and "eternal essence" are affirmed as coincident.
14. *Theology and the Kingdom of God,* 63f.
15. "Dogmatische Erwägungen zur Auferstehung Jesu," in *Grundfragen systematischer Theologie: Gesammelte Aufsätze,* vol. 2 (Göttingen: Vandenhoeck & Ruprecht, 1980), 171.
16. *Theology and the Kingdom of God,* 53.
17. "Zeit und Ewigkeit," in *Grundfragen systematischer Theologie,* 2:201.

to the apocalyptic seer. This points up the interpenetration of eternity into time, and calls even for the conclusion that therein eternity and time may be seen to "coincide" *(koinzidieren)*.[18] The conclusion reached is that the future of God, as "the parousia of God's eternity, already forms the depth dimension of the present time" and precisely "in its time-overlapping [*zeitübergreifend*] presence" is conceivable as God's eternity.[19]

In summary, the key terms that interpret the relation of time and eternity, and therefore of historical present and ultimate future, are *Gleichzeitigkeit* and *Verschränkung:* contemporaneity or compresence, and entwining or interweaving. Working from an essential identity between the concepts of eternity and ultimate futurity—or, more precisely, looking to the notion of God's eschatological future as a basis for redefining how eternity is to be conceived—Pannenberg interprets the penetration of the power of the future into the present as an interweaving of eternity itself into time, and therefore can speak of a co-inciding of the two. The answer to his question of "how the temporal difference between divine reality and the present is related to the difference between the divine as the 'Eternal One' and all time whatsoever"[20] is found in the overcoming of both indications of any dualistic differentness by the entwining compresence of the future of all into the temporal becoming of all.

III

The manner in which this ultimate future comes to be interwoven with every emerging present has to do with how God is the *power* of the future. From the outset of his work, Pannenberg has been concerned to reinterpret divine causality in such a way as to obviate the threat of divine determinism to responsible Christian faith.[21] Recognizing that any legitimate concept of God must be able to knock the props out

---

18. Ibid., 199f., the later notion being repeated on 202.
19. Ibid., 202 (the last clause appears in question form in the text but the indicative is implicitly legitimated by the context).
20. Ibid., 190.
21. See, for example, "Der Einfluss der Anfechtungserfahrung auf den Prädestinationsbegriff Luthers," *Kerygma und Dogma* 3 (1957): 136f.

from under an atheism of human freedom, he continued to be keenly committed to circumventing the pitfalls of a deterministic notion of deity. The very attractiveness of the possibility of God's essential futurity is discernible in the prospects it holds out for grounding human freedom.

Accordingly, the question which focuses this inquiry into Pannenberg's concept of God's future as *powerful* is precisely the one he set out from: How is power to be understood here, such that the freedom of the other is genuinely authenticated and not made to vanish into the ether of divine determinism? It is perhaps not an exaggerated claim to propose that the whole of Pannenberg's rather brilliant theological enterprise stands or falls on the adequacy and conceptual consistency of the answer he works out to this pivotal issue—for he himself suggests no less.[22]

Pannenberg worked for a time with designations of God as "all-embracing power" *(die alles umgreifende Macht)*[23] and the "power over everything," the latter being conjoined explicitly with the issue of human freedom.[24] He was still utilizing that phrase extensively in the year following his penetration into the *essential* futurity of God's power in "The God of Hope."[25] Already in the immediately preceding essay on "The Question of God," however, there is brief reference to God as *"alles bestimmende Wirklichkeit,"* the "all-*determining* reality."[26] And it is this theme which soon comes to predominate his interpretation of the nature of the power of the future: God can be meaningfully conceived as God only as *die alles bestimmende Macht*—the all-determining power of the whole of reality.[27] It is the meaning he

---

22. See, for example, "Speaking about God in the Face of Atheist Criticism," in *The Idea of God and Human Freedom*, 106.

23. *Grundzüge der Christologie* (Gütersloh: Gütersloher Verlagshaus Gerd Mohn, 1964), 43, in a sentence unaccountably omitted from *Jesus—God and Man:* "Gott *heisst* ja die alles umgreifende Macht" (emphasis added).

24. The German is, "Die Macht über alles Wirkliche," in *Grundfragen systematischer Theologie*, 1:378 ("The Question of God," in *Basic Questions in Theology*, 2:223).

25. This is the phrase that appears throughout Pannenberg's "Response to the Discussion," in *Theology as History*, ed. James M. Robinson and John B. Cobb Jr., New Frontiers in Theology 3 (New York: Harper & Row, 1967), from 1965 to 1966.

26. "The Question of God," in *Basic Questions in Theology*, 2:201.

27. The key phrase puts in an appearance in "On Historical and Theological Hermeneutic" *(Basic Questions in Theology*, 1:156-158, 178), an essay hailing from 1964 but extensively revised for publication in *Basic Questions in Theology*. It is also anticipated in a footnote in

intends this phrase to convey which holds the key to unraveling the mystery of divine power conjoined with human freedom.

The phrase is not easily clarified. As with the duality of meanings inherent in the corollary noun *Bestimmung* ("destiny" and "determination"), so here also, with *bestimmend,* we face a pair of possible interpretations—though this time both are incorporated in the single English equivalent, "determining." On the one hand, Pannenberg may intend to assert only that, since it is the ultimate future which finally decides the essence of what becoming occurrences in history actually *mean,* therefore the future possesses the power of *ascertainment* of the true character of all reality.[28] Not existence per se but the *essence* of what comes to exist is fully a consequence of God's all-determining power, under this perspective. For the sake of convenience, I shall designate this way of understanding his notion of all-determining power as "soft determinism."

On the other hand, there is the strong possibility that what he really has in mind is nothing less than a kind of "hard determinism," that is, the understanding *that the power of the future is a genuine force of creativity out of which history is fully and concretely constituted.* Indeed, the passages that tilt in this direction are truly numerous. Pannenberg can typically allude to the power of God as that which "dominates all" and is "master over all,"[29] and can ascribe to God "constitutive" *(konstituierend)* significance over all of history.[30] Present events are said to "spring from" the infinite future which "separates

"Response to the Discussion" where Pannenberg speaks of the future as "the power determining the present" (*Theology as History,* 267, n. 77). It becomes especially prominent in *Theology and the Kingdom of God,* the content there dating from 1966, and its use is widespread in Pannenberg thereafter. The point of these references is to clarify that the definition of God as all-determining power, though anticipated earlier, comes to decisive expression only subsequent to the penetration into God as "die Macht der Zukunft"; i.e., it is explicitly as the power of the future that God can be comprehended as the all-determining power of the whole of reality. (In a recorded conversation, 21 October 1982, Pannenberg observed that he regards the understanding of God as "all-determining power" to embody "a minimal description of what the concept of God logically must contain, while 'die Macht der Zukunft' is meant to comprise, though not to spell out in detail, a distinctively Christian understanding of God.")

28. See, for example, *Theology and the Kingdom of God,* 60; *The Apostles' Creed in the Light of Today's Questions,* trans. Margaret Kohl (Philadelphia: Westminster, 1972), 38.

29. *Theology and the Kingdom of God,* 55.

30. "On Historical and Theological Hermeneutic," in *Basic Questions in Theology,* 1:157, 158; "A Liberal Logos Christology," in *John Cobb's Theology in Process,* ed. David Griffin and Thomas Altizer (Philadelphia: Westminster, 1977), 136.

itself from the finite events which until then had been hidden in this future but are now released into existence."[31] The impression one receives is that such a deity is solely accountable for what emerges into being in every historical present.

One possible qualification might be entertained. Perhaps only the *that* of an event is released into existence, with some degree of self-determination also at hand in regard to its particular contours. But Pannenberg will not acknowledge that. It is essential for him that "the power of the future should not only create possibilities, but actualities as well," establishing "the *complete dependence* of everything real upon God."[32]

A significant impetus to this view of the nature of God as the all-determining one is discernible in Pannenberg's thoroughgoing emphasis on the doctrine of the absolute freedom of God. From early on, he has championed what he calls "the freedom of God's active omnipotence,"[33] accenting God's transcendence over finite reality in terms of a "living, ever new carrying out of his freedom."[34] Precisely as final future, God is to be thought of as "pure freedom," as "freedom itself."[35] Indeed, viewed in this light, much of his discussion about the contingency and novelty of events in history seems to be oriented toward establishing the freedom of God active therein to bring forth the new rather than be circumscribed by the givenness of what already is. It is "the otherness of the freedom of God precisely in his acts"[36] which establishes the contingent character of *God's* activity and *therefore* the contingency of the events themselves. What is at stake is not the genuineness of contingent novelty but the theological affirmation that the freedom of God is in no way held in check by realities external to God's own being. To maintain that some cause other than God's future could also be involved in the becoming of the present would

---

31. *Theology and the Kingdom of God,* 59.

32. Pannenberg and Lewis Ford, "A Dialog about Process Philosophy," *Encounter* 38 (1977): 319, 320 (emphasis added).

33. "The Appropriation of the Philosophical Concept of God," in *Basic Questions in Theology,* 2:175.

34. "Response to the Discussion," 250.

35. *Theology and the Kingdom of God,* 63, and *Theology and the Philosophy of Science,* trans. Francis McDonagh (London: Darton, Longman & Todd, 1976), 309, n. 615.

36. "The Appropriation of the Philosophical Concept of God," in *Basic Questions in Theology,* 2:181.

entail that the ultimate truth of God, as unifying unity of history, incorporates components not exclusively derivative from God, and this would infringe upon the absolute freedom of God not to be in any way determined by anything other than godself.

Even so, a key passage in *Theology and the Philosophy of Science* contains the germ of an idea that opens up provocative possibilities for further exploration. Pannenberg extends there his definition of God as all-determining power in the direction of divine self-limitation: implicit in the claim that the power of the future is the power behind everything "is the idea that this all-determining power is itself determined only by itself and not subject to determination by anything else, *unless it determines that it should be determined by something else.*"[37] I propose that no more crucial qualification has been presented in Pannenberg's reconceiving of the notion of divine power than this. There is no evidence of his having extended his reflections about divine and nondivine causation along those lines. But this would appear to offer a significant concession to the view that what comes into momentary existence in history's myriad becoming can be traced also to additional agents or efficient causes in relationship to which God's power is ever at work.

I have identified the element of ambiguity present in Pannenberg's doctrine of God as the all-determining power of the future, recognizing the possibilities of "hard" and "soft" determinism therein. In the one case, God is interpreted as fully constituting what emerges in history; in the other, God finally decides what those emergent realities ultimately mean, what their essence is. I wish now to probe this pair of alternatives, particularly drawing out the implications of the fruitful but undeveloped concession in *Theology and the Philosophy of Science*, to see where the two options of hard versus soft determinism take us concerning an understanding of divine power and its consequences.

IV

If the fundamental concession that the all-determining power resolves to be determined in part by anything other than itself is finally disa-

---

37. *Theology and the Philosophy of Science,* 302 (emphasis added).

vowed, then the consequence seems absolutely unavoidable that Pannenberg is unable to circumvent the verdict of many of his critics that the "openness" of the future is, as in the perception of Langdon Gilkey, merely epistemological and not ontological, that is, decided out of God's time-intersecting eternity but simply not yet known by us.[38] If the concession is not a real one, then the meaning of the contingent novelty of events has reference only to *God's* freedom of nonnecessity—a sort of eschatologically recentered nominalism—and not at all to the conventional understanding of the nonnecessity of the events themselves. In this mode of interpretation of his intent the conclusion seems inescapable that human openness *to* the future is nothing more than a process of discovery of what will come to be but is actually already decided (in God's future), in which case the much-heralded concern to develop a doctrine of God that overcomes the atheism of human freedom is vitiated.[39] The final outcome of this line of thought is that Pannenberg has merely substituted for the unpalatable tradition of divine predeterminism an equally odious divine *postdeterminism* which amounts to the same thing—what Gilkey aptly tags "a kind of Calvinism set into temporal reverse gear."[40]

But perhaps Pannenberg *has* opened a door to a quite different set of possibilities. What if, on the other hand, one were to develop the implications allowed for by the consideration that the all-determining power may *will* to give over to the creaturely realm a share in deciding the shape of what comes into being? Immediately a radically different set of factors comes into play. The whole notion of an appeal

---

38. Langdon Gilkey, "Pannenberg's *Basic Questions in Theology:* A Review Article," *Perspective* 14 (1973): 46, 53.

39. Pannenberg's tape-recorded comments (21 October 1982) repudiating an opening toward a degree of human self-determination only reinforce this conclusion. Polk: "Is there any degree of self-expression that is not determined by God?" Pannenberg: "No, I don't think so. . . .Even everything we do in shaping our lives is an effect of God's creative action. They don't work on the same level, and therefore they can't possibly be in competition. If the human person is a creature of God, so everything that belongs to that creature, including its self-creative, self-determining potential, is already an effect of the work of the creator."

40. Gilkey, "Pannenberg's *Basic Questions,*" 53. Pannenberg objects strongly to this interpretation of his position, insisting that the temporal shift is vitally important in the overcoming of deterministic thinking. In conversation with me in 1982, he called the attribution of "postdeterminism" an illusory notion; "to change the temporal mode has consequences concerning the nature of causality," in that the cause now no longer is understood to come before its effect. But how this by itself denies what "postdeterminism" expresses remains a mystery to me.

to persons to be open to the offer of the reign of God in our lives takes on genuine meaning: the possibility of not doing so is really there. In this perspective, sense can be made of the idea that present (or rather, immediately past) reality acts as a drag on our response to the power of the future to free us from imprisonment in the already-at-hand. Though the effort by Lewis Ford to draw out Pannenberg's reflections in this direction was explicitly rejected by him,[41] the option nevertheless seems a real one: God as all-determining power need not *fully* constitute the actuality of what becomes in history *if it is God's absolutely free determination not to do so*.

The significance of this direction of thought is enhanced when one considers the matter from the standpoint of Jesus' message of God and God's coming rule. If it is appropriate to maintain that it is *as love* that God is powerful, then that perception is utterly consistent with Pannenberg's unexplored proviso. For to will others to participate in the deciding of their own becoming is precisely to indulge in the *risk* of love. The offer may very well be abused. But the meaning of existence itself is infinitely intensified thereby: what would otherwise be a drama written by a single author and played out on a cosmic stage now becomes a true adventure into creative novelty, and the participants speak lines of at least partly their own devising. Thereby, the coming of the reign of God as *judgment* makes genuine sense, for there are decisions other than God's whose adequacy is to be continually evaluated. And equally the coming of the reign of God as *grace* is genuinely affirmed—for the context of possibility of deciding *for* God's oncoming, in-breaking love is no other than the sustaining and *empowering* love that is of God (1 John 4:19).

Within this orientation, Pannenberg's particular exploration into the true nature of human freedom not as willful self-determination but as a matter of being freed by the power of the future to actualize one's proper destiny is not necessarily repudiated but even underscored: our resistance to the power of the future may be not so much an expression of our willful and free self-determination but a consequence of our unfree entrapment by the seductiveness of our past and present environment or our bondage to the safely familiar.

---

41. See above, n. 32.

V

To say that the aporia of divine causality and human freedom is readily solved in this way, by seizing upon God's willing to share decisions of causal efficacy with other centers of power *that God godself creates,* thereby reflecting a position of soft determinism, is hardly so simple, however. There is another major implication which flows from this alternative perspective on Pannenberg's meaning, necessitating the surrender of a feature of his theology that is less easily relinquished than a notion of strict determinism. It concerns the capacity of God, as the ultimately powerful future of all that comes to be, to experience within godself the emergent contingencies of historical becoming. In short, does not soft determinism entail the attributing of change to God?

From the outset of Pannenberg's assessment that history itself is the locus of God's self-disclosure, he attempted to come to terms with the question of how that history genuinely contributes to the being of the God revealed therein. Under his second thesis on revelation, as happening ultimately at the end of history, he observed that history itself does not merely contribute to the disclosure of God extrinsically but belongs to the very essence of God, "which has a history in time." [42] Temporal history is affirmed as "of decisive importance for God himself," and "the eternity of God is itself still *dependent on* the future of the world." [43] But is that not a denial of God's essential immutability? Pannenberg has never been open to that possible consequence. The concept of immutability, he pointed out, needs to be redefined, not simply as enduring sameness but as a corollary of God's self-determined constancy, God's freely enacted faithfulness. [44] In the freedom of God's contingent acting that discloses God as "wholly other," "God assumes properties into his eternal essence through such deeds in that he chooses these and no other events as the form of his contingent operation." [45]

---

42. "Dogmatische Thesen," in *Offenbarung als Geschichte* (Göttingen: Vandenhoeck & Ruprecht, 1961), 97 (cf. *Revelation as History,* trans. David Granskou [New York: Macmillan, 1968], 133f.).

43. *The Apostles' Creed,* 174 (emphasis added).

44. "The Appropriation of the Philosophical Concept of God," in *Basic Questions in Theology,* 2:161f.

45. Ibid., 181.

Therefore, "the particular, the unique, and the accidental are included in God's eternity,"[46] inasmuch as true being, the truth of God, essentially incorporates into itself the historical.[47]

But to this point, the issue has only been joined, not resolved. The question presses itself forward: *How* does this incorporation of historical/temporal truth into the essential/eternal truth of God not *require* divine becoming, change, process? Pannenberg's answer is already forthcoming, however briefly, in his Christology, where, in the context of a discussion of the implications of the incarnation for understanding God's eternality, he states:

> That an element of God's becoming and being in the other, in the reality differentiated from himself, is one with his eternity requires that what newly flashes. into view from time to time in the divine life can be understood at the same time *as having always been true in God's eternity.*[48]

That is drawn out in further detail in *Theology and the Kingdom of God,* in the context of a brief critical engagement with the process philosophy of A. N. Whitehead. Pannenberg wants to affirm the process contribution of "incorporating time into the idea of God,"[49] but precisely without allowing for the seemingly incumbent consequence of acknowledging development within God. He avoids that by recapitulating and extending the notion of *retroactive permanence* set forth in the Christology:

> The very essence of God implies time. Only in the future of his Kingdom come will the statement "God exists" prove to be definitely true. But then it will be clear that the statement was always true. . . . It is true that, from the viewpoint of our finite present, the future is not yet decided. Therefore, the movement of time contributes to deciding what the definite truth is going to be, also with regard to the essence of God. But—and here is the difference from Whitehead—what turns out to be true in the

46. *What Is Man?* trans. Duane A. Priebe (Philadelphia: Fortress, 1971), 76.
47. "What Is Truth?" in *Basic Questions in Theology,* 2:9, 10.
48. *Jesus—God and Man,* 32 (emphasis added).
49. *Theology and the Kingdom of God,* 62.

future will then be evident as having been true all along. This applies to God as well as to every finite reality.[50]

Therefore eternity is not the antithesis of change but takes up into itself change—unchangingly!

Now we see why the aporia of divine determinism cannot be so quickly resolved in the direction I have indicated: *Pannenberg's doctrine of God's changeless eternal co-presence to every moment depends utterly on the hard meaning of God's all-determining power.* It is only because God, in God's eternity, *totally* determines all that emerges as historical truth—truth incorporated into its ultimate consummation—that the novelties of history make no contribution of their own to God's fullness of being. Process and change come to be incorporated as constitutive for ultimate truth only because it is ultimately God who is fully constitutive of process and change.

Acknowledgment that God wills to allow other instances of causal agency than God's own to contribute to the becoming of history would lead inexorably to the realization that history is also the *divine* adventure, full of novelty and uncontrolled twists and turns even for God. Such a perspective would explicitly overturn the distinction between merely (mis-)perceived and truly real development in God, and would call for the irresistible conclusion that time, precisely in its temporal distinctions of already and not yet, affects God also. For if what God "releases" into existence from out of God's powerful future were to include the provision for a degree of self-determination in the shape of what comes into being at that moment, then God would be increased by the knowledge of the decision now made which God wills not to control. God would therefore be affected by what is brought forth "from time to time" within the temporal process.

The notion that the historical is the real, which began to focus Pannenberg's energies over a quarter of a century ago, would be decidedly enhanced in this interpretation. But that gain is in direct tension with a thesis he holds onto with great tenacity: the lack of real development within the deity. I cannot avoid the conclusion that he can retain this facet of his doctrine of God only by denying not only the

---

50. Ibid., 62f.

alternative possibility of soft determinism in the becoming of events in history but even also the truly genuine and distinctive reality of temporal process itself.

In summary, the argument of this brief critical analysis is simply that, given the possible alternative meanings of God as all-determining power of the future, either "all-determining" means that every possible facet of temporal becoming is exhaustively attributable to God, in which case the atheism of human freedom is not truly surmounted after all; or it conveys a less exclusive expression of divine determination as allowed for by the concession offered in *Theology and the Philosophy of Science,* in which case Pannenberg's insistence on the absolute immutability of God vis-à-vis historical becoming must necessarily be surrendered. It is this latter step which offers the genuine prospect of carrying through on his initial intent to develop a theological perspective in which truth is to be found precisely in what is historically real, not in timeless essence above (or ahead of) temporal process.

6

PANNENBERG
on
REVELATION AND FAITH

Avery Dulles, S.J.

◆

olfhart Pannenberg's theology of revelation, from one point
of view, may be described as a prophetic reaction against
certain aberrations that have appeared in modern Protestantism, partly as a result of Kant's critique of knowledge. For Søren
Kierkegaard and many like-minded theologians, the decision of faith
is a purely subjective act that can scarcely escape the charge of being
arbitrary and whimsical. Pannenberg wishes to offset the privatization
that occurs when faith is presented as a mere wager or a groundless
commitment rather than as a response to objectively sufficient evidence.[1]

The Catholic cannot assume that Pannenberg is speaking to a
purely Protestant problem. Since Vatican Council II, subjectivism has
invaded many sectors of Catholicism, with the result that concern for
universally valid truth has greatly receded. Many of the faithful feel
justified in holding a particular position as "true for me" without any
sense of accountability to public criteria. Faith becomes a matter of
private feeling.

---

1. Pannenberg, "Wahrheit, Gewissheit und Glaube," in *Grundfragen systematischer Theologie,* vol. 2 (Göttingen: Vandenhoeck & Ruprecht, 1980), 245.

Against the tendency of many linguistic analysts, such as R. B. Braithwaite and R. M. Hare, Pannenberg stoutly defends the cognitive character of religious language.[2] To adhere to a religious faith, he argues, is to make implicit claims about the nature of reality—claims that can and should be spelled out in creedal statements.[3] The decision to believe, moreover, must be based on intelligible grounds so that it can be defended against the charge of capriciousness.

The Pannenberg project, seen in this perspective, harmonizes excellently with the Catholic mentality, which has, at least until very recently, been characterized by universalism and rationality. Catholics who are anxious to defend or recover their own best tradition have much to learn from Pannenberg, who has done perhaps more than any other theologian of our time to vindicate the objective basis for Christian faith and the relevance of faith for the universal human quest for truth. He has brilliantly shown how reason, as the faculty of criticism, deliberation, and judgment, can be integrated into a revelation-centered theology.

In the past, theologians who have cherished the universality and rational cogency of their religion have tended to emphasize the close correspondence between Christian faith and natural religion. Deists and idealists have exalted rationality at the expense of historical particularity. Pannenberg, on the contrary, rejects natural theology. He insists that God cannot be known at all except through revelation, that revelation must be historical, and that the sole historical revelation is that given in Jesus Christ. In some respects, therefore, Pannenberg remains close to Karl Barth.

Many apologists, seeking to vindicate the intelligible grounds for revealed religion, have appealed to the authority of divinely accredited teachers. They have built their systems on extrinsic signs, such as biblical miracles and prophecies. Pannenberg, however, disavows authoritarianism in all its forms. He enthusiastically accepts the critical tools of modern scholarship. Rejecting biblical inerrantism and magisterial infallibilism, he admits no claims of authority that cannot be

---

2. Ibid., 227.
3. Pannenberg, "The Place of Creeds in Christianity Today," in *Foundation Documents of the Faith,* ed. C. S. Rodd (Edinburgh: T. & T. Clark, 1987), 141-152; esp. 144, 148.

verified by rigorous critical testing. Words must be verified by deeds, and the meaning of deeds must be ascertained from the deeds themselves. Thus Pannenberg diametrically opposes authoritarian or extrinsicist apologetics, which establishes the contents of faith from the testimony of divinely accredited legates.

Already in his early work, published in the late 1950s and in the early 1960s, Pannenberg proposed to effect a synthesis between reason and revelation by a highly original line of argument that he has never renounced. Let me begin, therefore, with a somewhat oversimplified presentation of the basic position set forth in Pannenberg's early writings and then, in the light of some criticisms, show how the argument can be modified and enriched so as to achieve greater adequacy and wider acceptance. We shall see how Pannenberg himself, in dialogue with his critics, has nuanced his own positions.

I

At the heart of Pannenberg's proposal lies a crucial distinction between direct and indirect revelation. Direct revelation, he states, is that in which the content is the revealer himself. "The Word of God would be direct communication if its content were directly connected with God himself, somewhat in the sense of a self-presentation of the divinity."[4] Indirect revelation occurs when a word or action having a content that is other than God also expresses something about God as its originator.

While holding that all revelation is self-revelation, Pannenberg insists that revelation in the Bible is indirect.[5] In the Old Testament God is indirectly revealed through historical events such as the exodus and the conquest. The later Old Testament writings look forward to a future self-vindication of God through a decisive event at the end of history. According to the New Testament, God is indirectly revealed in the career and fate of Jesus, in which the eschaton breaks through into time.

---

4. Pannenberg, "Introduction," *Revelation as History* (New York: Macmillan, 1968), 15.
5. Pannenberg, "Dogmatic Theses on the Doctrine of Revelation," in *Revelation as History*, 125. Cf. *Faith and Reality* (Philadelphia: Westminster, 1977), 56.

God, in indirect self-revelation, speaks the language of facts. But the facts do not exist without words which predict, accompany, and report them, sometimes developing their implications for the direction of human conduct. The word of God pertains to revelation but, Pannenberg insists, the word adds nothing to the meaning of the events on which it builds. In many of his writings Pannenberg returns to the theme that revelatory events are not ambiguous in themselves and do not require an inspired interpretation for their meaning to be discerned. Thus word-revelation in Pannenberg's theory has no independent status.

The advantage of this maneuver for Pannenberg's project is that it frees him from the necessity of relying on authoritative testimony. If the meaning of the events could not be unlocked except through an inspired interpretation, Pannenberg would be forced to submit, in the end, to authority. But this he apparently finds unacceptable in view of the Enlightenment principle, *sapere aude*. In his own words:

> But for men who live in the sphere in which the Enlightenment has become effective, authoritarian claims are no longer acceptable, in intellectual as little as political life. All authoritarian claims are on principle subject to the suspicion that they clothe human thoughts and institutions with the splendor of divine majesty.[6]

The entire burden of revelation must therefore be borne by events. God proves himself not by what he says but by what he does. For Pannenberg, what God does appears in history, for reality as a whole is historical. There is no cosmic order of incorruptible entities (such as the heavenly spheres in ancient Greek cosmology) or of purely repetitive action, such as nature was long thought to be. Everything is caught up in a relentless process of change, and nothing has meaning except in terms of the goal to which it is tending.

The centrality of history had previously been recognized by the Protestant "salvation history" school (J. C. K. von Hofmann, O. Cullmann, and others). Like Ernst Troeltsch before him, Pannenberg is critical of this school for making an artificial split between the sacred and the profane and for giving special treatment to the former as attested

---

6. Pannenberg, "Response to the Discussion," in *Theology as History,* ed. J. M. Robinson and J. B. Cobb Jr. (New York: Harper & Row, 1967), 226.

and interpreted by Holy Scripture.[7] For Pannenberg, this theory rests on a false supernaturalism. History must be treated as a continuous whole in which every event is open to investigation by established historical methods. Pannenberg refuses to take refuge in what he calls the "ghetto of redemptive history."[8]

Because of his universalistic approach to history, one might expect Pannenberg to look for revelation in the nonbiblical religions, but in fact he insists on the uniqueness of biblical religion. Precisely through an "unprejudiced understanding of the total process of the universal history of religion"[9] Pannenberg finds it possible to establish the historical particularity of Christian revelation. He is highly critical of the phenomenology of religion on the ground that it draws unwarranted parallels between widely separated religions on the basis of superficial structural similarities. He ridicules the naming of Asclepius, Apollo, and Jesus side by side as "savior figures," and dismisses the facile equation made by one comparativist between "the Pope and the Dalai Lama."[10] The religions differ radically in the ways in which they conceive of the appearance of the divine power in history. The nonbiblical religions, imprisoned in a primordial or archetypal concept of the sacred, remain closed to their own future transformation, and are therefore destined to become obsolete.[11] Biblical faith, on the other hand, perceives human existence as a history moving toward a definitive goal. For this reason the latter is able to focus on the transcendent divine mystery, which the other religions confuse with the particular finite medium through which the transcendent appears. Falling into polytheism and idolatry, these religions neither express nor communicate revelation. The most that Pannenberg will say of them is that they "have to do with the same divine reality as the message of Jesus."[12]

Considering the attention that he devotes to the Old Testament in

7. Ibid., 247-248; cf. E. Troeltsch, *The Absoluteness of Christianity and the History of Religions* (Richmond: John Knox, 1971).

8. Pannenberg, "Redemptive Event and History," in *Basic Questions in Theology,* 2 vols. (Philadelphia: Fortress, 1970), 1:69.

9. Pannenberg, "Toward a Theology of the History of Religions," in *Basic Questions in Theology,* 2:69.

10. Ibid., 74, referring to Gerardus van der Leeuw, *Religion in Essence and Manifestation* (New York: Harper Torchbooks, 1963), 220.

11. Ibid., 107.

12. Ibid., 115.

his writings on revelation, one might expect Pannenberg to speak very positively of the revelation of God to ancient Israel. In fact, however, Pannenberg is surprisingly reserved about Old Testament religion. While acknowledging that Israelite faith was concentrated on the great deeds of God in history, and especially upon God's expected action bringing universal history to a climactic end, Pannenberg points out that the prophets and seers of the Old Testament always spoke with a certain provisionality. Until God had definitively proved his divinity by his transforming intervention at the end of history, there was as yet no unambiguous disclosure. What passes for revelation in the Old Testament, therefore, stands in need of future confirmation. Thus Pannenberg can conclude that in comparison with Jesus Christ, all earlier self-manifestations of the divine are "purely provisional; they are not a definitive self-disclosure, and therefore cannot be called in a strict sense God's self-revelation." [13]

In Pannenberg's system this relativization of the Old Testament is connected with a thesis taken over from Karl Barth, that God is revealed only in Jesus. "The very concept of self-revelation," writes Pannenberg, "really implies that it cannot take place in manifold forms, but that if it happens at all, it can only be in a single form." [14] Elsewhere he states:

> The concept of self-revelation includes the fact that there can be only a single revelation. God cannot disclose himself in two or more different ways as the one who is the same from eternity to eternity. When someone has disclosed himself ultimately in a definite, particular event, he cannot again disclose himself in the same sense in another event different from the first. Otherwise, he has not disclosed himself fully and completely in the first event, but at most partially. [15]

Although Pannenberg recognizes that in the phenomenology of religions one may speak about revelations in the plural, he holds that in Christian theology the term must be used in the singular. [16]

---

13. Pannenberg, *Faith and Reality*, 60; cf. 52.

14. Ibid., 60.

15. Pannenberg, *Jesus—God and Man* (Philadelphia: Westminster, 1968), 129.

16. Pannenberg, "Offenbarung und 'Offenbarungen' im Zeugnis der Geschichte," in *Handbuch der Fundamentaltheologie*, ed. W. Kern et al. (Freiburg: Herder, 1985), 2:105.

After having restricted revelation to God's self-disclosure in Jesus Christ, Pannenberg goes on to narrow the concept yet further. In the public life of Jesus, as in the Old Testament and in the ministry of John the Baptist, there was as yet no definitive gift of the eschaton. God's reign was present only by anticipation in the proclamation of Jesus and in the miracles he worked. A certain ambiguity therefore remained. Unless the expectations awakened by Jesus had been fulfilled by the Easter event, trust in his call would have to be judged misplaced.[17] The end did not come about in the way that Jesus and his contemporaries would have expected, and therefore we must look for the revelation not in the provisional anticipations but in the surprising fulfillment. Thus Pannenberg can conclude:

> Therefore, Jesus' resurrection from the dead, in which the end that stands before all men has happened before its time, is the actual event of revelation. Only because of Jesus' resurrection, namely because this event is the beginning of the end facing all men, can one speak of God's self-revelation in Jesus Christ.[18]

By concentrating revelation in the one event of Jesus' resurrection, Pannenberg can dispense himself from having to defend anything else as revelation. He can freely admit that the non-Christian religions are distorted, that the Old Testament abounds in legend and myth, that Jesus himself was unoriginal and confused, and that the miracles attributed to the prophets and to Jesus lack probative force.

What becomes all-important in Pannenberg's doctrine is to ascertain the fact and the meaning of the resurrection of Jesus. With Paul, Pannenberg can assert that if Jesus did not rise from the dead the preaching of the apostles and the faith of Christians are in vain (1 Cor. 15:14).[19] On the other hand, if the resurrection is a fact, then all the Christian assertions about Jesus follow. Through community with him we may have sure hope in our future destiny.[20]

In demonstrating the facticity of the resurrection, Pannenberg has

---

17. Pannenberg, "Focal Essay: The Revelation of God in Jesus of Nazareth," in *Theology as History*, 111-114.
18. Pannenberg, *Jesus—God and Man*, 129.
19. Pannenberg, "Did Jesus Really Rise from the Dead?" *Dialog* 4 (1965): 128.
20. Ibid., 135.

to contend with a number of familiar objections, which need not be detailed here. One general problem is the uniqueness of the event, which appears to have no analogies elsewhere in history or experience. How can reports of such an event escape being discredited in advance? In reply, Pannenberg observes that history by its very nature deals with nonhomogeneous and singular events. In the history of revelation the theologian's interest focuses especially on the particular and the novel. The fact that God brings about something radically new in the resurrection of Jesus is not a valid motive for contesting its facticity.[21] In several places Pannenberg has made detailed studies of the biblical testimonies to the resurrection. He finds the event well attested by the standards of critical historiography.

For the correct interpretation of the significance of the resurrection Pannenberg points to the framework of apocalyptic expectation in which the event occurred. "The story of the conversion of Paul shows how in the horizon of the apocalyptic expectation the fact of the resurrection of Jesus has a ready-made eschatological meaning."[22] Viewed in its actual context, according to Pannenberg, the event can have no other meaning except that God has inaugurated in Jesus the final glorious transformation that awaits creation as a whole. The resurrection is therefore the revelation of God's divine power, the transcendence of Jesus, and the ultimate future of history as a whole. It can no longer be doubted that the God in whom Israel and Jesus put their faith is indeed the Lord of history. Retroactively, therefore, the resurrection validates the provisional revelation of the prior biblical tradition and in so doing provides a solid footing for the apostolic preaching and for the creeds of the Christian church.

II

Pannenberg's theology of revelation, which I have attempted to outline, is original, challenging, coherent, and profound. But it is also contestable at many points. Here I can only indicate a few of the points at which the system is, in my judgment, vulnerable. Yet the criticisms, as we shall see, are not fatal. By attending to the criticisms Pannenberg

21. Pannenberg, "Redemptive Event and History," 45-49.
22. Pannenberg, "Dogmatic Theses," 146; cf. "Focal Essay," 125.

himself has to some extent moved to more adequate and balanced positions. I shall suggest ways in which he may continue to do so in the future.

To begin with a very basic criticism, one may ask whether the terms "direct" and "indirect" revelation are well chosen. In insisting that biblical revelation is indirect, Pannenberg gives the impression that God has not positively willed to communicate with human beings but has, accidentally as it were, allowed himself to be discovered in his historical activity. Some readers have even thought that, for Pannenberg, God's self-revelation is a mere inference from the course of events.[23] Pannenberg, rejecting this interpretation of his position, affirms that the divine makes itself immediately perceptible through events. To indicate this he might better have used some other category, such as symbol. Although Pannenberg was originally on guard against the idea of symbolic revelation, which he suspected of Gnostic overtones, he has recently moved toward a clear acceptance of this category. He writes:

> The revealing event as symbol indicates the plenitude of meaning that surpasses its own finite form as an individual, isolated event. This holds true also for the history of Jesus Christ insofar as in him is summarized and mediated to us "the fullness of all revelation" [Vatican II, *Dei Verbum*, 2], namely eschatological salvation, which constitutes the content of the divine activity in history that leads to this goal, and is recognizable in relation to this goal.[24]

The category of symbol, as Pannenberg himself has said, "stands on the border between direct and indirect communication. When a symbol is supposed to have divine content, it is direct revelation to the extent that it surpasses its own primary and unsymbolic meaning in favor of its symbolism."[25] Symbolic communication has unique

---

23. For the allegation see J. M. Robinson, "Revelation as Word and as History," in *Theology as History*, 89-92, with references to Moltmann. For Pannenberg's reply see his "Response to the Discussion," ibid., 254-255.

24. Pannenberg, "Offenbarung und 'Offenbarungen,' " 102. For Pannenberg's previous reservations about symbol as carrier of revelation see "Introduction," *Revelation as History*, 11 and 15.

25. Pannenberg, "Introduction," *Revelation as History*, 15.

power to effect a mysterious encounter with the transcendent. It betokens the involvement of God himself in revelatory action. The symbolic has particular importance in connection with Jesus Christ as the "revealed revealer." In dealing with him we have to do with the "revelational presence" of the divine. "Self-revelation in the strict sense," says Pannenberg, "is only present when the medium through which God makes himself known is not something alien to himself, brings with it no dimming of the divine light, but, on the contrary, results in the knowledge of the divinity of God for the first time."[26] Speaking in these terms, Pannenberg approximates the symbolic realism or sacramentalism of Eastern Orthodox and Catholic Christianity. He also qualifies his own doctrine that revelation is necessarily indirect.[27]

One limitation of symbol is its inability to present its deeper, divine content with full clarity. This holds even for the resurrection, central as it may be for God's self-revelation in Christ. Pannenberg has frequently argued that the resurrection as a historical event is transcendent and eschatological. In reply it seems correct to observe that the historically accessible aspects of the resurrection, although they powerfully intimate the transcendent, themselves pertain to human and worldly history. The historically tangible aspects of the resurrection are the negative fact of the empty tomb and the positive fact of a series of apparitions. Taken in combination, these two aspects symbolically point to the transhistorical reality of the risen Lord. But, like other symbolic events, they cannot situate the eschaton within cosmic or human history. The eschaton itself begins only at the point where history leaves off.

A second consequence of the symbolic approach may now be stated. If the resurrection, insofar as it is historically perceptible, is a symbolic revelation of God, it does not have the absolute and exclusive character with which Pannenberg seems to endow it. Precisely because

---

26. Pannenberg, *Jesus—God and Man*, 129-130. See p. 127 on Jesus as "revelational presence."

27. Pannenberg, "Offenbarung und 'Offenbarungen,' " 102. Pannenberg at this point in his text raises some questions about my own views on "symbolic disclosure." These questions, I trust, have been sufficiently answered in my *Models of Revelation* (Garden City: Doubleday, 1983), a book which Pannenberg had apparently not seen. He refers to an article of mine in *Theological Studies* (erroneously abbreviated *JThS*) 41 (1980): 51-73.

it is a symbol, it is not exhaustive; it does not exclude God's self-revelation through other phenomena. On the contrary, the resurrection itself would not have its revelatory power were it not for the whole stream of revelatory history to which it belongs. The core revelation is not the resurrection but rather the individual who has risen. From some of Paul's letters one gets the impression that for him it is the cross, rather than the resurrection, that constitutes the center of faith and proclamation (1 Cor. 1:23; 2:2; Gal. 6:14). Many of the faithful are drawn to God's presence as they perceive it in the preaching and public ministry of Jesus. The revelatory power of the Christ figure is diminished if one concentrates too narrowly on the resurrection. In some of Pannenberg's writings it might seem as though the mere fact that someone was reliably reported to have risen from the dead, taken in the context of apocalyptic expectation, would suffice to ground the sole and absolute revelation of God.

Pannenberg is correct, however, in insisting that the many revelatory events and symbols do not constitute an irreducible plurality. They coalesce into a single multifaceted revelation. But it needs to be said that the revelation is not constituted by Jesus alone, and still less by the resurrection alone. As Vatican II said in its Constitution on Divine Revelation, the revelation is perfected in Jesus "by his words and deeds, his signs and wonders, but especially through his death and glorious resurrection from the dead and the final sending of the Spirit of truth" (*Dei Verbum,* 4). The consummation of the revelation in the paschal event does not deprive the other elements, whether found in creation or in the earlier stages of salvation history, of their revelatory status. Without these additional elements, I would argue, the Christ event would not be recognizable as final revelation.

As mentioned above, Pannenberg regards events, not words, as the prime medium of revelation. The dispute about the relative primacy of word and deed in revelation cannot be adequately treated here. In my own view the two modes are inseparable and cannot be weighed in the scales against each other, as Pannenberg seems to do. The concise statement of Vatican II is as satisfactory as any:

> This plan of salvation is realized by deeds and words having an inner
> unity: the deeds wrought by God in the history of salvation manifest and

confirm the teaching and realities signified by the words, while the words proclaim the deeds and clarify the mystery contained in them. (*Dei Verbum, 2*)

Pannenberg, in a recent article, quotes this sentence, but he interprets it as giving priority to the deeds. The words, he points out, must convey the mystery contained in the deeds.[28] Yet it is equally true, I would hold, that the deeds are in need of being elucidated by revelatory words. In many cases, as Pannenberg asserts, the words do not add anything extrinsic to the meaning that already belongs to the events to which they refer.[29] But it does not follow that everyone who learns of the events is by that very fact sufficiently equipped to discern their full meaning. The authority of insight, therefore, has its place. The biblical accounts frequently represent divinely gifted prophets, seers, or apostles authoritatively interpreting the meaning of events that are opaque to others. In his recent writing Pannenberg seems to recognize this. He quotes Jesus as saying to Peter: "Blessed are you, Simon Bar-Jona! For flesh and blood has not revealed this to you, but my Father who is in heaven" (Matt. 16:17).[30] Thus the meaning inherent in the events may require a kind of "private" revelation for its disclosure.

The credibility of the proclaimed word does not have to rest on a naked claim to authority. Like a commentary on a poem, it can justify itself by its illuminative power, especially if this power is felt by very many inquirers over a long period of time. On occasion Pannenberg seems to approach the canonical accounts with an attitude of excessive suspicion, as though the meaning had to be derived ever anew from the facts themselves. From this view I would distance myself. The biblical facts are so intermeshed with theological interpretations that it is often impossible, even with the best use of modern critical tools, to reconstruct what was originally experienced. Theological interpretation has overlaid and enriched the initial deposit, so that one cannot

28. Pannenberg, "Offenbarung und 'Offenbarungen,' " 101.
29. Ibid., 100.
30. Ibid., 97.

accept the events as a basis for faith except with their traditional interpretation. The modern student is no longer able to reenter the situation of the first witnesses.

Considerations such as these have some bearing on Pannenberg's contention that critical historical research is the only reliable avenue of access to the past. With this assertion he apparently rejects the trustworthiness of other channels, such as the apostolic witness, the Christian tradition, and the creeds. Yet it is on these other sources that most Christians rely for their convictions about the saving events that sustain their faith. Very few have the skills or leisure to conduct personal research evaluating the authenticity of the Gospel accounts. Possibly—as Troeltsch and Pannenberg suggest—the nonspecialist may derive some comfort from a general impression that experts have engaged in this type of scholarly inquiry.[31] But many, I suspect, continue to believe in spite of a realization that their commitments receive only meager and ambiguous support from scientific history. For them the testimony of Scripture and tradition is a reliable avenue to truth about matters of faith, even when that testimony cannot be corroborated by academic history.

In some of his essays Pannenberg is severely critical of the kerygmatic theology of Martin Kähler and others. Doubtless the kerygmatic movement had its excesses and defects, but it seems to have correctly identified the limitations of scientific history and the comparatively greater power of the apostolic proclamation to elicit the assent of faith. Rare indeed is the individual who comes to Christian faith from a detached historical analysis of Christian origins such as one finds in the work of E. P. Sanders.[32] The ordinary catalyst of faith is the religious testimony of convinced believers.

At certain points in Pannenberg's writings one finds hints of a richer approach, influenced, perhaps, by Martin Luther. Pannenberg says, for instance, that the word of proclamation has power from the Spirit, and brings with it the possibility of sharing in the same Spirit.[33] Even though Pannenberg adds that the Spirit is inherent in the word,

---

31. Pannenberg, "Redemptive Event and History," 56-57.
32. E. P. Sanders, *Jesus and Judaism* (Philadelphia: Fortress, 1985).
33. Pannenberg, "Offenbarung und 'Offenbarungen,' " 97; cf. *Jesus—God and Man,* 174.

not added to it, he can acknowledge that faith, in the ordinary case, comes from hearing the word of Christian proclamation (Rom. 10:8-17).[34] Somewhat as Jesus spoke with authority in the power of the Spirit, so too the apostles, with the assistance of the same Spirit, were able to proclaim the gospel with boldness and confidence *(parrēsia, plērophoria)*. The unction of their words and of the apostolic writings preserved in the canonical Scriptures is still able to awaken faith in readers who remain quite unpersuaded by the findings of academic history. The inspired words of the prophets and apostles are not mere reports of historical events. Charged with the power of the divine pneuma, they symbolically evoke the sense of the transcendent.[35]

Pannenberg's work raises very acutely the problem of the competence of historical method. He argues against a highly specialized conception of history on the model of the empirical sciences. In his opinion the conventional dichotomies between fact and value, or between occurrence and meaning, are obsolete and untenable.[36] Strictly speaking, there is no such thing as an uninterpreted fact.

While this may be conceded, one must add that there are many different levels of interpretation. Thus it does not follow from what has been said that the historian has the responsibility to pronounce on the ultimate religious meaning of the events being studied. According to Pannenberg the historian must interpret events in their context, and the full context includes the whole of history. Since the unity of history is grounded, for Pannenberg, in the transcendent, it follows for him that the historian must make reference to the concept of God. More than this, the historian "will have to take a stand on the deity of the God of Israel in contrast to the gods of other religions."[37]

These statements would seem to imply that only the biblical monotheist could be truly qualified as a historian. If the historian did not begin with an attitude of faith, historiography itself would bring about

---

34. Pannenberg, "Wahrheit, Gewissheit und Glaube," 240.

35. Pannenberg seems to recognize this in "Offenbarung und 'Offenbarungen,' " 102, but I regard this as a departure from his earlier position that the word of proclamation is not revelatory by reason of its quality as a call or challenge but only "on the basis of its content, on the basis of the event that it reports and explicates" ("Dogmatic Theses," 155).

36. Pannenberg, "Focal Essay," 126-127.

37. Pannenberg, "Redemptive Event and History," 77.

this attitude. The non-Christian would lack the proper framework needed to comprehend events in their full context, and thus in their true meaning. Here, I suspect, Pannenberg somewhat exaggerates the unity of knowledge. To pronounce on the divine or transcendent significance of past events would take the historian beyond his proper competence and would involve a philosophy or theology of history. If history as such has any specific area of competence, this would have to be understood in terms of innerworldly causes and effects.

Pannenberg has frequently discussed the competence of the historian with regard to the resurrection of Jesus, "the sustaining foundation of Christian faith."[38] The resurrection, for him, is a historical event, and its plain significance, in the context in which it occurs, is to constitute Jesus as the final self-revelation of God.[39] To establish the resurrection as a particular occurrence in past time, Pannenberg continues, we must evaluate the assertions made in the New Testament. "The examination of such assertions, however, can be carried out solely and exclusively by the methods of historical research."[40] In various books and articles Pannenberg dispassionately sifts the evidence provided by the Gospels and St. Paul. His conclusion is surprisingly modest:

> It is perfectly possible to arrive at the opinion that, when one has subjected the early Christian traditions to a critical examination, the description of the event in the language of eschatological hope still proves itself to be the most plausible, in the face of all rival explanations. Nobody could call this opinion indisputable. The matter is not historically decided, or decidable, in the sense that all further discussion about it is superfluous.[41]

Even to establish this much, Pannenberg feels it necessary to go beyond what is usually regarded as historical inquiry. "The possibility of an event such as is reported in the Christian message of Easter," he concedes, "can only be seriously considered if the general resurrection of all men (or at least of the righteous) from the dead is meaningful

---

38. Pannenberg, *The Apostles' Creed in the Light of Today's Questions* (Philadelphia: Westminster, 1972), 97.

39. Pannenberg, "Did Jesus Really Rise?" 135.

40. Pannenberg, *Apostles' Creed*, 108; cf. *Jesus—God and Man*, 109.

41. Pannenberg, *Apostles' Creed*, 113-114.

in itself, and if it is conceivable in the context of a contemporary understanding of reality." [42] To ground the antecedent possibility, Pannenberg engages in a philosophical analysis of the common human aspiration to an existence beyond death and in a discussion about whether such survival would necessarily include bodily life. [43] Thus in the end his demonstration does not seem to be made "solely and exclusively by the methods of historical research."

Pannenberg frankly admits a difficulty that occurs for Christians living centuries after Jesus. The resurrection was originally viewed as the dawn of the eschaton. "The fulfillment, which had begun for the disciples, which was almost in their grasp, in the appearances of the resurrected Lord, has become promise once again for us." [44] We can no longer connect the appearances with the imminence of the parousia. As a result the resurrection itself "has become more problematic again." [45] The question whether we can believe the resurrection has to be answered "by theology as a whole, and not only by theology, but also by the way in which the faith of Christians, which is grounded upon the truth known in the past, stands the test today in the decisions of life." [46] Here Pannenberg, if I am not mistaken, is admitting the insufficiency of pure historical research to achieve definitive knowledge about the resurrection of Jesus as a past event.

From the question of faith and history we may now pass to a final question which concerns the relationships between knowledge, faith, and certitude. In his early work Pannenberg seemed to propose a rather simple two-step process: first knowledge, then faith. By knowledge we would be assured of God's mighty acts in history, including his raising of Jesus from the dead. Then by faith we would respond by entrusting our lives to the God who had thus demonstrated his power and his purposes for the world. In this view faith would not be cognitive. While resting on a cognitive basis, it would itself be purely fiducial. Thus Pannenberg was able to write:

> The proclamation of Christ presents, for those who hear it, a fact (taken to be reasonably and reliably true) that in the fate of Jesus of Nazareth,

---

42. Ibid., 104.
43. Ibid., 106; cf. "Did Jesus Really Rise?" 130-131.
44. Pannenberg, *Jesus—God and Man,* 108.
45. Ibid.
46. Ibid, 107.

God has been revealed to all men. The proclamation of the gospel cannot assert that the facts are in doubt and that the leap of faith must be made in order to achieve certainty. . . . The proclamation must assert that the facts are reliable and that you can therefore place your faith, life, and future on them.[47]

This way of putting the matter gave rise to a number of difficulties. Biblically, Pannenberg's language agrees with certain texts but stands in tension with others. According to many texts Christians are to "believe that" God has raised Jesus from the dead (e.g., Rom. 10:9; 1 Cor. 15:11, etc.). In the Johannine writings faith and knowledge seem to interpenetrate. Thus Jesus can say to the Father about the disciples: "I have given them the words which thou gavest me, and they have received them and know in truth that I came from thee; and they have believed that thou didst send me" (John 17:8). The idea of "believing that" certain things are factually true is perpetuated in the creeds and in much of the Christian tradition. The purely fiducial concept of faith, therefore, does not do full justice to the testimony of Scripture and of tradition.[48]

A further difficulty arises from the point of view of certitude. Pannenberg in many of his writings holds that the contents of revelation are known only through a clear-headed rational analysis of the objective evidence, with the help of scientific historical method. But such method alone, as he himself recognizes, can yield only probability.[49] It cannot therefore provide certitude about the resurrection of Jesus. Since the resurrection is "the sustaining foundation of Christian faith," the entire edifice of faith then appears to rest on a dubious foundation. If the fact of the resurrection is only probable, and involves "an element of hypothesis, of subjective conjecture, which must be confirmed—or refuted—by subsequent experience,"[50] the believer would seem to be

---

47. Pannenberg, "Dogmatic Theses," 138.

48. Although texts such as the ones quoted in this paragraph have often been cited as evidence against Pannenberg's positions in his earlier writings, he himself now uses these texts to clarify his own position. See "Wahrheit, Gewissheit und Glaube," 239-240.

49. Pannenberg, "Response to the Discussion," 273.

50. Pannenberg, *Theology and the Philosophy of Science* (Philadelphia: Westminster, 1976), 310.

faced by a dilemma. One could content oneself with a conditional or hypothetical act of faith, but this would be contrary to the nature of faith as complete and unconditional trust, corresponding to the eschatological meaning of the history of Jesus.[51] Faith, therefore, seems compelled to go "beyond its own criteria, abandoning not only self but also the particular form of knowledge of its object from which it started."[52] But if such a further move is justified, and is anything more than a Kierkegaardian leap, there is need for faith to be undergirded by something more than the tentative deliverances of academic history.

In Pannenberg's recent work one senses an increasing sensitivity to this problem. He gives continually greater emphasis to the element of hope that is embedded in the judgment that Jesus has been raised from the dead. This judgment is never a merely historical one about an objective occurrence (though it is that too). In the concrete it is also an expression of hope about the future salvation to which we are called in Christ. The judgment therefore depends in part upon "an anticipatory gift of divine truth"[53] that encounters us, calling us to wholeness and salvation. This intimation, however, does not become true and certain until the self-evidence of divine truth is mediated historically, as happened in the resurrection of Jesus. For its firmness, therefore, faith does depend in part upon historical revelation.

If this summary of Pannenberg's present position is accurate, he now recognizes a dialectical interplay between faith and knowledge rather than positing the two successive stages previously referred to. To say yes to the resurrection as a historical fact is always also to place one's trust in the life it promises. Knowledge and faith are intertwined, each sustaining, and being sustained by, the other. One may of course bracket the existential question and consider the resurrection simply as a historical event, but such a consideration will not of itself result in

51. Pannenberg, "Response to the Discussion," 273. In his "Postface" to Ignace Berten, *Histoire, Révélation, Foi: Dialogue avec Wolfhart Pannenberg* (Brussels: CEP, 1969) 105-115, Pannenberg has an interesting discussion of "hypothèses engagées" that apparently involve firm commitment but do not exclude theoretical doubt. To my mind he does not here sufficiently explain how anyone is justified in making such a commitment to a mere hypothesis.

52. Pannenberg, *Apostles' Creed*, 12.

53. Pannenberg, "Wahrheit, Gewissheit und Glaube," 263. In the present paragraph I am summarizing what I interpret Pannenberg as saying in this important but difficult page of his article.

full conviction. The "fiducial" ingredient of trust or commitment is indispensable to the religious certitude.

I would hope that as Pannenberg continues to add to his already impressive output on the subject of revelation and faith, he will write more fully on the epistemological implications of the existential hope that seems continually to spring up within the human breast. Does hope itself, as Newman maintained, give rise to an antecedent probability about what may be found in history? If so, does hope confer added credibility on the historical signs and testimonies? Does this existential hope have its adequate source in our common human nature or does it derive, at least in part, from a free and unmerited bestowal of divine grace? Does grace, as Thomas Aquinas and others hold, afford a foretaste of eternal life and thereby attune one in a special way to the gospel tidings?

By greater attention to theological questions such as these, Pannenberg might be able to flesh out his account of faith, which has been, up to the present, primarily focused on the objective, rational aspect. I am intrigued by the use he has recently made of insights borrowed from John Henry Newman's theory of conscience and of the illative sense.[54] By further explorations of the subjective and personal component in religious knowledge, Pannenberg may eventually find it possible to incorporate into his system, in some manner, the positions of Augustine and Aquinas regarding the cognitive importance of God's free self-bestowal in grace. If Pannenberg's theology were to develop in this direction, many of the difficulties raised in the preceding pages would be resolved. He would overcome the last elements of that Hegelian rationalism which initially burdened his system.

---

54. Ibid., 260-261. J. H. Walgrave has shown how Newman's entire apologetic takes the form of a "dialectic of conscience." See his *Newman the Theologian* (New York: Sheed & Ward, 1960), 201-240. Walgrave also shows here how Blondel's approach to faith confirms and complements that of Newman (239-240). I mention this because Blondel's reflections on the relations between faith and history are a factor in my own critique of Pannenberg.

7

JESUS IN THE TRINITY: WOLFHART PANNENBERG'S CHRISTOLOGY AND DOCTRINE OF THE TRINITY

Robert W. Jenson

♦

I

It is always a good maxim when reading Wolfhart Pannenberg: remember that it has been his overriding concern to assert the *universality* of the Christian claim, and indeed of any claim that speaks of God. Accordingly, he has denounced every retreat of theology into isolation from other intellectual enterprises, and has determined to make no claims that are plausible only inside a "storm-free refuge" from otherwise valid standards of truth. Some of those who, like myself, came into the theological enterprise just after him and regard him as in some degree an exemplary ally have been attracted by precisely this characteristic of his thought. In no *loci* of Pannenberg's theology is it more determinative than in Christology and the doctrine of Trinity.

It is also a good maxim to reread Pannenberg's books from the back, for in longer works it is his invariable method to let the explicit theologoumena emerge only at the end, from exhaustive—and sometimes exasperating—recountings of the relevant intellectual history. His major treatment of Christology, *Grundzüge der Christologie* (ET: *Jesus—God and Man*) thus gets around to a strictly systematic summary only on page 362:

> Jesus is the Son of the eternal Father only in total resignation to the will of the Father, a resignation which corresponded to the unconditionality of Jesus' historical sending and which, in view of the earthly wreck of that sending, had to become a complete abandonment of his self to the Father. Jesus' absolute practiced unity of will with the Father, as this was confirmed by God's raising him from the dead, is the medium of his unity of essence with the Father and the basis of all assertions about Jesus' divine sonship.[1]

It will be seen how the concern named in my first maxim determines the position thus summarized. What Jesus in fact willed is as amenable to historical investigation as what any other past figure willed, provided the documents are there and we do not follow a—chimerical, in any event—psychologistic understanding of "will." That his mission ended with abandonment and objective despair is a fact the ascertaining of which needs no special access. And on these, together with the resurrection, Pannenberg proposes to build the whole of Christology, and that not only noetically but also ontically. "Christology," he says, "is concerned not only with explicating the church's confession of Christ, but above all with providing its *grounds, from the past fact of Jesus' work and fate"* (emphasis added).[2]

II

In the list of facts on which Christology is to be built, there appear, to be sure, not only Jesus' openly enacted will and his manifest disaster, but his resurrection. If my maxim is right, Pannenberg must take also this event to be knowable in the usual ways of cognition; and he does just that, notoriously. Taking my citations from the discussion in

---

1. Wolfhart Pannenberg, *Grundzüge der Christologie* (Gütersloh: Gerd Mohn, 1964), 362; ET *Jesus—God and Man*, trans. Lewis L. Wilkins and Duane A. Priebe (Philadelphia: Westminster, 1968; 2d ed. 1977).
2. *Grundzüge*, 22

Jesus—God and Man we read: "There is no justification for asserting that the resurrection of Jesus really happened, if this cannot be asserted historically. Whether or not a particular event happened 2000 years ago is not decided by faith or sheer certainty but only by historical investigation. . . ."[3] Accordingly, the truth of Pannenberg's Christology depends on the truth of his assertion—repeated in one form or another throughout his writings—that since "the appearance of primal Christianity . . . can, despite all critical testing of the tradition-materials, only be made intelligible if considered in light of the eschatological hope for a resurrection from the dead," precisely such an event must be considered "an historical occurrence, even if we know nothing more about it."[4]

Pannenberg's famous claim that historical investigation must affirm Jesus' resurrection has found few willing even to consider it seriously. Ironically, precisely this lynchpin of his program—to say nothing unintelligible or in principle implausible to the total community of truth—has made him implausible to that community. It is therefore a temptation for admirers and friendly colleagues of Pannenberg to slide over the offensive contention, to bracket it out as an allowable eccentricity. The evasion, however, will not do. Without the historical verifiability of Jesus' resurrection, the structure of Pannenberg's doctrines of Christ and God would have to be altered radically.

I will in the course of this essay raise a series of questions about Pannenberg's systematics, some only as questions, others provided with what I propose as answers. Several are already urgent.

First, must we indeed include the resurrection among the founding facts of Christology? Few would propose that there would be any occasion of Christology had Jesus been universally thought dead and gone, but that is a different matter. Is the resurrection something that happened *to* the one *homoousios* with the Father, or does it belong to the *homoousia*? Soteriologically, did Jesus accomplish his redeeming work on the cross, and rise only to "apply" it, or is the proclamation "Jesus is risen" itself the message of salvation? One need but remember

---

3. Ibid., 96.
4. Ibid., 95.

Anselm's soteriology and its dominance in the Western church to see how close the first alternative always is in Western theology. In this paper I will merely say that I, like Pannenberg, find only the more radical alternative now viable. Resurrection belongs to what it *means* that Jesus is God the Son.

Second and third, is it likely that Pannenberg's understanding of historical method, according to which it must lead in the matter of Jesus' resurrection to positive results, is wholly right if it isolates him from most historians? And *how* radically would the structure of his thought have to change, if the resurrection were not verifiable by the canons of historical inquiry? Suggesting any answer to the latter question would spring the assigned limits of this essay. To the former, I will venture a lamentably cryptic answer.

In that the proposition "Jesus is risen," whether uttered by those who experienced his appearances or by us, predicts the intersubjectively perceivable event of his final triumph, it is indeed informatively meaningful. And that is much of Pannenberg's concern. But this event is to occur only after all historical cognition. And the discontinuous "visionary" character of the witnesses' experiences of his risen reality prohibits any other predictions being drawn from them about what may or may not now appear in the tradition or in the present state of affairs. Therefore, despite all good will, I am yet to be convinced that "Jesus is risen" is an assertion which a historian can confirm.

III

I have space in this essay to sketch and question only the bare systematic bones of Pannenberg's version of Chalcedon. I will follow the quoted summary. Pannenberg begins with the man Jesus, who like every human has a divine sending; that he is sent by God to a mission over against his sisters and brothers does not diminish his cohumanity with us, it constitutes it. Nor is the historical particularity of Jesus' mission in itself distinguishing; every human is historically particular.[5] Specific is the *content* of his particular human "office": it was "Jesus' office, his earthly sending . . . to call human persons into the imminent rule

---

5. Ibid., 195-217.

of God." A human calling with such content is, necessarily, unconditional; it calls for "commitment" that is "clear and grasped with the whole heart."[6]

Many programs of "Christology from below" make foundational moves already at this point: Jesus' unity with God is grounded in the perfection of his human relation to God. Thus Schleiermacher made Jesus' deity consist in the perfection of his God-consciousness, of which Jesus' death was but the final proof and of which his resurrection is the communication. Pannenberg's version of Christology from below proceeds differently: "Not already" with the character of his life, "but only in his commitment to God's will in the darkness of his destiny to crucifixion, which had primally to mean the *catastrophe* of his sending, did Jesus' commitment to God acquire the character of self-surrender."[7] And only in *that* character is a human personal reality achieved that can be identical with another personal reality, with God or any other.

Pannenberg sets the human reality here identified for Jesus and in his case identifiable with God under the modern concept of *person;* its identity with God he accordingly conceptualizes as a "personal union."[8] Despite the verbal similarity and historical connections of the modern concept of person with the *persona* or *prosōpon* of the Christological and trinitarian tradition, it is a very different concept, as Pannenberg knows and insists: "The choice of the concept of personal union . . . is not yet justified by the mere fact that the Christological tradition has designated the unity of God and humanity in Jesus as 'hypostatic' or 'personal.' We will use the concept of 'person' . . . in a sense distinct from that of the tradition."[9]

It has, indeed, been one of Pannenberg's major projects to mold the modern concept of personhood into its most appropriate form; *Anthropology in Theological Perspective* is mostly devoted to the task. In that work and elsewhere, he works from the equally modern concepts of the "I" and the "self," developed both in German transcendental philosophy and in psychoanalytic theory. The "I" is the subject that is given; the "self" is what this subject "is"—which, since the subject

---

6. Ibid., 346.
7. Ibid.
8. Ibid., 335-378.
9. Ibid., 336.

is placed in time, means "is to be." For a convenient statement of what then the "person" according to Pannenberg is, I turn to an earlier and decisive article: "Neither the I nor the self, taken alone, is personal. The person is the presence of the self in the always momentary reality of the I. It subsists in the claiming of my I by my true self and in anticipatory consciousness of my identity."[10] Again: "The I does not have personality from itself. To be a person comes to the I only from a specific content of life, which transcends the I and founds its true selfhood."[11]

The I, the sheerly given subject of consciousness, if it could subsist in itself, would be timeless in its moment. The self, the destined authenticity of the I, would, if it could subsist in itself, be transcendentally future. Personal identity is the historical unity of the I with its self. And the *person* exists in the anticipation of that unity. And then a further point: the "call" to me as the I that I am, to be the self that I am to be, is delivered by "you," by the presence to me of an other person precisely in his or her selfhood.[12] It is "persons" in this sense of which there is only one in Christ and three in the triune God.[13]

Given what a person is, it is clear that if one person's will were to be so directed to the will of another person as to be in "absolute practiced unity of will" with the other, achieved in "complete abandonment of self" to that other, *and* if that unity of will were confirmed by the other, this would amount to the reality of a personal being which is one for both persons, to a "personal union." In that the Father confirmed Jesus' self-abandonment to him, by raising him from the death in which it was actualized, Jesus and his Father are in this way one.

But now note that *this* personal union is not the union we may have been expecting Pannenberg to be steering toward, between "the Logos" and Jesus; it is a union between the *Father* and Jesus. It is a major, though not wholly unprecedented, departure of Pannenberg's·

---

10. Wolfhart Pannenberg, "Person und Subjekt," *Neue Zeitschrift für systematische Theologie* 18 (1976): 144.

11. Wolfhart Pannenberg, "Die Subjektivität Gottes und die Trinitätslehre," *Grundfragen systematischer Theologie,* vol. 2 (Göttingen: Vandenhoeck & Ruprecht, 1980), 109.

12. Pannenberg, "Person und Subjekt," 144.

13. Pannenberg, "Subjektivität Gottes . . . ," 111.

Christological and trinitarian thought: "The question of the unity of the man Jesus with the eternal Son of God cannot be directly set or answered." All theories must fail which "attempt to think the unity of God and humanity in Jesus by starting with the notion of the incarnation of the Logos. . . . The unity of the man Jesus with the eternal Son of God emerges only roundabout . . . , by way of Jesus' relation to . . . the God of Israel, whom he called 'Father.' Only the personal fellowship of Jesus with the Father shows him as himself identical with the Son of this Father." [14]

Just this self-giving to the Father, and the Father's acceptance of it, constitute the one divine essence which is common to the Father and the Son. For such personal fellowship "is simultaneously essential fellowship." [15] This is so because, first, it is precisely "the essence of the person itself, to exist in commitment to another," and because, second, such sinking of the I in a you as has been described must mean "participation" in the other's essence. [16] According to Pannenberg, it is precisely the fellowship of the divine *persons,* using that concept in the full modern sense, and indeed in an intensified version thereof, which *is* the oneness of God, as that oneness has been named with the traditional concept of "essence." [17]

These moves are a truly remarkable revision of traditional Christology. The personal unity between the Father and the man Jesus, which out of its authenticity as a mutual personal act constitutes an "essential" union, is remarkably like that which the Antiochene theology described between the *Logos* and the man Jesus. Scholars have regularly found something attractive in Antiochene theology, have intuited some legitimate concern at the heart of its plainly inadequate propositions. By the time Antioch had become Nicene and turned to Christology, the term *Logos* had ceased to be felt as denoting the deity *of Jesus;* "the Logos" had become an extra metaphysical entity that would have been the "person" he was with or without the man Jesus; and Jesus' relation to God was grasped as his relation to *this,* "second" God. In effect,

---

14. Pannenberg, *Grundzüge,* 346 (ET *Jesus—God and Man*).
15. Ibid., 347. See also the massive discussion of "Offenbarungseinheit" and its relation to "Wesenseinheit," 124-157.
16. Ibid., 347.
17. Ibid.

Pannenberg recapitulates the Antiochene description of Jesus' relation to God, but takes this biblically, as Jesus' relation to the God he called "Father," and then makes *this* relation the basic Christological relation.

What traditionally has been the central Christological move Pannenberg then dispatches with astonishing abruptness: it is in the carrying out of this personal relation to the Father that Jesus is "identical with the correlate already implicit in the understanding of God as Father, with the Son—whose essential mark it is, not to live of his own but wholly from the Father." [18] Within his Christological reflections themselves, Pannenberg does not specify any particular sense for this "identity" of Jesus with the Father's Correlate; the traditionally central Christological analyses of "hypostatic union" and "communication of natures/attributes" are only historically treated. Thus it is not that Pannenberg simply uses the modern concept of person where the tradition had its predecessor; Pannenberg has altogether abolished the locus of reflection at which the tradition used its person-concept; Christologically he uses *no* concept in the way in which the tradition used its "person."

One is tempted to say that for Pannenberg there finally is no Christological problem as that problem was anciently felt, because for Pannenberg it directly is the person Jesus who, by virtue of his life and destiny, "is one of the Trinity." But we are also intended to take that "correlate" with ontological seriousness; for the sake of the difference between time and eternity, Pannenberg holds it "unavoidable that we distinguish between Jesus' eternal sonship and his humanity, which came into being only at a particular time." [19] We are, after all, to think of *some* sort of *logos asarkos*. Within his Christological analyses Pannenberg provides no specification of what sort that is to be.

Plainly, a new set of questions is before us.

First: Is the demotion of the incarnation concept from its foundational role right? Judgments will separate here, and the separation will mark fundamental divisions in contemporary theology. I must myself record entire agreement with Pannenberg's move. The concept of

---

18. Ibid., 347-348.
19. Ibid., 335.

incarnation can never found a Christology adequate to the actual confession of Christians. If you start from the posit of two entities, "the Logos" and "the human nature of Jesus," Christology becomes inquiry into how these two can have become one; this is a hopeless enterprise. These two entities *cannot* in fact become one, in any sense of "one" compatible with the confession of "one Lord, one Christ."

Second: Is the way in which Pannenberg does this, by making Jesus' personal relation to the Father the foundational Christological unity, the right way? I think it is, and can hardly think otherwise, since I have been led, though by other considerations, to a similar position.

Third: Should we conceive Jesus' personal relation to the Father as the relation of a "person" *in the modern sense* to an "other"? Unless there is something fundamentally misguided about the modern concept of "person," how should we not, once the concept is there? I think it right: the "one person" of Christ is the one personality. From this, however, it does *not* follow that the "three persons" in God need be similarly conceived. Here is a key place where Pannenberg's Christology leads into his doctrine of Trinity and perhaps also into its problems. Indeed, what his Christological propositions themselves mean must remain in some degree unclear until he also tells us how their terms are to be used in that doctrine.

Fourth: What is that "Correlate"?

IV

We need not decide whether, biographically, Pannenberg's version of Chalcedon led to his version of Trinity, or vice versa; I in fact suppose the latter. Since, in accord with my assignment, I began with Christology, I will follow the systematic line from it to Trinity. There is a further difficulty, that a complete treatment of Trinity like that of Christology has not yet appeared. Much of it exists, as part of the forthcoming dogmatics, and one chapter has been available to me in draft. I will in the following limit myself to contentions that have appeared in print, using the draft manuscript only to control and expand their presentation; I will on such occasions paraphrase but not cite.

If Pannenberg's Christology is on the right track, then we must drastically revise the traditional Western understanding of the relation between the Trinity-as-such, the "immanent Trinity," and the triunely plotted saving events, the "economic Trinity." For if Jesus is the Son precisely by virtue of his human obedience and prayer to the Father, then that prayer and obedience are themselves the "relations" which in classical trinitarianism constitute the "persons." The foundation of the doctrine of Trinity will be exactly the same as the foundation of Christology: Jesus' relation to his Father, comprehending mission, death, and resurrection.[20]

Karl Rahner has provided a maxim for much contemporary trinitarian theology: "The immanent Trinity *is* the economic Trinity." Pannenberg is among those who have adopted it. Whether, as Pannenberg says, Rahner did not succeed in drawing out the consequences of his own thesis,[21] or Pannenberg and some others of us have adopted the verbal formula in a sense unintended by Rahner, we may leave undecided.[22] By adopting the maxim, Pannenberg both states a goal of his own trinitarian thinking, and explicitly aligns himself with an identifiable current in contemporary theology (in a lecture I will be drawing on heavily, he cites Eberhard Jüngel, Jürgen Moltmann, and Robert Jenson). Such theologians are engaged in reestablishing and recasting the doctrine of Trinity as "the starting point for a critical reexamination of the traditional contrast between an eternal and in himself immutable God and the changes of time and history,"[23] even as a "resource which allows Christian theology to make constructive use of antimetaphysical and atheistic criticisms of the concept of God" in order "to make possible a deeper appropriation of the specifically Christian concept of God. . . ."[24]

The demanded rethinking, according to Pannenberg, is first of all sheer acknowledgment that "the eternal self-identity of God" cannot

---

20. Pannenberg, "Der trinitarische Gott," draft of chap. 5 of the forthcoming dogmatics.

21. Pannenberg, "Probleme einer trinitarischen Gotteslehre," in *Weisheit Gottes—Weisheit der Welt I, Festschrift für Joseph Kardinal Ratzinger* (St. Ottilien: EOS Verlag, 1987), ET "Problems of a Trinitarian Doctrine of God," trans. Philip Clayton, *Dialog* 26 (1987): 250-257, see p. 251. In this instance the English text is equally authoritative and will be cited in this chapter.

22. I must for honesty's sake record, however, that in my understanding Rahner intended *is* in his maxim analogically, so that our appropriations of it at *least* stretch it very far.

23. Pannenberg, "Problems," 251.

24. Ibid., 250.

properly "be conceived independently of the salvation-historical work-ings of the Son and of the Spirit. . . ."[25] Also in this, Pannenberg moves with the just-mentioned theological current. We must be clear how drastic a critique of the Western tradition is being conducted by these theologians.[26] It has been since Augustine an overriding rule that no proposition about Christ or the Trinity can be true from which it would follow that God is any different on account of incarnation—or the mission of the Spirit—than God would have been without it. In consequence, as Pannenberg put it in a decisive essay, "the Trinity was hypostatized . . . into a Prius of all history, even though the doc-trine of Trinity describes the God who is revealed in history."[27] Pre-cisely this rule Pannenberg and others propose to reject: "If nothing changed for God through the incarnation, so that God would be in the same sense God without the incarnation as he is in his incarnation, the very concept of an incarnation of God would be canceled. . . ."[28]

Although such critique of the tradition is widespread in contem-porary theology, Pannenberg argues the position in his own way, from the very center of his theology, that is, from the ontologically consti-tutive force of the resurrection. Jesus' crucifixion put the "divine au-thority" he claimed into question. When the Father confirmed that claim by raising Jesus, the first thing revealed was that, since Jesus' claim was *true*, "also the deity of the Father himself" had been in question. "Therefore the resurrection of Jesus is just as constitutive for the deity of the Father as for the divine sonship of Jesus. Without Jesus' resurrection, the Father Jesus proclaimed would not be God." And that in turn "means that in the history of the Son the deity of the Father is implicated."[29]

A sizeable question is already posed, to which, unfortunately for the suspense of this essay, my answer is predetermined: Is Pannenberg right in joining this current? In a way, you pay your money and you take your choice: Are the theological "acids of modernity" mere ene-mies of the gospel, to be conquered or succumbed to, or are they also

25. Ibid., 251.

26. My own version of the technical critique of Augustine and the subsequent tradition is in Robert W. Jenson, *The Triune Identity* (Philadelphia: Fortress, 1982), 114-131.

27. Wolfhart Pannenberg, "Der Gott der Geschichte," *Kerygma und Dogma* 23 (1977): 83.

28. Pannenberg, "Der Gott der Geschichte," 83.

29. Ibid., 87-88.

allies or even fruits of the gospel, in its polemic relation to religion? How one answers that question will depend mostly, I think, on how much of the 20th-century's Christian critique of religion, and of its Marxian and Nietzschean cognates, one has in one. Much exposure to Barth, the great virtuoso of that critique, inoculated many of us; that cannot be the whole explanation in Pannenberg's case.

As to Pannenberg's argument from the meaning of Jesus' resurrection also for the Father, it is of course valid within his systematics. I have to say that he seems to me to argue from the more difficult to the less; at least in my own case, it is the Lutheran conviction that the human person Jesus is "one of the Trinity" that compels me to say that if Jesus had not risen the Christian God would not be, rather than the other way around. I do not know if that is a quibble.

V

Three innovations of trinitarian teaching follow from Pannenberg's resorption of Christology into the doctrine of Trinity. I will discuss them in order of ontological difficulty.

First, that the deity of the Father is as dependent on the triumph of the Son as that of the Son is on his sending by the Father—and analogously with the Spirit—means that the inner-trinitarian "relations" are *reciprocal*. The point is more than an analytical observation. Acknowledging the reciprocity of the inner–triune relations goes to the heart of the new trinitarianism Pannenberg and others are working on. For, in Pannenberg's formulation, it is the "reciprocity in the relationship of the divine persons" which "makes room for the constitutive significance of the central salvation-historical events for the Godhood of God and . . . for the significance of time and change for the divine eternity."[30]

Readers will recall that the standard Western doctrine of inner-triune relations lists: the Father begets the Son, the Son is begotten of the Father, the Father and the Son breathe forth the Spirit, and the Spirit proceeds from the Father and the Son. Notably, the flow of deity runs, as it were, all one way: from pretemporal eternity into time and

---

30. Pannenberg, "Problems," 252.

not vice versa. By the traditional predicates, the Father is rightly described as *fons trinitatis*, but the Son and the Spirit have no coordinate dignity. Yet so far as the formal structure is concerned, there is indeed room for other "predicates" stating the *mutual* dependence of the hypostases.

In his forthcoming dogmatics, Pannenberg will argue that the inner-trinitarian relations must include, beside the traditional ones, relations in which the Son and Spirit are active over against the Father, and relations that are not relations of origin. The Son is not merely "begotten," but "obeys" and "glorifies" the Father. The Spirit is not merely "breathed," but "fulfills" the Son and "rests" on him. It does not appear that Pannenberg thinks there is any one decisive set of such relations, rather that whatever relations prove exegetically appropriate for describing the saving triune history are to be posited as in God.[31]

Second, Pannenberg's concern is much more with what he takes to be an immediate consequence of inner-triune reciprocity: that the triune God is not as such one personal being, in the modern sense of "person." There are *three* (modern) persons in God, whose *fellowship* constitutes the one divine essence. Perhaps the single most important of his trinitarian essays to date is "Die Subjektivität Gottes und die Trinitätslehre," of 1977; there he formulates: "The triune God is indeed but one God, and this God is not impersonal. But this God is each time person only in the form of one or another of the triune persons, since each of the persons of the Trinity possesses not only his personhood but also his deity only mediated by his relation to the two others."[32]

In the dogmatics, Pannenberg will accordingly found the immanent tripersonality of God by finding in the relations between Jesus and his Father and their Spirit that act of distinguishing the self from an other, in order just so to be person by and for that other, which constitutes personhood. Each person in a unique way distinguishes himself from each of the other persons as from the one God of Israel:

---

31. Pannenberg, "Der trinitarische Gott." In *The Triune Identity*, 138-143, I proposed that as the Father is "unoriginate" so is the Spirit "unsurpassed," and that as the Father and the Son "breathe" the Spirit so the Spirit and the Son "free" the Father. This proposal differs from Pannenberg's insofar as it intends to maintain the classic structure in which the persons can be defined by and understood as ontologically constituted in the relations.

32. Pannenberg, *Grundfragen*, 2:110.

the Son points away from himself to the Father as to the one God, the Spirit praises the Son as in his obedience one with the Father, the Father gives over his kingdom to the Son, so that now the Son is the power and wisdom that makes godhead. And just so, each is established as in his personhood very God.[33]

Pannenberg acknowledges Karl Barth's role as the great renewer of trinitarianism for the theology of our century. But he conducts a vehement critique of what he takes to be characteristic of Barth's specific trinitarianism: that Barth presents God's triune life, in the line of German idealism, as the unfolding of a single divine subject.[34] He finds continuance of this error also in Moltmann and Jenson. An announced goal of his trinitarian reflection is fully to expunge it.[35]

In the dogmatics, the critique of this recent tradition will broaden into a critique of *any* derivation of the triune distinctions from a concept of the one reality of God, and so into a critique that touches nearly the whole Western tradition. Every such derivation either draws the deity of the Son and the Spirit from that of the Father, and must finally be subordinationist, or draws the deity of all three from a common deity and must finally be modalist. Moreover, the very organization of standard Western treatments, which puts the doctrine of God's one being first and only then comes to his trinitarian reality, historically depends on this derivation, and when the latter is eschewed divides the doctrine of God into what amounts to the doctrine of two separately describable Gods.[36]

It is time again to stop for questions. *Are* the inner–triune relations reciprocal? And does that mean that the one God is not one person, or even one subject?

Both by Pannenberg's sort of argument and by other considerations, I have for some time been persuaded that the one-way flow of the traditional description of triune deity is inadequate to the gospel. If deity is to be interpreted by what happened and happens with Christ, then obedience must as much constitute deity as command, suffering as action. Then the Father's deity must as much depend on what the

---

33. Pannenberg, "Der trinitarische Gott."
34. Pannenberg, *Grundfragen,* 2:96-108.
35. Pannenberg, "Problems," 252.
36. Pannenberg, "Der trinitarische Gott."

Son does as the Son's deity depends on what the Father does. And if that is true, then the Spirit, who is the mutuality of this command and obedience, more *defines* deity than do either the Father or the Son; "God *is* Spirit," and that must be recognized in trinitarian dialectics.[37]

I cannot, however, say that I am yet persuaded to adopt the second innovation. I doubt that the modern term "person" can be substituted for the tradition's term "person" to denote the three in God. I do not see that Pannenberg has as yet adequately argued the substitution.[38] Nor am I yet willing to give up the tradition which from Augustine on has regarded the one God as personal, in what has come to be the modern sense, and has explored the trinitarian dialectics as constituting the life of the one Creator.

Against Barth and those who agree with him, Pannenberg says: "The classical doctrine of Trinity attributed no unique personhood to the common divine essence, along with that of the three persons."[39] But this gets us nowhere, since the classical doctrine of the Trinity did not attribute personhood in the modern and Pannenbergian sense to the *three* either; it did not use the concept at all. If we are to take the affirmative features of classical doctrine as given, then the starting situation is: there are three "persons," in the old sense, in God. Pannenberg and I are then further agreed: at least one of these, Jesus the Son, is "a person" in the modern sense and is of one essence with the others by the dialectics of his personhood. The remaining question is: Would we rightly conceive the other two identities by conceiving them also as persons in the modern sense? I confess that Pannenberg's interpretation of, for example, the Spirit's glorification of the Son or the Father's giving over of rule to the Son as acts of personal self-distinction seems to me a bit stretched, though I am delighted with its ingenuity.[40]

It is a consequence of Pannenberg's position that the one-to-one correspondence between the codified trinitarian relations and the persons is broken. Each person is related to the others, and therein constituted both in personality and deity, by a multiplicity of relations, of

---

37. If the Father is the "source" of deity, the Spirit must be goal. And of the *triune* God, why is not the goal as much if differently originating as is the source? Jenson, *Identity,* 140.

38. Also not in the deservedly praised article on "Person" in *Religion in Geschichte und Gegenwart,* 3d ed., 5:230-234. I am unable to judge the forthcoming dogmatics on this point.

39. Pannenberg, *Grundfragen,* 2:109.

40. Pannenberg, "Der trinitarische Gott."

various sorts.[41] I do not know if it is a drawback of Pannenberg's proposal that it breaks the old correspondence of one relation with each person[42]—the Father begets, the Son is begotten, the Spirit is breathed—and that this correspondence was somehow aesthetically pleasing. More serious is that the key doctrine of classical Western trinitarianism, that the persons *are* "subsisting relations," must, I think, be abandoned; I regard this doctrine as a major achievement of Western thought.

The matter cannot, of course, be responsibly argued in the space of this essay. I will only suggest that another conception than Pannenberg's is possible, one which may seem to satisfy the criteria Pannenberg's work and this essay have affirmed. Also on Pannenberg's scheme, the three are not in the same way persons: "self-distinction" does not mean quite the same in each case, and "personhood" has a different structure in each.[43]

If we retain the old sense of "person" for the three, a similar differentiation is possible within the Trinity conceived as personal in the modern sense. We might conceive the Father as an "I" in the sense Pannenberg analyzes, as a universal consciousness. Such an entity is a *necessary factor* of personhood in the modern sense. Jesus the Son, who is indeed a person in the modern sense, is then the one in whom the Father sees his "self." And so there is a universal person, the triune God. The person this God *is,* is Jesus.[44]

Nor, in order to conceive the one God as personality, do we need to *derive* the three as the factors of that personality. We can very well conclude *to* the personality of the one God from the triune pattern of what happens with Christ over against his Father in their Spirit.

Third and finally, Pannenberg drastically reconceives the relation between the one being of God and the pluralities, of triune persons and of soteriological "attributes," by which God is concrete for and among us. Also in this matter Pannenberg draws creatively and profoundly on German idealism, but here I must go straightway to the

41. Ibid.
42. Ibid.
43. Ibid.
44. This is a schema drawn from analyses scattered through Jenson, *Identity,* but see esp. 173-175. In his critique of this book, "Problems," 252, Pannenberg does not refer to these considerations.

dogmatic outcome. It follows directly from the foregoing, although Pannenberg never in published writings proceeds so abruptly: "being" is an intrinsically *relational* concept.[45]

The "being" or "one essence" of anything is always just that, the essence *of* some reality that can be indicated.[46] In the case of the biblical God, it is the actor of saving history *whose* being is the one essence of God.[47] The relation between the immanent Trinity and the economic Trinity "belongs to the concept of the divine essence itself."[48] Once that is faced without evasion, much becomes soluble.

In particular, the cure of an ancient theological ill becomes possible. In God "himself" traditional theology has posited, if grudgingly, that there must be those relations—"begetting," "being begotten," etc.—by which the three identities subsist. But in obedience to the metaphysical prejudice that "being" is self-enclosure, transcendence of relation, it has rigorously distinguished these inner-divine relations from a different set of divine characteristics, the "attributes" which describe God's relation to his creation, "righteousness," "mercy," "wisdom," etc. Meanwhile, yet another set of characteristics, attributes such as "omnipotence" and "omniscience," have been said to denote the one essential being of God. The structure is both clumsy and perilously coherent in itself, and formalizes the splits between eternity and time, the "immanent" Trinity and the historical Trinity, the being of God and the relations of God, against which resurgent trinitarianism protests.

I must brutally summarize Pannenberg's cure. It consists of two analyses.

Pannenberg first attacks the division between two sets of attributes.[49] The attributes of the one set, the "omni-" attributes, all, he notes, "relate back to the concept of infinity."[50] But the infinity which such predicates could by themselves determine would be false, for it would be limited by its opposite, merely set over against the finitude

45. Pannenberg, "Problems," 254-256.
46. Ibid., 253-254.
47. Ibid., 254.
48. Ibid.
49. Ibid., 254-256.
50. Ibid., 256.

stipulated in its own concept.[51] "Truly infinite is only that which is distinguished from the finite yet also transcends the distinction and is itself present on the side of the finite." We have a word for such a relation, where it is concretely realized: "love." Thus "the phrase 'God is love' represents the concretization of the abstract structure of the concept of infinity." But such relational attributes as "righteousness" and "mercy" are precisely "concretions of love." Thus the relational attributes are but specifications of deity's intrinsic infinity, insofar as this is real and not merely abstract.[52]

The second analysis goes very quickly. Love is now "perceived to be not merely one attribute of God among others, but . . . identical with the divine essence." But the inner-triune relations between Father, Son, and Spirit are all reducible to their mutual love. "The phrase 'God is love' " is equally "to be understood as the·comprehensive expression of the trinitarian fellowship. . . ." Thus the inner-triune fellowship *is* the one divine essence, of which the attributes which state the one God's relation to his creation are but the concrete stipulations.[53] The fissures and antinomies of traditional doctrine are overcome.

It is, according to the forthcoming dogmatics, impossible appropriately and consistently to conceive God's oneness at all without the Trinity. The reversal is complete. It is not that we first conceive the oneness of God and then inquire how he can be three; rather, it is precisely the doctrine of Trinity which works out the oneness of that God who reveals himself in Jesus Christ. It is only with the question about the nature and characteristics of the God who among us is Father, Son, and Spirit that his oneness first becomes thematic.[54]

It is always hard to know how to judge such metaphysical sequences—which does not, in my judgment, make them meaningless or useless. I believe the sequence just summarized to be right, and propose to incorporate it into my own ventures on such lines. If asked *why* I think it right, I could only respond that the key move, the identification of love as authentic infinity, is one I had some time ago

---

51. In this analysis Pannenberg is, of course, conversing with Hegel (ibid).
52. Ibid.
53. Ibid.
54. Pannenberg, "Der trinitarische Gott."

been led by other warrants to make,[55] so that Pannenberg's paths to and from it necessarily seem to me to have a right goal and a right starting point. To others, I can only commend them for trial.

Finally, it is at this point that I must note that the dogmatics will indeed tell us more about that "Correlate," the *logos asarkos*. What is said in the draft chapter available to me suggests that Pannenberg and I may have a very deep metaphysical disagreement, about the concept of "eternity." But since none of the comments to which I would refer is published, and since discussion would lead very deep into the doctrine of God's being and attributes, which is the assignment of another essayist, I must leave the matter as a reference to possible future discussion.

VI

This volume embodies an American "reception" of Pannenberg's work—or the lack thereof. I must be brief in the extreme. Nothing, it seems to me, is so desperately needed in American Protestantism, and in much Protestantized American Catholicism, as recovery of that primal point, that the gospel is about the Lord Jesus. Christians do not have "a God," about whose ideas Jesus then perhaps contributes some information. They have the particular God of whom the man Jesus is one identity, and who therefore is triune in the first rather than the second place. No contemporary theologian has worked harder, more creatively, or more successfully than Wolfhart Pannenberg, at the highest intellectual level, to make these points.

---

55. Jenson, *Identity*, 168-176.

8

PANNENBERG'S ECUMENISM

Geoffrey Wainwright

◆

I. GERMANY AND AMERICA

Wolfhart Pannenberg gained his initial ecumenical inspiration from his mentor Edmund Schlink, the Heidelberg dogmatician who belonged from its beginnings in 1946 to the Jaeger-Stählin circle of German Catholics and (predominantly) Lutherans, and who was a prominent figure in the Faith and Order Commission of the World Council of Churches in the 50s and 60s and served as its vice-chairman from 1961 to 1968. Since 1975 Pannenberg has been a member of the WCC Faith and Order Commission, with a place on its standing commission, and in 1980 he succeeded Schlink as "academic leader" of the Jaeger–Stählin study group on the Protestant side.

It is not possible to make a simple and direct application of Pannenberg's ecumenical interests to the United States. For one thing, American Lutheranism is not the same as German Lutheranism, nor American Catholicism the same as German Catholicism. Yet American Lutherans and Catholics participate in the global conversations between the Lutheran World Federation and the Roman Catholic church, so that Pannenberg's participation in bilateral studies in Germany may give him something to say—refracted, if need be, through the international dialogue—to Lutherans and Catholics in their specific relations in the

United States. Then again, the broad denominational pluriformity of the American scene is far removed from the largely bi-confessional pattern of Germany. Yet this very fact may make of the United States a better testing ground than his own Germany for the results of those multilateral exercises in ecumenism in which Pannenberg has significantly shared through his work in the Faith and Order Commission of the WCC. The United States constitutes, moreover, the prime case of that understandable but finally (self-)deceptive "religious neutrality" and of that inevitable but dangerous "civil religion" which resulted by reaction from the interconfessional conflicts of 16th- and 17th-century Western European Christendom and that now need rethinking, according to Pannenberg, in terms of Christian ecumenism and the desirable contribution of the Christian faith and the world religions to the unity of humankind.

We shall shortly examine two major projects of Faith and Order in which Pannenberg has been and remains engaged, namely, "Baptism, Eucharist and Ministry" and "Towards the Common Expression of the Apostolic Faith Today" (III). Then I shall turn more narrowly to questions of Catholic–Protestant relationships (IV). First, however, it is necessary to describe briefly Pannenberg's eschatology and ecclesiology, his view of the Church and its relation to the kingdom of God (II). And to this will correspond a later section on the links he makes between ecclesial unity and human community (V). Finally, in relation to our professional calling, I will take the case of Pannenberg as a systematic theologian to illustrate the importance of his discipline for ecumenism as well as the importance of the ecumenical dimension for theology (VI). Throughout I shall look for the contributions Pannenberg has to make, *mutatis mutandis,* to our American situation and the challenges we present to his positions.

II. ESCHATOLOGY AND ECCLESIOLOGY

Pannenberg's fundamental ecclesiology comes to expression in his *Thesen zur Theologie der Kirche* (1970) and finds instantiation in his collected papers on *The Church* (1983; German 1977) and later treatments of particular questions. Ecclesiology is firmly set in an eschatological perspective. As early as his *Jesus—God and Man* (1968, 1977; German 1964), Pannenberg considers the resurrection of Jesus—which was God's confirmation of his message and the divine acceptance of his life and death—as the beginning of the end. The Church then explicitly becomes the community of believers in Christ who in faith and love share by anticipation in the final reign of God that will be marked by justice and peace. As such, the Church is a present *sign* of God's kingdom. The sign comes to its densest expression in the worship assembly, and particularly in the celebration of the Lord's Supper. The sacramental divisions of Christians and Christian communities are a countertestimony to the gospel. The ecumenical movement is a proper and necessary attempt to render more visible the believed unity of the Church which is constituted by Christ as himself the object of the Christian faith.

Pannenberg's position is basically scriptural, traditional, and (to me) systematically congenial. But some problems attach to his use of the category of sign. First, Pannenberg is willing to speak of "Christians without the Church." In the German situation, he has sympathy with the long-term victims of the disgust with the institutional, confessional churches that was provoked by the wars of religion. But too ready an allowance of Christianity outside the Church threatens, in fact, the "central"—and, I would say, constitutive—place of the eucharistic celebration in the Christian sign-complex. In the American situation—where there is little anti-institutional feeling towards the denominational churches, since these are "free"—Pannenberg's position would risk giving comfort to those liberal Protestant views which vaguely include "all persons of good will" within "the Church." Certainly the Church or churches should welcome into membership all who come in repentance and faith towards Christ, but the fudging of boundaries impairs the Church's identity and thereby its character as sign. It may happily be noted that Pannenberg in fact repeatedly pleads for the upbuilding of eucharistic communities through regular Sunday celebration.

Second, Pannenberg's favorite notion of *manifesting* an *already existing* unity that is, perhaps to a large extent, *invisible* may not give the best account of the ecumenical process, even though it may find some support in the New Delhi description of 1961 ("The unity which is both God's will and his gift to his Church is being made visible as . . . "). One may question how *real* the unity *is*, which is not visibly expressed. While institutional unity without spiritual unity would be a mere facade, it is the nature of faith, hope, and love to express themselves. Imperfection or absence of expression suggests a substantive lack. While respecting Pannenberg's placing of the Church's significative character under the eschatological reserve, we must beware of encouraging a pluralistic American acquiescence in the present visible *dis*unity of Christians and their churches. It may happily be noted that Pannenberg is well aware of the need for making and living new *forms of expression* of Christian unity. These should enhance the Church's sign character because they increase its *being*.

Third, Pannenberg objected to the claim made at the Accra meeting of the WCC Faith and Order Commission in 1974 that some Christians may be closer to non-Christians engaged in the struggle for freedom than they are to other Christians not so engaged. Insofar as his objection is related to the *ambiguity* of signs in the political arena, his point may be appreciated. But if the Church's calling is to be, as Pannenberg allows, an "*effective* sign," then many American Christians will (I think rightly) expect that some *action* is required, risky though it be.

III. FAITH AND ORDER

1. The Apostolic Faith

Under the aegis of the joint working group between the World Council of Churches and the Roman Catholic church, Pannenberg wrote already in 1970 a major paper on "The Importance of Eschatology for the Understanding of the Apostolicity and Catholicity of the Church." He argued that the definitive and universal significance of Jesus Christ gave to the apostolic message concerning him an eschatological scope. The apostolicity of the Church implies, therefore, not only a backward-looking and formal dependence on its apostolic origins, but also a forward-looking and material orientation to the final kingdom of God. In the accomplishment of its catholic mission, the Church has the freedom and the need to *reformulate* its proclamation in order to reach all cultures.

Pannenberg was present (and it is there, on a personal note, that I first met him) at the World Council of Churches/Roman Catholic church meeting in Venice in June 1978, which formulated the project "Towards a Confession of the Common Faith" (Faith and Order Paper 100). Later in that year in Bangalore, and then again in 1982 in Lima, he was among those who fought hardest in the plenary commission meetings of Faith and Order for making the Nicene-Constantinopolitan Creed the "basis and instrument" of the resultant Faith and Order study, "Towards the Common Expression of the Apostolic Faith Today." This procedure imposed itself over the problems Western liberals have with the substance of the creed, and over the difficulties many Africans in particular have with its "Greek" conceptuality. (A Jamaican Baptist declared that, despite his suspicion of the creedal form, he stood with the divinity of Christ over against reductionist accounts.) There may have taken place a slight shift of emphasis on Pannenberg's part as the true colors of liberalism became more evident to him. He has always maintained that "personal confession of Jesus" *(Bekenntnis zu Jesus)* suffices for access to the Church and its sacraments. Already in a paper of 1973 on "Confessions and the Unity of Christians," however, he recognized that, as early as the New Testament period itself, willingness to use the language of the Church *of the time* was a necessary test in order to ensure that the would-be believer intended the object of the Church's proclamation (e.g., Mark 8:29; Rom. 10:9; 1 Cor. 12:3; 1 John 4:15). Pannenberg's enthusiasm for the Nicene-Constantinopolitan Creed may betoken a deeper appreciation for the *diachronic continuity* needed at the linguistic level—somewhat along the lines of the Church as a cultural-linguistic tradition, as in George Lindbeck's *Nature of Doctrine*—in order to maintain the identity of the Church's message and faith. It may also show a greater sensitivity to the need to make explicit the trinitarian dimensions of "confession of Jesus."

Such an emphasis would certainly be valuable in the United States. A typescript draft for the liturgical inauguration of the interchurch covenant proposed by the Consultation on Church Unity *nowhere* invoked the Trinity by its scriptural and traditional name. When shown the text, I suggested several places in which this might be done, including the recitation of the creed. The draft published in "Covenanting towards Unity: From Consensus to Communion" (1985) does now include the Nicene Creed. For the proposed rapprochement between the denominations to be clearly located within the historic Christian tradition, it would be good if its doctrinal basis could make bolder use of the declarations in "The COCU Consensus," which in its 1976 and 1980 versions specified that baptism takes place "in the name of the Father, the Son, and the Holy Spirit," with a confession of faith in the same, and dared to admit that "the Church confesses and worships in glad celebration the one God, Father, Son, and Holy Spirit." One fears that the move will be rather in the other direction, as when the 1986 *Book of Worship* of the United Church of Christ bowdlerizes scriptural and traditional language and retains as the sole naming of "the Father, the Son, and the Holy Spirit" the baptismal formula—and that, allegedly, purely "for ecumenical reasons." Such an isolated use will fossilize the formula, the vitality of which depends on its relation to the continued telling of God's story in those terms and the use of the Name in the regular prayer life of the Church. The loss of Christian substance is a real danger in a culture where the faculty of a leading divinity school, scarcely disguised, can be said by John Updike, in *Roger's Version,* to consist of "lapsed Unitarians" (Fawcett Crest edition, p. 28). Unless memory deceives me, it was by Pannenberg's formulation that the following crucial paragraph appears in the current version of the thoroughly trinitarian WCC text on the apostolic faith:

> In Jesus' language about God, "Father" is not only an image, it is primarily the *name* of the God to whom he relates in his mission and whose kingdom he proclaims. It is the name used to address God in prayer. In its function as a name, the name of God in Jesus' own teaching and prayer, the word "Father" cannot be replaced by another one. It would no longer be the God of Jesus to whom we relate, if we were to exclude the name Jesus himself used.

(Faith and Order Paper 140 [1987])

2. The Lima Text

Pannenberg did not belong to the small drafting group for "Baptism, Eucharist and Ministry"; but he contributed to special preparatory studies, he spoke to the subject in plenary meetings of the Faith and Order

Commission, and since its appearance in 1982 he has energetically advocated the Lima text and defended it in face of German Protestant criticisms. His article "Lima pro und contra" in *Kerygma und Dogma* 1986/1 is particularly important. It is ironic that, against those who desire, for instance, a stronger insistence on the dominical institution of Baptism and the Lord's Supper, Pannenberg should have needed to point out that it was precisely as a result of the near-universal influence of German Protestant historical-critical exegesis that the Lima text adopted such delicate phraseology at these points and "rooted" baptism more comprehensively in the life, death, and resurrection of Jesus and showed the broader continuity of the Eucharist with all the significant meals in his ministry. Pannenberg has been deft, too, at quoting the Reformers back at those who claim that Lima positions are "unacceptable" to "the churches of the Reformation." Thus he can show the compatibility of Lima's eucharistic anamnesis with Luther's view that we lay our offering of praise and thanks upon Christ as our mediator (WA 6, 368f.), and of Lima's notion of ordained ministers as representatives of Christ with the Apology of the Augsburg Confession 7, that "they do not represent their own persons but the person of Christ, because of the Church's call, as Christ testifies: 'Whoever hears you hears me' (Luke 10:16). When they offer the word of Christ or the sacraments, they do so in Christ's place and stead."

With regard to baptism, in particular, Pannenberg opines—in face of those who fear the loss of the divine action and a drift towards works-righteousness—that the Lima text "offers for the first time the basis for an agreement" between pedobaptists and Baptists which "respects the need to keep baptism and faith together, while not reducing baptism to a supplementary act of confession on the part of the believer, but rather holding fast to its character of a work of God towards the human being, its transmission of the Spirit, and its unrepeatability." It is gratifying to remember that the decisive pre-Lima consultation on this point took place on American soil, at Louisville, between equally strong contingents on each side. It is noteworthy, too, that it is in this country that, given the denominational configurations, the most significant construction could eventually take place, if Lima provides the "base" that Pannenberg hopes it will for the resolution of the "infant" versus "adult" problem.

With regard to the Eucharist, Pannenberg stresses that it is "the Lord's table" and regards "confession to Christ" as the sufficient condition of Communion. He expects that a table mutually open to their respective members will allow the divided churches to be brought—by this divine mystery which in any case passes understanding—to closer unity in the Lord. I myself used to take such a "productive" view of intercommunion, but I have become much more hesitant. A historian colleague of mine at Duke holds that it is time—given the ease with which Americans practice intercommunion and the transfer of membership across denominations—for official ecumenism to do what perhaps the United States government should have done in Vietnam, namely "declare victory, and pull out." For my part, I am suspicious of the current doctrinal indifferentism and institutional minimalism. For *doctrine* and *institution* come close to *faith* and *order,* which are integral to Christianity. Eucharistically, I am concerned for the *identity* of the celebrating community and therefore of the message it is proclaiming.

With regard to the ordained ministry, Pannenberg insists on its traditional role as a sign and agent of ecclesial unity, on local, regional, and universal planes. He objects to the misinterpretation of the *satis est* in the seventh article of the Augsburg Confession which would relegate the ministry to the indifferent level of ceremony. While showing considerable sympathy for the threefold pattern, he wishes to keep open the Reformation position that bishop and presbyter are essentially the same order. I will reserve for later discussion the relation between structures of ministry and models of unity. Suffice it here to say that Pannenberg's views on episcopal, and even primatial, ministry are likely to find more understanding in the English-speaking world, familiar with the Chicago–Lambeth Quadrilateral, than they have so far found in Middle European Protestantism.

IV. PROTESTANTS AND CATHOLICS

Pannenberg writes as a Lutheran, but he is more willing than some to let the Reformed come to voice when it comes to presenting a Protestant position, and he generally highlights the harmony between and among the Reformation traditions. Vis-à-vis Roman Catholicism, Pannenberg stresses the substantive continuity which the Augsburg Confession (and indeed Calvin) claims with the patristic church; and on this basis he extends to Protestants, and to other doctrinal themes, the famous remark made by Joseph Ratzinger in his Graz lecture of 1976 that the Orthodox should not be asked for more in the matter of primacy than Rome expected of them in the first millennium.

Let us look at Pannenberg's position on three topics in Protestant/ Catholic relations: justification, papal primacy, and the teaching office.

1. Justification

On justification "um Christi willen . . . ohne Verdienst . . . durch den Glauben," said Luther as late as the Smalcald Articles of 1537, stands "alles, . . . was wir wider den Papst, den Teufel und die Welt lehren." It is Pannenberg's perception that "this Lutheran doctrine of justification no longer counts as church-dividing in the theological discussion of today." For this he gives credit to such Roman Catholic scholars as Joseph Lortz, Hans Küng, Otto Hermann Pesch, and Vinzenz Pfnür . . . and to Karl Barth! While he does not cite a reciprocal remark from a Lutheran scholar concerning the teaching of Trent on the matter, Pannenberg reckons that Roman Catholic theologians now largely accept that Luther's thoughts concerning justification—albeit in an unfamiliar form which made their reception difficult for the scholastic tradition—"express a fundamental Christian truth," and he looks for an official Roman Catholic confirmation that Luther's teaching is "in its substance catholic."

When, however, Pannenberg goes on to the "Christian freedom" which corresponds to Luther's teaching on justification, he draws some consequences which might (I imagine) make many Catholics call back into question the basis on which the conclusions rest. This may be especially the case when Pannenberg declares that "Christian freedom, and what goes inseparably with it" is the particular, and apparently the only, contribution which Protestantism has to bring into a renewed Christendom. Although the believer's "immediacy to God" requires the human mediation of preaching, it appears to allow such a variety (which Pannenberg approves) in the relation of the Christian faith to social life, in the understanding of faith and in theology, and in the forms of the Church that, as the course of history after the Reformation and to this day seems to show, it is hard to stop a slide into that individualism with which old-fashioned Catholics reproach Protestants and which Pannenberg himself regrets. Justification through faith, in its Lutheran understanding, and applied, as Lutherans are wont to apply it, as a single criterion for every point of doctrine and life, produces strange results that are hard to square with a more comprehensive and nuanced version of Christianity.

The United States dialogue between Lutherans and Catholics was a little more reticent in its claims concerning the amount of agreement achieved on the subject of justification. In "Justification by Faith" (1983), the group was able to agree on a "fundamental affirmation":

> Our entire hope of justification and salvation rests on Christ Jesus and on the gospel whereby the good news of God's merciful action in Christ is made known; we do not place our ultimate trust in anything other than God's promise and saving work in Christ (§§4, 157).[1]

Yet the dialogue has explicitly *not* reached agreement on "faith *alone*," and does *not* claim its agreement is "fully equivalent to the Reformation teaching on justification" (§157). Oddly, the text also refers—without disowning it—to a recent trend in Lutheran thinking, that "God's word does what it proclaims or, in modern terminology, the gospel message is performative; it effects the reality of which it speaks. The preaching of the gospel has the force of decreeing the forgiveness of sins for Christ's sake. . . .In this hermeneutical perspective even the faith which receives the promise is not a condition for justification" (§§88-89). When salvation is thus reduced to coming within earshot of the gospel, the *sola fide* becomes a *sine fide*. Ironically, we there have the (mistakenly conceived) *ex opere operato* against which Lutherans used to rail and which responsible Catholic thought denies. It is doubtful that Pannenberg would subscribe to this strange interpretation of justification which would seem to make it harder for even the most sympathetic of good Catholic thinkers in their search for a convergence with Protestant understandings.

---

1. *Justification by Faith*, ed. H. George Anderson, T. Austin Murphy, and Joseph A. Burgess (Minneapolis: Augsburg, 1985), 16, 72.

2. Primacy

Pannenberg is persuaded of the need not only for a local and a regional but also for a universal ministry of unity, and he is open to the bishop of Rome's playing this role in a reformed and renewed way. Here he is not so different from the American Catholic/Lutheran dialogue reported in "Papal Primacy and the Universal Church" (1974).

When the Roman see is allowed a "primacy of honor" only, and an infallibility that appears limited to what is already (or nowadays, one perhaps has to say, still!) believed by "the Church as a whole" (a question-begging term!), and a jurisdiction that at best extends to "the Latin patriarchate" and remains radically open to question by mature and critical believers, then we may wonder how this vision of Pannenberg's differs from the popular adulation accorded John Paul II by American Catholics and their widespread ignorance or rejection of his significant, albeit not formally "infallible," teaching on important issues of faith and morals. But surely this is not very satisfactory.

3. Magisterium

Neither Pannenberg nor the international Lutheran/Catholic Commission have given such sustained treatment to the question of magisterium as is found in the American Catholic/Lutheran study "Teaching Authority and Infallibility in the Church" (1978).

In what Pannenberg does write on the matter, I find that he tends not adequately to distinguish and relate faith, doctrine, and theology. In this he may be handicapped by the German Protestant usage of the word *Lehre,* which shades toward (individual) theology rather than (official) dogma. At any rate, Pannenberg tends to pair doctrine and theology under the single head of "understandings of the faith," but the resultant weakness on the dogmatic side of doctrine leaves "simple believers"—and theologians in their capacity as believers—without firm guidance in matters of faith, and the Christian community or communities without instances to settle new, difficult or disputed questions.

In the 120th of his "Theses on the Theology of the Church," Pannenberg shows himself well aware of the dilemma in which the

Protestant churches in particular—but perhaps also the contemporary Roman Catholic church—find themselves:

> Since the Scripture principle gained autonomy from the Church's magisterium through the development of an academic exegesis of the Scriptures in the Middle Ages, and especially since the development of historical-critical scholarship on the Scriptures in the seventeenth and eighteenth centuries, the testing of the unity of the contemporary Church with its origin has in practice been performed by theology. Bishops no longer need to guarantee this unity, for this task has fallen to theology in a combination of historical criticism and the systematic and practical disciplines. Yet theology, for its part, has in no way thereby taken over the function of authoritative teaching. Rather, such a function has become quite unacceptable in an intellectual situation determined by the Enlightenment.[2]

When the 19th-century Russian Orthodox theologian Aleksei S. Khomyakov—without the intention of flattering either side—predicted that once the papal magisterium declined, Roman Catholics would turn out to be thoroughly "Protestant" in their approach to the Christian faith and life, he was putting his finger on the problem of how to maintain any pastoral teaching at all within a cohesive ecclesial community in the modern West.

As yet, Pannenberg has not, to my knowledge, offered even a sketch to the resolution of this dilemma. He insists that in the coming unity of the Church there shall be variety of "doctrine" (I hope he means theology). He is certainly concerned for the continuing freedom of theology, but attempts no theoretical justification that would encourage theologians in their *responsibility* to advise the bishops or councils in the maintenance or recovery of the faith. Small wonder that so many of our pastoral leaders remain *ratlos* in this bewildering time. Happily, Pannenberg's practical engagement in the cause of faith and order is making an important contribution to doctrinal unity at the ecumenical level. It would be interesting to hear what concrete form he envisions for ongoing and final dogmatic authority in a united Church.

---

2. Pannenberg, *Thesen zur Theologie der Kirche* (Munich: Claudius Verlag, 1970), 45-46.

How is the commensurability, the compatibility, and finally the agreement, of different doctrinal formulations and theological positions to be determined? Vagueness here is one of the problems with the kind of proposals made by K. Rahner and H. Fries in their *Unity of the Churches—An Actual Possibility*.[3] The Congregation for the Doctrine of the Faith, or its future equivalent, would have an even more difficult task than now. Given the inherited historical diversity among the churches, given the apparently insatiable individualism even of Christians in the modern West, given the speed of intellectual and cultural change in our time, and given the shift of Christianity towards parts of the world where the faith is encountering other religious traditions, it is hard to think that a universally united Church in the foreseeable future could ensure its own doctrinal consistency and cohesion with only the same procedures as have obtained in Eastern Orthodoxy since the Seventh Ecumenical Council. It may be that the procedures necessary within a united Church will and can only *emerge* as part of the process of attaining unity in the first place.

V. CHURCH UNITY AND HUMAN COMMUNITY

According to Pannenberg, the best contribution the Church has to make to human community is, by its own being and life, to signify the unity which belongs to the kingdom of God. He can call Christian unity "the principal task of the Church in our century."

What form should Christian unity take? Among proposed models, Pannenberg rejects both "reconciled diversity," since that seems to underplay the need for change and renewal, and "organic union," if that is understood as organizational merger. The "mutual recognition" for which he works and pleads is to be grounded in the basic faith, but will allow considerable variety in theology, styles of worship, and structures of common life.

We have seen Pannenberg attaching vital importance to a ministry of unity. What would that mean, concretely, at the episcopal level? He is not much clearer than the international commission between the

---

3. K. Rahner and H. Fries, *Unity of the Churches—An Actual Possibility* (Philadelphia: Fortress; and New York: Paulist, 1985; German, 1983).

Lutheran World Federation and the Roman Catholic church, in "Das geistliche Amt in der Kirche" (1981) and "Einheit vor uns" (1985), as to whether this would mean confessionally "parallel" and geographically "overlapping" episcopates, or rather a fully integrated episcopal ministry with a single bishop in each unitary place. His "conciliar fellowship of bishops" is not precise on this matter.

I wonder how Pannenberg would respond to my own vision—similar to the one developed by Richard Norris, with an eye to the United States scene[4]—of a

> web of "dioceses" (probably much smaller than the dioceses, or equivalents, of any single existing denomination), each containing "congregations" in various liturgical, spiritual, and cultural styles, with free interchange of affiliation among individual members, and each diocese being in conciliar communion with all other dioceses in the land and indeed in every part of the world where unity among Christians had progressed thus far. . . . Full Christian unity includes a complete sharing of faith and life, and that ultimately entails a unified structure of order and governance. At each geographical level, Christian communities should regulate all that lies within their own competence (such is the principle of subsidiarity), while an ever-widening network of relationships is needed to ensure catholicity.[5]

The bishop would constitute the unifying ministerial presence in the diocese, the basic "unit," while the presbyters and the parishes would embody, where appropriate, the diversity of the traditions. Any transdiocesan structures that were deemed necessary in the united Church for preserving the positive values of the previously separate traditions might resemble the "religious orders" within the present Roman Catholic church and would certainly carry less ecclesiological weight than existing denominational structures. In a letter to me of June 2, 1987, Pannenberg speaks of the possibility of "an autocephalous status for the Protestant churches on conditions that have to be spelt out"—which is weightier than I myself would think desirable.

For Pannenberg, the preservation of confessional inheritances is

---

4. "What Is 'Church Unity'?" *One in Christ* 18 (1982): 117-130.
5. G. Wainwright, *The Ecumenical Moment* (Grand Rapids: Eerdmans, 1983), 10-12.

important not only out of fidelity to God's grace towards us even in our times of separation, and as a recognition of the "partial" character of our Christian knowledge and life before the final coming of God's rule, but also as part of the legitimate pluriformity that would help to make Christianity tolerant and attractive in its relations with other religions and society at large.

Pannenberg considers religious liberty—grounded, as we saw, in the immediacy to God implied by the doctrine of justification—as a vital contribution of the Protestant Reformation to the later history of the Church and of humankind, even if it "needed" the wars of religion to establish the principle and practice of toleration. Pannenberg makes the internecine conflicts among Christians to a large degree responsible for the unfortunate *secularization* of the concept of freedom in the modern world. The "free society," it is becoming increasingly evident, is a colossus with feet of clay. The concept of freedom has become "contentless," a "hollow form of individual whim." Phenomenologically and anthropologically, Pannenberg argues for a fresh recognition of the ineluctably *religious* basis of society and the commonwealth.

Here Pannenberg introduces the notion of "truth," commitment to (the search for) which should provide a common context for Christians, adherents of other religions, and people with no historic religious allegiance. This certainly raises problems, on the one hand, for proponents of philosophical perspectivalism, who deny the possibility of locating an objective truth, and, on the other hand, for Christians who hold that, with due allowance for the eschatological reserve, Jesus Christ is already the anticipatory revelation of the all-determining reality which is God. Nevertheless, the very prospect of debate on these matters should challenge American Christians and churches to hold their place in the academy and the public square.

VI. ECUMENISM AND THEOLOGY

Wolfhart Pannenberg belongs to the rapidly and regrettably declining number of theologians who cannot be suspected of engaging in ecumenism because of their incapacity for the ostensibly harder intellectual task of a more philosophically oriented reflection. His participation, helps to keep ecumenism doctrinally honest and, in turn, allows his own broader theological work to stay in touch with the living ecclesial tradition.

Pannenberg continues to advocate the restoration of Faith and Order to the central position it held before the restructuring of the World Council of Churches by the Uppsala Assembly in the "revolutionary" year of 1968. It is indeed curious that Faith and Order should still need to fight against its in-house marginalization when the Lima text on "Baptism, Eucharist and Ministry" has proved to be the most exciting and widely discussed document in modern ecumenical history, translated into some 40 languages, and already having its effect on catechetical and liturgical revisions and in interchurch dialogue. In the United States, we may be grateful for the tireless and imaginative efforts of Brother Jeffrey Gros in the Faith and Order office of the National Council of Churches, an organization which has been principally oriented to social ethics since its beginnings.

Despite his advocacy of an immediate opening of eucharistic communion to individual believers, Pannenberg is well aware that full "mutual recognition" from church to church demands hard theological work at the level of doctrine. By precept and example, he maintains the importance and the quality of such work. He thereby demonstrates the inadequacy of a sentimental or practical ecumenism that would reduce unity to feeling or collaboration. Both temptations beset American Christianity. Christianity would die if the opinion ever came to prevail that every doctrinal formulation, every theological position was just as good—which would mean just as empty—as any other. An ecumenism bought at that price would be worthless. We must therefore be particularly grateful for the serious doctrinal effort that has gone into the Consultation on Church Union (and hope that it will not be derailed by current pressures), and for the quite remarkable products of the national Lutheran/Roman Catholic dialogues that have been published since 1965.

There are many signs in Pannenberg's theological writings that as a Lutheran he has benefited from engagement with the Eastern Orthodox churches and, even more, the Roman Catholic and other Western churches. Here he sets an important example to us all for the ecclesial and ecumenical location of Christian theology. It is, however, noteworthy that he has never lived or taught in Africa, Asia, or the Pacific, where he might have drawn on the life of the churches in less classical form. By this I do not mean to suggest that an—allegedly "Western"—intellectual approach to Christianity has anything less than universal value. But a fully catholic theology will integrate the *thinking* that takes place in the life situations of the churches throughout the world. Like all of us to varying degrees, Pannenberg is limited in this respect. But it may be that our internal pluriformity in the United States makes Americans sensitive to the need.

Over a decade I have, by grace of the Faith and Order Commission of the World Council of Churches, enjoyed the personal, academic, and ecumenical friendship of Wolfhart Pannenberg, and I express my gratitude by saluting him through this chapter written for his 60th birthday. *Vivat et floreat!*

PART III

APPLICATIONS

9

THEOLOGY
for
CHURCH AND POLIS

Richard John Neuhaus

◆

In preparing for this essay I went back, for the first time in years, to "A Profile of a Theologian," which I wrote exactly 20 years ago and which was intended to introduce Wolfhart Pannenberg to an American readership.[1] I suppose that it might be called an authorized profile, since it was approved by Pannenberg in its final form, but it was also a very personal statement of my undisguised excitement about the promise of Pannenberg for American religious thought. Whether it is boast or confession, whether it is reason for embarrassment or confidence, 20 years later there is very little that I would change in my understanding of Pannenberg's project and its high promise for Christian theology, and for the reconstruction of a philosophy for the public order.

And yet, in terms of the reception of Pannenberg's work, it must be admitted that that promise is still very much a promise. In one sense, that is appropriate, since Pannenberg first gained attention as a proponent of the "theology of promise," or, as it was more commonly

---

1. Richard John Neuhaus, "Profile of a Theologian," in *Theology and the Kingdom of God* (Philadelphia: Westminster, 1969).

226

called in the 1960s, the "theology of hope." Others were more prominent in that connection, notably Jürgen Moltmann, Johann Baptist
Metz, and, in his more historical moments, Karl Rahner. But the theologically literate were aware of Pannenberg in the background. He was
presumably working on the philosophical underpinnings of the theology
of hope which, as presented by Moltmann and others, was more or
less another theme of biblical theology. Two decades later, with very
important exceptions (including contributors to the present volume),
Wolfhart Pannenberg remains a figure in the background of the consciousness of North American theologians and religious ethicists. My
distinct impression is that he is more respected than read. Certainly he
has not been "discovered" as a theological celebrity and, for reasons
I will come to, that is not likely to happen—which may be just as well.
More troubling in my experience is the number of serious theological
thinkers who admit, usually with a measure of uneasiness, that they
have not yet gotten around to dealing with Pannenberg as earnestly as
they suspect they should. There is nothing like a Pannenberg "school"
in this country. His work is widely acknowledged as a major "option"
on the theological scene, but it is seldom engaged on its own terms as
a challenge to the idea that theology consists in the entertainment of
options.

Of course I may underestimate the influence of Pannenberg on
American theological thought, but I think not. If my reading of the
situation is marked by a note of disappointment, it is because I thought
more than 20 years ago, and I think now, that Pannenberg's is the single
most ambitious and impressive project in constructive theology in the
Christian world today. Through his writings and in person, I have over
the years learned more by arguing with Pannenberg than by agreeing
with any other living theologian. It is worth exploring briefly why that
enthusiasm is not more widely shared. It was more easily explained
in 1968 when only one of Pannenberg's major works, the Christology,
had appeared in English. But now 13 books, plus occasional writings,
are readily available. I have not counted, but I would not be surprised
if the Christology, *Jesus—God and Man,* received more, and more
extended, reviews than all the other books combined. Indeed one recalls
that for a little while even some writers of a fundamentalist disposition
celebrated Pannenberg because of his argument for the historical evi-

dence of the resurrection. He was lauded as the "theologian of the resurrection" until these admirers discovered that his position on the "historicity" of the resurrection had nothing to do with their understanding of biblical inerrancy.

The relative neglect (relative, that is, to what is warranted) of Pannenberg's work to date has several explanations. He is—it is commonly said and can hardly be protested—hard to read. Not only are the ideas demanding, but the style is, as they say, "Germanic"—heavy, ponderous, lumbering, persistently winding in its interconnectedness. In some instances he has been poorly served by translators, but it cannot be denied that his German is rigorous and his written English not felicitous. Given the relaxed standards of contemporary theological education, that explains in large part why Pannenberg is not the rage in seminaries and divinity schools. But it does not explain why he is also neglected by more thoughtful people not so easily intimidated by stylistic obstacles.

Pannenberg offends against the cult of specialization that has in recent decades gripped the theological guild. This too is related to the above-mentioned interconnectedness of his work. Pannenberg is something of a polymath and asks his reader to join him in reaching to make connections between usually disparate disciplines of a maddening variety. (Those who are voguishly "interdisciplinary" in their approach discover the meaning of the term in encountering Pannenberg.) The interconnectedness of Pannenberg's thought is not the product of intellectual pretension nor simply a matter of personal disposition. It is at the heart of his argument that theology is the science of the meaning of all things. His is a theology of history understood as the totality of reality. Pannenberg is keenly aware of the limits of any person's knowing and has no illusions about being a universal man in the sense of being a universal expert. But, to use another term that suffers from voguish employment, his work is profoundly dialogical. Theology must engage, enter into, other *logoi,* which is both possible and imperative because of the universal reason symbolized by the *Logos* in whom all truth is engaged and comprehended.

Put differently, Pannenberg's work is not amenable to what the French call the *bricollage* treatment. It cannot, like a Tinkertoy, be eclectically taken apart and put together differently. The pieces do not readily lend themselves to uses apart from the whole. The result is that to engage Pannenberg seriously is to make a major investment of time and energy. In a world in which most theologians struggle to "stay on top" of their own specialities, the prospect of such an investment is forbidding. I have heard this described as an aspect of the "imperialism" of Pannenberg's enterprise; it simply demands too much on its own terms. It seems likely that more people will be persuaded to make the requisite investment when the number of those who have discovered its rewards reaches a kind of critical mass in American theology. That has not happened to date, although it may be hoped that the present book will contribute to its happening. An additional obstacle, of course, is that, after the passing of such as Barth and Tillich, it was announced and widely believed that the age of the great systems in theology is definitively past. Such an announcement has a self-fulfilling effect and is, needless to say, exceedingly convenient in a theological multiverse increasingly fragmented by specialization. In such a situation, Pannenberg's project is defiantly—some think outrageously—architectonic in its systematic aspiration.

Pannenberg's being German is no doubt both advantage and disability. While in the past streams of American theology had their source in European thought, and German scholarship possessed a most particular panache, there is an ambivalence toward the post–World War II Germany of which Pannenberg is a representative. The Europeans who for a time cast a long shadow in this country were heroes and expatriates in relation to the Hitler era, such as Bonhoeffer, Barth, and Tillich. For those who came after the Hitler era there was no similarly clear-cut test of personal and intellectual authenticity. Since the politically pressurized 1960s, American theology—both in old-line Protestantism and, increasingly, in Roman Catholicism—has become quite explicit in applying political tests of orthodoxy. Although a theology of politics is not Pannenberg's central concern, and he rejects political theology in principle, he has run up against that orthodoxy on occasion. His understanding of the delicate connections between Christian truth claims, liberal democracy, and the role of the United States in world-historical change, for example, is not tailored to fit the regnant prejudices in American academic religion. In both intellectual style and substance, then, Pannenberg is moving against the stream. He has no constituency, so to speak, apart from readers concerned for the ideas that constitute the Christian construction of reality. The truths that most interest him are not instrumental truths, they are not immediately useful for any purpose other than understanding the truth. His uncompromising rejection of the claim that truth is defined by the *praxis* of sociopolitical consequence creates a deep breach between Pannenberg and much of contemporary theology. He is not "doing" a genitival "theology of" for any group or class or cause. Not surprisingly, proponents of genitival or unabashedly partisan theologies reject the possibility of simply practicing Christian theology and thus suspect him of false consciousness or, worse, bad faith. (Of course, "simply" practicing theology is by no means simple, as Pannenberg's work amply demonstrates.)

To suggest that Pannenberg is indifferent to the historical, including the political, consequences of Christian theology would be a grave error. He is a theologian of the Church in the sense that he understands himself to be, as a *Christian* theologian, the servant of an historically identifiable tradition and of the community that bears that tradition. One must immediately add, however, that devotion to that tradition and that community is only warranted if they bear the truth about the world, about all reality. The Church is for the world, but it must frequently, in both appearance and fact, be against the world at those points where the world misunderstands or refuses to accept the truth about itself. The gospel of God's self-revelation in Jesus and the promise of the coming kingdom is the truth about the world—or so Christianity and Christians claim. Our aspiration to be liberated encounters the promise that that truth will make us free. That truth defines the meaning of freedom. Our inclination, however, is to get this entirely backwards. We think we know what freedom means, and whatever contributes to our understanding of freedom we then declare to be the truth. Thus the relationship between freedom and truth is exactly inverted, which is one definition of sin. It is the structural sin, so to speak, of much that is called liberation theology today.[2]

2. Wolfhart Pannenberg, "Christianity, Marxism and Liberation Theology," unpublished manuscript, 1987; cf. idem, "The Future and the Unity of Mankind," in *Ethics* (Philadelphia: Westminster, 1981), 175ff.

In Pannenberg's thought, the world has an enormous stake, indeed it has everything at stake, in the future of the gospel, if, as claimed, the gospel is the truth about the world. This is the connection that makes necessary Pannenberg's deep concern for ecumenism. The unity of Christians is an anticipation of and a sign of promise for the unity of humankind. The reconciled diversity of the Church models the reconciled diversity of the polis. Marxists and others are correct to say that human beings are alienated, from one another, from society, from reality. But their understanding of the cause and remedy of such alienation is profoundly wrongheaded, Pannenberg contends. Their analysis "does not uncover the real causes of the typically modern experience of alienation, causes that lie in the abstraction of our public culture from its religious roots."[3] As to Marxism's proposed remedy, Pannenberg argues that it rests upon an anthropology that is "inherently atheistic and unacceptable from the point of view of Christian personalism." "The Marxist economic description is not, as many liberation theologians assume, an ideologically neutral, analytic instrument. It is not in that sense scientific. If one does not subscribe to the anthropological presuppositions, empirical evidence will lead to quite different descriptions of the economic process."[4] It is also ecumenically significant that Pannenberg is generally well disposed to the two "instructions" on liberation theology issued by the Vatican's Congregation for the Doctrine of the Faith in 1984 and 1986. While he believes that "a more detailed critical assessment of Marxist theory" is required, he writes that "in general the warnings of the Congregation are appropriate."[5]

Marxists of various sorts are not alone in proposing what is the cause and what is the remedy of human alienation. On the non-Marxist left and on the right, ideas are set forth to advance the unity of humankind. Some such ideas are hard utopian, some soft utopian, some technological or pragmatic. The temptation of Christians is to reduce the gospel to being an appendage to such proposals and programs. Pannenberg has long been active on the Faith and Order side of the

---

3. "Christianity, Marxism and Liberation Theology," 13.
4. Ibid., 9.
5. Ibid., 16.

World Council of Churches, and has long been concerned that the WCC has relentlessly subordinated theological reflection, and the gospel itself, to understandings of the human project that are uninformed by, if not explicitly opposed to, the Christian construction of reality. Thus he suggests that the ecumenical theme, "The Unity of the Church— The Unity of Humankind," has, in effect, been inverted. "In the WCC, as well as in Vatican Council II, the ecumenical emphasis was that the Church, as a sacramental reality, symbolizes the future unity of a new humankind in the Kingdom of God. . . . But now that theme is turned around. It is said that the unity of humankind is to be envisioned in secular, largely economic and political terms, quite apart from the symbolism of the Church. Some even go further and say that the unity of the Church must be defined in terms of agreement in the struggle to achieve this unity of humankind. The implications of this reversal are vast, and I do not think that we have given careful thought to it."[6] The vast and perfectly logical implication is made explicit by those liberation theologians who reconstruct Christian ecclesiology in terms of "the partisan church."[7]

So again it appears that Pannenberg is moving against the stream. The objection may be raised that, for someone to whom the future is such a critical referent, that is the wrong direction in which to be moving. But such an objection belies a very short-range understanding of a future determined by existent currents and trends. The time frame in which Pannenberg locates his enterprise includes millennia of human reflection on the meaning of reality and, more specifically, of Christian reflection. The future toward which Christian theology points is the Absolute Future that is God in the fullness of his rule over all things. This temporal spaciousness for theology's work provides ample room for critical distance from the clamorous immediacies of the historical moment. Pannenberg has been accused of remaining "aloof" from some of the current "options" in the theological world that many

---

6. Richard John Neuhaus, "Pannenberg Jousts with the World Council of Churches," *The Christian Century*, February 17, 1981, 174ff.

7. For a detailed critique of the idea of "partisan church" which draws on Pannenberg and relates specifically to the German experience, see the author's "A Cautionary Tale," in *The Catholic Moment: The Paradox of the Church in the Postmodern World* (New York: Harper & Row, 1987).

consider not to be optional at all. Usually mentioned in this connection are feminist theology, third-world theologies, and similar undertakings. It is a mistake to think that Pannenberg is indifferent to such movements and the excitement they generate in the contemporary Christian world. As we have seen, he has directly and indirectly addressed the proposals of various liberation theologies in considerable detail.

Within the entire range of history, Pannenberg takes the historical moment that is his very seriously indeed. He does not dismiss as mere fads or trendiness movements that claim the attention of many serious people. He knows that in some circles he is accused of being exclusively preoccupied with "white, male, North Atlantic theology." To this he responds that ecumenical theology must include the widest possible range of theological reflection: "Everybody knows that some of the most vital Christian forces in today's world are in Africa and Asia. Their theological work is making a difference and will make a bigger difference. Nobody who is theologically serious can resist it. The problem is with the definition of Christian theology itself. Christian theology has a specific history. Theological reflection must make its contribution within the context of that history."[8] The last sentence underscores that, far from being "arrogant" or "imperialistic," as some charge, this understanding of the theological task is profoundly modest. We cannot change the definition of Christian theology at will, no matter how much we might want to. There is a history, typically a very troubling history, that is a given, and those who would be Christian theologians must understand that they are part of that history. This Pannenberg posits against the gnosticism that is an ever-present temptation in the life of the Church. In recent history, elements of German theological thought, he is keenly aware, succumbed for a time to the gnostic temptation in trying to "de-Judaize" Christianity. Our time is no different from other times in producing "radical" theologies that are quite the opposite of being radical in that they cut themselves off from the historical roots of theology and, in a manner all too familiar since the earliest years of Christianity, set forth a *gnosis* which is declared by the knowing to be true Christianity.

---

8. "Pannenberg Jousts," 175.

These movements cannot be lightly dismissed. Since they importantly influence the life of the Christian community, they must be of great pastoral and catechetical concern. But Pannenberg's self-understanding is that he is a theologian working within and from a historically specifiable discourse that is Christian theology. Part of his responsibility as a theologian is to raise the question about forms of theology that are beyond the boundaries of that historical community of discourse. This has everything to do with the public nature of Christian theology and the claims that it makes. Christianity is not a private knowledge or experience that can be arbitrarily expressed in any form we may choose. Here we can understand the importance of Pannenberg's sustained critique of "pietism." What Pannenberg means by pietism in theology is very close to what George Lindbeck describes as the typically liberal "experiential–expressive" mode of theology.[9] In that mode, theology is essentially reflection on religious experience which is presumed to be universal and can be expressed, more or less adequately, in any set of religious symbols. By contrast, Pannenberg insists that the Christian message is in fact a message, that it contains truth claims that are public in nature and are therefore accessible and vulnerable to critical reason.

Pannenberg's understanding of the theologians' task, then, is both more modest and more audacious. Contra gnostic flights and pietistic poesy, the subject matter and form of theology are historically defined. And yet, most audaciously, Christian theology claims to engage the ultimate meaning of absolutely everything, and declares itself ready to dispute in public alternative definitions of reality. This is a high-risk understanding of theology that stresses vulnerability, and it is therefore curious that it is sometimes confused with "triumphalism." Pannenberg would contend, correctly I believe, that it is the pietist or experiential-expressivist who is the true triumphalist. In that theological mode, one always holds trump, which is an invulnerable religious experience that is impervious to critical reason or historical falsification. Here it is important to underscore that one has not understood Pannenberg's project until it is understood that, in his view, Christianity could turn out to be wrong. To put it quite bluntly, it is conceivable that Jesus is not

9. George Lindbeck, *The Nature of Doctrine* (Philadelphia: Westminster, 1984).

raised from the dead and the kingdom of God is not coming after all. That is why Christians live by faith and hope. Faith and hope are not the product of private inspiration but are premised upon public evidence and reason and will be vindicated or falsified in public.

Christians are frequently embarrassed by the audacity of Christianity's claim. This is particularly true in a time of pervasive relativism such as ours. In an odd twist, however, many of those who suggest that religious symbols and statements are relative turn out not to be relativists at all. They have simply retreated from public discourse, relocating the absolute in the sphere of private experience where it is safe from intersubjective challenge by public reason and evidence. Pannenberg, by contrast, believes that it is not triumphalism but a decent respect for the truth that should prevent Christianity from trimming its claims when it encounters other ways of understanding reality, including other religions. It is certainly the case that in the dialogue between Christianity and other world religions all the parties to the dialogue are changed. Christianity and Christian theology have by no means reached their definitive form. Indeed we may well be the early Church. But Christianity has a specific history and what it becomes will be in a continuity of identity with what it is and has been. And, yes, there finally will be or will not be a triumph. Every knee will or every knee will not finally bow at the name that is, through all the changes worked by time, historically identifiable as that of Jesus the Christ. And, to the unspeakable joy or embarrassment of those of us who are Christians, everybody will know how it turned out.

Pannenberg's theological work is, as he repeatedly says, "from below." Here is his decisive break from Barth, who was his teacher and for whom Pannenberg continues to express a respect bordering on reverence. It is precisely from this earth-bound and history-bound perspective, however, that we perceive our dependence upon the transcendent. The earth-bound nature of our reflection in no way shuts us off from the transcendent, for, as the psalmist says, the earth is full of the glory of the Lord. Pannenberg's insistence upon the rationality of faith in no way confines Christian truth claims or experience to the canons of scientific rationality as found, for example, in the natural sciences.[10] Reason vibrantly exercised is touched by the wingtips of angelic hosts. Once again, it is a mark of the ambition of Pannenberg's project that he challenges conventional antinomies such as the particular against the universal, the immanent against the transcendent. Pannenberg warmly welcomed the "Hartford Appeal for Theological Affirmation" of 1975 that descried a "pervasive and debilitating loss of transcendence" in contemporary Christian thought. He noted two common aberrations in modern Christianity and acclaimed the Hartford Appeal as "a remarkable event because it attacks both aberrations at the same time."[11]

The first aberration, he wrote, "is to compromise with the intellectual fashions of the day in the hope of gaining at least temporary relief from the growing tensions between secular thought and the Christian tradition." The second, "which arises especially when the potential dangers of compromise are realized, is the temptation to throw the Christian fundaments into the face, so to speak, of modern thought." The second is most evident in forms of pietism and sectarianism, but both aberrations constitute a surrender. "Neither comes to terms with the requirements implicit in the fact that the affirmations of the Christian faith make a claim to truth." Pannenberg's thought, I believe, allows for and even nurtures dimensions of Christianity usually associated with an accent on the transcendent—spirituality, worship, and even mystical experience. And yet it must be admitted that his writings on these subjects are among his least successful. There are no doubt a number of reasons for this, but I expect the chief reason is that Pannenberg, like most of us, tends to accent that which he thinks is most dangerously neglected by others. Large sectors of contemporary Christianity are awash in a "spirituality" of unbridled subjectivism. It is against this danger that Pannenberg so forcefully emphasizes the rational and public nature of Christianity, sometimes running the risk of being misunderstood as a rational*ist* who denies or neglects the angelic presences that fill the worlds of which our world is part. I am convinced that that is a misunderstanding, but I admit that I am convinced more

---

10. This is worked out in great detail in Pannenberg, *Theology and the Philosophy of Science* (London: Darton, Longman & Todd, 1976).

11. Pannenberg, "Breaking Ground for Renewed Faith," *Worldview*, June 1975, 37f.

on the basis of personal knowledge of Pannenberg than on the basis of his writings.

In his historical essay on the Hartford Appeal, George Lindbeck wrote, "The Hartford Appeal is *sui generis* because it battles for the possibility of theology rather than itself proposing a theology."[12] The theological situation that has to date been largely resistant to Pannenberg's influence is one that tends to deny the possibility of theology. Theology is construed to be many things—critical reflection on religious experience, passion and poetry in support of programs of sociopolitical change, heightened expression of processes of self-actualization, philosophical underpinning for systems of morality—but it is very frequently not *theo*logy. When theologians have nothing to say about God, it is doubtful that they have anything to say at all *as theologians*. The offense of Pannenberg is that he is determined to speak of God in public. Given the theological situation, I expect he will continue to offend many. Of course that situation can and will change, and it may change for the better. Lindbeck's "postmodern" proposal of "cultural–linguistic traditions" in *The Nature of Doctrine* is, I believe, a promising portent. Similarly, aspects of the emphasis on narrative theology can contribute importantly to a reappropriation of the historical context in which Christian theology again becomes identifiable and possible. Other changes not yet perceptible may well be underway.

But, whatever changes may or may not be in the offing, Wolfhart Pannenberg will continue to go on with his life project. This single-mindedness is awesome. Pannenberg believes that he knows his place within the historical scheme of theology, and he knows that that place is assured. It is assured not because of the brilliance of his work but because that is simply how the history of thought works. There is something new under the sun. There are historically particular thoughts that have not been thought before in relation to other thoughts, there are lines of inquiry that have not been pursued before in relation to other lines of inquiry. One is reminded of Isaiah Berlin's famed image

---

12. George A. Lindbeck, "A Battle for Theology: Hartford in Historical Perspective," in *Against the World for the World,* ed. Peter L. Berger and Richard John Neuhaus (New York: Seabury, 1976).

of the hedgehog and the fox. Pannenberg is both hedgehog and fox. He is fox in discovering connections and analogies of the most disparate variety, but he is most of all hedgehog, bringing everything into the service of working through the ramifications of a few key proposals central to the Christian construction of reality.

Few would deny that Pannenberg is a premier presence in contemporary theology. He has not to date, however, been as effective a presence as his work warrants. I have tried to suggest some of the reasons why this might be so. We do not know what the future holds, but there are several reasons to hope that the influence of the Pannenberg project is on the increase. He will, *deo volente,* be active and productive for many years (the first volume of the systematic theology appears only this year). In this country the achievement of the aforementioned critical mass of theological attention may be near. But most of all—and I admit this may be wishful thinking—one senses that thoughtful people are weary of derivative and auxiliary theologies, of theologies that are drawn from and ancillary to definitions of reality unrelated to the Christian proposition. There may be a new climate of Christian readiness, and cultural readiness, for the audacity of truth. If so, that should translate into a new openness to the Pannenberg project. And that in turn will, I am confident, redound to a renewed understanding of both Church and polis—and, by no means incidentally, to the glory of God.

10

PANNENBERG'S
ESCHATOLOGICAL ETHICS

Ted Peters

◆

s we approach the dawn of the third millenium we strain to
see what the first rays of new light will reveal about our future.
Our apocalyptic anxiety engenders the fear that we will create
our own artificial light—a temporary thermonuclear light—which may
shortly plunge us back into an oblivion of darkness. And, if we are
successful at postponing such a holocaust, we still fear that we may
stumble on in a self-inflicted darkness that hides the hovels of the poor,
covers over the scars of oppression, disguises the tyranny of an ex-
ploitative economic order, and camouflages the forces that make for
injustice.

These concerns, combined with the ecological concerns which the
Club of Rome a decade and a half ago dubbed the *world problematique,*
have produced a contemporary consciousness that is global, pluralistic,
wholistic, futuristic, and apocalyptic. Our consciousness is *global* because we realize that the economy and safety of every location in the
world are interdependent, that a major upheaval in one land necessarily
affects life everywhere. It is *pluralistic* because of the rising tide of a
sense of entitlement, the spreading conviction that ethnic and cultural
traditions have a right to extend themselves without the domination of
a single cultural or political empire. As the flip side of pluralism, our

consciousness is *wholistic,* because we recognize that the protection of one group's integrity is incumbent upon all groups, and that all together make for a richer whole. It is *futuristic* because we recognize the open-endedness of events and because we believe that creative action by the present generation can lead to something new and better in the decades to come. Finally, it is *apocalyptic,* because what might happen could be of ultimate significance to the future of the human race and perhaps even to life in general on our planet. Ours is a time calling for serious thinking about matters ethical and political, about ultimate values and social commitments, about the will of God and the deeds of humanity. Christians along with all other people of good will need to ponder the theory and inspire the action appropriate to the challenges of the 21st century.

What we need today are ethical sanctions which justify as well as inspire the call to a future-oriented, global-oriented co-creatorship. By the term *sanction* here we mean something close to what Amos Wilder does, namely, an intersubjective consideration, tacit or expressed, which enforces a moral imperative.[1] In other words, a sanction provides the reason for pursuing what is good while defining what is good. The fundamental biblical imperative is no secret: love God and neighbor. This imperative, which Jesus calls the two great commandments, is no matter of personal taste. Nor is it an obligation enjoined only upon those individuals who happen to have chosen to follow Jesus. It is an imperative enjoined upon us all. What is its sanction? We will suggest here that the command and paradoxical freedom to love creatively are grounded in—and sanctioned by—God's promise for the consummate fulfillment of all things.

What we need, then, is an eschatological grounding for ethics which, on the one hand, takes seriously the contributions of human activity in mundane history while, on the other hand, affirming that eschatological salvation is a free act of God which comes to us as a gift regardless of human contributions to it. We need in addition a universal ethical vision with compelling power, an inspiring vision which in itself calls for and enlists the support of people of good will.

---

1. Amos N. Wilder, *Eschatology and Ethics in the Teaching of Jesus* (New York: Harper, 1939, 1950).

Our thesis here is that, of the contemporary alternatives, the proleptic eschatology of Wolfhart Pannenberg most adequately serves to establish the foundation for such an ethical vision. It is more adequate than a more disjunctive eschatology, such as that of John Howard Yoder, because the Pannenberg approach affirms human effort aimed directly at the secular world and is not limited to the church alone. It is also more adequate than the strictly conjunctive eschatology of John Cobb which, because it lops off the consummate end to history, viscerates the power of the symbol of God's kingdom to sanction ethical commitment. It is also more adequate than the combination conjunctive–disjunctive eschatology of the liberation theologians, because the Pannenberg approach better takes into account the global and wholistic dimensions of political intentions. I will also suggest in passing that Pannenberg's ethics provides much more support for the revolutionary agenda of liberation theology than his critics or even Pannenberg himself will normally admit. It is to the basic structure of Pannenberg's ethics that we first turn.

THE HEART OF PANNENBERG'S ARGUMENT

Pannenberg works with an axiological ethic, a theory of the ground of value. The fundamental problem is to establish the ground for valuing independently from the arbitrariness of subjective preference. We need an ontological foundation for ethics. What this means is that we need to locate the point of convergence between the source of the good and the source of being. The point of such a convergence for any Christian theologian, of course, is going to be God. It is God who determines both what is and also what is good.

That convergence cannot be located in the present state of being, however. What exists now is not itself good. We are constantly seeking for what is good, for a good which we at present do not have. Socrates even defined the good as that which all people lack and after which they strive. Present being is not good enough. We must go beyond. The source of the good is transcendent. Where Pannenberg takes us is to the future which transcends the present. The being of the future has a priority over everything extant. It is the future of God which determines the good.

His [God's] rule, and therefore the full revelation of his existence too, is still future. This corresponds to the futurity of the good which is not conclusively possessed but always the object of our striving. Thus it may be asserted that God, as identical with the coming of his imminent Kingdom, is the concrete embodiment of the good. This good has priority over against all human striving for the good. In this sense the Kingdom of God defines the ultimate horizon for all ethical statements.[2]

Pannenberg's next step is to move from the transcendent source of being and goodness in the future to the situation in the present. The present is slated for transformation. God loves the world. So do we. "The striving for God as the ultimate good beyond the world is turned into concern for the world."[3] It is God's intention to transform the world through his rule of the world. The most constructive consequence of such an ethic is the Christian idea of love which affirms the present world while seeking its transformation. The individual moves beyond the pale of his or her own personal happiness in the present, realizing that the fulfillment of the individual is interdependent with the fulfilling of the whole of creation. Pannenberg calls this a "conversion to the world."

Pannenberg stresses that our love for the world participates in God's love for the world. Loving God and loving the world are not two separate things. Pannenberg's ontology seeks to correct a past error here. In the past Christians have been tempted to think of God as a transcendent *being,* an entity which exists in some heavenly realm separate from the world in which we live. When God is so conceived, ethicists can speak of a "vertical" love for God in combination with a second love, a "horizontal" love, which we have for one another. This is a mistake. We can remedy this mistake by conceiving of God proper as God's rule. Pannenberg identifies the being of God with the coming kingdom or rule of God. By loving one another and by loving our world now, we are actually participating in the transforming power of God's rule, of God's love.

---

2. Wolfhart Pannenberg, "The Kingdom of God and the Foundation of Ethics," in *Theology and the Kingdom of God* (Philadelphia: Westminster, 1969), 111. Cf. *Ethics,* trans. Keith Crim (Philadelphia: Westminster, 1981), 181.

3. Pannenberg, *Theology and the Kingdom of God,* 111.

We need more clearly to see that love for fellowmen is participation in God's love; that is to say, love for fellowmen is participation in the coming Kingdom of God. The priority of God's coming Kingdom and the possibility of our participating in the coming Kingdom is, properly understood, the meaning of grace.[4]

This means that the absolute good transcends the relative good as the ultimate future transcends the dynamic present. The way we express our love and participate in God's love, then, is to throw ourselves into what is temporal, changing, and provisional. Commitment to what is provisional is essential to Christian faith in the coming kingdom of God. To withhold such a commitment because we are waiting for something transcendent would mean betraying the kingdom. And yet it is the special contribution of the eschatological understanding of the yet outstanding kingdom that it does not allow for any particular social institution to become absolute. Everything we accomplish and appreciate now is provisional. It is subject to transformation by a still higher good. This wipes away the ground for any conservatism which seeks to maintain the established order at all cost. The futurity of God's rule actually serves to open up possibilities for ethical action while still denying any human institution the glory of perfection which might warrant its making an absolute claim on us for obedience. The kingdom of God, just because it is eschatological, draws us beyond the present state of being and prohibits the claim to totalitarian rule by any temporal dictator.

These qualities of openness and provisionality serve to give love a dynamic and creative character. There is no divine law or moral code which can in advance delineate what a loving person ought to do. Loving is not conforming. It is creating. Pannenberg says that love involves "creative imagination." While commenting on the question in Luke 10 which led to Jesus' telling of the parable of the good Samaritan, "Who is my neighbor?" Pannenberg says we should not simply wait around for our neighbors to show up and identify themselves. We should be going out to create new neighbors.[5] Love is

---

4. Ibid., 113.
5. Pannenberg, *Ethics*, 65.

creative and aggressive and ever seeking new ways to cultivate domains of communal wholeness.[6] "True love nurtures wholeness," he writes.[7]

This leads, then, to what we are calling a *proleptic ethic*. It is an ethic of anticipation, participation, and creation. We begin by recognizing that God loves the world with a creative communion. We participate in this communion of creative transformation. God loves with a "creative love which supports all creatures, grants them their limited duration, and brings them to fulfillment of life by relating them to one another. . . . His love is creating unity, the particular unities which go to make up the individual, and the unities which integrate individuals in society. . . . If a particular action springs from the spirit of creative love and contributes to individual and social integration, unity, and peace, then that particular action expresses the spirit of God's Kingdom."[8] When we as parts contribute to the harmony of the whole, we participate anticipatorily in the unity which all things will ultimately find in the eschatological kingdom of God. Ethical action in the present is proleptic in structure.

PROLEPTIC POLITICS

This has implications for politics. Citing Plato and Aristotle, Pannenberg holds that the human being is a "political" animal; and he agrees with Reinhold Niebuhr that the human community is primordial.[9] This corresponds appropriately to his belief that the eschatological kingdom of God will be as wide as the creation. It will be inclusive and unitive. It will not give priority to the interests of the individual person or the individual nation over against those of the whole community. A foundational principle of Pannenberg's political ethics is that the unity of the human race corresponds to the universality of the one God. This

---

6. Pannenberg analyzes Jesus' golden rule (Matt. 7:12; Luke 6:31) to show how it is rooted in divine love; then he argues that the religious foundation for ethics is laid when this love produces our readiness for community.

7. Pannenberg, *Theology and the Kingdom of God*, 118.

8. Ibid., 117f.

9. Wolfhart Pannenberg, *Anthropology in Theological Perspective*, trans. Matthew J. O'Connell (Philadelphia: Westminster, 1985), 445. "Human beings are indeed destined for a social life, and only in society can they live in a way that accords with their destiny. Their destiny is therefore in fact political . . ." (ibid., 476).

means that the global human community is given priority over national, ethnic, and class interests.

Hence, concern for the commonweal, understood primarily in terms of peace and justice,[10] ought to be elevated above the sovereignty of the people. The common good takes precedence over what any individual might perceive to be his or her own private good. It takes precedence over the programs of special-interest groups. "Politicians must have the courage to recognize the difference between the wishes of the people, even of a majority of the people, and the common good. . . . In its relevance to a particular social situation, the Kingdom of God is manifest in the common good."[11]

On this basis Pannenberg pits nationalism over against internationalism. He strongly favors the latter. Nationalism divides. Internationalism unites and thereby corresponds anticipatorily to the universal unity indicative of the coming kingdom of God.

> It has been the distinctive message of Jesus that the coming Kingdom of God as something future is already determining the present. In the light of the originally political nature of the hope for the Kingdom, this must hold true also for political life, and not only for the private life of Christians. And in political life the supreme concern will be the quest for a universal order of peace and justice.[12]

Concomitant with his stress on a *universal* rather than just a local or national order of peace and justice, Pannenberg finds theological support for the concept of democracy and its ethical ideals of *liberté, egalité, et fraternité*. Democracy is inherently universal in its conception, because it is based upon the dignity and rights of individuals regardless of their respective ethnic history or national citizenship. Even though empirically we can see that many people in our world today do not in fact enjoy freedom and equality, we recognize that such is their God-appointed destiny. All "are called to a freedom and equality

---

10. "There is a correspondence between the justice of the state and the divine will to justice, the definitive accomplishment of which Christians await in the future of the reign of God" (ibid., 449).

11. Pannenberg, *Theology and the Kingdom of God*, 123.

12. Pannenberg, *Ethics*, 135.

before God, which is not yet present, but in which they believe."[13] What this means for us ethically and politically is that when confronted with actual enslavement and inequality, we are called to work creatively to make freedom and equality a historical reality. "Equality in the Christian sense means that everyone should be raised up through participation in the highest human possibilities. Such equality must always be created; it is not already there."[14] To pursue creatively the task of making freedom and equality an actuality gives expression to our sense of solidarity, our sense of brotherhood *(fraternité)*, our sense of the oneness which the human race enjoys before God.

DISJUNCTION AND CONJUNCTION

One of the abiding questions raised by any eschatological theory which takes temporal movement seriously is the relationship between future and present. Is it disjunctive, i.e., will the ultimate future be so radically different from the present that there will be little or no continuity? Or is it conjunctive, i.e., will actions in the present have significance for the reality yet to come? If the relationship is totally or strictly disjunctive, then it would follow that present ethical actions would be irrelevant to God's future; eschatology could not function as a sanction for intrahistorical ethics. If the relationship is strictly conjunctive, then we could argue that present ethical actions would have a determining impact on what will ultimately come; but we would do so at the risk of collapsing eschatology into history and losing the salvific contribution of divine grace. There is no doubt that an ethic based upon Christian eschatology must affirm both. One of the merits of Pannenberg's proleptic eschatology is that he can affirm both in a healthy complementarity.

On the one hand, Pannenberg certainly assumes a disjunction. One of the constant themes throughout his work is the contrast between the future kingdom of God and present reality. He warns us not to confuse them. Present reality is at best provisional. It will not endure.

> The human destiny of the individual can never be adequately fulfilled by the political order. The latter has but a provisional function: to ensure

13. Ibid., 140.
14. Ibid.

a peaceful communal life for human beings. Human salvation, however, can only be awaited in the coming world of God, and any participation in that future world is mediated in the present life not by the state but only by the sacramental and symbolic communion of the church.[15]

Pannenberg argues that the church should exist as an institution independent of the state just so it can remind the state of its provisionality. No temporal power is ultimate. No present institution is eternal. The church must exist as a prophetic witness and critic, reminding us of the disjunction between the divine future and the human present.[16]

The above-cited statement needs some further interpretation, however. He says that participation in the future world is mediated to us in the present. It is mediated by the sacramental and communal life of the church. This is what motivates Pannenberg's passion for ecumenism. We should seek Christian unity, he argues vehemently, because such unity embodies ahead of time the same unity which will characterize the unity of humanity in the coming kingdom of God.[17]

It would seem from this quotation that participation in the future kingdom is not mediated by the state. Elsewhere, however, Pannenberg comes close to saying that nonecclesial social structures such as the body politic can in fact anticipate the eschatological kingdom of God. In particular, international political structures which correspond to the universal domain of divine lordship provide contemporary expression of God's kingdom. This is in contrast to the individual nation-state which tends to exalt itself and then in the arena of competing nation-states pursue domination. Nationalism is divisive; internationalism is unitive.

Neither the United States of Europe nor the transformation of the United Nations into an organization that truly transcends national sovereignty with specific supreme laws would finally usher in the Kingdom of God on earth. But it might well be the case that efforts should be made in

---

15. Pannenberg, *Anthropology*, 477.

16. Wolfhart Pannenberg, *Jesus—God and Man*, 2d ed. (Philadelphia: Westminster, 1977), 377; and *Human Nature, Election, and History* (Philadelphia: Westminster, 1977), 31, 67, 81.

17. Pannenberg, *Ethics*, 19; *The Church*, trans. Keith Crim (Philadelphia: Westminster, 1983), 20f., 151f.

this direction which would lead to the form of the promised Kingdom of God that while still temporary, would be its best possible expression in our day.[18]

If this form of internationalism could count as the "best possible expression in our day" of the "promised Kingdom of God," then it appears that for Pannenberg there must be conjunction between eschatology and history, even secular history. The conjunction is proleptic in character. The point of prolepsis is that the future enters the present and exerts influence.[19] The role prolepsis plays for Pannenberg is akin to that which the incarnation plays in classical theology. Its significance is that the holy has entered profane history and claimed it. Should there follow a radical disjunction in which the future departs completely from present history, then the incarnation would be erased. Therefore, we could argue, there must be at minimum a continuity between the historical Jesus Christ and the eschatological salvation which he came to effect. In addition, there must be some continuity with the tradition of the effects which Jesus has had on human history *(Überlieferungs-geschichte)*. This would include, among other things, later developments in cultural ideals and ethical systems. It would include as well contemporary visions of a united humanity, of a single body politic for the whole world. This would seem to indicate that contemporary ethical behavior, influenced by the inspiration of Jesus which reaches us through the transmission of tradition, would have to have some eschatological significance.

Terms such as *consummation* and *fulfillment* would be appropriate for developing this notion of continuity. They indicate that the present is incomplete. It lacks its full quiddity. Present reality is provisional, awaiting something different. But that which we await is not a total departure but rather a completion of what has been started, a fulfillment of that for which we hope.

What concerns Pannenberg—and what should concern us—is the primary direction of causal efficacy. It is important for Pannenberg to observe that God's future has had and continues to have an impact

---

18. Pannenberg, *Ethics*, 136.
19. Pannenberg, *Jesus—God and Man*, 66, 206, 367; "The Revelation of God in Jesus of Nazareth," in *Theology as History*, New Frontiers in Theology 3, ed. James M. Robinson and John B. Cobb Jr. (New York: Harper & Row, 1967), 125.

upon our present situation. The direction of force comes from the future. God's tomorrow will not be the mere product of what we humans do today. The political systems we create, the international peace we establish, the social justice we achieve and other such accomplishments will not in themselves bring the kingdom of God into existence. Rather than causing God's future, Pannenberg would have to say, such accomplishments are better thought of as effects of God's future. They at best anticipate a fullness which is yet outstanding. They participate proleptically in what is yet to come. By giving priority to the future, Pannenberg can preserve emphasis on the initiation of God, on divine grace.

DISJUNCTION: JOHN HOWARD YODER

On the contemporary theological scene there are alternative ways to conceive of the relationship between eschatology and ethics. Some tend more toward excessive disjunction and others more toward excessive conjunction. Mennonite John Howard Yoder, for example, tends to drive such a wedge between eschatological salvation and social ethics that the tie becomes severed.

Yoder advocates an ethic of discipleship. As disciples of Jesus we conform to the law of love and thereby participate in the divine reality of love. What is relevant about Yoder's view is that he understands discipleship eschatologically.

In his book *The Politics of Jesus,* Yoder states that Jesus inaugurated the eschatological kingdom of God in his person. He brought the order of God's future aeon to bear on the present, but, according to Yoder, the order of God's rule is simply not comprehensible within our present aeon. The future and the present are fundamentally alien to one another. To be a disciple of Jesus, then, consists in embodying the new and strange amidst the old and familiar. It consists in radical obedience to God's future in direct conflict with all that the reality of the present world stands for. The church, which is made up of Jesus' disciples, becomes a deviant community. It does not complement the world. It contends against the world.

Yoder believes Jesus' disciples must make a hard choice between effectiveness and obedience. We cannot be effective in the present world, he contends, because the present aeon is fundamentally and irredeemably opposed to the eschatological aeon. All that we can do is be obedient. All that we can do is exhibit our citizenship in the future city of God while living now in an alien land. This path will lead undoubtedly to social rejection and our own condemnation to the cross.

A significant corollary for Yoder is that as disciples of Jesus we should not attempt to guide the course of historical events. We should not employ coercive political action for the purpose of trying to create a better world. It is not our task to manage world affairs. In fact, only when we have been freed "from the compulsiveness of the vision of ourselves as the guardians of history" can we "see ourselves as participants in the loving nature of God as revealed in Christ." Because we are plagued by the "urge to manage the world" we are unable to recognize God's "invitation to a servant stance in society." [20] Yoder is serious about Christians playing the servant role, but as servants we are not supposed to guard, guide, or manage. Here we must pause to ask Yoder: How then should we serve? This question reveals a problem with Yoder's position.

There is a fallacy in Yoder's argument. It is the fallacy of false alternatives. On what grounds must we decide between management and servanthood? Is it not possible to engage in both? When Joseph served Pharaoh—a slave to the Egyptian king—he worked as an executive manager of court affairs. Joseph was a steward. The concept of steward in the time of Jesus incorporated the combination of servanthood and management, and stewardship is often used as a metaphor for the life of faith. We might even observe that management and servanthood imply one another. How can one be a servant unless one does something? What is the opposite of management? Mismanagement? Nonmanagement? Noninvolvement? Twiddling one's thumbs while letting someone else do it? What does servanthood mean if it takes no responsibility for the course of ordinary historical events? If servanthood consists solely in obedience to a future reality which is alien to the present aeon, then it eviscerates any sense of stewardship of present resources and responsibility for the wider society of which

---

20. John Howard Yoder, *The Politics of Jesus* (Grand Rapids: Eerdmans, 1972), 248.

we are a part. Direct social or political action lacks an eschatological sanction.

In his more recent work, *The Priestly Kingdom,* Yoder argues that the reason we cannot manage the world is that we—members of the post-Constantinian church—are too small a group. We are a minority. We are impotent. Nevertheless, the church wishes to be "an instrument for serving and saving the larger culture."[21] The means for doing so is through a "modeling mission," i.e., existing now in the form that the world will exist ultimately.[22] There is a proleptic tone to what Yoder is proposing here, but it applies only to the company of Jesus' disciples and is not understood as having any direct effect on the world. Whereas in Yoder's earlier work we find the radical disjunction cast between future and present, here in his later work it is cast more as a disjunction between church and world.

The severity with which Yoder separates future from present seems to break the continuity between our obedient servanthood and the world around us which "God so loved" that he sent his Son into it. Much more amenable to what we are doing here is the work of James McClendon. McClendon follows Yoder in developing an eschatological ethic based upon the resurrection of Jesus, what he calls an "anastatic" ethic. Like Yoder he affirms the notion of the two aeons and the disjunction between Jesus' resurrection and ordinary life in the present aeon. But McClendon does not stop here. He presses on to ask just what implications the eschatologically new reality has for our day-to-day responsibilities to the world of nature and to human society.[23] Like Yoder he starts with the church, but McClendon moves more directly toward our responsibilities for the social world.

The reason we need an approach which is distinctively proleptic is the recognition that, even though we are dealing with two otherwise discontinuous aeons, the new aeon has entered the old and has left an impact, the impact of divine love upon it. Yoder would agree with this in part. But where he would differ with Pannenberg is that for Yoder

21. John Howard Yoder, *The Priestly Kingdom* (Notre Dame: University of Notre Dame Press, 1984), 11.

22. Ibid., 92.

23. James William McClendon Jr., *Ethics,* vol. 1 of *Systematic Theology* (Nashville: Abingdon, 1986), 248-253, 266.

this proleptic impact belongs strictly to the church. For Pannenberg, in contrast, it belongs to the church, to be sure, but to the world as well. If the state—or better, an international order—exercises justice, for example, it too participates anticipatorily in the eschatological justice of God. Even though the church is a leaven, so to speak, it is still the case that prolepsis is creation-wide.

Thus, there is a subtlety regarding the nature of our call to love that is overlooked by Yoder. If we pose the question, "Should we love the world?" we could line up both negative and positive answers and support both with biblical references. Texts such as 1 John 2:15 tell us not to love the world. The meaning in this case is plainly to avoid concupiscence or the type of love that seeks to possess that which is alien to God. But there is another dimension of God's *agapē* that leads to a positive love for the world. It is the divine love which led God himself down the path of the cross towards the redemption of this world, toward the fulfillment of God's creation. It is this of which John 3:16 speaks. It is this to which our ethical sanctions appeal. Alien or not, this is a world which we are commanded to love as God loves and, if we respond to the command in obedience and stewardly service, then we will actually participate in the divine *agapē*. And when we participate in the divine *agapē* our love for God, for the world, and for one another becomes authentic self-realization, an expression of who we truly are as human beings. It goes almost without saying that this will require involvement and even what Yoder disparagingly calls "management."

CONJUNCTION: JOHN COBB

Whereas with Yoder we see excessive disjunction, in the process theology of John B. Cobb Jr. we find such a degree of conjunction that the transcendent eschaton loses all force. Eschatology is almost exhaustively collapsed into the world process. What human beings do on the plane of history, then, becomes nearly decisive for our destiny, a strictly historical destiny.

Process theists in general, and John Cobb in particular, applaud Alfred North Whitehead for providing grounds for hope in history. Whitehead does this by asserting the openness of the future. This means that we are free to fill the future with the results of our decisions and the outcomes of our actions. We are free to write new chapters in the history of the world. This means that genuine progress is possible. Institutions and ideals can be changed for the better. The present is always ready for new acts which will transform the today and create a different tomorrow. And, as a special bonus, the products of these transformative acts have an impact upon God: they are retained in the everlasting divine memory. All this openness inspires hope in the likes of John Cobb.[24]

The only drawback, of course, is that such openness also means we can choose the opposite of progress. There is no assurance that the human species will move forward. We may choose to perpetuate human misery through political tyranny and economic exploitation, to increase our contamination of the biosphere with pollutants, or to burn it all in a thermonuclear firestorm. Progress is not guaranteed. Only process is.

The key point in process eschatology is that there is no end, no consummate fulfillment to conclude the present temporal process.[25] God is constantly at work in the world, of course, seeking to lure all occasions toward their proper fulfillment through the power of divine persuasion. God is constantly redeeming our experience for perpetual remembrance in the divine memory, transforming mundane enjoyment as well as mundane suffering into heavenly enjoyment. But there will never come a time when God will so act as to put a temporal end to sin, evil, suffering, and death. Rather, as the process continues unabated, God will take our evil experience up into the divine memory in such a way as to transform it into positive divine enjoyment.

Process theism . . . cannot provide the assurance that God's will is always done. It does affirm that, no matter how great the evil in the world, God acts persuasively upon the wreckage to bring from it whatever good is possible. . . . Because of God, life has meaning in the face of victorious evil. That meaning is that both in our own enjoyment and through our

---

24. John B. Cobb Jr. and David R. Griffin, *Process Theology* (Philadelphia: Westminster, 1976), 112.
25. Ibid., 117. "The process of the world does not aim at some remote Omega point. Its teleology is simply the creation of values moment by moment" (Charles Birch and John B. Cobb Jr., *The Liberation of Life* [Cambridge: At the University Press, 1981], 189).

adding to the enjoyment of others we contribute everlastingly to the joy of God.[26]

Thus, salvation, in the sense of actually overcoming evil, is something God enjoys even if we do not. This contrasts with Pannenberg, for whom the consummate end to history signals salvation for the world, not just for God.

What is significant for our discussion here is that for Cobb the sanctioning or drawing power of the future does not reside in some future actuality. In fact, if such a future actuality were promised, then this would contravene human freedom and openness for the future, at least as Cobb understands them. What the idea of the kingdom of God does for Cobb is to present us with an ideal, with an image, with a transcendent lure to draw us continually forward. The kingdom is not, however, a forthcoming actual state of affairs. The process as presently constituted, evil and all, is everlasting.

Cobb recognizes that what he shares with Pannenberg is an emphasis on the future, on the possibility of novelty and the power of the not-yet to shape what happens now. But what Cobb cannot accept is Pannenberg's insistence on an eschatological end, on the divinely promised consummation of history. To Cobb this seems to reduce or eliminate openness, not enhance it. In his essay in this book, Cobb says he associates openness *to* the future with openness *of* the future. As evidence he remarks that the danger of human self-destruction is a very real one, as if to say that if such self-destruction would occur then the consummation could not. Cobb's implied argument misses the point, I think, because one point of positing the eschatological end is to emphasize disjunction: if God can transform Calvary into Easter then God can transform human self-destruction into consummation.

With regard to the problem of freedom, Pannenberg's case is built on the observation that determination by the consummate end opens present history to freedom. It does not close it off. If the course of events were determined in advance, say by an act of predestination fixed in the past, then we would not have freedom in the present. But by positing an eschatological end which is essentially transformatory,

---

26. Cobb and Griffin, *Process Theology,* 118, 123.

in that it introduces salvific newness, and by positing that this future transformatory work of God is effective now proleptically, in that it shares with us now its power to create the new, then it is the eschatological reality which provides the condition for the possibility of authentic freedom within history.

What Cobb has done is take the notion that the kingdom of God is calling us forward and jettison the promise that someday God's will will "be done on earth as it is in heaven." Cobb admits that Jesus' original message regarding God's kingdom included the expectation of "the consummation of all things" which would be a "sharp break with the past." But due to certain reasons, e.g., the failure of the kingdom to arrive in Jesus' own imminent future and also the rise of modern consciousness which puts a gulf between ancient and modern understandings of how the world works, theologians today cannot simply repeat Jesus' beliefs. We need a formulation for our time. So Cobb proposes that we focus on the *call forward,* which is understood as a dynamic principle common to human experience and indicative of the world process as a whole. God is the one who calls us forward. How far forward is God calling us? All the way to the end, i.e., all the way to the consummation of history? No. We are being called forward to a certain quality of life within history. "The call forward is toward intensified life, heightened consciousness, expanded freedom, more sensitive love. . . ."[27]

This I would dub the fallacy of unwarranted abstraction. Cobb has abstracted the call forward along with his own version of the fruit of the Spirit, but he has discarded the essential content which gave the symbol of the kingdom of God its power in the first place, namely, God's promise that it would actually come. We now have the call, but we have lost the kingdom which originally issued the call. If we think that the kingdom will never come in actuality, then it functions only as an unrealistic ideal and it loses its power to sanction and inspire ethical principles in the present.

Cobb does not think so, of course. He plunges on to provide theoretical justification for what may be the most comprehensive and wholistic ethical vision in contemporary theology. He combines the

---

27. John B. Cobb Jr., *God and the World* (Philadelphia: Westminster, 1969), 56; cf. 44ff.

political and economic aspirations of the liberation theologians with the ecological concerns put forward by scientists and futurists. Using the powerful metaphor of "the web of life," Cobb and his colleagues follow the World Council of Churches in emphasizing the twin concerns for justice and sustainability.[28] We must pursue justice to make life worth living; yet we must pursue ecological sustainability if there is to be a just life to live. It is the concept of cosmic connectedness and the doctrine of internal relations in Whiteheadian philosophy which makes the transfer to a wholistic ethic so easy for Cobb. Everything is related to everything else; so all it requires is one small step to affirm that everyone has a responsibility for everyone else.

In many ways Cobb has given more attention than Pannenberg to working out the middle axioms and practical applications of his ethical principles. Even so, the Pannenberg ontology is no less universal or less wholistic than Whiteheadian metaphysics. Its applications are equally as broad. In addition, the Pannenberg eschatology provides stronger sanctions and a more powerful lure because of the divine promise of fulfillment.

In sum, by eliminating the notion of an eschatological end, Cobb has turned the symbol of the kingdom of God into a cipher for an unreachable ideal. He then places the whole weight of his ethics into the intrahistorical process. The result is total conjunction, i.e., we free human beings have the power to create a future destiny, a destiny which may be either utopia or oblivion, but it will be a destiny which we will have to live (or die) with. God's activity in behalf of the kingdom cannot significantly alter the course of events as far as we are concerned. Yes, of course, God can transform such events as they are absorbed into the divine memory, but the only effect this has on us is in their reappearing as a persuasive lure. There will never occur for us any freedom from or victory over the viscissitudes of the historical process.

LIBERATION THEOLOGY: CONJUNCTION PLUS DISJUNCTION?

One salient feature of the many current liberation theologies—Latin American, feminist, and black—is the unabashed eschatological excitement. José Miguez Bonino, for example, says that an eschatological

---

28. Birch and Cobb, *Liberation of Life*, 234.

faith makes it possible for us to invest our lives in the building of temporary and imperfect political orders with the certainty that this work is not meaningless or lost, that as stewards of the creation we actually participate "in love, the final justification of all fight against evil and destruction." [29] Rosemary Radford Ruether assigns a utopian function to the eschatological vision, a prophetic "vision of the new age to come in which the present system of injustice is overcome and God's intended reign of peace and justice is installed in history." [30] Letty Russell uses the term "advent shock" to make this same point, i.e., we in the present are maladjusted when compared to the anticipated future fulfillment which God has promised. [31] And James Cone explains how the promised eschatological fulfillment functions as both judge and lure:

> If death is the ultimate power and life has no future beyond this world, then the rulers of the state who control the policemen and the military are indeed our masters. They have our future in their hands and the oppressed can be made to obey laws of injustice. But if the oppressed, while living in history, can nonetheless see beyond it, if they can visualize an eschatological future beyond the history of their humiliation, then "the sigh of the oppressed," to use Marx's phrase, can become a cry of revolution against the established order. It is this revolutionary cry that is granted in the resurrection of Jesus. [32]

What the eschatological vision does for the liberation theologian is employ God's promise for a transformed future as the key which unlocks the fetters binding us to the present and past. The newness of the new creation provides us with critical distance over against the old forms of political tyranny and economic oppression. For us in our present generation to take up arms against injustice is to participate in the divine plan to establish a kingdom of justice in history. Gustavo Gutierrez draws the connection: "The attraction of 'what is to come'

29. José Miguez Bonino, *Doing Theology in a Revolutionary Situation* (Philadelphia: Fortress, 1975), 152.

30. Rosemary Radford Ruether, *Sexism and God-Talk: Toward a Feminist Theology* (Boston: Beacon, 1983), 24.

31. Letty Russell, *The Future of Partnership* (Philadelphia: Westminster, 1979), 102.

32. James H. Cone, *God of the Oppressed* (New York: Seabury, 1975), 160.

is the driving force of history. The attraction of Yahweh in history and his action at the end of history are inseparable."[33]

The decisive move in liberation theology is to draw a close connection between eschatological salvation at the end of history and political liberation within history. The precise nature of that connection is subtle, perhaps even ambiguous, and hence it has become the focus of considerable debate.

To ferret out the nature of this connection, we begin by noticing what position the liberation theologians oppose. They oppose an eschatology of radical disjunction, especially one which so spiritualizes the kingdom of God that it has no impact on our current social and political life. Gutierrez says that "a poorly understood spiritualization has often made us forget the human consequences of the eschatological promises and the power to transform unjust social structures which they imply. The elimination of misery and exploitation is a sign of the coming of the Kingdom."[34] Furthermore, Gutierrez says that the impact of the eschatological kingdom is not simply beyond history; it is within history. "The grace-sin conflict, the coming of the Kingdom, and the expectation of the parousia are also necessarily and inevitably historical, temporal, earthly, social, and material realities."[35]

The practical objective of the liberation theology project is the creation of a new humanity, a social humanity; it is the establishment of a truly human and humane society, one characterized by political and economic justice and by the freedom to be free.[36] This is God's work. It is our work. They are conjoined. Hence, Gutierrez can define "liberation" with reference to

> three levels of meaning: political liberation, the liberation of man throughout history, liberation from sin and admission to communion with God. . . . These three levels mutually affect each other, but they are not the same. One is not present without the others, but they are distinct: they are all part of a single, all-encompassing salvific process, but they are to be found at different levels.[37]

---

33. Gustavo Gutierrez, *A Theology of Liberation* (Maryknoll, N.Y.: Orbis, 1973), 164.
34. Ibid., 167.
35. Ibid.
36. Ibid., 22, 67, 238.
37. Ibid., 176.

It is at this point that the critics attack liberation theologians in general, and Gutierrez in particular, for excessive conjunction, i.e., for unnecessarily conflating eschatological salvation beyond history with liberation within history. Pannenberg is one such critic. With regard to Gutierrez's above-mentioned three levels of liberation, Pannenberg complains that there may be no more than a mere verbal connection between them. He inquires about the warrant for seeing these three as different levels of the same process. He asks, "What if the conception of human history as a process of human self-liberation emerged in diametrical opposition to the Christian affirmation that human beings become free, not by themselves, but only by the spirit of Christ? How is it possible to harmonize such a conflict by speaking of 'levels' in one and the same process? But Gutierrez does not try to harmonize, he merely overlooks the problem."[38] In other words, we get our modern ideas of freedom from the Enlightenment and from Marxism. But the Enlightenment was critical of Christ-centeredness and Marxism was outright atheistic. From the driver's seat of history they removed God and substituted human self-initiation. Human freedom is now assumed to be the accomplishment of human freedom. So, Pannenberg is asking, if Christians begin with the axiom that true freedom is found in Jesus Christ, and if Jesus Christ plays no role in the Enlightenment and Marxist views of freedom, then how can Gutierrez so glibly identify both of these as belonging to the same process?

Pannenberg renders a second criticism. He argues that Gutierrez and others fail to work from an adequate theory of justice, and this makes them unable to discriminate between legitimate and nonlegitimate claims to represent genuine liberation. Or, to put it another way, there is nothing in the process of liberation so conceived which will protect us against the rise of a new tyranny. "It [liberation theology] does not offer any means to prevent tyrannical rule by an elite that might obtain power under the pretext of 'liberating' the people from oppression. . . . Some liberation theologians are so unaware of the dangers at this point that they even reject the distinction in European eschatological theology between the ultimate future of God's Kingdom and the provisional and fragmentary anticipations of that future in

---

38. Wolfhart Pannenberg, *Christian Spirituality* (Philadelphia: Westminster, 1983), 65.

human action."[39] Langdon Gilkey's criticism is parallel. He too objects to

> the apparent *identification* of liberation and especially of political and social liberation with the salvation promised in the gospel. This is expressed through the identification of the eschatological kingdom with a perfect historical society, a fully just political and social reality. . . . [This view] forgets that self-determination is the ground not only of the fullest humanity but also of sin—for it is in our use of our *freedom* that we each sin against our neighbor. . . . The freeing of freedom frees us for sin as well as for good works, for the creation of injustice as well as the creation of justice. . . . Thus the "freeing of freedom" in human society, even if it were to be achieved, and however valid a political and a Christian goal it may be, would by no means represent the final redemption of mankind or of history; for it is in freedom that we all sin. . . . Only a new relation of mankind to God, to self, and to the neighbor can achieve that goal, an achievement far beyond the range of political activity.[40]

What Pannenberg and Gilkey are saying is that it would be a big mistake to conflate eschatological salvation with intrahistorical liberation, i.e., to have exhaustive conjunction with no remaining disjunction. Even the greatest achievement of political and historical freedom would not touch the fundamental problem of human sin, the fundamental problem of alienation between one human being and another and between all of us and God. Freedom is as much the condition for the possibility to sin as it is the redemption from sin. Whatever eschatological salvation is, it must be more than what can be achieved through political and social transformation within history.

But, we might ask, have the liberation theologians actually conflated eschatology and history? One critic, Dennis McCann, interprets Gutierrez as distinguishing though not separating the two. He notes that here Christian eschatology and utopian aspirations are intimately correlated but not identified. What they have in common is that "history is one," but they are distinct in that Christian eschatology remains in

---

39. Ibid., 63. At this point Pannenberg refers us to Hugo Assmann, not Gutierrez.
40. Langdon Gilkey, *Reaping the Whirlwind: A Christian Interpretation of History* (New York: Seabury, 1976), 236f., Gilkey's italics.

tension with political aspirations. This tension is maintained, not by contrasting history with an eschatological reality beyond history, but rather by perpetuating the revolutionary process of liberation. Liberation becomes a process, not an achievement. Each achievement will be open to further transformation. All social and political gains are still surpassable. "The eschatological promise, in other words, symbolizes transcendence, but a transcendence immanent to history itself."[41] In short, the McCann critique is that although Gutierrez retains a disjunctive or transcendent component to his eschatology, it does not bespeak an actual end to history or consummation to history. It is rather a mere cipher for the ongoingness of the transformation process. Or, to put it another way, Gutierrez comes out looking a lot like John Cobb.

I believe the McCann interpretation is closer to accuracy than that of Pannenberg and Gilkey, but it is not close enough.[42] Gutierrez does not simply conflate salvation and liberation. Eschatology is not exhaustively swallowed up by history. Eschatological salvation still counts for something which intrahistorical liberation cannot of itself achieve, and this would ordinarily imply that there must be an actual consummation for it to count. Gutierrez does not actually deny a temporal consummation.

> This is not an identification. Without liberating historical events, there would be no growth of the Kingdom. But the process of liberation will not have conquered the very roots of oppression and the exploitation of man by man without the coming of the Kingdom, which is above all a gift. Moreover, we can say that the historical, political liberating event *is* a salvific event; but it is not *the* coming of the Kingdom, not *all* of salvation.[43]

That there remains some sort of disjunction between temporal

---

41. Dennis P. McCann, *Christian Realism and Liberation Theology* (Maryknoll, N.Y.: Orbis, 1981), 193. The heart of McCann's criticism of Gutierrez is that he fails to clarify the theological relationship between liberation and salvation (ibid., 4).

42. Matthew Lamb will not grant that McCann even comes close. He objects vehemently to McCann's contention that transcendence for Gutierrez is immanent to history itself. Lamb cites Gutierrez to the effect that salvation in Christ conducts history "above and beyond itself" to a fulfillment that is not within the reach of human foresight or any human effort ("A Distorted Interpretation of Latin American Liberation Theology," *Horizons* 8:2 [Fall 1981]: 359).

43. Gutierrez, *Theology of Liberation*, 177.

achievement and eschatological grace should be clear. Thus, the Pannenberg and Gilkey criticisms—especially if applied to Gutierrez—border on commiting the straw theologian fallacy here. If Gutierrez and other liberation theologians exhaustively collapsed eschatological salvation into political liberation, then their criticisms would definitely apply. But this is not the position Gutierrez actually takes. He is aware that an intrahistorical utopia is beyond the scope of sinful human striving and that the gospel includes, among other things, the promise of divine grace to achieve what we cannot on our own achieve. If there is a weakness in the Gutierrez project, it is his failure to spell out with clarity just what are the conjunctive and disjunctive components of his eschatologically inspired process of liberation. But they are both there.

It would seem to me that a carefully thought-through liberation theology—especially with its emphasis on revolution—should be a logical extension of Pannenberg's eschatology. Pannenberg's view provides both the vision for transformation as well as the critical judgment that renders all temporal achievements as but provisional anticipations of what is yet to come. On the one hand, we want to acknowledge that the power of God's eschatological future is being mediated to human history proleptically and that this has a transforming effect on the course of events. On the other hand, because salvation itself is a free act of God's grace, the eschatological kingdom cannot be exhaustively actualized prior to the end of history as we know it.

Perhaps El Salvadoran liberation theologian Jon Sobrino takes better account of these concerns. He employs his own version of the "eschatological reservation" in order, first, to affirm that the kingdom of God is mediated to history through liberation politics while, second, providing the judgment that no social achievement within history can be considered the last word. The eschatological kingdom of God does not confirm the present reality of oppression; but rather it passes judgment on that reality in order to recreate it. It also involves a "temporal fulfillment of the world which, strictly speaking, is not the work of people insofar as it is a fulfillment. It is the work of the God who comes." He recognizes the "tension between fashioning the Kingdom on the one hand and asserting that God is drawing near in grace on the other. On the basis of Jesus' own eschatology we can say that both aspects are real and important. . . ."[44] Such a position ought to escape the criticism of Pannenberg. It should, because Sobrino borrowed it from Pannenberg.

Certainly Carl Braaten saw the revolutionary potential in Pannenberg's eschatology when he wrote his "little dogmatic," *The Future of God*, nearly 20 years ago, at a time before the term "liberation theology" became a commonplace.[45] He argued that it was Pannenberg's understanding of the future which marks the "breakthrough" to a theology of revolution. Braaten said that once we grasp the significance of eschatological newness we will see how it applies to social and political transformation within history. Yes, of course, Braaten shares with Gilkey and Pannenberg the criticism that liberation theologians risk losing the significance of human sin and the need for grace proclaimed in the gospel; that they risk losing the disjunction between history and eschatology. But he applauds them for recognizing that God is pressing for the historical liberation of human beings, not just through the church, but even through a host of secular media.[46] The liberation theologians have recognized that the gospel has called Christians to the front lines of history to practice the good news of liberation for all humankind, beginning with the poor and the oppressed.

With this in mind Braaten goes on to offer a "holistic theology of the Kingdom of God" through which he hopes to give expression both to the depth dimension of the eschatological idea of salvation as well as to the breadth dimension of the historical concern for liberation. "Holistic salvation is both other-worldly and this-worldly, present and future, somatic and spiritual, personal and social, religious and secular, historical and eschatological. Persons cannot be saved minus their world. Thus, *liberation* is not a new word *for* salvation; it *is* salvation under the ambiguous conditions of history."[47]

What the Pannenberg vision could add to the liberation vision is universality and the kind of wholism of which Braaten speaks. The

---

44. John Sobrino, *Christology at the Crossroads* (Maryknoll, N.Y.: Orbis, 1978), 65f.; cf. xviii, 355.

45. Carl E. Braaten, *The Future of God* (New York: Harper & Row, 1969), 12.

46. Carl E. Braaten, *Principles of Lutheran Theology* (Philadelphia: Fortress, 1983), 134.

47. Carl E. Braaten, *The Flaming Center: A Theology of the Christian Mission* (Philadelphia: Fortress, 1977), 150.

ethical limitation of liberation theology is that it presupposes the class struggle as axiomatic, so that the Christian must always choose to side with one historical group over against another. The group we should choose is the poor, say the liberationists, because God too chooses the poor. We side with the poorer classes within a given nation, and we side with the poorer nations against the richer nations. The liberation theologian can at best give only lip service to the concept of a single universal humanity. Our actual ethical decision-making is limited to an advocacy which perpetuates competition. The result is pluralism to the exclusion of wholism.

The Pannenberg ethic, in contrast, is universal and wholistic. The eschatological vision of the coming kingdom of God in Pannenberg's thought is as comprehensive as the human race itself, as comprehensive as even the creation itself. Consequently, the burden of proleptic ethics is on those principles and actions which move us toward greater unity, toward overcoming class divisions for the edification of everyone and not just the underclass. The justice he seeks is a universal justice which goes beyond mere redress for the victims of oppression. This universalist thrust should also press our ethical vision beyond justice concerns to include ecological concerns. John 3:16 reports that God loved the *world*, not just some of the people within the world. It is the universality of this vision which corresponds to—and hence participates proleptically in—the coming kingdom of God.

CONCLUSION

In sum, what Pannenberg shares with the disjunctive eschatology of John Howard Yoder is the proleptic task enjoined upon the church to witness to God's future and to decry all claims to absolutism by political regimes by reminding them of their provisionality. What Pannenberg should share with the conjunctive process theology of John Cobb is a more intentional interweaving of political and ecological agendas. Similarly, Pannenberg should recognize there is a greater affinity than he usually admits between himself and the liberation theologians on the call for revolution in the name of justice.

The achievement of Pannenberg has been to lay a foundation for a universal ethic based upon the promised eschatological act of God whereby history will be consummated and reality will attain its final quiddity. It is a view which maintains the disjunction between history and eschatology, between human achievement and divine gift, between sin and grace. It recognizes the necessary newness which the final advent of the kingdom of God will embody, a newness required if it is to be identified with salvation. Yet this view also maintains the notion of conjunction. It does so with the idea of prolepsis. What prolepsis takes from eschatology and invokes within history is the dynamic of newness, the dynamic of creativity as an expression of freedom and as a force for healing. Revolutionary work within history can, if it issues from the anticipated justice and peace of the promised kingdom of God, actually participate in the divine love which transforms the world. It is this vision of what is to come which provides the sanction for a political and even an ecological ethics.

11

THE ROLE OF SCIENCE IN PANNENBERG'S THEOLOGICAL THINKING

Philip Hefner

◆

This essay will set forth a thesis concerning the significance of the sciences for the body of theological thinking which Wolfhart Pannenberg has given us over the past 25 years. The significance of his way of handling the sciences for theology generally will be the subject of the concluding section.

The thesis is expressed both in a formal and in a material statement. Formally, it can be said that Pannenberg's theological thinking makes a statement about the empirical world; that is, it claims to add to our knowledge of empirical reality. Consequently, science is important as a realm within which theological issues arise, and science can either lend credence to theological statements or falsify them. In its material form, the thesis suggests that Pannenberg's theological production is focused on the phenomena of contingency and field, and could indeed be viewed from this perspective as a theology of contingency and field. Since these phenomena are empirically discernible data, the scientific understandings of contingency and field are of importance to Pannenberg. In his final achievement, Pannenberg's concept of eschatology and God's relation to it, as revealed in Christ and his resurrection, form his theological way of making sense of contingency and field. The knowledge which Pannenberg's theology contributes to our scientific understandings of contingency and field is the suggestion that they are signals of the eschatological character of creation, which in turn is an eschatological order that is rooted in God and an order whose meaning is made clear proleptically in the resurrection of Christ. If we follow St. Thomas's definition of theology as the discipline whose distinctiveness lies in its speaking of all things in terms of their relation to God, then Pannenberg's theological achievement is that he has related these phenomena, as they occur in the natural world, to God, and he has suggested that when related to God, they are a testimony to the knowledge which Pannenberg claims theology can add to our understanding of the empirical world.

I. CONTRIBUTING TO KNOWLEDGE AS A GOAL OF THEOLOGY

The intention of Pannenberg's theological program to maintain theology as full partner in the community of disciplined rational discourse is well known. "Language about God no longer becomes privy to faith or imprisoned in the church and its confessional theology. For this reason he argues that theology belongs as one of the academic disciplines of a university."[1] This theme runs throughout his work. In his latest massive work, *Anthropology in Theological Perspective*, Pannenberg writes:

> If it can be shown that religion is simply a product of the human imagination and an expression of a human self-alienation, the roots of which are analyzed in a critical approach to religion, then religious faith and especially Christianity with its tradition and message will lose any claim to universal credibility in the life of the modern age. Without a sound claim to universal validity Christians cannot maintain a conviction of the truth of their faith and message. For a "truth" that would be simply my truth and would not at least claim to be universal and valid for every human being could not remain true even for me. This consideration

---

1. Carl E. Braaten, "Wolfhart Pannenberg," in *A Handbook of Christian Theologians*, ed. Martin E. Marty and Dean Peerman (Nashville: Abingdon, 1984), 653-654.

explains why Christians cannot but try to defend the claim of their faith to be true. It also explains why in the modern age they must conduct this defense on the terrain of the interpretation of human existence and in a debate over whether religion is an indispensable component of humanness or, on the contrary, contributes to alienate human beings from themselves.[2]

He goes on to say:

The aim is to lay theological claim to the human phenomena described in the anthropological disciplines. To this end, the secular description is accepted as simply a provisional version of the objective reality, a version that needs to be expanded and deepened by showing that the anthropological datum itself contains a further and theologically relevant dimension. *The assumption that such aspects can be shown to exist in the facts studied by the other disciplines is the general hypothesis that determines the procedure followed in my own study;* the hypothesis must, of course, prove its validity in the discussion of the particular themes discussed.[3]

The "hypothesis" described here is, in a sense, the hypothesis of Pannenberg's entire theological work, particularly if one includes, in addition to the significant methodological efforts, the concrete material which Pannenberg proposes in his Christology (and elsewhere in his work) as the content of that "further and theologically relevant dimension."

The point to be made here very emphatically is that this approach, which stands right at the heart of his theological effort, places Pannenberg's work squarely on the interface of theology with the sciences. If the "secular descriptions" derived from the sciences are to be considered by the theologian "simply" as provisional versions of reality, and if this considered opinion must "prove its validity," then the theologian must be expected not only to be informed about those secular descriptions but also to be able to engage in meaningful and persuasive

2. Pannenberg, *Anthropology in Theological Perspective*, trans. Matthew J. O'Connell (Philadelphia: Westminster, 1985), 15; also idem, *Theology and the Philosophy of Science*, trans. Francis McDonagh (London: Darton, Longman & Todd, 1976), 326-345.

3. Pannenberg, *Anthropology*, 19-20, emphasis added.

argumentation with them. Even though these "descriptions" are, in the *Anthropology,* more or less restricted to the sciences that are related to anthropological studies (in itself no mean feat!), the principle enunciated here amounts, in fact, to an elaboration of what Pannenberg has intended throughout his career.

The thrust that is so strikingly set forth in the opening pages of the *Anthropology* is already explicit in the concept of revelation that was argued in the early programmatic work, *Revelation as History,* in 1961. Thesis 3, as formulated by Pannenberg, states: "In distinction from special manifestations of the deity, the historical revelation is open to anyone who has eyes to see. It has a universal character."[4] Revelation dare not be considered to be "an occurrence that man cannot perceive with natural eyes and that is made known only through a secret mediation." Any concept of revelation that "puts revelation into contrast to, or even conflict with, natural knowledge is in danger of distorting the historical revelation into a gnostic knowledge of secrets."[5] In a somewhat perplexing argument that has often been misunderstood and contested, he asserts that revealed truth "lies right before the eyes, and . . . its appropriation is a natural consequence of the facts."[6] It is true that many persons do not see the truth, but that is not because they lack faith, but rather because their reason is blinded, for some inexplicable reason. In any case, "theology has no reason or excuse to cheapen the character and value of a truth that is open to general reasonableness."[7]

The concept of revelation at work here is a subtle one. Pannenberg is not arguing that certain historical facts can be isolated and used as the foundation of revelation, simply on the basis of their facticity. The argument, rather, is that when the events of nature and history are properly understood, in and of themselves, knowledge of their being rooted in God and God's will is conveyed. This knowledge is not complete in any single event or series of events, but only in the totality of all events, that is, it is not complete until history is completed. The

---

4. Pannenberg, with Rolf Rendtorff, Trutz Rendtorff, and Ulrich Wilkens, *Revelation as History,* trans. David Granskou (New York: Macmillan, 1968 [German original, 1961]), 135.

5. Ibid.

6. Ibid., 136.

7. Ibid., 137.

proper understanding of nature and history is enabled by interpreting the "natural consequence of the facts" through the event of Jesus Christ and his resurrection. The apocalyptic dimension of the resurrection establishes the eschatological character of the revelation. When one is in relationship with Christ, one is also in touch with the movement of history toward the meaning and fulfillment that will come to pass when God's work is completed. This meaning and fulfillment that center in Christ's revelation form the focus which also encompasses the reality that concerns the "secular descriptions" of nature and history found in the sciences. The reality that science provides knowledge of is part of the history that is on the trajectory of God's will and fulfillment which is revealed proleptically in Christ and his resurrection.[8]

The foregoing discussion gives the content to our thesis that Pannenberg conceives of theology as claiming to add to our knowledge of empirical reality. If theology is to lay claim to the phenomena described by the sciences, and if it views the secular scientific descriptions of reality as provisional versions that wait upon the expanding and deepening that theology can provide, then it is very clear that theology contributes to our knowledge of the phenomena that the sciences describe. This is precisely what revelation, as conceptualized in *Revelation as History,* is supposed to accomplish. What we observe here provides both a breathtaking program and also the criteria by which to assess whether Wolfhart Pannenberg has succeeded in accomplishing what the program intends.

Some explanation about our approach in this essay is in order. We will devote more attention to analyzing the program and Pannenberg's execution of it than to assessing the adequacy of his performance. The grounds for this imbalance rest on our judgment that this aspect of his program has generally not been recognized for the breathtaking venture that it truly is. Further, since the sources we will rely on are not everywhere so well known, we will include generous long quotations from them. Finally, although the complete range of the sciences, natural and social, falls within Pannenberg's purview (and ours, as well), we will put more emphasis on the natural sciences, partly because

8. See n. 37.

of limitations of space and also because his treatment of the social sciences is more widely discussed in other places.

II. THE PHENOMENA OF CONTINGENCY AND FIELD

We have said that Pannenberg's theological thought puts a high premium on coming to terms with the events of nature and history as described by the various sciences. The breadth of his knowledge of the range of these events is impressive, even staggering. His scope of vision aims to cover the entire range of human knowledge. The outcome of this broad-gauged survey of knowledge, however, is a focus, again and again, upon the various phenomena that can be placed first of all under the rubric of *contingency*, and secondly under the rubric of *field*. He is not interested, apparently, in all of the data which the sciences churn up, but rather is selective in concentrating upon those which are most useful for theological construction. The most useful factors in the data seem to be contingency and field theory.

In his theological writings, he speaks of the phenomena of contingency and field in several domains: physics, biology, anthropology, psychology, and history. In terms of quantity, the bulk of his attention has been given (in this order) to history, anthropology/psychology, physics, and biology. We will survey the way in which Pannenberg deals with the data in each of these fields. Even though it is most important to Pannenberg, history will receive less attention here, since several other essays in this book deal with it.

Physics

In his 1970 book, *Erwägungen zu einer Theologie der Natur* (which also features an essay written by the co-author, physicist A. M. Klaus Müller), Pannenberg writes: "A common field should be sought on which the natural sciences and theology can relate themselves without losing sight of the specific differences between the two ways of thinking. In what follows, an attempt will be made, provisionally, to lay out such a field. *The field will be characterized through the relationship of contingency and lawfulness.*"[9] He believes that contingency is a

---

9. Pannenberg, with A. M. Klaus Müller, *Erwägungen zu einer Theologie der Natur* (Gütersloh: Gütersloher Verlagshaus Gerd Mohn, 1970), 37, emphasis added.

basic consideration for the Christian outlook, because the understanding of God which was bequeathed to the Christian church from Israel was one in which "the experience of reality was primarily through contingency, and particularly through the contingency of historical happenings. Always, there came the new and unforeseen, which were experienced as the workings of the almighty God." [10] Lawful regularities were recognized, as well, but they are also contingent upon the action of God. The reality of the future also arose in this context, because the Israelites were aware that they were part of a continuum that was not yet complete.

Two recent essays raise similar considerations, "Theological Questions to Scientists" [11] and "The Doctrine of Creation and Modern Science." [12] In these essays, too, the concern is whether the physical sciences can be reconciled with the biblical understanding of reality as historical, the historical being the work of God as creator and sustainer (*creatio ex nihilo* and *creatio continua*). The question of inertia arises, since that physical principle seems to suggest that events are fully caused by the nexus of physical reality, leaving no possibility for divine causality.

These concerns take on deep significance when one thinks back to the early, formative essays that Pannenberg wrote, particularly the 1959 piece, "Redemptive Event and History." In that monumental essay, the point is also made that Christians, like the Israelites, experienced reality as historical. "History is the most comprehensive horizon of Christian theology." [13] There, too, history is made up of the contingent and the continuous. Both have their origins in God: "The God who by the transcendence of his freedom, is the origin of contingency in the world, is also the ground of the unity which comprises the contingencies as history. This history does not exclude the contingency of the events bound together in it. It seems that only the origin of the contingency of events can, by virtue of its unity, also be the origin of its continuity without injuring its contingency." [14]

---

10. Ibid., 37.

11. Pannenberg, "Theological Questions to Scientists," in *The Sciences and Theology in the Twentieth Century*, ed. A. R. Peacocke (Notre Dame: University of Notre Dame Press, 1981).

12. Pannenberg, "The Doctrine of Creation and Modern Science," *Zygon* 23 (1988): 3-21.

13. "Redemptive Event and History," in *Basic Questions in Theology*, 2 vols., trans. George H. Kehm (Philadelphia: Fortress, 1971), 1:15.

14. Ibid., 74-75.

Why would the theologian be so concerned to discuss contingency and lawfulness with the physicist? Because the Christian view of God and the world puts contingency and the lawfulness that is also contingent at the center. We note, however, that the aim is not simply to gain reinforcement for Christian theological belief or scriptural affirmation from the sciences. Without any question such a simplistic motivation founders on the rocks of philosophical analysis! On the contrary, harking back to the understanding of revelation that also emerged in these years, the point is that theology has something to contribute to the provisional descriptions of the physicist, and this "something" is knowledge. As we shall note, the contingency of events is a fundamental clue to events being rooted in a source of that contingency, namely, the action of God. The descriptions of the cosmologists are only provisional until they are conjoined with the theological commentary.

The discussion of field theory and inertia has the same concern.[15] Field theory (which will receive greater attention in the next section) suggests that causes do not originate in entities nor do they operate only on individuals, but rather factors in the field which is the ambience of the entity can be causes, and they work on the entire ambience. This, too, is a clue that the biblical imagery of all things being rooted in the source of nature and history, God, not only has a point of contact with the scientific understandings of reality, but also has something to contribute to those understandings: the insight that the largest field of all, which embraces all of reality, is God.

In the discussion both of contingency and of field, the final theological point to be made seems to be that both concepts point toward a ground upon which both are dependent, namely, God. The contribution of theology in both cases is to call attention to and say something about this ground in God. In his most recent work, Pannenberg begins to relate this concern to the very important and complex set of issues that pertain to the unity of space and time. Drawing upon a wide range of authors, stretching from Plotinus through Augustine, Duns Scotus,

---

15. See Pannenberg, "Theological Questions to Scientists," 7-10, and "The Doctrine of Creation and Modern Science," 7-11.

Ockham, and up to contemporary physics and philosophy, he juxtaposes for discussion the attempts of physics to speak about the cosmic field of space and time, on the one hand, to the Christian theological concepts of God, the divine Spirit, and the eschatological future, on the other.[16] He suggests for discussion two sets of questions in particular: "The question of how the different parts of the cosmic field are related to that field itself and . . . [the question] of the role of contingency and time in the understanding of a cosmic field."[17]

Throughout his years of dialogue with scientists, Pannenberg has also called attention to an insight that he derived from his conversations in the interdisciplinary group that met in Heidelberg in the early 1960s. This insight deals with the character of scientific statements. He writes:

> An agreement was formulated to the effect that each scientific hypothesis of law describes uniformities in the behavior of the object of such hypotheses. The object itself, however, is contingently given in relation to its hypothetical description as a case where the affirmed law obtains. This element of contingency in the givenness of the object, however, is usually not explicitly focused upon in scientific statements. The focus is rather on the uniformities that can be expressed in equations. *It is accepted as a matter of fact that those uniformities occur in a substratum that is not exhausted by them* [there follows a description of examples which make his point]. . . . *This means that the descriptions of nature by hypothetical statements of natural law presuppose their material is contingently given.* These statements do not focus on this contingency, however, because their intention is the formulation of uniformities that occur in the natural phenomena, their contingency notwithstanding.[18]

This argument is important because it serves to make credible the notion that theology, particularly a theology that speaks of contingency, has something legitimate to contribute to the enhancement of scientific knowledge. In this connection, we note the style in which Pannenberg relates science and theology. It is not one that employs a "God of the gaps" strategy, nor that of perceiving science and theology as "two worlds." Rather, it immerses itself fully in the contributions that science

---

16. Pannenberg, "The Doctrine of Creation and Modern Science," 8-18.
17. Ibid., 14.
18. Ibid., 10, emphasis added.

makes to our understanding of the world, and it seeks to bring theology to bear in a constructive and cooperative manner upon the descriptions which science provides. It does so in the conviction that theology has something to contribute which will otherwise be wanting. Such a style of approach, upon which we will comment more fully later, is thoroughly consistent with the program which Pannenberg has set for himself.

Biology

Although he has devoted the least attention to the biological realm in his published works, some of Pannenberg's most insightful and persuasive arguments emerge from this area. The chief sources for this aspect of his thought are the 1962 book, *What Is Man?* the 1985 *Anthropology;* the 1970 essay, "The Working of the Spirit in the Creation and in the People of God"; and the generally overlooked but nevertheless extraordinary essay, "The Doctrine of the Spirit and the Task of a Theology of Nature," which appeared for the first time in 1972.[19]

The issues of contingency and field are dominant for Pannenberg as he approaches the biological sciences. The discipline of biology governed as it is by evolutionary modes of interpretation, and overlapping at important points with anthropology, provides Pannenberg a rich and complex set of ideas within which to pursue his concerns for contingency and field. He has obviously learned greatly from this realm of reality, just as he has chosen to express some of his formative ideas in its context.

In the context of biology and anthropology, the concepts of *openness* and *ecstatic, ecological self-transcendence* receive brilliant articulation. These articulations take on even deeper meaning if we keep in mind all the while the larger reaches of Pannenberg's theological system—the concepts of revelation, eschatology, and God as the all-determining reality (and hence the ground of the unity of all reality).

---

19. Pannenberg, *What Is Man?* trans. Duane A. Priebe (Philadelphia: Fortress, 1970 [German, 1962]); idem, "The Working of the Spirit in the Creation and in the People of God," in Pannenberg, Avery Dulles, and Carl Braaten, *Spirit, Faith, and Church* (Philadelphia: Westminster, 1970); idem, "The Doctrine of the Spirit and the Task of a Theology of Nature," *Theology* 75 (1972): 8-21.

Evolutionary modes of thinking lend themselves to the articulation of these concepts, because (1) the processes of nature so perceived are intrinsically contingent, both in the sense that the new and the unforeseen is, as in history itself, always occurring, and also in the sense that all evolutionary events take place in a larger environment upon which they are dependent for their origin and sustenance; (2) the notion of this larger environment leads directly to the concept of field; and (3) the dynamics of evolution lay the groundwork for the empirical actuality of openness.

The evolutionary pathway is one in which the organism interfaces with its physical world through its own physical shape (phenotype), and in this situation, it is continuously being drawn outward. This "drawing out" is the biological basis for and correlate of openness, and in the course of being drawn out, the organism has no recourse but to transcend itself.

> All human life is carried out in the tension between self-centeredness and openness to the world. In order to understand man's unique situation correctly, one must note that man shares this tension in its main features with all organic life. On the one hand, every living organism is a body. which, as such, is closed to the rest of the world. On the other hand, every organism is also open to the outside world. It incorporates its environment, upon which it is dependent for food and growth into the cycle of its biological functions. Thus every organic body, whether it is animal or plant, simultaneously lives within itself and outside itself. To live simultaneously within itself and outside itself certainly involves a contradiction. But it is a contradiction that really exists in life. All life, even human life, as we have seen, is carried out within this tension.[20]

The ground of this tension and its meaning are found, finally, for Pannenberg in the concept of God.

The concept of openness that is intrinsic to the evolutionary-biological process is the direct descendant of the concept of contingency that was the subject of discussion with physics. There, the concept of contingency was primarily correlated to God's working as origin of the new and unforeseen. Here a nuance is added: the concept of being

---

20. Pannenberg, *What Is Man?* 56-57.

drawn out and thereby constituted is correlated to the "Spirit of God as the creative origin of all life."[21] Here the concepts of ecstatic and ecological self-transcendence should be considered. Ecstasy is intrinsic to life, particularly to human life, and it is manifested in the phenomenon of living beyond oneself.

> Every living organism lives beyond itself, for every organism needs an appropriate environment for the activity of its life. When kept in isolation, no organism is fit for life. Hence every organism lives beyond itself. A particular aspect of this ecstatic character of life is to be found in its relation to time: every organism relates itself to a future that will change its present conditions. This is evident in the drives and urgencies of life, but also in negative anticipations such as fear and horror.[22]

Ecstasy is a mark of the spirit. Pannenberg elaborates this further:

> The element of transcendence in spirit suggests that after all it might be neither necessary nor wise to admit a fundamental distinction between a human spirit and a divine spirit. The ecstatic, self-transcendent character of all spiritual experience brings sufficiently to bear the transcendence of God over against all created beings. *The spirit never belongs in a strict sense to the creature in his immanent nature, but the creature participates in the spirit—and I venture to say: in the divine spirit—by transcending itself, i.e., by being elevated beyond itself in the ecstatic experience that illustrates the working of the spirit.* . . . Thus the idea of spirit allows us to do justice to the transcendence of God and at the same time to explain his immanence in his creation.[23]

What we have here, when put in the context of Pannenberg's other writings, is a theological interpretation, in the concept of "spirit," of one very important component of the evolutionary process that is observed empirically by the sciences. The train of thought is carried further in the essay, "The Doctrine of the Spirit and the Task of a Theology of Nature":

> Modern biology does not exclude everything that transcends the living cell from the analysis of life. Although life is taken as the activity of

---

21. Pannenberg, "The Doctrine of the Spirit," 17 et passim.
22. Pannenberg, "The Working of the Spirit," 18.
23. Ibid., 21, emphasis added.

the living cell or of a higher organism, that activity itself is conditioned. It is conditioned particularly by the requirement of an appropriate environment. When kept in isolation, no organism is fit for life. In this sense, every organism depends on specific conditions for its life, and these conditions do not remain extrinsic to its own reality, but contribute to the character of its life: an organism lives "in" its environment. It not only needs and actively occupies a territory, but it turns it into a means for its self-realization, it nourishes itself on its environment. *In this sense, every organism lives beyond itself. Again it becomes evident that life is essentially ecstatic: it takes place in the environment of the organism much more than in itself. But is there any relation of this ecological self-transcendence of life to the biblical idea of a spiritual origin of life? I think there is.*[24]

The phenomenon of field is in these reflections given even greater significance for theology, fully as important as the phenomenon of contingency. It is clear that the significance of both phenomena is rooted in their relevance to the reality of God. Pannenberg goes on to introduce the phenomenon of the future into the biological scheme: "by turning its environment into the place and means of its life the organism relates itself at the same time to its own future and, more precisely, to a future of its own transformation. . . . By his drives an animal is related to although not necessarily aware of his individual future and to the future of his species."[25] This insight lays the foundation for relating eschatology to the biological realm. This is clear as he goes on:

Hence, the element of truth in the old image of breath [which he has elsewhere related to the biblical concept of spirit and the scientific concept of field] as being the creative origin of life is not exhausted by the dependence of the organism on its environment, but contains a deeper mystery closely connected with the ecological self-transcendence of life: the temporal self-transcendence of every living being is a specific phenomenon of organic life that separates it from inorganic structures.[26]

What should be clear at this point is that in his rather extensive discussions of physics, cosmology, and biology, Pannenberg has laid,

---

24. Pannenberg, "The Doctrine of the Spirit," 17, emphasis added.
25. Ibid., 18.
26. Ibid.

to his own satisfaction, at least, the basis for correlating to the empirical phenomena *as described by the sciences* the realities that are spoken of in theological discourse in the concept of God, Spirit, creation (both *creatio ex nihilo* and *creatio continua*), transcendence, and eschatology.

Anthropology/Psychology/Social Theory/History

Our analysis must be satisfied with an even more summary discussion of anthropology, psychology, social theory, and history as they fit into the vast Pannenbergian scheme. There is some overlapping of the inter-pretations taken from anthropology with what we have already con-sidered, since the trends in anthropological thinking that he seizes upon build upon the phenomenon of openness, world-relatedness, and self-transcendence, for which the evolutionary biological descriptions lay a sort of foundation. In the context of anthropology and psychology, he elaborates the concept of relatedness to and openness to the world with great learning and subtlety, in a way that is provocative of further insights.

> The concept of human self-transcendence—like the concept of openness to the world which is to a great extent its equivalent—summarizes a broad consensus among contemporary anthropologists in their effort to define the special character of the human.[27] It was this transcending of every particular object—a transcending that is already a condition for the perception of the individual object in its determinacy (and thus in its otherness and distinctness)—that I had in mind when I wrote in 1962 that the so-called openness of the human being to the world signifies ultimately an openness to what is beyond the world, so that the real meaning of this openness to the world might be better described as an openness to God which alone makes possible a gaze embracing the world as a whole.[28]

Contingency and field still figure as foundational concerns. In the important realms to which psychological and anthropological descrip-tions are relevant, the challenge to discover and actualize the unity that

---

27. Pannenberg, *Anthropology*, 63.
28. Ibid., 69.

binds together the contingencies is at the center of human existence and reflection. The field, as the environment or ambience which is causative and sustaining, is even more intensely the focus of Pannenberg's reflection and argumentation. Some of the most important examples of this trend of his thought can be highlighted:

(1) The phenomenon of openness to the world and the attempt to unify the disparateness of the world through human dominion are linked to the biblical affirmation that humans are created in the image of God.[29]

(2) In the formation of identity, the individuals must differentiate themselves from the world, gain independence, "while not destroying that symbiotic connection" with their world which makes life possible. Trust is definitely a matter of relatedness to the field in which the individual lives—physical and cultural. The religious dimension is visible here, because "trust is, by reason of its lack of limits, *implicitly* directed beyond mother and parents to an agency that can justify the unlimited character of trust."[30] This argument concerning trust is not meant as a proof for the existence of God, but rather it shows "that the theme of 'God' is inseparable from the living of human life. . . . *There is an original and at least implicit reference of human beings to God that is connected with the structural openness of their life form to the world and that is concretized in the limitlessness of basic trust.*"[31]

(3) The primary challenge facing human cultural life is the establishment of the unity of culture, that is, of articulating the field or unity which sustains culture and gives it meaning. This is where religion becomes meaningful for culture. Religion is the factor that can give legitimacy to the culture. To understand this, the function of religion within the cultural system must be understood.

> This function is to be seen, first, in the fact that religion has for its object the unity of the world as such in relation to its divine source and its possible fulfillment from that same source.[32]

Because religions are concerned with the unity of all reality, it is

---

29. Ibid., 76f.
30. Ibid., 233.
31. Ibid., emphasis added.
32. Ibid., 473.

possible and necessary to seek and find in religion the ultimate frame of reference for the order of human life in society.[33]

As with the issue of the trust which makes individual identity possible, this unifying within the cultural system is basically the challenge to make clear the field in which life's origin and sustenance are to be found and describing the field in ways that are persuasive and add the knowledge of it to what the sciences can describe of it.

(4) History becomes at a higher, more complex, and (in the epoch in which humanity is the dominant species) more critical level, what the physical and biological processes were for preceding levels. History is a realm of self-transcendence, ecstasy, openness, subject formation, contingency, and the operation of the field.[34] This is not surprising, since Pannenberg used the historical order as the analogy for understanding contingency and field in the physical realm.[35]

III. THE TOTALITY OF MEANING

Pannenberg himself uses the term that is the title of this section to refer to God; we are using it to refer to a summary of the total system of meaning which he presents to us, bits and pieces of which we have discussed in this essay thus far. If there were space, we would argue that what Pannenberg has provided is what the philosopher of science, Imre Lakatos, has termed "a research programme."[36] A research program is constituted by a "hard core" of assertions and a set of auxiliary hypotheses which surround the core. The hard core rises to the top of the heap of theories in its field and surpasses others, because it is able to provide "dramatic, stunning, and unexpected" interpretations of the world, which do as a result provide "new facts" that had not been known before (the "positive heuristic"). This hard core is never subjected to the process of scientific falsification; its activity is rather to

33. Ibid., 474.
34. See ibid., 485-532.
35. See p. 271 above.
36. Imre Lakatos, *The Methodology of Scientific Research Programmes* (Cambridge: At the University Press, 1978); Nancey Murphy, "Acceptability Criteria for Work in Theology and Science," *Zygon* 22 (1987): 279-297.

provide the stunning and unexpected interpretations. The auxiliary hypotheses carry the brunt of the falsification process, and thereby lend credibility to the hard core and to the research program as such (the "negative heuristic"). I will attempt to summarize Pannenberg's proposals for global meaning in the form of a Lakatosian research program. I will not always use Pannenberg's own terminology to summarize his contribution.

A. *The Hard Core* (the source of stunning, dramatic interpretations):
1. God is the all-determining reality which constitutes the field in which everything that exists derives its being and in which all the contingencies of nature and history have their origin.
2. The medium in which God's all-determining work (both as *creatio ex nihilo* and *creatio continua*) has been cast is that of an eschatological historical continuum, wherein the meaning is in the as-yet-uncompleted totality of reality. Within this continuum, the resurrection of Jesus Christ is a revelation of that meaning.[37]
3. Included in God's all-determining work is the fulfillment of the eschatological continuum.

B. *Auxiliary Hypotheses* (these may be falsified in appropriate ways; this listing is by no means complete):
1. Drawn from the Biblical/Theological Tradition—
  a. The biblical picture of God as Lord of history and creator supports the concept of God that is contained in the hard core.
  b. The biblical picture of the divine spirit as the creative source of all life supports the hard core.
  c. In Jesus Christ and his resurrection we encounter a proleptic

---

37. Any discussion of Pannenberg's use of science must take note of his remarkable discussion of the resurrection of Jesus Christ. This discussion demonstrates how his Christology is the nodal point, where his concern for secular knowledge and Christian tradition intersect most intensely. Consequently, one can say that he has been consistent in following out the concept of revelation that he set forth in his earliest work. His interpretation of the New Testament texts, utilizing his version of the apocalyptic framework of the early first century, brings to bear the quintessence of what we have elucidated in section II concerning contingency and field. What Pannenberg thus gives us is a neatly dovetailed tapestry of meaning: contemporary scientific understandings (as Pannenberg interprets them) are subtly employed to interpret the texts, and the texts (interpreted in the light of Pannenberg's understanding of apocalyptic) result in a message of the resurrection that reveals the meaning of the eschatological reality in terms that make sense also to contemporary secular knowledge. This means that the Christ-resurrection-revelation is the point where the two sets of auxiliary hypotheses meet; it also explains why Christ appears both in the hard core and in the first set of auxiliary hypotheses (see Pannenberg, *Jesus—God and Man*, 2d ed., trans. Lewis L. Wilkins and Duane A. Priebe [Philadelphia: Westminster, 1977], 53-114).

embodiment of the totality of reality and of God's will for it and fulfillment of it, when interpreted in the light of the apocalyptic framework in which it was originally experienced. Therefore, Christ and his resurrection qualify as God's revelation, i.e., God's own indirect self-revelation.

    d. The biblical concept of the kingdom of God is a symbolic representation of God's eschatological work and of God's relation to it.

2. Drawn from Scientific Descriptions of Reality—

    a. In their character as contingent and field-dependent, physical processes leave open the conjecture that they manifest the effects of God's all-determining totality.

    b. In their character as contingent and field-dependent, biological evolutionary processes leave open the conjecture that they manifest the effects of God's all-determining totality. Ecological self-transcendence is an important aspect of this manifestation.

    c. In their character of openness to the world, to others, and to the future, the process of society and history leave open the conjecture as described in (a) and (b) above.

    d. In its dependence upon the reality of trust, the process of identity formation in the individual human person leaves open the conjecture as described in (a) and (b).

    e. In their dependence upon a perception of unity, the processes of human culture leave open the same conjecture.

    f. A comparable hypothesis may be made about history, except that it would be more complex.

The magnitude of this program is stunning in its own right. As this Lakatosian elaboration reveals, Pannenberg's central core of contributed insight does attempt to throw light on the nature of all things, and it demonstrates its seriousness by suggesting hypotheses that cover broad ranges of biblical-theological and scientific materials. I suggest that this way of representing Pannenberg's theological thought is not simply a perspective that grows out of the consideration of his use of the sciences, but rather that it does more justice than many other perspectives to the genuine intent of his theological work and its genuine significance. This elaboration shows the justification of his claim that theology deserves a place in the university because of its contribution to knowledge, that is, because of its cognitive claims.

IV. ASSESSING PANNENBERG'S HANDLING OF SCIENCE

In a brief sketch, we may suggest several ways in which Pannenberg's handling of science can be assessed.

First, we must recognize that in contrast to the vast majority of mainline Christian theologians of his generation, Pannenberg genuinely opens his theological work to the impact of science by inviting falsification on the basis of science. He has not retreated behind the prevalent "two worlds" approach to the sciences, which builds an insuperable wall between science and theology by making some version of the claim that the two kinds of discourse are so utterly different that they cannot exist on the same interface. Furthermore, while he has opened himself to falsification from the side of the sciences, he has also assimilated himself so fully to the theological tradition that he also courts falsification from that sector as well. I suggest that there is no other school of theological thought at work today that opens itself so fully to this dual falsification—from the side of the sciences and also from the side of the biblical-theological tradition. If one believes, as this writer does, that the primary challenge to theology in our epoch is to open itself to the greatest extent possible to both the contemporary world and to the Christian tradition, then Pannenberg's premier position vis-à-vis the dual falsification suggests that he has produced a research program in theology that surpasses any other current program.

Second, we should examine the rather full discussion that Pannenberg has given us of how his theological statements can be subjected to scientific methods of validation to see if they are adequate. This discussion is set forth in *Theology and the Philosophy of Science.*[38] Although we cannot go into this question here, the four basic tests, which he outlines in this work,[39] conform to the Lakatosian structure we have utilized in our analysis: conformity to the tradition, connection

---

38. Pp. 326-345.
39. Ibid., 344-345.

with present experience (which I interpret to include scientific experience), integration with the appropriate area of experience, and comparison with other existing research programs. The third criterion is the only one to which this essay has not given attention.

Third, granted that Pannenberg's design for his theology proposes a brilliant engagement with science, the major test is whether he actually brings off what he has attempted. I suggest a number of concrete assessments.

(1) Even though the range of the auxiliary hypotheses in Pannenberg's program is very impressive, he will surely need to develop more. The emerging field of thermodynamic thinking bids fare to become the foundation of a unified science, that is, a unified view of the entire cosmic order. This new field is of such great pertinence to Pannenberg's program that he can scarcely overlook it.[40] One might also suggest he will want to probe more fully the relationship between culture and the biogenetic background of the human central nervous system. His reflection upon biological evolution[41] does recognize that the concepts of openness and self-transcendence, which are so central to his interpretation of society and history, have significant roots in the biogenetic evolution and structure of human life. The anthropologist Victor Turner recognized this shortly before his death.[42] He was greatly influenced by the work of Ralph Burhoe[43] and Eugene d'Aquili.[44] It would be a natural step for Pannenberg to take this interrelationship of culture and biogenetic backgrounds more seriously.

(2) Pannenberg tends to give the impression that the biblical-theological tradition is a given in the quest for knowledge which at the formal level changes little, even though in material expressions he suggests dramatic reformulations of the tradition. Is it not a contradiction of the standards that he applies to his own theological program

---

40. Jeffrey Wicken, *Evolution, Thermodynamics, and Information* (New York: Oxford University Press, 1987).

41. Pannenberg, "The Doctrine of the Spirit."

42. Victor Turner, "Body, Brain, and Culture," *Zygon* 18 (1983): 221-245.

43. Ralph Burhoe, "The Source of Civilization in the Natural Selection of Coadapted Information in the Genes and Culture," *Zygon* 11 (1976): 263-303.

44. Eugene d'Aquili, "The Neurobiological Bases of Myth and Concepts of Deity," *Zygon* 13 (1978): 257-275; idem, "The Myth-Ritual Complex: A Biogenetic Structural Analysis," *Zygon* 18 (1983): 247-269.

to protect the tradition, even the biblical traditions, from validation and falsification procedures that are in use today?

(3) Physicists have raised a number of questions about Pannenberg's discussion of contingency and inertia. Robert Russell[45] has suggested that Pannenberg's discussions,[46] while provocative, would benefit from a fuller and more complex attention to what physicists today are saying about inertia and contingency. Jeffrey Wicken[47] also finds Pannenberg's questions fruitful, but he believes that, on the one hand, Pannenberg is not careful enough in his use of the concept of field, while, on the other, more attention should be given to the "ontological room" that science necessarily leaves for theology in probing the "sensitive dimension of nature that is the source of feeling, perception, and consciousness." David Breed[48] has argued that current cosmological thinking suggests that contingency includes limitations upon the action of God which would qualify the claim that God is all-determining. These examples are cited in order to suggest that Pannenberg's dialogue with the scientists is by no means at an end. The further developments in the process of give-and-take between him and scientists are eagerly awaited.

The magnitude of Wolfhart Pannenberg's theological enterprise is clearly revealed when we view it from the perspective of his stance toward the sciences. His program merits the most serious attention and dialogue. Let the conversation continue!

---

45. Robert Russell, "Contingency in Physics and Cosmology: A Critique of the Theology of Wolfhart Pannenberg," *Zygon* 23 (1988).

46. Pannenberg, "Theological Questions," and "The Doctrine of Creation and Modern Science."

47. Jeffrey Wicken, "Theology and Science in the Evolving Cosmos: A Need for Dialogue," *Zygon* 23 (1988): 45-55.

48. David Breed, "Reflections on Theology and Science in Wolfhart Pannenberg's Thought," unpublished paper (1985).

12

THE PLACE OF CHRISTIANITY AMONG THE WORLD RELIGIONS: WOLFHART PANNENBERG'S THEOLOGY OF RELIGION AND THE HISTORY OF RELIGIONS

Carl E. Braaten

◆

I. THE QUEST FOR A NEW PARADIGM IN THEOLOGY

Theologians who hearken to the prophecy that a new age is aborning are urging a corresponding shift to a new theological paradigm. For lack of a better name, the emerging new age is commonly called "post-modern." The word *paradigm* is borrowed from Thomas S. Kuhn, who defined it as "an entire constellation of beliefs, values, techniques, and so on shared by members of a given community."[1] The call for a "post-modern paradigm" in theology suggests that something of epochal significance is happening. All of a sudden, "modernity" has become a bad word as somehow synonymous with the "entire constellation" of Western religious superiority, cultural

---

1. Thomas S. Kuhn, *The Structure of a Scientific Revolution* (University of Chicago Press, 1962; 2d enlarged edition, 1970), 175.

enlightenment, scientific optimism, and technological progress. All of these things which seemed so great and glorious in the old paradigm appear now as the demons of death and damnation in the new paradigm.

In the 1960s Bob Dylan taunted middle-class people with a song whose refrain went like this: "Something is happening, and you don't know what it is, do you Mister Jones?" Something is bestirring theology, and we don't know what it is, whether a revolution of countercultural prophets, whether a mere ripple in the history of modern times, or whether the bellwether of a new age. Langdon Gilkey speaks of it as "the new watershed in theology."[2] George Lindbeck sees that we are in need of a "theology for a post-liberal age."[3] Trutz Rendtorff proposes that we speak rather of "the middle age of modernity."[4] Whatever the label, there is no consensus about the essence of post-modernity. Gordon Kaufman locates it in the notion of "historicity."[5] Ted Peters avers that the prime candidate is "wholistic thinking."[6] Catherine Keller, seeing through feminist eyes, chooses "post-patriarchy" as the most fitting term for a really new paradigm.[7] Hans Küng outlines the features of a new paradigm in theology and calls it a "modern critical ecumenical theology."[8]

In many respects, the new-age prophets tend to cancel each other out. They have different motives for urging a paradigm shift beyond modernity, and they couch their arguments in different matrices of beliefs and values. This becomes particularly clear with respect to the

2. Langdon Gilkey, *Society and the Sacred* (New York: Crossroad, 1981), 13-14.

3. George Lindbeck, *The Nature of Doctrine: Religion and Theology in a Postliberal Age* (Philadelphia: Westminster, 1984).

4. Trutz Rendtorff, "Beyond Modernity? The Historical Consciousness of Twentieth Century Theology Re-evaluated," an unpublished paper presented at the seminar of the Institute for the Advanced Study of Religion, The University of Chicago, February 1986.

5. Gordon Kaufman, "Towards a New Paradigm in Theology," a paper prepared for the "Workgroup on Constructive Theology" convened at Vanderbilt University.

6. Ted Peters, "Theology in the Context of Transition from Modern to Post-Modern Culture," a paper presented at the Second East–West Religious Encounter Conference, January 1984, at Honolulu, Hawaii.

7. Catherine Keller, "Toward a Postpatriarchal Postmodernity," a paper presented at a conference on "Toward a Post-Modern World," sponsored by the Center for a Post-Modern World, January 1987, Santa Barbara, Calif.

8. Hans Küng, "Paradigm Change in Theology," a paper delivered as a public lecture at the University of Tübingen, 1980, and developed further while Küng was a visiting professor at the University of Chicago Divinity School, 1981.

issue of religious pluralism. Perhaps everyone senses a profound shift underway in thinking about the place of Christianity among the world religions. Of course, there is nothing new about a plurality of religions. What is new is the relativism that characterizes many of the positions formulating the relationship of Christianity to other religions. As the dominant religion of the Western world, Christianity encumbered itself with all the liabilities charged to modernity, including that of alleging its own superiority to other religions or claiming to be their absolute fulfillment. This provides a broad and easy target for the post-modern pluralists who call for a new paradigm in which all religions enjoy a relationship of equality. Gilkey writes, "The encounter is now fully one of equals."[9] Gilkey has in mind not merely a sociological but also a soteriological meaning of equality. "What is new about this encounter is the equality among religions that characterizes it, equality, one might say, of truth and grace, of illuminating and of healing power."[10] Gilkey goes on to say that "this situation is, therefore, quite new. It represents a veritable uncharted sea for theology. . . . What this situation calls for theologically is by no means clear."[11]

Gilkey's concept of a "rough parity" among the religions lies at the heart of the pluralist paradigm advocated by most post-modernists. John Hick speaks of a "Copernican revolution" to express the shift from a Ptolemaic Christ-centered interpretation of the religions to a theocentric pluralism which places God at the center of the "universe of faiths."[12] Paul Knitter also commends this movement from a Christocentric to a theocentric perspective, in order to gain the most adequate basis for what he calls a "unitive pluralism of religions."[13] He traces the progress of Christian thinking about the religions from the traditional Catholic *(extra ecclesiam nulla salus)* and Protestant *(sola fide)* types of exclusivism to the more recent inclusivist theories of Paul Tillich (latent church) and Karl Rahner (anonymous Christianity) and,

---

9. Langdon Gilkey, *Society and the Sacred,* 12.
10. Ibid.
11. Ibid., 13.
12. John Hick, *God and the Universe of Faiths* (New York: Macmillan, 1973), 121.
13. Paul Knitter, "Christianity as Religion: True and Absolute? A Roman Catholic Perspective," in *What Is Religion? An Enquiry for Christian Theology, Concilium,* ed. Mircea Eliade and David Tracy (New York: Seabury, 1980), 18.

like John Hick, finds them woefully deficient for the new age of interreligious dialogue. The sacrifice to be made for the sake of a global theology in the new paradigm, responding to the challenge of the plurality of religions, is the traditional Christian belief in the finality and normativity of Jesus Christ.[14] Wilfred Cantwell Smith agrees with Hick and Knitter in substituting theocentricity for Christocentricity. In *Towards a World Theology*, Smith says, "My proposal is unabashedly theocentric. . . . I wonder whether I need shrink from saying: if Christians insist that Christ is the centre of their lives, it is time that we rediscovered that God is at the centre of the universe."[15] The result of such a view is that all religions are seen as different but equal expressions of the same deep mystical experience of "faith." Ironically, Smith appeals to Martin Luther's emphasis on "faith alone" as the essence of real religion. The positive religions are "cumulative traditions" that enshrine the faith experiences of individuals, the common denominator of which we may call "God" but certainly not "Christ." God unites; Christ divides.

The voices are legion today that say that Christ must decrease so that God might increase in an age when all religions are searching for common ground. The common opinion seems to be that Christians must substitute God for Christ at the center of a theology of the world religions.

This introduction has set the stage for considering the relevance of the theology of Wolfhart Pannenberg on the question of the place of Christianity in the world of religions. In many respects, Pannenberg's theology addresses the questions that motivate the call for a new paradigm in theology. His is an example of a theology that takes seriously

---

14. Having the teaching of Hick and Knitter clearly in mind, Hans Küng has this to say: "What is proclaimed today as 'brand new' teaching often proves to be the old teaching from the liberal Protestant side. Such people do indeed hear God speaking through Jesus 'as well' but have abandoned his normativity and 'finality' (conclusiveness). They have put him on the level of other prophets alongside others (Christ together with other religions or other revealers, saviours, Christs) and so have lost all criteria for the discernment of spirits. Against such liberalism the protest of Karl Barth and 'dialectical theology' (Rudolf Bultmann and Paul Tillich) was a necessary corrective. To go back in this direction is no progress" (Hans Küng, "Toward an Ecumenical Theology of Religions: Some Theses for Clarification," *Christianity among World Religions, Concilium*, ed. Hans Küng and Jürgen Moltmann [Edinburgh: T. & T. Clark, 1986], 121-122).

15. Wilfred Cantwell Smith, *Towards a World Theology* (Philadelphia: Westminster, 1981), 177.

the basic questions arising from the scientific disciplines of our time and still attends to the indispensable conditions of a Christian theology that remains continuous with its Christian origins. If the new paradigm in theology is characterized by the themes of historicity, wholism, self-transcendence, openness to the world, no one among contemporary theologians is Pannenberg's equal in dealing with these issues with such remarkable depth of insight and breadth of knowledge. Yet, with equal insistence, he retains continuity with the classical Christian faith that originated in historic events interpreted by the apostolic traditions and transmitted by Christian witnesses down through the ages. Pannenberg is committed to a rational account of the truth of the Christian faith at once theocentric and Christocentric, neither one without the other. For Pannenberg, Christology is the interpretation of the historical person of Jesus of Nazareth who mediates the cause of God to humanity and the cause of humanity to God, and is thus both *vere deus et vere homo*. For a Christian theologian, there is no such thing as a paradigm shift or revolution in scientific thinking that requires a surrender of the claim of the gospel and the centrality of Jesus Christ as the foundational principle of Christian identity. The religious pluralists and relativists who herald a new paradigm intend to ease the way of Christians into the so-called post-modern world. However, they have loosened the links with the Christian tradition, which is ultimately based on the apostolic message concerning Jesus of Nazareth as the Christ of God and the Savior of the world.

The aim of this essay is to take the measure of Pannenberg's theology of Christian identity in relation to the meaning of religion as an essential structure of human being and to the history of religions as the context in which the Christian faith must legitimate its claim to universal validity and truth. Pannenberg himself has advocated the need for a new theology of religion and the religions. In the first section, we will deal with Pannenberg's methodology; in the second, with his apology for religion in the face of modern atheistic criticism; in the third, with his theology of the history of religions and his view of the place of Christianity within its framework. There follows a conclusion of an interrogatory nature.

291

II. METHODOLOGY

Pannenberg describes his approach to questions about the essence of religion and the truth claims of the religions as a "fundamental-theological anthropology." [16] This is a strategy that resumes the conversation with the philosophical-theological traditions of the 19th century going back to Kant, Hegel, and Schleiermacher, a conversation that, to a large extent, was aborted by the vehement strictures of Karl Barth against all natural theology. Today, Barth's approach is being continued by the neo-confessional narrativist theology of Hans Frei and George Lindbeck, backed up by the neo-pragmatist, anti-foundationalist perspectives of Richard Rorty and Richard Bernstein, as well as the cultural linguistic theory of Clifford Geertz. It enjoys some kind of unholy alliance with deconstructionist thinking, which rejects onto-theological metaphysics and the referential theory of meaning and truth. Pannenberg's titanic struggle with Barth's method puts him decidedly in opposition to this neo-Barthian trend in American theology.

Pannenberg's opposition to the confessional dogmatic approach, which presupposes by *faith* what needs to be established by *reason*, has nowhere been more clearly stated than by Eberhard Jüngel. He notes: "There are two approaches in contemporary theology by which the attempt is being made to think God again. The one way, pursued by Wolfhart Pannenberg with impressive consequentiality, is to think God 'God having been removed' *(remoto deo)* in order to arrive at the disclosure of the thought of God which then functions as the framework of the Christian faith's own understanding of God. The studies in this book [Jüngel's *God as the Mystery of the World*] will take the opposite approach. The thinking here pursues a path which, one might say, goes from the inside toward the outside, from the specifically Christian faith experience to a concept of God which claims universal validity. The goal of the intellectual route adopted in this book is not to demonstrate the thinkability of God on the basis of general anthropological definitions, but rather to think God and also man on the basis of the event of God's self-disclosure which leads to the experience of God, and thus

---

16. Wolfhart Pannenberg, *Anthropology in Theological Perspective*, trans. Matthew J. O'Connell (Philadelphia: Westminster, 1985), 21.

to demonstrate that the Christian truth is universally valid on the basis of its inner power."[17]

Pannenberg has restored *religion* to its rightful place as an indispensable theme of theology. He says, "Theology as a science of God is therefore possible only as a science of religion, and not as the science of religion in general but of the historic religions."[18] After Ernst Troeltsch, theology and religious studies were placed on different tracks. Now, when Pannenberg brings them back to the same track, he is committed to a theological reflection on the empirical findings of the psychology, sociology, phenomenology, and history of religions. This reunification of theology and the sciences of religion flies in the face of Barth's restriction of theology to the theme of revelation. For Barth, the only subject matter of real theology is divine revelation and not human religion. There seems to be something almost blasphemous about theology's attempt to base its study of God's word on the study of religion. It is hardly fitting to clothe the mystery and majesty of God in the beggarly rags of religion. Pannenberg agrees with Barth that theology should properly concentrate on God and God's self-revelation. As clearly as anyone in the Protestant tradition, Pannenberg defines theology in the strict sense as the *logos* of *theos (Gotteswissenschaft)*. Theology is not a mere transcript of religious feelings and experiences but, finally, a "science of God." However, "the question is only whether we have any knowledge of divine revelation in any other form than that in which it has already been received by men."[19] There is no way to examine divine revelation except as refracted through human religion.

Pannenberg is more worried about subjectivism than even Barth. Barth assumed that, by diverting theology's attention away from religion to revelation, he was securing an objective basis and content for theology, thus escaping Feuerbach's reduction of theology to anthropology. Barth, thereby, achieved only the appearance of success. His positivism of revelation is itself a form of subjectivism. "A positive

---

17. Eberhard Jüngel, *God as the Mystery of the World*, trans. Darell L. Guder (Grand Rapids, Mich.: Eerdmans, 1983), viii.
18. Wolfhart Pannenberg, *Theology and the Philosophy of Science*, trans. Francis McDonagh (Philadelphia: Westminster, 1976), 31.
19. Ibid., 319.

theory of revelation not only is not an alternative to subjectivism in theology, but is in fact the furthest extreme of subjectivism made into a theological position. . . . Barth's apparently so lofty objectivity about God and God's word turns out to rest on no more than the irrational subjectivity of a venture of faith with no justification outside itself."[20]

Pannenberg's method takes the risk of placing all his theological principles on the open market of public accountability, holding nothing back on a private Christian reservation. The commitment of faith, however existentially meaningful, cannot be used as an argument for the validity and truth of a proposition. Of course, every scholar of religion inevitably brings along a set of commitments and convictions; that is granted. Nevertheless, their function is strictly heuristic, and they should not be smuggled into one's conclusions. One wonders whether such an ideal distinction between the passionate commitments of faith and the objective findings of reason can be observed in actual practice.

Pannenberg is striving for a method of a *theology* of religion and religions that can claim intersubjective validity in the midst of all the scientific approaches to religion, psychology, sociology, phenomenology, and history. If Pannenberg could succeed in gaining broad acceptance of his vision of theology as a science among the sciences, it would bring about a revolution in theological studies. At the present time, there is a bifurcation, on the one hand, of theological studies, in which God and the revelation of God are the primary theme of the curriculum and, on the other hand, of religious studies, in which religion and the religions are analyzed as expressions of human experience and human society. In recent decades, the religious studies approach has enjoyed phenomenal growth and has come to dominate the teaching of religion in the universities. In contrast, the seminaries of the churches are, by design, theological schools more or less restricted to a hermeneutic of the Christian tradition. Pannenberg sees this as an unhealthy division. Religious studies are becoming increasingly detached from theology and radically secularized; theology is becoming wholly subservient to the practical needs of the church to train its leaders, disengaged from the public discussion concerning the truth of

---

20. Ibid., 273.

religion in a secular age. In Pannenberg's futuristic vision, a scientifically based theology of religion and religions would become the essence of a fundamental theology on which could be built a special theology of Christianity as well as each of the other religions. As the interreligious dialogues intensify, we can imagine that Pannenberg's vision will come closer to reality.

If the modern sciences of religion provide the data base for theology, we are faced with two seemingly insuperable problems. The first is that we have a variety of scientific approaches to the study of religion—philosophy of religion, psychology of religion, sociology of religion, phenomenology of religion, and the history of religion—each of which deals with its raw data from different methodological assumptions and procedures, so that they offer no unified picture. The second problem is that these disciplines have been further divided into subspecializations, yielding an explosion of knowledge which no single discipline can hope to survey and incorporate into a comprehensive system. Yet, in principle, this is what Pannenberg's approach seems to require of a theology for our time. As a matter of fact, however, Pannenberg does limit his conversation with the sciences and their results, and has his own favorite selection of dialogue partners.

Pannenberg works particularly with the phenomenology and the history of religions. He says, "Today, the phenomenological method is obviously the dominant one among the sciences of religion."[21] But what does theology have to do with the method and results of phenomenology? Paul Tillich used the phenomenological method to deal with the history of religions, but Pannenberg finds Tillich's approach deficient on two counts. First, it falls short of being a *theology* of the history of religions, focusing more on the human response than on the divine reality to which religious experience is directed. Second, it neglects the dimension of *history*, and thus can hardly do justice to the function of Christianity within the world of the religions.

None of the methods or the results of the sciences of the religions can be taken by theology at face value.[22] Theology has both a critical

---

21. Wolfhart Pannenberg, *Basic Questions in Theology*, 2 vols., trans. George H. Kehm (Philadelphia: Fortress, 1971), 2:72.

22. Pannenberg speaks of a "critical appropriation" of nontheological anthropological findings. Theologians "may not indiscriminately accept the data provided by a nontheological anthropology and make these the basis for their own work, but rather must appropriate them in a critical way" (Pannenberg, *Anthropology*, 18).

and a constructive task. A theology of religion must be critical of the reduction of the concept of religion to anthropology. From a theological perspective, the sciences of religion view human experience in too dim a light when they focus exclusively on human feelings, actions, and experiences. As Pannenberg points out, even the great Dutch phenomenologist of religion, Gerardus van der Leeuw, objected to the fact that the modern sciences of religion are methodologically at odds with the intention of the religions themselves.[23] Nothing less than a *theology* of religion is necessary if justice is to be done the essence of religion, which points first of all to the action of God in relation to humanity. None of the sciences of religion as practiced today succeeds in thematizing the primacy of the divine reality in religious experience, the underlying assumption being that religions are fundamentally expressions of the human spirit. Nor do the sciences understand themselves as partial and preliminary, requiring completion and fulfillment in a theology of religion and the religions. My suspicion is that the ranking scholars involved in the scientific study of religion—historians, phenomenologists, sociologists, etc.—are not yet prepared to be convinced that their disciplines are methodologically reductionistic, nor are they open to linking their sciences to theology as the "science of God."

Pannenberg's program for a theology of religion and the religions stands as a challenge to the current working models in vogue in the schools of religion. Pannenberg will be criticized by both theologians and scientists—by theologians who wish to do pure theology as a confessional discipline devoted to Scripture and tradition for the sake of the church and by scientists who cherish the autonomy of their own disciplines for the sake of pure science. Although I have spent most of my theological career working within a confessional setting, I have been committed at the same time to the apologetic and fundamental tasks of theology, along the lines of Tillich and Pannenberg, who build bridges to those who think and teach outside the walls of the church.

The lack of receptivity to Pannenberg's unifying scheme of theology and the sciences of religion, both in the seminaries and the

---

23. Wolfhart Pannenberg, *Systematische Theologie*, vol. 1. The as yet unpublished manuscript was made available to me by the author, with permission to use it in the writing of this chapter.

schools of religion, is due largely to its innovating features. It breaks with the dualistic schemes which keep theology and the sciences guarding their different terrains. After all, the very expressions, "theology of religion" or "theology of the history of religions," are relatively new terms, standing for new disciplines. Traditionally, religion was dealt with as a piece of the philosophy of religion, relegated to a few paragraphs in the prolegomena to theology, and the religions came into view as an appendix to missiology. When Tillich, in his last public lecture, discussed "The Significance of the History of Religions for the Systematic Theologian," he expressed his hope that, in the future of theology, there would be an "interpenetration of systematic theological study and religious historical studies."[24] He acknowledged that his own thought had been devoted mainly to "the apologetic discussion against and with the secular. Its purpose was the discussion or the answering of questions coming from the scientific and philosophical criticism of Christianity."[25] Pannenberg's thought continues but goes beyond Tillich's apologetic intentions and begins in his theology of the phenomenology of religion and the history of religions to make a down payment on Tillich's hope for the future of theology.

Tillich stood "on the boundary" between the clashing movements and ideologies of his time, between church and society, theology and philosophy, religion and culture, idealism and Marxism, and many others that he described in his autobiography, but he never stood on the boundary between Christianity and the world religions (although in his aging years he went to Japan for a dialogue with Buddhist thinkers). Today, theology must move to the front line of dialogue, for the days of religious and cultural isolationism are over. Theology is involved in this dialogue not merely for the sake of pure science but also for the sake of the mission of the church. Pannenberg's proposal for a theology of the religions combines both factors, believing that science is to mission what reason is to faith. Without the former, the latter becomes useless passion and empty subjectivism.

---

24. Paul Tillich, "The Significance of the History of Religions for the Systematic Theologian," in *The Future of Religions* (New York: Harper & Row, 1966), 91.
25. Ibid.

III. WHAT IS A THEOLOGY OF RELIGION?

The concept of religion is notoriously difficult to define. On allegedly scientific grounds, Wilfrid Cantwell Smith objects to the very notions of "religion" and "religions" because they are abstract and harmful reifications, accounting for the "we–they" mentality evidenced in the competition and hostilities between the historic religions.[26] For "religion," he would speak of "faith as a universal quality of human life,"[27] and, for "religions," he would prefer "cumulative traditions"—the historical systems of rituals and beliefs. On theological grounds, Karl Barth placed "religion" and the "religions" under God's blanket condemnation of all human self-righteousness and attempts at self-salvation. This judgment holds also against Christianity as a religion, but, insofar as Christianity accepts God's revelation, Christianity is to be qualitatively distinguished from other religions. "There is faith in this promise, and, in this faith, the presence and reality of the grace of God, which, of course, differentiates our religion, the Christian, from all others as the true religion."[28] It is but a small step from this negative verdict to Bonhoeffer's attempt to interpret Christianity in nonreligious terms, as a force for secularization driving beyond religion. John Cobb senses acute problems with the word *religions* and proposes instead to call them "Ways," the earliest term to designate the Christian movement (Acts 19:9); and, in many places, Jesus is called the "Way." Cobb's suggestion, then, is to speak of Christianity as "the Way of creative transformation as The Way which is Christ."[29]

In spite of all recent criticisms of the word *religion*, Pannenberg has decided to retain its use and to concentrate on its meaning in light of its history, its structural significance in human existence, its role in human society, and its function in theology.[30] What matters is the reality to which the word points, and, moreover, there is no better word to take its place. Pannenberg traces religion back to its ancient roots.

---

26. Wilfrid Cantwell Smith, *The Meaning and End of Religion* (New York: New American Library, 1964).
27. Wilfrid Cantwell Smith, *Toward a World Theology*, 113.
28. Karl Barth, *Church Dogmatics*, trans. G. T. Thomson and Harold Knight (New York: Scribner's, 1956), vol. 1/2, 327.
29. John Cobb, "Is Christianity a Religion?" in *What Is Religion?* 9.
30. The following discussion on the nature and truth of religion is based on Pannenberg's *Systematische Theologie*, chap. 3.

Cicero defined religion as the "cult of the gods" *(cultus deorum);* Augustine, in his writing *de vera religione,* went beyond Cicero and included *doctrine* together with *worship* as essential to religion, which has been truly realized in the church. Pannenberg then traces the history of the concept of religion through the Middle Ages and modern times, showing its permutations through Scholasticism, Protestant Orthodoxy, rationalism, romanticism, and 19th-century developments from Schleiermacher to Barth.

As usual, Pannenberg surveys the whole waterfront in the process of setting his sights on the target of his concern. Paradoxical as it may sound, Pannenberg acknowledges that, in some sense, both Schleiermacher and Barth are right; he unites the thesis of Schleiermacher that religion is an essential dimension of human life with the antithesis of Barth that upholds the primacy of God over against all religion, in a synthesis in which the primacy of the reality of God appears in the medium of religious experience as its fundamental orientation, in spite of all ambiguities and distortions manifest in the history of religions. Pannenberg's persistent quarrel with Barth has less to do with dogmatic content than with method of procedure. Pannenberg holds that Barth is certainly right in maintaining that the divinity of God stands and falls with the primacy of the reality of God and his revelation in relation to religion. But, in refusing to argue this on the basis of general anthropological foundations, Barth's position has the character of a mere subjective assertion. *Argument* and not *assertion* is what is required in the religious situation of our day. "This is the task: How can theology make clear the primacy of God and God's revelation in Jesus Christ and vindicate its claim to truth in a time in which all speaking about God is reduced to subjectivity, as is shown both by the history of modern society as well as the modern fate of the proofs of God and of philosophical theology?"[31]

On the other side, the problem with Schleiermacher's approach is its tendency to define religion without primary reference to the idea of God.[32] Although it rightly viewed religion as an essential dimension

---

31. Wolfhart Pannenberg, *Systematische Theologie,* 133-134 (in manuscript, my translation).

32. Pannenberg does acknowledge, however, that Schleiermacher, in his *Speeches on Religion,* does relate his idea of religion as "feeling of absolute dependence" to an extra-mental reality referred to as the "Universum."

of human experience, it fails to express the orientation of the religious consciousness to the numinous mystery of reality beyond personal subjectivity.[33] Pannenberg is critical of the dominant tendency of modern times to reduce the concept of religion to anthropology. Religious phenomena do express human feelings, attitudes, and actions, but God—hidden or manifest—is the unifying ground and source of meaning behind the gods of the religions. In a carefully developed argument interwoven with the thoughts of Schleiermacher, Otto, van der Leeuw, Troeltsch, and many others, Pannenberg tries to salvage the concept of religion from its anthropocentric bondage and reunite it with its originating roots in the appearance of the divine reality in which humans participate. Religion is the medium of the appearance of the divine in human experience and history.

It is only in modern times, through the process of secularization, that scholars have seriously entertained the hypothesis that the religion within the religions can be accounted for without reference to the reality of God. Pannenberg's argument for religion in a secular culture is constructed as a countercriticism to the Big Four modern critics of religion—Feuerbach, Marx, Nietzsche, and Freud. It is not enough to prove that humans are incurably religious, or that religion can be socially useful. The question is nothing less than the *truth* of religion, whether it refers to reality beyond human subjectivity. Pannenberg's massive *Anthropology* is, in a profound sense, an attempt to hoist the modern critics of religion on their own petard, to prove that their atheistic hypothesis does not fit the facts of religion which they try to explain and, in fact, to explain away. Pannenberg says, in the "Introduction" of his *Anthropology in Theological Perspective:* "If it can be shown that religion is simply a product of the human imagination and an expression of a human self-alienation, the roots of which are analyzed in a critical approach to religion, then religious faith and especially Christianity with its tradition and message will lose any claim to universal credibility in the life of the modern age. The Christian faith must then accept being lumped together with any and every form of superstition."[34]

---

33. This was Rudolf Otto's criticism of Schleiermacher's notion of religion.
34. Wolfhart Pannenberg, *Anthropology*, 15.

Anyone sharing Pannenberg's views on the truth of religion must be discouraged by the trends of the times. A 1987 poll taken in the Federal Republic of Germany indicates that 46 percent of people now consider religion obsolete (according to the Institute for Public Opinion Research). Only one-third of West Germans believe that religion has an answer for the problems of today. Two-thirds said they believe in God, but only one-third said they stand by the teachings of the church. Fifty-seven percent said they rarely or never attend worship. The statistics are more or less similar for other European countries, but somewhat less grim in the United States. Religion is faring much better in most third world nations. It seems that the modern radical criticism of religion is favored by such statistical reports. Enlightenment seems to promote atheism, whereas religion flourishes in the backwaters of primitive culture. Critics of Pannenberg will undoubtedly view his defense of religion in the face of atheistic criticism as rearranging the deck chairs on the sinking Titanic. Nevertheless, those who are still committed to the viability and truth of the Christian message should be sympathetic with Pannenberg's strategy of taking a stand and fighting the criticism rather than running and hiding in the inaccessible asylum of personal subjectivity. "For a 'truth' that would be simply my truth and would not at least claim to be universal and valid for every human being could not remain true even for me. This consideration explains why Christians cannot but try to defend the claim of their faith to be true."[35]

Confessional or church theologians who eschew apologetics and anthropological studies of religion fool themselves if they imagine that Christianity somehow holds a trump card against the modern criticism of religion that other religions lack. The retreat to religious experience or personal faith is no guarantee against the common suspicion that religious assertions are either nonsense or untrue, that is, unrelated to reality. If truth is what discloses itself only to those who already believe, how shall we have a meaningful conversation with those who do not yet believe? This would make God, as the object of theology, present and available only to those who have made the right decision of faith. God, who is supposed to be the *author* of faith, then turns out to be

35. Ibid.

the *product* of faith. Christian subjectivism proves to be no match for the modern criticism of religion, and it is fast losing ground.

Will Pannenberg's countercriticism work? In turning against a purely subjectivistic account of religion that explains it as nothing more than a matter of wishes, needs, compensations, neuroses, or illusions, Pannenberg's argument is an appeal to the self-understanding of the religious consciousness itself. A purely functional psychological or sociological explanation of religion does not do justice to religion as religion, which stands and falls with the claim to the truth concerning the reality and activity of God. No one who participates in religion today will honestly continue to do so after learning that it is a human projection without grounding in truth and reality. Religious people would never regard their own subjectivity as self-justifying without relation to the reality of its object. The radical critics of religion assume that religion is alien to the essence of being human, and that to propagate religious belief in a secular culture is to infantilize human beings. It would be just a question of time before the practice of religion and its belief in God would wither away.

Pannenberg's counterview argues that religion belongs to the essence of humanity and is, therefore, constitutive of a full human life and human society. However, the finding that religion is, from the outset, human—and fundamentally so—is only a necessary but never a sufficient condition for the truth of religious assertions about the reality of God. This is particularly true of the biblical-Christian faith, which asserts that God is the creator of the world, the power determining all reality, and not merely the source of religious piety or creaturely consciousness. At this point in his argument, Pannenberg turns to the world, beyond the limits of human subjectivity, as the locus for authenticating speech about God, but not in the antiquated sense of a cosmological proof of God's existence. How then? When Pannenberg talks about the world as the creation of God, he has in mind the world as a historical process in which the power of God is proving itself. The idea of God cannot be limited to human subjectivity. The question of the truth of religious statements can be answered only in the open field of history, the context in which the "gods" of the religions express their power. A religion is verified, or its statements are verified or not, in the course of the historical process. Religions are not eternal but temporal; they come and they go; they are born and they change in the flux of history. This is true of Israel, Christianity, and all religions. Only a moving picture can represent them in their contingent historical reality, and not a series of snapshots of their essential immutable structures. What is needed, even more than a theology of religion as of the essence of humanness, is a theology of the history of religions as the sphere in which the Godhead of God is self-authenticated through the power of his actions.[36]

IV. THEOLOGY OF THE HISTORY OF RELIGIONS

Christianity can be assigned its proper place only within a history of the religions. Pannenberg has stated: "History is the most comprehensive horizon of Christian theology."[37] A theology of the religions constructs the framework within which the uniqueness, truth, and particular mission of Christianity must be developed. In the age of Christendom, the truth of Christianity stood beyond question. Today, that truth is very much in dispute all over the world. We are now closer to the New Testament situation when the truth of the Christian faith had to vindicate itself in face of the competing truth claims of other religions. When the cultural props for Christianity have been stripped away, and the Christian religion is no longer buttressed by political, economic, and military advantages, the question of the truth of Christianity and of each and every other religion appears in a new light, raising the issue of how they shall properly be related to each other.

Pannenberg would use the word *syncretism* to characterize the growth and interaction between religions in the universal stream of history, except for its bad connotations. He quotes Hermann Gunkel's saying, "Christianity is a syncretistic religion,"[38] which was vehemently protested, because it seemed to threaten the uniqueness of Christianity. But "syncretism" may actually be turned to good account. "The fact that Christianity is syncretistic to an unusual degree thus expresses not a weakness but the unique strength of Christianity."[39] A

---

36. Wolfhart Pannenberg, *Basic Questions in Theology*, 2:104.
37. Ibid., 1:15.
38. Ibid., 2:87.
39. Ibid., 2:88.

perfect example is the use of the Hellenistic concept of *Logos* to express the universal relevance of Jesus of Nazareth. The missionary encounter of Christianity and the religions gives numerous examples of the syncretic process. Today, Christianity is engaged in a dialogue with the religions, showing that this process is still in progress.[40] Since religions meet each other as total views of reality, the interreligious dialogues inevitably become a medium in which their respective "gods" are being put to the test, but not in the same bloody way, we hope, as in the contest between Yahweh and the Baalim in ancient Israel. When religions meet, there is no telling beforehand what will happen. Sometimes they agree to coexist, limiting their influence to their respective circles of devotees. Sometimes they fuse and an amalgamation process takes place in which a principle of interpretation is at work to relate the new situation to the old. Something like this happened in primitive Christianity, where the Christological principle interpreted the Hebrew past, the Christian present, and the world's future. Sometimes one religion destroys and replaces the others through war and conquest. Examples are not hard to find.

Now, what is Pannenberg's view of the proper place of Christianity in the religious history of the world? The first thing to be said is a matter of fact. Christianity has contributed, through its worldwide mission, to a common religious situation of the whole of mankind. Even the secularizing process that draws regional cultures together through science and technology into a new international situation is itself a by-product of Christianity, albeit fraught with great tensions and ambiguities. Today, virtually all nations of the world have been confronted in some fashion with the Christian tradition as well as with the secularized culture that has developed in Western society.

The sustaining power of Christianity to endure in world history lies in its openness to the future, a feature rooted in Israel's interpretation of divine revelation as promise. A religion that lives by promise toward the future can cope with the vicissitudes of the historical process better than religions related to the past-oriented myth of primordial time. "Whoever lives on the basis of the archetypal and strives to achieve for the present only its optimal participation in the archetypal

---

40. Wolfhart Pannenberg, *Theology and the Philosophy of Science*, 361.

reality, lives unhistorically. To this extent, archaic peoples close themselves off from the historic future."[41] The revelation of God as promise grounds and mediates the historicity and openness of religious experience. This is the unique element in Israel's particular experience of God. Israel came to view reality as history moving toward a future goal which had not yet appeared and, at the same time, would not be a recurrence to a primordial and archetypal time. Israel, however, oscillated between seeing the revelation of God in the law given at Sinai and in the coming of the Messiah who would inaugurate the future of God's reign. A similar kind of dialectical tension repeated itself in Christianity, which split its eschatology between what had already occurred in Jesus and what was still to happen in the eschatological future of God's kingdom. The future of the reign of God proclaimed by Jesus was not determined by the established traditions of Israel. It was, rather, the other way around; the future held the power to reinterpret the past. On account of Jesus' unique relation to the future of God's rule, sacrificing himself for its mission, Jesus is the revelation of the coming of God in the midst of history, before the end. Christology is the point of tension between the historical particularity of Jesus' person and ministry and the eschatological universality of God's coming and rule. The rule of God which Jesus proclaimed and pioneered in his own life, death, and resurrection can be seen in light of the apostolic message as the power at work in all the religions of humanity. This Christocentric perspective does not prevent Pannenberg from acknowledging that the God revealed by Jesus is identical with the God at work in all the religions other than Christian. Although all the religions are striving after the same divine mystery as revealed in Jesus, something unique and definitive happened in the message and history of Jesus. Pannenberg makes the bold assertion that the special place of Jesus Christ in world history is a phenomenon that can be examined on generally applicable methodological grounds, without recourse to specifically Christian dogmatic principles. No special Christian spectacles are presumably required for one to see the facts that disclose the place of Christianity in the history of religions.

In disclaiming a dogmatic standpoint from the outset, Pannenberg

---

41. Wolfhart Pannenberg, *Basic Questions in Theology*, 2:109.

is setting himself at a polar opposite position from Hendrik Kraemer's expressed in *The Christian Message in a Non-Christian World*. There Kraemer asserted that Christian theology has a perfect right to formulate a Christian theology of the religions on the basis of its own presuppositions. A Christian qua Christian can think only within a circle of which Christ is the center, however vast the circumference of that circle might be. The difference between Kraemer and Pannenberg is that what for Kraemer is a premise of faith (the Christological starting point) is for Pannenberg a conclusion of reason. Both function with a high Christology. Consider Pannenberg's statement: "Jesus of Nazareth is the final revelation of God because the end of history appeared in him. It did so both in his eschatological message and in his resurrection from the dead. However, he can be understood to be God's final revelation only in connection with the whole of history as mediated by the history of Israel. He is God's revelation in the fact that all history receives its light from him."[42]

Pannenberg's inductive historical approach to Christology "from below to above" remains within the framework of a Christocentric view of the place of Christianity in the history of world religions. However, the God who is definitively revealed by the Christ event is the same divine mystery who appears in various ways in other religions. The difference for Pannenberg has to do with the way eschatology figures into his interpretation of history. The eschatological kingdom proleptically present in Jesus can be seen retrospectively to be active in all epochs prior to Christ and in all religions as the power of their end. Christianity can be assimilative of the elements of truth in other religious traditions, because they too function as witnesses, in their own proleptic way, to the coming of the fullness of truth beyond their own limitations. Since the God of the future was present in Jesus as the eschatological power of salvation, demonstrated by God's raising of Jesus from the dead, a fact which is also open to historical-critical inquiry, Jesus holds a place of unique significance as the key to the future of the world and its salvation.

---

42. Wolfhart Pannenberg, "The Revelation of God in Jesus of Nazareth," in *Theology as History*, ed. J. M. Robinson (New York: Macmillan, 1967), 104.

V. QUESTIONS IN LIEU OF A CONCLUSION

I have tried to portray Pannenberg's thinking on the relation of Christianity to other religions through a combination of quotations, paraphrases, commentaries, comparisons, and interpretations, and have done so with a fundamentally sympathetic attitude. My theological conversion to Pannenberg's overall theological perspective goes back to the early 60s, when I was searching for a more adequate place for the historical Jesus in systematic theology than I could find in Barth, Bultmann, or Tillich. After much resistance on my part, Pannenberg won me over to the importance of taking history seriously. My first monograph, *History and Hermeneutics,* was a tribute to his persuasiveness. It is this same feature of his thought that appeals to me on the role and future of Christianity in world history. In this chapter, we have covered sketchily the anthropological, theological, Christological, and eschatological links between Christian theology and the challenge of religious pluralism. There is no space to draw out the ecclesiological and missiological implications of this approach—which I have done in many writings, but chiefly in two of my books, *The Flaming Center* and *The Apostolic Imperative.* I hope that, throughout, I have amply acknowledged my indebtedness to Pannenberg's work.

Yet, my own appropriation of Pannenberg's conceptualization continues to generate questions to which I look for more explicit and complete answers in his books and essays.

1. My own view of the relation between Christianity and the religions has been stamped by the Lutheran tradition, a tradition which Pannenberg, of course, shares and knows in its detail as well as anyone. In this tradition of thinking, certain themes stand out and impress themselves forcefully on every aspect of thought, themes like law and gospel, the three *solas*—grace alone, faith alone, Scripture alone— theology of the cross, and the two kingdoms. Pannenberg's method calls for a suspension of these principles so that, presumably, his examination of religious phenomena would not be laden with dogmatic prejudgments. My question is: What is the use of these principles if they don't function to interpret the data of religious experience? Can they really be bracketed if they thoroughly permeate one's mind and soul? Should they not function at the outset in guiding the application of general methodological rules, at least in the formation of hypotheses

to be tested? Pannenberg admits that such confessional principles may have a heuristic function and do inevitably enter into the psychological matrix of inquiry, but do they not also possibly have material significance as binding interpretations of divine revelation which have come to expression in the message of Jesus and the apostolic tradition? If it is granted that there can be no presuppositionless approach to the history of religions, then why should not those presuppositions that arise out of the historic encounter with the God disclosed in Jesus of Nazareth enjoy the same rights as those that stem from some other religious or nonreligious perspective? Is it not the case that these presuppositions do, in fact, guide Pannenberg's analysis like a director behind the scenes who does not appear in full view with the actors? The once-for-allness of the Christ event and the principle of justification by faith alone are two such principles which play a normative role in Pannenberg's theology. Are they received as gifts from the tradition or are they products of theological work?

My question can be otherwise formulated as the relation between faith and reason, a theme which Pannenberg frequently discusses. Pannenberg's great fear is fideism; it has bedeviled Protestant theology. But so has rationalism, and that looms up at the other end of the spectrum. I have frequently had the impression that, after a long and detailed argument, Pannenberg reaches a conclusion, which he claims to have demonstrated *sola ratione,* but somehow the ordinary layperson already holds the same conclusion *sola fide.* I have formulated the matter this way: "What reason sees is seen by reason, but *that* reason sees what it sees is made factually possible by faith." This seems to be most certainly true in the case of the resurrection of Jesus. Although I am fully in accord with Pannenberg's emphasis on the resurrection, I believe faith plays a role in its affirmation that transcends the demonstrations of historical reason. As Luther put it, "I cannot by my own reason and strength believe . . . but the Holy Spirit has called me by the gospel." I am still fond of Pascal's *pensée:* "Faith has its reasons which reason cannot know." I read Kierkegaard before I read Hegel— or Pannenberg—and I must confess that there remains a taint of that subjectivity which worries Pannenberg to the extreme. Having said this, I am grateful to those in the tradition who have argued for the reasonableness of the Christian faith.

2. Pannenberg agrees with many theologians in the Protestant tradition—Söderblom, Althaus, Tillich, and others—that there is genuine revelation of God within the history of religions. I certainly agree with that. Althaus used the idea of *Uroffenbarung* to express the belief that there is an original revelation of God based on creation. Others have called this "general revelation." This is universal and prior to the special revelation of God in the covenants with Israel and Jesus Christ. Pannenberg does not employ this language of "general" and "special" revelation, which has proved useful to make a proper distinction between First and Second Article concerns. My question is whether Pannenberg has found a clear enough way to speak of the distinction between God's revelation in the religions and God's unique revelation in Jesus Christ, which the New Testament calls "the gospel." Nor does Pannenberg use the distinction between law and gospel, so that everything has a relation to the gospel as question to answer, or as *praeparatio evangelica*.

Theologians in the ancient church adopted the Stoic idea of the Logos as the *tertium comparationis* to link God's revelation in the religions to God's revelation in Jesus Christ. The *logos spermatikos* that spread its seeds throughout humanity is identical with the *logos ensarkos* in Jesus Christ. This has continued down to our time and has found a new and creative expression in the Christology of John Cobb. Pannenberg is critical of this line,[43] although he affirms its basic intention to claim universal validity for the truth revealed in Christ. In his chapter in the *Festschrift* for John Cobb, Pannenberg develops a sharp critique of Cobb's "Liberal Logos Christology."[44] The Logos concept provides Cobb with a vehicle to control his interpretation of the figure of Jesus by Whitehead's metaphysics, and, thus, the historical particulars of Jesus' own history are suppressed. Rather than mediate

---

43. Pannenberg would agree, I think, with Ernst Benz, who made this statement: "The traditional Logos . . . proves itself to be a theological ell which is too short to measure our modern consciousness of history." Ernst Benz, "Ideas for a Theology of the History of Religion," in *The Theology of the Christian Mission*, ed. Gerald H. Anderson (New York: McGraw-Hill, 1961), 136.

44. Wolfhart Pannenberg, "A Liberal Logos Christology: The Christology of John Cobb," *John Cobb's Theology in Process*, ed. David Griffin and Thomas J. J. Altizer (Philadelphia: Westminster, 1977), 133-149.

Jesus' relation to God through the Logos, Pannenberg would deal immediately with Jesus' relation to the Father as the Son, and thereby lay hold of the root of his construction of the Trinity.[45]

What is the conceptual mechanism in Pannenberg's historical and eschatological outlook to coordinate God's revelation in the history of religions and God's revelation in Jesus' filial relation to the Father? The church fathers had the *logos asarkos* operating throughout the cosmos. The Reformers made a clear distinction between revelation through creation and law, on the one hand, and through gospel and church, on the other hand, a distinction which Gustaf Wingren has renewed to good effect in his theology. Liberal theology would make no distinction but rather identify all revelations as one. Jesus Christ is revealer of God, but so are many others, all on the same level, without qualitative distinction. How does Pannenberg's thoroughgoing historical model of interpretation solve this problem? I must leave it open as a problem to be solved in the historical process itself, through the missionary encounter of the gospel with all religions, the final outcome of which is a matter of the eschatological future. The particularity of the gospel does not exist in history without the particularity of the community of faith that mediates the unifying future of God to all religions and cultures. The question is how the experience of God apart from Christ is related to the experience of God in Christ.

3. My third question shifts the focus from revelation to salvation. There is a twofold revelation of God, through the universal history of religions and through the final revelation of God in Jesus Christ. But not all revelation is *saving* revelation. The revelation of God through creation establishes the law, maintains order, and strives for justice; the revelation of God through Jesus Christ inaugurates a new creation beyond law and order, and announces justification as a free gift of salvation apart from the worldly system of works and rewards. To get right to the point, Pannenberg affirms that there is divine revelation in all the religions. But are the religions also "ways of salvation"? If they are, why is Christ necessary? Pannenberg rejects Oscar Cullmann's clear-cut distinction between *Heilsgeschichte* and *Weltgeschichte*, thus

---

45. Wolfhart Pannenberg, "Problems of a Trinitarian Doctrine of God," *Dialog* 26 (1987): 250-257.

seeming to suggest that salvation history is a theme that runs throughout world history. I believe that the history of religions is oriented to salvation, as the history of the unending human quest for wholeness and fulfillment, in the spirit of Augustine's statement, "Our hearts are restless until they find their rest in God." But religions, as such, are not "ways of salvation." They are signposts marking the history of preparation for the coming of God's eschatological salvation announced by the gospel in the name of Jesus Christ.

Some Roman Catholic theologians, following Karl Rahner, are teaching that the religions are "ordinary ways of salvation," and Christianity is the "extraordinary way."[46] Salvation history is going on in all the religions and, thus, the religions, as such, are means of grace unto salvation. That is a novel teaching that goes beyond the statements of the Second Vatican Council on the non-Christian religions.[47] Nor, in the Protestant tradition, do we find so high an estimate of religions as "ways of salvation." Not even Christianity as a religion is capable of salvation. My question is: What is Pannenberg's view of the soteriological *efficacy* of the religions as organized systems of beliefs, rituals, and institutions? The older teaching that the religions are the "wiles and ways of the devil" may sound too harsh for modern sensibilities, but it continues to be true that the most heinous crimes against humanity are done in the name of the gods.

4. There is a slender line in the history of theology that holds out hope for universal salvation. Those who have held the belief in a universal consummation of the totality of reality *(ta panta)* in the final future of God have done so as a function of their "high" Christology. Karl Barth is the most splendid example of a Christocentric universalism. Pannenberg's theology of universal history would seem to lead to the same conclusion. We have called it an "eschatological panentheism." Yet, Pannenberg is more reserved than Barth in his speculations about the eschatological consummation, particularly with respect to the question whether at the end all shall be united through

---

46. Cf. Heinz Schlette, *Toward a Theology of Religions* (New York: Herder and Herder, 1966).

47. This is clearly demonstrated by Paul Hacker, "The Christian Attitude toward Non-Christian Religions," *Zeitschrift für Missionswissenschaft und Religionswissenschaft* (Münster) 55 (1971): 81-89.

Christ in the fullness of the divine life. There are universalist features in Pannenberg's thought from beginning to end, so that we might expect some clearer answers to the questions that trouble people about the universalist vision of eschatological hope.

I have explored Pannenberg's thinking on a theology of religions, because I believe it offers an alternative to the exclusivism of the evangelical conservatives to the right and to the relativism of the neo-liberal pluralists to the left. I have found Pannenberg's position attractive because his understanding of Christology calls for an openness to the future that does not fall back upon exclusivism and does not go headlong into a nonnormative relativism. Such a Christology that interprets Jesus as the "way, the truth, and the life" is in full accord with the central affirmations of the New Testament and the Christian tradition and, at the same time, is open to interreligious dialogue without nostalgia for the "good old days" of Christian imperialism that aimed to displace all other religions. What is needed, after all, is a Christian theology of religions that mediates the New Testament message of the normativity and finality of Jesus Christ under the conditions of the contemporary encounter of the world religions, worldviews, and ideologies. I believe that Pannenberg's theology is a timely summons to meet this challenge.

A RESPONSE
TO MY AMERICAN FRIENDS

Wolfhart Pannenberg

◆

It gives me a great deal of satisfaction to welcome in this collection of essays a testimony to the ongoing effort of Christian theology in a community of discourse of which I am happy to be a part. I am keenly aware of the limitations of my own personal contribution to this common task, but it is a pleasure to engage in a dialogue with colleagues and friends where it is not necessary first to complain about misreadings and misinterpretation before one gets to the real issues that should concern every Christian theology of this age. The awareness of such issues has united me to each one of the contributors of this volume as well as to many others.

The questions of how Christianity is related to the world religions and of the place of religion in general in human life belong to the most basic of these issues. Theological neglect of the issue of religion has only served to marginalize the importance of Christianity itself in the context of secular culture. To replace the term *religion* by *faith* confirms the general image of religious people as clinging to subjective preferences rather than to objective truth. In the spirit of the biblical religions it is certainly the reality of God that constitutes religious concern and not the other way around. But it is only in the form of religion and of *one* religion among others that the divine reality can be perceived by human beings. Religion, then, is the primary human form of perceiving the reality of God. As such, the issue of religion also belongs to anthropology. This is in itself a witness to the reality of God, the creator of everything; to argue that the human being is by nature the

313

religious animal is certainly not enough to demonstrate the reality of God, but is indispensable in any affirmation of that reality. The reason is that it is with the human being as religious animal that the reality of God becomes an explicit issue. Therefore, if the human being could do as well without relating his or her understanding of human existence and of the world of human experience to God, that in itself would be strong evidence against religious belief of any sort, even though it might not amount to a conclusive proof against the existence of a God. For this reason, anthropology has become the most prominent battleground in the contest between theists and atheists, and Carl Braaten rightly emphasizes that my entire book on anthropology was meant as a contribution to this dispute (p. 300).

The truth of a particular religious belief is, of course, another matter. It is my thesis that the question of the divine reality cannot be settled independently from dealing with the particular and antagonistic claims of the different religious traditions. All this is very well reported in Carl Braaten's essay. But in what sense, then, can we speak of "genuine revelation of God within the history of religions" (p. 309)? Hardly in the sense that the different truth claims of the religious traditions may be accepted equally: they cannot, because they fight each other. Therefore, the history of religions is a history of the disproof of religious truth claims as well as a history confirming (at least temporarily) some of them. This descriptive approach converges with the biblical view of history as theophany, as Mircea Eliade used to characterize the prophetic point of view. There, the expectation is that in the end it will be the God of Israel alone who will emerge as true God. And this end is said to be anticipated in Jesus Christ when the New Testament speaks of God's revelation in him. Therefore, there is finally only one revelation of God, in the view of Christianity; but since this summarizes the entire history of divine–human interaction, that Barthian affirmation should be presented in an inclusive rather than exclusive form.

I consider this the most important question asked by Carl Braaten, and it entails an answer to his third question (pp. 310f.). To me it seems unfortunate to distinguish between "revelation" and "saving revelation" in the sense that only the second expression relates to the uniqueness of Jesus Christ. The question of salvation is involved everywhere in religious life just as much as the experience of the truly divine, and the two are bound up with each other. But both of them are also a matter of continuing controversy. The Christian claim aims at the *finality* of revelation as well as of salvation, and as such it also includes a tendency towards "universal salvation" (pp. 311f.). But the historical process is still open in human experience, the controversy about the Christian (and other) truth claims is still continuing, and certainly there will be no salvation for anyone without going through divine judgment.

Is the theologian taking a confessional position (Braaten's first question, pp. 307f.) in working out the meaning structure inherent in the Christ event as anticipatory fulfillment of history? In a certain sense a confessional factor may already be involved in concerning oneself so intensely with Jesus Christ and with the foundations of the Christian truth claims. It may also be the case that one's own confessional tradition—e.g., being a Lutheran—influences the perspective of one's interpretation. But that can as easily result in distortion as in providing clues for deeper insight. Therefore, in devoting one's time confidently to the exploration of the meaning structure inherent in the Christ event, the theologian should be open to having his or her preconceptions corrected. This also applies to favorite doctrines of our Lutheran tradition, certainly to the teaching on law and gospel and the two kingdoms. On the other hand, such correction may be considered as a consequence of the principle of *sola scriptura*. But then, the scripture principle itself is deeply modified when we turn from the inspired authority of the Bible to the meaning inherent in the Christ event as a criterion to judge even the adequacy of the different scriptural witnesses. The doctrinal principles of the Lutheran tradition—like those of other churches—have served to introduce generation after generation into the Christian faith. But they are not more of a guarantee of truth than, say, Roman Catholic doctrines are. The truth of the gospel is to be found only in Jesus Christ himself, considered in the context of his history, and it has to be looked for again and again with fresh eyes. Even so, the question of its truth is not finally settled, but is in open dispute until he will come again in the glory of God's kingdom. God himself, if anybody, will take care of that, and we may leave it to him.

To accept the controversial status of Christian truth claims is the

price to be paid for preserving the cognitive character of the affirmations of the Christian faith. It is also a condition for reintroducing
the Christian truth claims into the area of public discourse, rather than
claiming some "supernatural" quality for the content of the Christian
faith. Treating the content of faith as something "supernatural" or—
if one prefers the Protestant equivalent—as a subjective truth that is
not open to public assessment and critique contributed significantly to
the marginalization of Christian theology in the course of modernity.
Louis Dupré clearly perceives that much of my endeavor has been
directed against that tendency. This applies to my criticism of the bifurcation of the supernatural and the natural, but also of the subjectivism
in the revivalist tradition of Christian thought. It emerges in the emphasis on reason and truth, in the use of critical rationalism in my
appraisal of theological method, but also in my criticism of the short-
comings of secularization. Dupré is correct in placing me in the tradition
of attempts to recapture the unity of nature and grace. It was, indeed,
the vision of the Christian humanists of the early Renaissance, as Dupré
eloquently points out. Was not their historical failure due to the fact
that—in spite of the work of Nicholas Cusanus—that vision was never
fully received in the theology of the church? I do not share Dupré's
negative evaluation of Ockham's theology, which has so often been
misrepresented; it was in fact an exciting attempt at a new Christian
synthesis. In the 15th century, however, the Platonic renaissance of
Florentine humanism should have induced a reappropriation of the
Platonic spirit of Greek patristic theology and of its unified Christian
vision of creation and human nature. In our century, such a rediscovery
took place in the work of French patristic scholars; as a student I was
deeply impressed by the unity of faith and reason in patristic theology.
Since that time I have considered the age of patristic theology as a
model of what Christian theology should achieve in our own time. In
Gregory of Nyssa, this patristic vision became a seedbed of the mystical
spirituality which Dupré rightly considers a decisive condition for restoring the unity of nature and grace. It is important that Gregory's
spirituality was not based on some irrational experience, but was intimately related to the rationality of the patristic vision of God and
creation.

In the 16th century the horizon had become more limited than in the century before, the spirituality moralized. Unfortunately, the Reformation shared in the typically Western overemphasis on morality and guilt-consciousness. It even helped to perpetuate it for centuries, in spite of Luther's rediscovery of the glory of Christian freedom. I share Louis Dupré's unhappiness with the concept of a merely imputative justification. In Luther's thought, the idea of imputation had been based on his mystical description of the union with Christ by faith, but, as early as in Melanchthon's thought, the moralism of the later humanists took over, and the arid concept of an isolated act of imputation resulted. But was the Roman Catholic theology of that time less moralistic? Both sides were caught in the narrowness of a primarily moral interpretation of Christian piety, and this seems to account for the limitations of Jansenism as well. In the long run, the dominant moralism of Christian piety was bound to result in a revolt against moral norms—a revolt such as we have experienced since Nietzsche. One precondition of a lasting revival of Christian spirituality in our time, and even of morality itself, in competition with Eastern religious mentalities, will certainly be that the limitations of a spirituality bound to guilt feelings and moralism be overcome. But neither is emancipation from such a mentality sufficient to constitute a new spirituality. For this purpose, a unified vision of God and the world is needed, a vision which also restores the place of aesthetics in religious awareness—a most neglected issue in modern Christian piety. But neither aesthetics nor mysticism will help as long as Christian theology cannot recapture the Christian truth claim to the dependence of all our awareness of ourselves and of our world on the reality of God.

Such a reinterpretation of reality is basic to the more specific cognitive claims of the Christian faith. Avery Dulles underlines the interconnection between this and my emphasis on historical events as mediating revelation. He has given a fair and balanced account of the difficulties inherent in such a position. He also notices a development of differentiation in my thought as compared to earlier assertions. I am in general agreement with his presentation. Certainly I never wanted to say that the resurrection of Jesus as an *isolated* event can be the only revelatory event. I always emphasized that it has to be seen in its historical context, in the context of Jesus' own history, but also in the broader context of Jewish history from the time of ancient Israel, and finally in the context of human history at large. In looking at these horizons of history, however, the Christian point of view is the resurrection of the crucified Jesus. Certainly there are parts of the New Testament witness where the resurrection is not explicitly mentioned, but there seems to be every good reason to assume that everywhere the perspective of presentation of the Jesus tradition was informed by the Christian Easter faith. The resurrection of the crucified Jesus also provides a different perspective for the interpretation of the history of ancient Israel than that of the Old Testament writings themselves. But still, that history of experiences of God's action in history is indispensable for understanding Jesus' message and his personal fate.

The historical context of Jewish history comprises not only physical events, of course, but also memories, beliefs, rules, expectations. There is no human history without language and, especially when it comes to religion, the symbolic element in language is highly important. In emphasizing the increasing priority of divine "deeds" or events in the development of biblical conceptions of revelation, I never wanted to disregard that it is only in language that the meaning of facts can be articulated. I fully agree with Dulles: " . . . it does not follow that everyone who learns of the events is by that very fact sufficiently equipped to discern their full meaning" (p. 180). I also agree that "credibility of the proclaimed word does not have to rest on a naked claim to authority" (ibid.). Unfortunately, however, the last-mentioned position was a view widely held in Protestant theology when I was a student, and in my opinion it contributed significantly to ruin the credibility of the proclaimed word. Instead, the proclaimed word should indeed "justify itself by its illuminative power," as Dulles says (ibid.). This "authority of insight" was what I wanted to restore, and certainly it is not only historical insight that is important in this matter, although a degree of historical insight on the part of theological reflection and a justified feeling of historical reliability concerning the basic Christian affirmations about Jesus on the part of every Christian are indispensable as long as we take seriously that Jesus is a historical person. This does not stand in contradiction to Dulles' statement: "The ordinary catalyst of faith is the religious testimony of convinced believers" (p. 181). But the assumption of basic reliability of the historical content of the gospel is implicit in the proper function of that ordinary catalyst.

The access to the historical basis of the Christian faith can be blocked by a narrow definition of historical reality in terms of a strictly secular notion of reality in general. Theologians have been somewhat shy in applying critical reflection to the ingredients of historical method, although it is generally admitted that the principles of historical method themselves are subject to a continuous process of reconsideration. In dealing with this issue, I consider it necessary that the divine reality which is the subject of religious traditions must not be excluded by a definition of reality before it even comes to specific historical investigation and judgment. In some of my earlier writings I expressed this concern in such a form that it seemed as if the historian were required to accept a Christian dogmatic conception of God as a presupposition of his work. More recently, I have tried to phrase my point more cautiously: in dealing with religious traditions, scholarly investigation and reconstruction should not preclude in principle the dimension of the divine and its interaction with secular reality. It may treat it as controversial, but not as nonexistent.

On the issue of faith and knowledge in general, my position did not change perhaps as much as Dulles seems to assume. Even in earlier statements I admitted that, psychologically considered, trust may precede knowledge, although with regard to the logic of faith trust presupposes some knowledge of the one to whom one entrusts oneself. Whether such knowledge is considered part of the concept of faith itself is a purely terminological question as long as the "dialectical interplay" between the two (Dulles, p. 186) is preserved. Finally, hope as an inherent factor in the act of faith (pp. 186f.) is bound up with its anticipatory nature. In the case of the Christian faith this corresponds to the anticipatory structure of the resurrection of Jesus as well as of his proclamation of the imminent kingdom of God. The proleptic presence of the eschaton in Jesus' history also seems bound up with the presence of the divine Spirit in its content, with the effect that the Spirit is communicated through the apostolic proclamation rather than supervening upon its content as an additional factor.

The importance of the concept of anticipation in my thought has been highlighted by Philip Clayton. He emphasizes correctly the strictly theological root of the concept of anticipation as I came to use it (p.

129), which was subsequently generalized to impinge even upon metaphysical principles (pp. 131f.). To do so appeared to me as inevitable, if Jesus' person and history are to be understood as final revelation of the divine Logos. It also prevented me from becoming a Hegelian (Clayton, pp. 132f., offers some of the most pertinent remarks on this issue), while encouraging a somewhat critical use of Dilthey's (and Heidegger's) hermeneutical philosophies (pp. 134f.).

Clayton is correct in describing my position in terms of "strong anticipation" (p. 131), while he himself seems to prefer "a weaker, 'epistemological' reading of anticipation" (p. 141). The latter would not be enough, I think, to express the truth claim that is inherent in the Christian affirmation that the God whose kingdom is still to come has been revealed definitively in the history and person of Jesus. That this is so is still a debated issue; the truth of the Christian affirmation depends on the future of the "second coming" of Jesus with the final consummation of God's kingdom. But if this Christian hope *will* come true, our present faith will have been more than pure guesswork. If we presuppose the advent of that future, which is still open in our actual experience, then—*but only on that condition*—it will mean indeed that "the gist of the final outcome has been decided (ontologically) in Jesus' resurrection" (p. 131). The condition is important, however, even metaphysically significant; it opens up the space for the work of the Spirit to complete the universal significance of what happened in Jesus.

Clayton comments on the notion of strong anticipation: "This is not an easy teaching" (p. 131). This is certainly a correct statement, and the five difficulties he raises (pp. 136ff.) are very real. But they do not compel one to surrender the notion of strong anticipation. They all derive from what Clayton mentions as a first difficulty: the use of the notion of anticipation in my published writings so far "suggests rather than presents a complete theory of reality" (p. 136). For many years, my American friends and others have urged me to spell out in more detail the metaphysical implications of that notion. Recently, I offered some approximation to this task in a series of lectures on God and Metaphysics, presented at the *Istituto degli studi philosophici* of Naples in April 1986, which will be published in German in 1988. To meet the task fully would require a complete metaphysics. But the lectures will at least indicate what such a metaphysics might look like.

What Clayton calls the two senses of anticipation (p. 137) is not the most difficult issue, because from the point of view of "strong anticipation" the subjective side of it corresponds to the ontological structure. The point of my thesis is precisely that the two belong together. In Clayton's view, this is considered to constitute another difficulty, which he calls the "idealist framework" (p. 138) of my thought. I am not sure whether every claim to truth in the sense of correspondence of thought to reality must be "idealistic." If so, everyone who does not surrender the notion of truth has to be called an idealist, and in that case I shall not be ashamed to be counted among that company. But normally, the notion of idealism is used in a somewhat narrower sense. I certainly do not want to equate thought and being in general. However, if some of our statements are in fact "true," then there must be some "link" between thought and being. At this point, the notion of anticipation seems helpful to clarify how this can be the case in light of the temporal nature not only of our experience and provisional insight, but also of the experienced reality itself. "Why should we expect the real to be thinkable, even in its entirety . . . ?" (p. 139). If we assume that at least some of our statements are true, and if truth involves coherence, it seems unavoidable to do so, if we want to be consistent.

Clayton's fourth difficulty relates to the theory of time and to the problem of determinism (pp. 139f.), and it is closely related to the issue of freedom with which his fifth point deals (pp. 140f.). Clayton correctly refers to my statements on the eschaton as coincidence of time and eternity. This is not the Augustinian view (p. 140), however. It is closer to Plotinus' theory of time, but deviates from it in important respects, because Plotinus did not develop a positive evaluation of time—a deficiency that may be due to his conception of God. The trinitarian conception of Christian theology offers additional possibilities at this point; especially, it provides a notion of created reality as different from but also united to God through the "economic" trinity, the "historical" aspect of the divine reality itself which nevertheless is one with the "immanent" trinity of God's eternal self-identity. Given this perspective, the finite (and temporal) may indeed be preserved as well as transcended when it obtains participation in eternity and thereby its own ultimate identity. Eternity, of course, is not only future, but also (as future) prior to the other modes of time. This has given rise again and again to suspicions of some inherent determinism in the thesis of an ontological priority of the future. But determinism is a clear idea only on the basis of a scheme where past events determine the future outcome of the process. "Determination" of the present by the power of the future is an almost completely different matter. Therefore, it is a mistake to apply the notion of determinism to this conception on the tacit assumption that it is of the same structure. Such an assumption amounts to saying that the difference of temporal direction does not matter. This is precisely where the mistake resides. "Determination" of the present by the future is not the same sort of determination as in the case of past events that determine the future outcome. It does not, therefore, prevent human freedom in terms of contingent decisions. To the contrary, it makes such freedom of decision possible. Nor does "the proleptic inauguration of God's rule" in the history of Christ (p. 141) destroy the openness of the historical process. The reason is that such a statement is based on the *condition* of a future that is still open in the course of our experience, the future arrival of God's kingdom in its fullness.

The supposed peril of determinism also stands at the center of the concerns expressed by the three process thinkers who contributed to this volume: David Polk, Lewis Ford, and John Cobb. Polk offers the most extensive discussion of the question. In approaching the issue, he takes into consideration the connection between (eschatological) futurity and eternity (pp. 156f.) and my intention to look at God's essential futurity as the source of human freedom (p. 159) as well as of contingency in general (p. 161). Understandably, as a process theologian he feels uneasy with the idea "that the power of the future is a genuine force of creativity out of which history is fully and concretely constituted" (p. 160). But he notices an escape from determinism in what appears to him as a "concession" (p. 162), i.e., that God might himself determine to leave "some degree of self-determination" (p. 161) to the creature. In my own view, this is not actually a concession, since even the strongest doctrine of creation *ex nihilo* must want to affirm that God creates his creatures as they are, which means in the case of the human creature that human freedom itself is to be conceived as God's creation. There can be no competition between God and the human person regarding his or her free activity, since they do not act on the same level. According to the concept of creation, if correctly understood, the creator intends the independent existence of his creatures, and the human case is the highest case of independent existence. David Polk indeed is in agreement with my own understanding of the Christian interpretation of God's "all-determining power" in terms of love (p. 164), a love waiting for the response of the creature. This is the reason why the creation of the world takes the form of a history of divine economy and why it takes the divine Logos himself to become a human person; in addition, it also requires the "persuasion" of others by the witness of the Spirit to obtain the intended response from the human creatures, a response which completes the independent existence of the creature in communion with God.

On the level of the economic trinity, there is undoubtedly an element of development and history within the divine reality itself. But the divine reality is also immanent trinity, eternal enjoyment of the fullness of its life. It is for this reason that I expressed reservations about the idea of a developing God, because this can only be one side of the picture if we are really talking about God in a way that avoids inferiority with respect to traditional standards of philosophical theology as well as to the biblical language about God. That God as economic trinity has a history is itself a facet of the abundance of the eternal life of the trinitarian God. In talking about the unity of economic and immanent trinity, however, one must never forget that the "place" of such identity is in the eschatological consummation of history, not in the past or present. It is also the "place" of God's "retroactive permanence" (p. 166). As soon as the idea of such permanence is cut loose from the eschatological future, it takes on the familiar features of a timeless eternity. But that involves a fatal loss of complexity. If the relation of eternity to time has to be accounted for by way of the eschatological future as point of their coincidence, then every attempt to talk about God's relation to the world of temporal processes that abstracts from that condition must end up in some impasse. It is my impression that this is behind the charge of "determinism."

The same range of problems emerges in the essay of Lewis Ford, but in a broader perspective. I admire Lewis Ford for what, to my knowledge, constitutes the most creative effort in American process thought towards further development of the Whiteheadian metaphysical scheme beyond Whitehead's own writings. In Ford's work this also includes, and increasingly so, the effort to integrate into the perspective of process metaphysics parts of the heritage of classical metaphysics that Whitehead did not incorporate into his thought or which he did not treat with full justice. Because I face the same task in relation to the metaphysical tradition, the progressive convergence of our views is perhaps not surprising. By means of exploiting the perplexities in Whitehead's notion of God as one actual entity, Ford is able to reconcile it to the Boethian notion of eternity as the simultaneous presence of the fullness of life (pp. 88f.) and even to the idea of divine infinity, though rephrased in terms of an infinity of becoming (p. 81). Furthermore, since God is to be considered as the metaphysical basis of all eternal objects, Ford envisages the possibility of combining this with the idea of a creativity of the future and arrives at a conception of God as "field" of the extensive continuum "lying in the future of a creative advance" and as self-creative, with the result that "this creativity becomes pluralized as the many independently active occasions of the present" (p. 80).

To realize the degree of convergence between Lewis Ford's process philosophy and my own view, it is informative to compare the brilliant essay of Philip Hefner on the impact of my dialogue with scientists on my theological thought. Daringly, but quite accurately, Hefner describes my theology as a "theology of contingency and field" (p. 266). For the first time he reveals in public that dialogue with science has not been a marginal aspect of my thought, but is of central importance in my metaphysical and theological vision. Hefner notices that even the hermeneutical concern for a dependence of each and all particular meanings on the framework of a totality of meaning is related to the field concept (pp. 281ff.), just as are the more recent reflections on the metaphysical and theological conceptions of space and time (pp. 273ff.). Given the limitations and fragility of my knowledge in all these different regions, I am, of course, aware of the audacity of the attempt at such a conceptual integration. But then, such is inevitable when a theologian even begins to realize what is required in talking about God. It is indeed no more than a "research programme" in the sense of Imre Lakatos (p. 281). Still, at least such a research program seems to be required in order to sketch out a framework that allows a theologian to talk about God in intelligible terms. Philip Hefner's interpretation will be vindicated by the fact that in my forthcoming *Systematic Theology* the nature of God as Spirit will be accounted for in terms of an infinite field of power.

I have to switch back again to Lewis Ford, because there are some additional problems to be mentioned. The first one (pp. 84ff.) relates once more to the question of freedom. Perhaps my comments on David Polk's paper provide some clarification here. But Ford asks specifically whether the power of the future as source of our freedom also gives the human person "his freedom from God" (p. 85). Here my answer would have to be developed in a sequence of steps. The first step is that freedom of decision requires an object to be given in some definite form. In such a way, our decisions normally relate to finite objects (or ideal possibilities), but not to God. The next step is that our decisions can hurt somebody whom we don't even know. In such a way, sin as self-centered concupiscence turns against God, although the intention of such behavior is directed to finite objects. Third step: when in religion the divine reality becomes an explicit issue to our mind, we are in a position to decide one way or another how to relate to the God of religion. But then, the religious mind achieves no more than at best a partial awareness of the divine reality. Therefore, to turn against the God of a given religious tradition does not necessarily involve opposition to God in his sublime reality. Finally, however, if the Creator wants his creature to respond to his love, there must be freedom to do so spontaneously. But whether those who do not respond still know what they reject is hard to tell. In each of these cases, human decisions contribute to constituting the character of the person, although there are other factors, too. The divine nature, however, is not constituted by our acts, but the divine economy encompasses all creation to let the creatures participate in communion with the eternal God, though not without undergoing judgment. This kingdom of God, then, is certainly essential in the satisfaction of his eternal nature.

The second problem is related to the question whether temporal sequence is finite or infinite (or, rather, indefinitely continues). Here

I may be more brief. Since Lewis Ford seems to accept the idea that time is intrinsically related to eternity, we should try to clarify this interrelation in connection with Plotinus' analysis of time: If the temporal is related to eternity in terms of its longing for wholeness and identity, then an infinite or indefinitely continued process of time would mean that wholeness ("salvation") will never be achieved. In the case of the individual creature as well as of the universe, the temporal process must be finite if wholeness is to be possible.

The last problem is a question I have to ask of Lewis Ford. He speaks of God in terms of an infinity of becoming, but not of being. This makes sense as far as one considers being in terms of finite being. But in talking about an infinite God, it still seems unavoidable (as long as one is not an atheist) to admit that God "is" becoming. Can there be a final dualism of being and becoming (as Ford's defense of Whitehead in the appendix to his essay assumes)? Or should the philosopher rather conceive of being itself in terms of becoming, or at least as integrating the aspect of becoming?

At this point, before turning to John Cobb, I have to comment on Robert Jenson's very careful and penetrating analysis of the interrelationship between my presentation of Christology and my ideas toward a revision of the doctrine of the Trinity. I referred to God as trinitarian several times in my discussion of the papers of Philip Clayton, David Polk, and Lewis Ford, and the relationship between God and creation does not become intelligible in my understanding without the trinitarian doctrine. But even the credentials for using the word *God* itself would appear to me *philosophically* weak without the trinitarian doctrine which allows us to conceive of "God" as both immanent and transcendent.

The trinitarian conception of God is based upon Christology. This is primarily a historical statement on the development of the doctrine, but it is also true systematically. In my view, as Jenson explains (pp. 193ff.), it is Jesus' relation to the "Father" that constitutes his own identity as "Son" of that Father as well as the impossibility of conceiving of the eternal Father otherwise than in relation to this Son. To reconstruct in this way the core of Christology and of the trinitarian doctrine involves, as Jenson emphasizes (pp. 195ff.), rather extensive revisions of traditional Christological and trinitarian conceptualities, though I hope not of their essential content. In addition, Jesus' claim upon the God of Israel as his "Father" was seriously questioned by the rejection he met, a rejection which culminated in his crucifixion. Therefore (and also as an advance on the imminent kingdom he had proclaimed), Jesus' resurrection is basic to Christology as well as to the Christian belief in the God whom Jesus proclaimed as his "Father." Although in the beginning of his paper Jenson raises the question whether it is indeed necessary to attribute such a crucial importance to the resurrection of Jesus (pp. 190f.), at a later point he agrees "that if Jesus had not risen the Christian God would not be" (p. 199). It is not on the assumption of some general father image, but only and strictly through participation in Jesus' relation to "God" as "Father" that we are entitled to speak of God the Father.

But what do we mean by *God,* if the term *God* applies to the Son as well as to the Father, and also to the Spirit who in the hearts of the faithful witnesses to both? In the discussion of the unity of divine "nature" in the three "persons" of Father, Son, and Spirit in my forthcoming *Systematic Theology,* the proposal will be that we should conceive of the "spiritual" nature of the one God in Father, Son, and Spirit in terms of a field of power rather than in terms of a single divine subject or person. This may be considered an even more radical revision of the traditional way of conceiving of God than what I proposed in my Christology. But I think that an interpretation of the divine nature in terms of an infinite "field" of power is closer to the biblical meaning of *Spirit* than are the images of a self-conscious subject, a supreme reason, etc. These images of the divine reality have been more closely related to Platonism than to the Bible, and they have become the main target of the modern critique of the traditional concept of God. This critique should help Christian theology develop an understanding of the divine reality that is closer to the Bible: it is "Spirit" in terms of a field of power that reveals itself as "personal" in being encountered in the way Jesus encountered the divine mystery as "Father" who relates to his "Son" and is glorified together with his Son through the "Spirit." Such an interpretation may help to restore the sense of mystery to Christian talk about God, but also to improve the Christian position in the upcoming period of dialogue and contest with other world religions.

Robert Jenson did not have this revisionist proposal for the re-statement of the idea of God before him when he wrote his essay. Philip Hefner obviously guessed it. I hope there will be opportunity for further discussion with Robert Jenson, to whom I owe important insights into the doctrine of the Trinity, concerning the question whether theology should continue, as he still does, with the image of God as one subject or whether it should rather replace that image by a more biblical inter-pretation of "Spirit."

There are many other points in Jenson's essay that invite further discussion. Only one of them, however, can be mentioned here: I am somewhat puzzled by Jenson's emphasis upon the contrast of a (or "the") modern concept of "person" to the traditional one (pp. 195f.; cf. pp. 202f.). There is a difference, of course, in that the traditional *hypostasis* was used primarily for the eternal Son or Logos who was said at Chalcedon in 451 to constitute the hypostatic union even in the incarnation, while today we use the word *person* primarily to refer to the concrete human "person" Jesus who, upon theological reflection, presents himself as the "Son" in relation to his divine "Father." But on the other hand, the trinitarian reinterpretation of *hypostasis* and *persona* resulted in the insight that relationship is constitutive of per-sonhood. And this insight has become basic in modern "dialogical" personalism, e.g., in Martin Buber, but previously in Fichte, Feuer-bach, and others. It is the famous idea that there can be no I without a thou. Therefore, there seems to be more continuity between the trinitarian (and Christological) concept of "person" and some modern conceptions of personhood than Jenson admits, although the idea of person as self-conscious subject may be a different matter.

John Cobb's contribution to this volume raises a number of ques-tions that have also concerned the other process thinkers. I need not repeat my earlier comments on the assumption of an end to temporal processes and on human freedom (see Cobb, pp. 59f., 67f.). But Cobb adds interesting remarks on both these issues.

Regarding the lack of "temporal closure" in Whitehead's thought, Cobb thinks it "related to his doctrine that there is closure in every moment" (p. 60). Does that provide definite identity, however? Cobb himself mentions that for each occasion "the role it will in fact play in the future" remains contingent (ibid.). Thus, there seems to be no final identity obtainable by anything except God, who endures forever.

In his discussion of freedom, Cobb characterizes my language about God as the power of the future as "a determinism based on the causal efficacy of the future" (p. 68). I dealt with this above, but Cobb offers additional ideas that are interesting. First, he agrees that "freedom" in the Bible "is not the formal freedom to choose between good and evil," but rather "the freedom to do good" (p. 68). But then he continues that formal freedom "seems clearly presupposed" (ibid.). I should tend to see it, in line with Kant, rather the other way around: the consciousness of the good opens up new possibilities for decision. But this may be a subordinate question. Cobb continues by rejecting a "freedom of indifference" (p. 69). Here a point of agreement emerges. But then he speaks of "subtler decisions" beneath the level of conscious choices (p. 69). Here I doubt that it is appropriate to speak of "decisions" on the subconscious or even elementary level in the same way as with conscious choices. I suspect that this language is based on Whitehead's generalization of certain notions from James' psychology by transferring them to the description of atomic events, a generalization that appears to me unwarranted, as I stated in my earlier critique of Whitehead. I would rather focus on the phenomenon of conscious choices. If such a choice is informed by some perception of what seems good to the choosing person, the question may arise whether there cannot be more or less responsiveness to the "call" (pp. 69f.). The problem here seems to be whether or not the call can be stated as objectively given in distinction from its subjective evaluation. I doubt that this is possible on the level of psychological description, because the notion of the good as such is relative to the one "for whom" something is considered to be good. Now the notion of choice seems to involve (as Cobb expects me to argue) the idea that choice consists in deciding what appears best to the one who decides. Only I cannot discover any circularity in this, as Cobb does (p. 70). If it is simply a matter of the notion of choice itself, there is no circularity. It is of course quite a different matter whether somebody chooses what is *really* best for him when he chooses what *appears* best to him. But that is a distinction which can only be made by an observer or, in retrospect, by the person who made the choice.

In the final section of his essay, John Cobb deplores that in my book on anthropology I have "closed" myself "to the voices coming from the third world and from women" (p. 70). I am not aware of a prejudice in either direction. My only criterion for selecting literature was relevance to the subject, and some prominent female authors were applauded for their contributions. I cannot accept the insinuation that my book deals only with "the male of the species" and more specifically with "North Atlantic 'man' " (ibid.). At this point I miss the usual fairness that otherwise distinguishes the style of my old friend. Everybody, of course, works and speaks out of his or her own context. As I cannot escape my identity as a German Lutheran, so John Cobb will always sound like a North American Methodist. Regarding the third world, it would amount to intellectual imperialism if any one of us would claim to do what only theologians from those regions can do for themselves in order to appropriate the gospel and the heritage of other cultures to their own context. Nevertheless, one can expect of everyone who writes on anthropology (or on any other issue) that, whatever the personal point of view might be, he or she write on the general subject rather than simply voicing a partisan view. I tried to do that as well as I was able to, and if John Cobb or others think that my approach is too limited, let us discuss the matter in terms of the issues rather than assailing each others' contextual roots. This is the difference which I always had in mind when I advocated objective rather than confessional argument (pp. 64ff.). Everybody's thought is historically and culturally conditioned, but it is something else to argue explicitly on the basis of partisan commitments. If that happens, the appropriate reaction might be that one partiality is as good as another, and then there can be neither genuine dialogue nor agreement anymore.

The choice or the range of subjects is another matter. Here John Cobb is certainly correct in pointing out that I am working primarily on what the heritage of the Christian cultural tradition (not only North Atlantic, since Israel, Egypt, and Greece are included) has to contribute to issues of general human concern. I am not far from John's feeling that our modern culture is in decay. My own response to that, however, is not only that we still need a worldview—a point that I share with

Cobb (pp. 58f.). My response, in addition, is to participate in re-covering and reexamining the rich heritage of our cultural tradition so as to keep it alive and make it available to future generations from all cultures as part of the heritage of human history at large. I recognize that there are other options, and I do not complain that John Cobb feels his vocation to be different. But there need not be sadness, since dif-ferent vocations might complement each other.

The specific focus of my theological and philosophical endeavors does not entail "insensitivity to suffering and injustice." It is not always easy, however, to distinguish appropriately between aspirations or claims on the one hand and their legitimate content on the other. If my energies had not been absorbed by reassessing foundational issues in philosophy and in theology, a clarification of the ambiguities of the concept of justice within the context of the social sciences and of political history would have been high on my agenda of urgent issues. Whether John Cobb's suspicion that my theological eschatology entails a neglect of "attention to those who demand justice now" (p. 73) is correct, may be pondered in comparison with Ted Peters' discussion of what he calls my "eschatological ethics."

Peters focuses his discussion on the reformulation of the concept of the "good" in terms of the future of the kingdom. He is right on target in claiming that this is "the heart" of my ethical argument (p. 241). In fact it combines the concept of the kingdom of God with the Platonic idea of the good to the effect that the temporal structure of the latter is emphasized. Peters puts it magnificently: "Present being is not good enough. We must go beyond" (ibid.). Going beyond, of course, must not mean destruction of the present, but rather the advent of its own future destiny. This happens in God's love, and Peters em-phasizes, as I do, that we are called to participate in God's creative and sustaining love for the world (pp. 243f.). Christian eschatological ethics does not overlook the present, as Cobb suspects, but "com-mitment to what is provisional is essential to Christian faith in the coming kingdom of God" (Peters, p. 243). Peters goes on to point out the implications for a "proleptic politics" of human universalism as opposed to nationalism, of peace and justice, freedom and equality (pp. 244ff.). I agree with his emphasis on "conjunction" between eschatology and history (p. 248): participation in God's future is me-

331

diated sacramentally in the life of the church (p. 247), but in another way it also impinges on the issues of the social and political order (pp. 284f.), though this remains at best incomplete and is continuously tempted to become demonic. I tend to emphasize this last point more than in earlier years, but it remains true that there is also a positive value in social order and change.

Now Peters thinks that on the basis of these principles there should be "a greater affinity" than I usually admit between my thought and the liberation theologians' "call for revolution in the name of justice" (p. 264). I do not deny the affinity, and perhaps my criticism of certain tendencies in liberation theologies has been rigorous precisely because of that affinity. Proleptic ethics must take pains to do justice to the ambiguities of the human situation, ambiguities that arise on all sides. A Christian anthropology which is not only a doctrine of universal sinfulness—though it certainly includes that issue—should provide the resources for paying attention to these ambiguities in the human situation. This is the remedy against ideological partisanship that looks at the world in terms of friends and foes and feels easily justified in taking refuge in violence. A Christian proleptic ethics, because it is aware of the inherent ambiguities in human life, will not fight the war of the children of light against the children of darkness, but seek reconciliation, a reconciliation, however, that changes what is intolerable in a given situation. I never excluded that in some situations the use of violence can be a last resort. But I am frightened to see people so confident of what they consider their righteous cause that they feel perfectly entitled to impose it upon others by means of violence.

My particular problem with most forms of contemporary liberation theology is their largely uncritical use of Marxist analysis of social reality. In that matter, I know what I am talking about. It is not only an expression of prejudice resulting from my biography and from German and East European experiences with Marxism in the course of this century. There was a time when I rather extensively studied Marxist literature, and I was not insensitive to the explanatory power of Marxist analysis. But I learned to recognize that Marxist analysis provides a systematically distorted picture of social reality. It is a relatively easy instrument to handle, and that contributes to its seductive power. But it does not satisfy the criteria of realistic analysis nor of Christian anthropological realism. In making this judgment, I am not defending capitalism. The stains of capitalism are many, and they are ugly enough. I should like to see a liberation theologian work out his or her own analysis of economic mechanisms and of their interaction with the social and political order without ideological commitment, but on the basis of a Christian anthropology and in combination with new proposals for a critical theory of justice. At present, the concept of justice itself is deeply controversial. It has to be reassessed in the context of Christian ethics and social theory. Under those conditions I could feel more at ease with Ted Peters' claim that "a carefully thought-through liberation theology—especially with its emphasis on revolution— should be a logical extension of Pannenberg's eschatology" (p. 262). Still, I would not be comfortable with the loose American usage of the word *revolution*. I know that Americans apply this word not only to violent change, but also to change by political pressure and persuasion, even to cultural and ideological innovation. I think that the difference between these uses is of enormous import, and especially so since it is almost impossible to contain and control the consequences of violent action in a situation of civil war.

Richard Neuhaus may be right that my way of dealing with questions of politics "is not tailored to fit the regnant prejudices in American academic religion" (p. 229). Moving against the stream, as he puts it (pp. 229, 232), does not give me particular satisfaction. I am not a protagonist of the traditional Lutheran two kingdoms doctrine, although I consider the distinction between the ultimate and the provisional— hence also between the church and the political order—to be essential and distinctive in all forms of Christian thought on society, even in the Byzantine Empire. But I also see that there is (and should be) a positive connection between the Christian faith and the cultural and social system wherever Christians have a chance to shape the order of society and culture. In the contemporary world, this responsibility is scarcely met, even in countries with vast Christian majorities such as in the two Americas. Perhaps the reason is, as Neuhaus says (p. 235), that "Christians are frequently embarrassed by the audacity of Christianity's claim." The tendency towards retreat from public discourse in questions regarding the truth of Christian affirmations, a truth that obliges not only the believer but also the world, seems to correspond to social

333

commitments that avoid the specifically Christian profile but accept without much critical reflection whatever counts for a generally human cause, be it in a liberal or Marxist fashion. The promise of the gospel that the truth will make us free has been "inverted," says Neuhaus (p. 230), and I certainly agree with him on that issue. The result is that the notions of freedom and of equality have become shallow.

Some of Peter Berger's works contributed significantly to convince me as well as Richard Neuhaus and others that a secular society that cuts itself loose from its religious roots cannot survive in the long run. The achievements of early modern history, the principles of toleration and of individual freedom, accompanied by increasing cultural pluralism, were bought at the price of a loss of religious unity at the basis of the social system. On the other hand, they require the continuous effect of a sufficient degree of social and cultural unity lest they eventually end up in the disintegration of society and culture. That basis of unity, however, can finally be provided only by religion, although in the course of modern history various forms of nationalism with more or less religious overtones have served as a temporary substitute for religion. Christianity can serve that function only on the condition of overcoming its dogmatic and confessional antagonisms. The antagonism between the churches resulting from the Reformation of the 16th century contributed more than any other factor to the privatization of religion in modern society and to the secularization of modern culture. This has become a key insight in the development of my thought and largely determines my attitudes to social and political ethics as well as to the ecumenical movement towards Christian unity. It cannot be repeated too often that the reunification of the Christian churches would be the most important Christian contribution in the area of social ethics, one that would give impetus to the future development of all human society, not only in the West.

Such a reunification requires the acceptance of pluralities that have been developed over the centuries. They cannot be accepted, however, by a surrender of doctrinal identity to relativism. Here I agree with Geoffrey Wainwright. The Christian conception of truth itself must legitimate a plurality of teaching and of liturgical life. This can be achieved by developing a more consistent awareness of the provisional status of all doctrinal expressions of faith this side of the eschatological consummation of history, one that is more consistent than the traditional Christian understanding of doctrinal truth. Such a reformulation of the concept of doctrinal truth does not mean to soften, but to strengthen Christian truth claims and their credibility in our contemporary world. It also legitimates the change of Christian attitudes toward other religions, without, however, surrendering the Christian truth claims themselves. Within the Christian family, such a modest formulation of the concept of doctrinal truth does not prevent but rather enhances the possibilities of expressing together what Christians have in common, with respect to Christian worship as well as the content and identity of the Christian faith through the centuries. Wainwright's description of my ecumenical activities may serve as an illustration of this. The reader of his paper will perhaps have received the impression that on the one hand my position on ecclesiological issues is almost "liberal," while on the other hand my emphasis on doctrine and especially on the importance of the Nicene Creed as a symbol of the unity of Christian faith through the centuries sounds "conservative." Therefore, the few remarks on the background of my commitment to the task of Christian unity within the framework of my general approach to theology may be helpful.

In conclusion, I may respond to Geoffrey Wainwright's question (p. 220) of how I envisage the form of ecumenical Christian unity that both of us work for. I think that his vision of a "web of 'dioceses' . . . each containing 'congregations' in various liturgical, spiritual, and cultural styles," while enjoying "conciliar communion" with each other, might be a possible result of a long range of developments. For a less distant future, however, the only realistic prospect I can imagine would be a mutual recognition among the present confessional families of churches. I therefore believe that concrete ecumenical progress will only happen in bilateral negotiations between particular churches. The World Council of Churches can only provide a framework for such a process. From the most recent phase of Roman Catholic–Protestant (Lutheran and Reformed) commission work in Germany, an extensive investigation has emerged that results in proposing as a first step to suspend the mutual anathemas which have separated the churches since the 16th century. The next step would be to reach agreement about concrete conditions of communion between the churches. At this stage the question of the papacy will have to be addressed, but in such a way that the Protestant churches might agree to the kind of symbolic primacy which could also be acceptable to the Eastern Orthodox churches (not the version of Vatican I). The condition would be, however, that the pope in his capacity as Latin patriarch would grant autocephalous status to the Protestant churches on the basis of their own organizational principles. Such a scheme should be applicable also to the relations between Rome and other Protestant churches. It would be less than institutional merger, which I think is neither realistic nor desirable, but it would be more than what sometimes has been understood by "reconciled diversity," which is not enough for a unity in faith and worship. Steps in that direction will be, I am sure, a necessary condition for a renewed hearing for the Christian message in our world.

A PANNENBERG BIBLIOGRAPHY

Compiled by
Philip Clayton

◆

The following bibliography contains works by and about Pannenberg. Works by Pannenberg published between 1953 and (roughly) 1986 are listed in chronological order, based on the date of publication in English. All of Pannenberg's books have been included, along with all articles that have appeared in English and virtually all untranslated ones more than five pages in length. Where a book or article has been translated, only the translation has been cited. The section "Monographs on Pannenberg" does not include some 35 unpublished dissertations on his work. Of necessity, I have been somewhat selective in the section on secondary works. The goal has been to include all major treatments of his work, as well as to provide a bibliography that is representative of the diversity of theological perspectives and critical reactions available in the secondary literature.

For assistance in compiling this bibliography I am grateful to David Polk and Stanley Grenz, who have shared their extensive bibliographical work on Pannenberg; to Jan Rohls and Gunther Wenz, editors of the German Festschrift for Pannenberg, *Vernunft des Glaubens: Wissenschaftliche Theologie und kirchliche Lehre,* 2 vols. (forthcoming from Vandenhoeck & Ruprecht, 1988); to Achim Dunkel and Bernd Burkhardt, who helped compile the bibliography for the German volume; and to Sarah McFarland of Williams College Library for a multitude of computer searches.

WORKS BY PANNENBERG (in chronological order)

"Zur Bedeutung des Analogiegedankens bei Karl Barth. Eine Auseinandersetzung mit Urs von Balthasar," *Theologische Literaturzeitung* 78 (1953), cols. 17-24.

"Mythus und Wort. Theologische Überlegungen zu K. Jaspers Mythusbegriff," *Zeitschrift für Theologie und Kirche* 51 (1954): 167-185.

Die Prädestinationslehre des Duns Skotus im Zusammenhang der scholastischen Lehrentwicklung. Göttingen: Vandenhoeck & Ruprecht, 1954.

"Christlicher Glaube und menschliche Freiheit," *Kerygma und Dogma* 4 (1961): 251-280.

"Person," in *Religion in Geschichte und Gegenwart,* ed. Kurt Galling et al., 3d ed. Tübingen: J. C. B. Mohr (Paul Siebeck), 1958, 5:230-235.

"The Crisis of the Scripture-Principle in Protestant Theology," *Dialog* 2 (1963): 307-313.

Dogma und Denkstrukturen. Festschrift für Edmund Schlink, coedited with Wilfried Joest. Göttingen: Vandenhoeck & Ruprecht, 1963.

"Theologische Motive im Denken Immanuel Kants," *Theologische Literaturzeitung* 89 (1964), cols. 897-906.

"Did Jesus Really Rise from the Dead?" *Dialog* 4 (1965): 128-135.

"A Dialogue on Christ's Resurrection," with Lawrence Burkholder, Harvey Cox, and J. N. D. Anderson, *Christianity Today* 12/14 (April 12, 1968), pp. 9-11 (681-683).

Jesus—God and Man, trans. Lewis L. Wilkins and Duane A. Priebe. Philadelphia: Westminster, 1968, 2d ed. 1977 (German, 1964).

Revelation as History, with Rolf Rendtorff, Trutz Rendtorff, and Ulrich Wilkens, trans. David Granskou. New York: Macmillan, 1968 (German, 1961).

"Apostolizität und Katholizität der Kirche in der Perspektive der Eschatologie," *Theologische Literaturzeitung* 94 (1969), cols. 97-112.

"Facts of History and Christian Ethics," *Dialog* 8 (Autumn 1969): 287-296.

"Reden von Gott angesichts atheistischer Kritik," *Evangelische Kommentare* 2 (August 1969): 442-446.

Reformation zwischen gestern und morgen. Gütersloh: Gütersloher Verlagshaus Gerd Mohn, 1969.

Theology and the Kingdom of God, ed. Richard John Neuhaus. Philadelphia: Westminster, 1969.

"Can Christianity Do without an Eschatology?" in *The Christian Hope,* ed. G. B. Caird et al. London: SPCK, 1970, pp. 25-34.

Erwägungen zu einer Theologie der Natur, with A. M. Klaus Müller. Gütersloh: Gütersloher Verlagshaus Gerd Mohn, 1970.

Spirit, Faith and Church, with Avery Dulles, s.j., and Carl E. Braaten. Philadelphia: Westminster, 1970.

Thesen zur Theologie der Kirche. Munich: Claudius Verlag, 1970.

What Is Man? trans. Duane A. Priebe. Philadelphia: Fortress, 1970 (German, 1962).

Basic Questions in Theology, 2 vols., trans. George H. Kehm. Philadelphia: Fortress, 1971 (German, 1967).

"Erfahrung der Wirklichkeit. Fragen an Carl Friedrich von Weizsäcker," *Evangelische Kommentare* 4 (1971): 468-470.

"Geist und Energie," *Acta Teilhardiana* 8 (1971): 5-12.

"Weltgeschichte und Heilsgeschichte," in *Probleme biblischer Theologie. Gerhard von Rad zum 70. Geburtstag,* ed. Hans Walter Wolff. Munich: Christian Kaiser, 1971, pp. 349-366.

The Apostles' Creed in the Light of Today's Questions, trans. Margaret Kohl. Philadelphia: Westminster, 1972 (German, 1972).

Christentum und Mythos. Späthorizonte des Mythos in biblischer und christlicher Überlieferung. Gütersloh: Gütersloher Verlagshaus Gerd Mohn, 1972.

"The Doctrine of the Spirit and the Task of a Theology of Nature," *Theology* 75 (1972): 8-21.

"Future and Unity," in *Hope and the Future of Man,* ed. Ewert H. Cousins. Philadelphia: Fortress, 1972, pp. 60-78.

"Die Geschichtlichkeit der Wahrheit und die ökumenische Diskussion," in *Begegnung. Beiträge zu einer Hermeneutik des theologischen Gesprächs,* Festschrift for Heinrich Fries. Graz, Vienna, Cologne: Verlag Styria, 1972, pp. 31-43.

"The Nature of a Theological Statement," *Zygon* 7 (1972): 6-19.

"A Theological Conversation with Wolfhart Pannenberg," with Lewis Ford, *Dialog* 11 (Autumn 1972): 286-295.

"Ein Briefwechsel zwischen Wolfhart Pannenberg und Gerhard Ebeling," *Zeitschrift für Theologie und Kirche* 70, Beiheft (1973): 448-473.

"The Christological Foundation of Christian Anthropology," in *Humanism and Christianity,* ed. Claude Geffre, Concilium, vol. 86. New York: Herder and Herder, 1973, pp. 86-100.

Gegenwart Gottes: Predigten. Munich: Claudius Verlag, 1973.

"History and Meaning in Lonergan's Approach to Theological Method," *The Irish Theological Quarterly* 40 (1973): 103-114.

The Idea of God and Human Freedom, trans. R. A. Wilson. Philadelphia: Westminster, 1973 (German, 1971).

Um Einheit und Heil der Menschheit, ed. with J. Robert Nelson. Frankfurt: Verlag O. Lembeck, 1973.

"Ekstatische Selbstüberschreitung als Teilhabe am göttlichen Geist," in *Erfahrung und Theologie des Heiligen Geistes,* ed. Claus Heitmann and Heribert Mühlen. Munich: Kösel Verlag, 1974, pp. 176-191.

Grundlagen der Theologie—Ein Diskurs, with S. M. Daecke, H. N. Janowski, G. Sauter. Stuttgart: Verlag W. Kohlhammer, 1974, pp. 29-41, 58-120.

"Lebensraum der christlichen Freiheit. Die Einheit der Kirche ist die Vollendung der Reformation," *Evangelische Kommentare* 8 (1975): 587-593.

"Reformation und Einheit der Kirche," *Una Sancta* 30 (1975): 172-182.

"A Theology of Death and Resurrection," *Theology Digest* 23, 2 (1975): 143-148.

"The Contribution of Christianity to the Modern World," *Cross Currents* 25 (1976): 357-366.

Theology and the Philosophy of Science, trans. Francis McDonagh. Philadelphia: Westminster, 1976 (German, 1973).

"Aggression und die theologische Lehre von der Sünde," *Zeitschrift für evangelische Ethik* 21 (1977): 161-173.

Faith and Reality, trans. John Maxwell. Philadelphia: Westminster, 1977 (German, 1975).

Human Nature, Election, and History. Philadelphia: Westminster, 1977.

"A Liberal Logos Christology: The Christology of John Cobb," in *John Cobb's Theology in Process*, ed. David R. Griffin and Thomas J. Altizer. Philadelphia: Westminster, 1977, pp. 133-149.

"Die Aufgabe einer politischen Theologie des Christentums," *Kerygma und Mythos* 7 (1979): 19-25.

Gottebenbildlichkeit als Bestimmung des Menschen in der neueren Theologiegeschichte, Sitzungsberichte der Bayerischen Akademie der Wissenschaften, Philosophisch-historische Klasse, Heft 8. Munich, 1979.

"Vom Nutzen der Eschatologie für die christliche Theologie. Eine Antwort," *Kerygma und Dogma* 25 (1979): 88-105.

"Antwort auf G. Sauters Überlegungen," *Evangelische Theologie* 40 (1980): 168-181.

"Foundation Documents of the Christian Faith: XI. The Place of Creeds in Christianity Today," *Expository Times* 91 (1980): 328-331.

"Heiligung und politische Ethik. Ein kritischer Blick auf einige Grundlagen der Befreiungstheologien im Protestantismus," in *Herausforderung: Die dritte Welt und die Christen Europas*, ed. F. Castillo et al. Regensburg: Pustet, 1980, pp. 79-107.

Ethics, trans. Keith Crim. Philadelphia: Westminster, 1981 (German, 1977).

"Freedom and the Lutheran Reformation," *Theology Today* 38 (1981): 287-297.

"God's Presence in History" (#17 in the series How My Mind Has Changed), *Christian Century*, March 11, 1981, pp. 260-263.

Judentum und Christentum. Einheit und Unterschied, with Pinchas Lapide. Munich: Christian Kaiser, 1981.

Ostern und der neue Mensch, with R. Schnackenburg. Freiburg: Herder Verlag, 1981.

Text und Applikation. Theologie, Jurisprudenz und Literaturwissenschaft im hermeneutischen Gespräch, Poetik und Hermeneutik, vol. 9, coedited with Dieter Henrich et al. Munich: Wilhelm Fink, 1981.

"Theological Questions to Scientists," *Zygon* 16 (March 1981): 65-77.

"Die theokratische Alternative. Die Einheit der Religion als Bedingung für die politische Einheit der Gesellschaft," in *Fortschritt ohne Mass? Eine Ortsbestimmung der wissenschaftlichen-technischen Zivilisation,* ed. R. Löw et al. 1981, pp. 235-251.

"Auf der Suche nach dem wahren Selbst. Anthropologie als Ort der Begegnung zwischen christlichem und buddhistischem Denken," in *Erlösung in Christentum und Buddhismus,* ed. Andreas Bsteh. Mödling: Verlag St. Gabriel, 1982, pp. 128-146.

"Eine geistliche Erneuerung der Ökumene tut not," in *Ökumene: Möglichkeiten und Grenzen heute,* Festschrift for O. Cullmann, ed. Karlfried Froehlich. Tübingen, 1982, pp. 112-123.

"Rezeptive Vernunft. Die antike Deutung der Erkenntnis als Hinnahme vorgegebener Wahrheit," in *Überlieferung und Aufgabe. Festschrift für E. Heintel zum 70. Geburtstag,* ed. Herta Nagl-Docekal. 1982, 1:265-301.

"Spirit and Mind," in *Mind in Nature,* Nobel Conference 17, ed. R. Q. Elvee. New York: Harper & Row, 1982, pp. 134-148.

"Bewusstsein und Geist," *Zeitschrift für Theologie und Kirche* 80 (1983): 332-351.

Christian Spirituality. Philadelphia: Westminster, 1983.

The Church, trans. Keith Crim. Philadelphia: Westminster, 1983 (German, 1977).

"Entwicklung und (Zwischen-)Ergebnisse der ökumenischen Bewegung seit ihren Anfänge," "Sakramente und kirchliches Amt," "Differenzen und ihre Folgen," and "Die Antwort der Kirchen auf die Herausforderungen der Zeit," in *Das Ringen um die Einheit der Christen,* ed. H. Fries. Düsseldorf: Patmos-Verlag, 1983.

"Gott und die Natur," *Theologie und Philosophie* 58 (1983): 481-500.

"Atom, Duration, Form: Difficulties with Process Philosophy," trans. J. C. Robertson and G. Valée, *Process Studies* 14, 1 (Spring 1984): 21-30.

"Schwerter zu Pflugscharen—Bedeutung und Missbrauch eines Prophetenwortes," Briefdienst 3/83 des Arbeitskreises "Sicherung des Friedens," Bad Böll, reproduced in part with Pannenberg's response to H. W. Wolff, *Evangelische Theologie* 44 (1984): 293-297.

"Constructive and Critical Functions of Christian Eschatology," *Harvard Theological Review* 77 (1984): 119-139.

Die Erfahrung der Abwesenheit Gottes in der modernen Kultur, ed. W. Pannenberg. Göttingen: Vandenhoeck & Ruprecht, 1984.

"The Historicity of the Resurrection: The Identity of Christ," in *The Intellectuals Speak about God,* ed. Roy A. Varghese. Chicago: Regnery Gateway, 1984, pp. 257-264.

"Reformation und Neuzeit (Troeltsch and Modernity)," in *Troeltsch-Studien,* vol. 3, ed. Horst Renz and Friedrich Wilhelm Graf. 1984, pp. 21-34.

"Die Theologie und die neue Frage nach der Subjektivität," *Stimmen der Zeit* 202, 12 (1984): 805-816.

Anthropology in Theological Perspective, trans. Matthew J. O'Connell. Philadelphia: Westminster, 1985 (German, 1983).
"Christentum und Platonismus. Die kritische Platonrezeption Augustins in ihrer Bedeutung für das gegenwärtige christliche Denken," *Zeitschrift für Kirchengeschichte* 96 (1985): 147-161.
"Meaning, Religion and the Question of God," trans. P. Clayton, in *Knowing Religiously*, ed. Leroy S. Rouner. Notre Dame: University of Notre Dame Press, 1985, pp. 153-165.
"Das theologische Fundament der Gesellschaft," in *Die religiöse Dimension der Gesellschaft. Religion und ihre Theorien*, ed. Peter Koslowski. Tübingen: J. C. B. Mohr (Paul Siebeck), 1985, chap. 3.
"The Doctrine of Creation and Modern Science," *East Asian Journal of Theology* 4 (1986): 33-46, in *Zygon* 23 (1988): 3-21.
"The Significance of the Categories 'Part' and 'Whole' for the Epistemology of Theology," trans. P. Clayton, *Journal of Religion* 66 (October 1986): 369-385.
"Die Theologie und die neuen Fragen nach Intersubjektivität, Gesellschaft und religiöser Gemeinshaft," *Archivio di Filosofia* 54 (1986).
"Problems of a Trinitarian Doctrine of God," trans. P. Clayton, *Dialog* 26 (1987): 250-257.
Metaphysik und Gottesgedanke. Göttingen: Vandenhoeck & Ruprecht, 1988.

MONOGRAPHS ON PANNENBERG

Berten, Ignace. *Geschichte, Offenbarung, Glaube. Eine Einführung in die Theologie Wolfhart Pannenbergs*, trans. from the French by Sigrid Martin. Munich: Claudius Verlag, 1970.
Galloway, Allan D. *Wolfhart Pannenberg*. London: George Allen & Unwin Ltd., 1973.
Klein, Günther. *Theologie des Wortes Gottes und die Hypothese der Universalgeschichte. Zur Auseinandersetzung mit W. Pannenberg*, Beiträge zur evangelischen Theologie, vol. 37. Munich: Chr. Kaiser, 1964.
McDermott, Brian O. *The Personal Unity of Jesus and God according to W. Pannenberg*. Ottilien, Germany: EOS Verlag, 1973.
McKenzie, David. *Wolfhart Pannenberg and Religious Philosophy*. Washington, D.C.: University Press of America, 1980.
Neie, Herbert. *The Doctrine of the Atonement in the Theology of Wolfhart Pannenberg*. Berlin, New York: de Gruyter, 1979.
Olive, Don H. *Wolfhart Pannenberg*. Waco: Word, 1973.
Robinson, James M. and Cobb, John B. Jr., eds. *Theology as History*, New Frontiers in Theology, vol. 3. New York: Harper & Row, 1967.

Tupper, E. Frank. *The Theology of Wolfhart Pannenberg.* Philadelphia: Westminster, 1973.

SELECTED SECONDARY WORKS

Ahlers, R. "Theory of God and Theological Method," *Dialog* 22 (1983): 235-240.

Allen, L. "From Dogmatik to Glaubenslehre: Ernst Troeltsch and the Task of Theology," *Fides* 12 (1980): 37-60.

Althaus, Paul. "Offenbarung als Geschichte und Glaube. Bermerkungen zu W. Pannenbergs Begriff der Offenbarung," *Theologische Literaturzeitung* 87 (1962), cols. 321-330.

Apczynski, J. V. "Truth in Religion: A Polanyian Appraisal of Wolfhart Pannenberg's Theological Program," *Zygon* 17 (1982): 49-73.

Betz, Hans Dieter. "The Concept of Apocalyptic in the Theology of the Pannenberg Group," trans. J. W. Leitch, *Journal for Theology and Church* 6 (1969): 192-207.

Bollinger, Gary. "Pannenberg's Theology of the Religious and the Claim to Christian Superiority," *Encounter* 43 (Summer 1982): 273-285.

Borowitz, E. B. "Anti-Semitism and the Christologies of Barth, Berkouwer and Pannenberg," *Dialog* 16 (1977): 38-41, 81.

Braaten, Carl E. "The Current Controversy on Revelation: Pannenberg and His Critics," *Journal of Religion* 45 (1965): 225-237.

————. *History and Hermeneutics,* New Directions in Theology Today, vol. 2. Philadelphia: Westminster, 1966.

————. "The Significance of Apocalypticism for Systematic Theology," *Interpretation* 25 (1971): 480-499.

————. "Toward a Theology of Hope," *Theology Today* 24 (1967): 208-266.

————. "Wolfhart Pannenberg," in *A Handbook of Christian Theologians,* ed. Martin E. Marty and Dean Peerman. Nashville: Abingdon, 1984.

Brown, Delwin. *The Divine Trinity.* LaSalle, Ill.: Open Court, 1985.

Burhenn, Herbert. "Pannenberg's Argument for the Historicity of the Resurrection," *Journal of the American Academy of Religion* 40 (1972): 368-379.

————. "Pannenberg's Doctrine of God," *Scottish Journal of Theology* 28 (1975): 535-549.

Carr, Anne. "The God Who Is Involved," *Theology Today* 38 (1981): 314-328.

Clark, Wayne R. "Christian Images of Fulfillment: Healing within Anticipation," *Religion in Life* 49 (1980): 230-241.

————. "Jesus, Lazarus, and Others: Resuscitation or Resurrection?" *Religion in Life* 46 (1977): 186-197.

Clayton, Philip. "Being and One Theologian," *The Thomist* 50 (October 1989).

_____. "The God of History and the Presence of the Future," *Journal of Religion* 65 (1985): 98-108.

Cobb, John B. Jr. Review of *Theology and the Philosophy of Science, Religious Studies Review* 3 (1977): 213-215.

_____. "Pannenberg's Resurrection Christology: A Critique," *Theological Studies* 35 (1974): 711-721.

_____. "The Meaning of Pluralism for Christian Self-Understanding," in *Religious Pluralism*, ed. Leroy Rouner. Notre Dame: University of Notre Dame Press, 1984, pp. 161-179.

_____. "Wolfhart Pannenberg's *Jesus—God and Man,*" *Journal of Religion* 49 (1969): 192-201.

Cousins, Ewert H., editor. *Hope and the Future of Man.* Philadelphia: Fortress, 1972.

Davis, Charles. "The Reconvergence of Theology and Religious Studies," *Studies in Religion* 4 (1975): 205-221.

Dillistone, F. W. Review of *Theology and the Philosophy of Science, Theology Today* 34 (1978): 218-222.

Dobbin, Edmund. "Pannenberg on Theological Method," *Proceedings of the Catholic Theological Society of America* 32 (1977): 202-220.

_____. "Reflections on W. Pannenberg's Revelation Theology," *Louvain Studies* 4 (1972): 13-37.

Drummond, R. H. "Christian Theology and the History of Religions," *Journal of Ecumenical Studies* 12 (1975): 389-405.

Dulles, Avery. *Models of Revelation.* Garden City, N.Y.: Doubleday, 1983.

Ebeling, Gerhard. "Die Krise des Ethischen und die Theologie. Erwiderung auf Wolfhart Pannenbergs Kritik," in *Wort und Glaube,* vol. 2. Tübingen, 1969, pp. 42-55.

_____. "Ein Briefwechsel zwischen W. Pannenberg und G. Ebeling," *Zeitschrift für Theologie und Kirche* 70 (1973): 448-473.

Eicher, Peter. "Geschichte und Wort Gottes. Ein Protokoll der Pannenberg-diskussion von 1961–1972," *Catholica* 32 (1978): 321-354.

Enquist, Roy J. "Utopia and the Search for a Godly Future," *Dialog* 19 (1980): 131-140.

Escribano-Alberca, Ignacio. *Das vorläufige Heil. Zum christlichen Zeitbegriff.* Düsseldorf: Patmos-Verlag, 1970.

Fischer, Hermann. "Fundamentaltheologische Prolegomena zur theologischen Anthropologie. Anfragen an W. Pannenbergs Anthropologie," *Theologische Rundschau* 50 (1985): 41-61.

Ford, Lewis S. "A Whiteheadian Basis for Pannenberg's Theology," *Encounter* 38 (Autumn 1977): 307-317.

_____. "Creativity in a Future Key," in *New Essays in Metaphysics,* ed.

Robert C. Neville. Albany: State University of New York Press, 1987, pp. 179-197.

————. "God as the Subjectivity of the Future," *Encounter* 41 (1980): 287-292.

Foster, Durwood. "Pannenberg's Polanyianism: A Response to John V. Apczynski," *Zygon* 17 (1982): 75-81.

Freyne, Sean. "Some Recent Writing on the Resurrection," *Irish Theological Quarterly* 38 (1971): 144-163.

Fuller, Daniel P. "A New German Theological Movement," *Scottish Journal of Theology* 19 (1966): 160-175.

————. "The Resurrection of Jesus Christ and the Historical Method," *Journal of Bible and Religion* 34 (1966): 18-24.

Galloway, Allan D. "The New Hegelians," *Religious Studies* 8 (1972): 367-371.

Geyer, Hans-Georg. "Geschichte als theologisches Problem. Bemerkungen zu W. Pannenbergs Geschichtstheologie," *Evangelische Theologie* 22 (1962): 92-104.

————. "Gottes Sein als Thema der Theologie," *Verkündigung und Forschung* 11, 2 (1966): 3-37.

Gilkey, Langdon. "Pannenberg's *Basic Questions in Theology:* A Review Article," *Perspective* 14 (1973): 34-56.

Goebel, Hans-Theodor. *Wort Gottes als Auftrag! Zur Theologie von Rudolf Bultmann, Gerhard Ebeling und Wolfhart Pannenberg.* Neukirchen-Vluyn: Neukirchener Verlag, 1972.

Greig, J. C. G. "Some Aspects of Hermeneutics: A Brief Survey," *Religion* 1 (1971): 131-151.

Griffiss, J. Review of *Basic Questions in Theology,* vol. 2, *Anglican Theological Review* 54 (1972): 219-225.

Gunton, Colin. "Time, Eternity and the Doctrine of the Incarnation," *Dialog* 21 (1982): 263-268.

Gutwenger, E. "Offenbarung und Geschichte," *Zeitschrift für Theologie und Kirche* 88 (1966): 393-410.

Halsey, Jim S. "History, Language and Hermeneutic: The Synthesis of Wolfhart Pannenberg," *Westminster Theological Journal* 41 (Spring 1979): 269-290.

Harder, H., and Stevenson, W. T. "The Continuity of History and Faith in the Theology of W. Pannenberg: Toward an Erotics of History," *Journal of Religion* 51 (1971): 34-56.

Hasel, G. F. "The Problem of History in Old Testament Theology," *Andrews University Seminary Studies* 8 (1970): 23-50.

Hefner, Philip. "The Concreteness of God's Kingdom: A Problem for the Christian Life," *Journal of Religion* 51 (1971): 188-205.

————. "Theological Reflections: Questions for Moltmann and Pannenberg," *Una Sancta* 25 (1968): 32-51.

Heinitz, K. "Pannenberg, Theology 'from Below' and the Virgin Birth," *Lutheran Quarterly* 28 (1976): 173-182.
Henke, Peter. *Gewissheit vor dem Nichts; eine Antithese zu den theologischen Entwürfen W. Pannenbergs und J. Moltmanns.* New York: de Gruyter, 1978.
Hesse, Franz. "Wolfhart Pannenberg und das Alte Testament," *Neue Zeitschrift für systematische Theologie und Religionsphilosophie* 7 (1965): 174-199.
Hill, William J. *The Three Personed God.* Washington, D.C.: Catholic University of America Press, 1982.
————. "The Historicity of God," *Theological Studies* 45 (June 1984): 320-333.
Hodgson, Peter C. Review of *Theology and the Philosophy of Science, Religious Studies Review* 3 (1977): 215-218.
————. "Pannenberg on Jesus: A Review Article," *Journal of the American Academy of Religion* 36 (1968): 373-384.
Hogan, John P. "The Historical Imagination and the New Hermeneutic: Collingwood and Pannenberg," in *The Pedagogy of God's Image,* ed. Robert Masson. Decatur, Ga.: Scholars Press, 1982, pp. 9-30.
Holwerda, David. "Faith, Reason and the Resurrection in the Theology of Wolfhart Pannenberg," in *Faith and Rationality,* ed. A. Plantinga and N. Wolterstorff. Notre Dame: University of Notre Dame Press, 1983.
Jellouscheck, H. "Zum Verhältnis von Wissen und Glauben," *Zeitschrift für katholische Theologie* 93 (1971): 309-327.
Jenson, Robert W. *The Triune Identity.* Philadelphia: Fortress, 1982.
————. "Gott als Antwort," *Evangelische Theologie* 26 (1966): 368-378.
————. "The Futurist Option in Speaking of God," *Lutheran Quarterly* 21 (1969): 17-25.
Jentz, Arthur H. Jr. "Personal Freedom and the Futurity of God: Some Reflections on Pannenberg's 'God of Hope,'" *Reformed Review* 31 (1978): 148-154.
Johnson, Elizabeth A. "Resurrection and Reality in the Thought of Wolfhart Pannenberg," *Heythrop Journal* 24 (1983): 1-18.
————. "The Ongoing Christology of Wolfhart Pannenberg," *Horizons* 9, 2 (1982): 237-250.
————. "The Right Way to Speak about God? Pannenberg on Analogy," *Theological Studies* 43 (December 1982): 673-692.
Jüngel, Eberhard. "Das Dilemma der natürlichen Theologie und die Wahrheit ihres Problems. Überlegungen für ein Gespräch mit W. Pannenberg," in *Denken im Schatten des Nihilismus,* ed. Alexander Schwan. Darmstadt, 1975, pp. 419-440.
Kegley, Charles W. "Theology and Religious Studies: Friends or Enemies?" *Theology Today* 35 (1978): 273-284.
Kehm, G. H. "Pannenberg's Theological Program," *Perspective* 9 (1968): 245-266.

Kienzler, Klaus. *Logik der Auferstehung; eine Untersuchung zu R. Bultmann, G. Ebeling und W. Pannenberg.* Freiburg: Herder, 1976.

Klappert, Bertold. "Tendenzen der Gotteslehre in der Gegenwart," *Evangelische Theologie* 35 (1975): 189-208.

Klooster, Fred H. "Aspects of Historical Method in Pannenberg's Theology," in *Septuagesimo Anno,* Festschrift for G. C. Berkhouwer, ed. J. T. Bakker et al. Kampen, 1973, pp. 112-128.

_____. "Historical Method and the Resurrection in Pannenberg's Theology," *Calvin Theological Journal* 11 (1976): 5-33.

Knauer, P., s.j. Review of W. Pannenberg, *Wissenschaftstheorie und Theologie, Theologie und Philosophie* 49 (1974): 602-603.

Knitter, P. "What Is German Protestant Theology Saying about the Non-Christian Religions?" *Neue Zeitschrift für systematische Theologie und Religionsphilosophie* 15 (1973): 38-64.

Koch, K. "Gottes Handeln in der Geschichte und die Bestimmung des Menschen. Zur geschichtstheologischen Neuinterpretation des christlichen Erwählungsglaubens bei Wolfhart Pannenberg," *Catholica* 33 (1979): 220-239.

Konrad, Franz. *Das Offenbarungsverständnis in der evangelischen Theologie.* Munich: M. Huebner, 1971.

Kühn, Ulrich. "Die Kirche als Ort der Theologie," *Kerygma und Dogma* 31 (1985): 98-115.

Kugelmann, Lothar. *Antizipation. Eine begriffsgeschichtliche Untersuchung.* Göttingen: Vandenhoeck & Ruprecht, 1986.

Ladner, Benjamin. "Religious Studies in the University: A Critical Reappraisal," *Journal of the American Academy of Religion* 40 (1972): 207-218.

Lash, Nicholas. "Up and Down in Christology," in *New Studies in Theology,* vol. 1, ed. Stephen Sykes and Derek Homes. London, 1980, pp. 31-46.

Leuze, Reinhard. "Möglichkeiten und Grenzen einer Theologie der Religionsgeschichte," *Kerygma und Dogma* 24 (1978): 230-243.

Lönning, Per. "Zur Denkbarkeit Gottes: ein Gespräch mit Wolfhart Pannenberg und Eberhard Jüngel," *Studia Theologica* 34 (1980): 39-71.

Löser, W., s.j. Review of W. Pannenberg, *Gottesgedanke und menschliche Freiheit, Theologie und Philosophie* 49 (1974), 604-606.

Macquarrie, John. "Theologies of Hope: A Critical Examination," *Expository Times* 82 (1971): 100-105.

_____. "What Is a Human Being?" Review of W. Pannenberg, *Anthropology in Theological Perspective, Expository Times* 97 (1986): 202-203.

McCann, Dennis P. Review of W. Pannenberg, *Ethics, Journal of Religion* 66 (1986): 348-349.

McCullagh, C. B. M. "The Possibility of an Historical Basis for Christian Theology," *Theology* 74 (1971): 513-522.

McDermott, Brian. "Pannenberg's Resurrection Christology: A Critique," *Theological Studies* 35 (1974): 711-721.

McGrath, Alister E. "Christology and Soteriology: A Response to Wolfhart Pannenberg's Critique of the Soteriological Approach to Christology," *Theologische Zeitschrift* 42 (1986): 222-236.

McKenzie, David. "Pannenberg on God and Freedom," *Journal of Theology* 60 (1980): 307-329.

Michalson, Gordon E. "Pannenberg on the Resurrection and Historical Method," *Scottish Journal of Theology* 33 (1980): 345-359.

Migliore, D. L. "How Historical Is the Resurrection: A Dialogue," *Theology Today* 33 (1976): 5-14.

Milbank, John. "The Second Difference: For a Trinitarianism without Reserve," *Modern Theology* 2, 3 (April 1986): 213-234.

Miller, E. L. "Salvation-History: Pannenberg's Critique of Cullmann," *The Iliff Review* 37 (1980): 21-25.

Mudge, Lewis S. Review of W. Pannenberg, *The Church, Journal of Religion* 65 (1985): 425-426.

Muschalek, G., and Gamper, A. "Offenbarung in Geschichte," *Zeitschrift für Katholische Theologie* 86 (1964): 180-196.

Mühlenberg, Ekkehard. "Gott in der Geschichte. Erwägungen zur Geschichtstheologie von W. Pannenberg," *Kerygma und Dogma* 24 (1978): 244-261.

Neuhaus, Richard John. "History as Sacred Drama," *Worldview* 22 (1979): 23-26.

————. "Pannenberg Jousts with the World Council of Churches," *Christian Century* 99 (1982): 74-76.

Nicol, Iain G. "Facts and Meanings: Wolfhart Pannenberg's Theology as History and the Role of the Historical-Critical Method," *Religious Studies* 12 (June 1976): 129-139.

Nierth, W. "Die Differenz zwischen Theologie und Anthropologie als Kriterium fur die Adäquatheit einer Lehre vom Menschen," *Kerygma und Dogma* 22 (1976): 317-334.

Nobuhara, Tokiyuki. "Analogia Actionis: A New Proposal for Christology 'from Below,'" *Union Seminary Quarterly Review* 39 (1984): 269-285.

North, R. "Pannenberg's Historicizing Exegesis," *The Heythrop Journal* 12 (1971): 377-400.

O'Collins, G. "Revelation as History," *The Heythrop Journal* 7 (1966): 394-406.

————. "The Christology of Wolfhart Pannenberg," *Religious Studies* 3 (1967): 369-376.

Obayashi, Hiroshi. "Future and Responsibility: A Critique of Pannenberg's Eschatology," *Studies in Religion* 1 (1971): 191-203.

————. "Pannenberg and Troeltsch: History and Religion," *Journal of the American Academy of Religion* 38 (1970): 401-419.

Obitts, Stanley. "Apostolic Eyewitnesses and Proleptically Historical Revelation," in *The Living and Active Word of God,* ed. M. Inch and R. Youngblood. Winona Lake, Ind.: Eisenbrauns, 1983, pp. 137-148.

Oeing-Hanhoff, Ludger. "Hegels Trinitätslehre. Zur Aufgabe ihrer Kritik und Rezeption," *Theologie und Philosophie* 52 (1977): 378-407.

Olson, Roger E. "Pannenberg's Theological Anthropology: A Review Article," *Perspectives in Religious Studies* 13 (1986): 161-169.

_____. "The Human Self-Realization of God: Hegelian Elements in Pannenberg's Christology," *Perspectives in Religious Studies* 13 (1986): 207-223.

_____. "Trinity and Eschatology: The Historical Being of God in Jürgen Moltmann and Wolfhart Pannenberg," *Scottish Journal of Theology* 36 (1983): 213-227.

Osborn, Robert. "Pannenberg's Program," *Canadian Journal of Theology* 13 (1967): 109-122.

Owen, J. M. "A First Look at Pannenberg's Christology," *Reformed Theological Review* 25 (1966): 52-64.

_____. "Christology and History," *Reformed Theological Review* 26 (1967): 54-64.

Park, A. P. "Christian Hope according to Bultmann, Pannenberg, and Moltmann," *Westminster Theological Journal* 33 (1971): 153-174.

Parker, T. D. "Faith and History: A Review of Wolfhart Pannenberg's *Jesus—God and Man,*" *McCormick Quarterly* 22 (1968): 43-82.

Pasquariello, Ronald D. "Pannenberg's Philosophical Foundations," *Journal of Religion* 56 (1976): 338-347.

Peters, Ted. "Jesus' Resurrection: An Historical Event without Analogy," *Dialog* 12 (1973): 112-116.

_____. "The Use of Analogy in Historical Method," *The Catholic Biblical Quarterly* 35 (1973), 475-482.

_____. "Truth in History: Gadamer's Hermeneutics and Pannenberg's Apologetic Method," *Journal of Religion* 55 (1975): 36-56.

_____. "Whirlwind as Yet Unnamed," *Journal of the American Academy of Religion* 42 (1974): 699-709.

Petri, H. "Die Entdeckung der Fundamentaltheologie in der evangelischen Theologie," *Catholica* 33 (1979): 241-261.

Placher, William C. Review of W. Pannenberg, *Anthropology in Theological Perspective, Encounter* 47 (1986): 172-173.

_____. "Pannenberg on History and Revelation," *Reformed Review* 30 (1976): 39-47.

_____. "The Present Absence of Christ: Some Thoughts on Pannenberg and Moltmann," *Encounter* 40 (1979): 169-179.

Preston, R., ed. *Theology and Change.* London: SCM, 1975.

Puntel, Lorenz Bruno. "Wissenschaftstheorie und Theologie: zu W. Pannenbergs gleichnamigen Buch," *Zeitschrift für Katholische Theologie* 98 (1976): 271-292.

Queirunga, Andres Torres. "La teoria de la revelacion en W. Pannenberg," *Estudios Eclesiasticos* [Madrid] 59, 229 (1984): 139-178.

Reitz, H. "Biblical and Cosmological Theology: A Process View of Their Relatedness," *Encounter* 36 (1975): 407-432.

Rhem, Richard A. "A Theological Conception of Reality as History—Some Aspects of the Thinking of Wolfhart Pannenberg," *Reformed Review* 26 (1972): 178-188, 212-223.

Richardson, Alan. "The Resurrection of Jesus Christ," *Theology* 74 (1971): 146-154.

Ross, J. Robert. "Historical Knowledge as Basis for Faith," *Zygon* 13 (1978): 209-224.

Russell, John M. "Pannenberg on Verification in Theology: An Epistemic Response," *The Iliff Review* 43 (1986): 37-55.

Sauter, Gerhard. *Zukunft und Verheissung. Das Problem der Zukunft in der gegenwärtigen theologischen und philosophischen Diskussion.* Zurich: Zwingli Verlag, 1965.

————. "Fragestellungen der Christologie," *Verkündigung und Forschung* 11 (1966): 37-73.

————. "Überlegungen zu einem weiteren Gesprächsgang über 'Theologie und Wissenschaftstheorie,'" *Evangelische Theologie* 40 (1980): 161-168.

Scaer, David P. "Theology of Hope," *Tensions in Contemporary Theology,* ed. Stanley Gundry. Chicago: Moody, 1976.

Scharlemann, R. *The Being of God.* New York: Seabury, 1981.

Schmid, G. "Erkennen und Erwagen. Überlegungen zum Verhältnis von Religionswissenschaft und Theologie," *Zeitschrift für Religons- und Geistesgeschichte* 30 (1978): 289-305.

Schönborn, Christian. "'Aporie der Zweinaturenlehre?' Überlegungen zur Christologie von W. Pannenberg," *Freiburger Zeitschrift für Philosophie und Theologie* 24 (1977): 428-445.

Schwarzwäller, Klaus. *Theologie oder Phänomenologie.* Munich: Christian Kaiser, 1966, pp. 90-118.

Seckler, Max. "Die letzte Bestimmung des Menschen," *Lebendiges Zeugnis* (April 1973): 31-38.

Simpson, Gary M. "Whither Wolfhart Pannenberg? Reciprocity and Political Theology," *Journal of Religion* 67 (1987): 33-49.

Slenczka, R., ed. "Zur Theologie von Wolfhart Pannenberg [A Symposium]." *Kerygma und Dogma* (1978): 229-320.

Stead, Christopher. "Die Aufnahme des philosophischen Gottesbegriffes in der frühchristlichen Theologie. W. Pannenbergs These neu bedacht," *Theologische Rundschau* 51 (1986): 349-371.

Steiger, Lothar. "Offenbarungsgeschichte und theologische Vernunft. Zur Theologie W. Pannenbergs," *Zeitschrift für Theologie und Kirche* 59 (1962): 88-113.

_____. "Revelation–History and Theological Reason: A Critique of the Theology of Wolfhart Pannenberg," in *History and Hermeneutic*, vol. 4, ed. R. Funk. New York, 1967, pp. 82-106.

Stock, Konrad. "Ist die Bestimmung der Person noch offen?" Review of W. Pannenberg, *Anthropologie in theologischer Perspektive*, *Evangelische Theologie* 45, 3 (1985): 290-297.

Suhl, Alfred. "Zur Beurteilung der Überlieferung von der Auferstehung Jesu in W. Pannenbergs 'Grundzüge,'" *Neue Zeitschrift für systematische Theologie und Religionsphilosophie* 12 (1970): 294-308.

Tracy, David. Review of *Jesus—God and Man* and *Revelation as History*, *Catholic Biblical Quarterly* 31 (1969): 285-288.

_____. Review of *What Is Man?*, *Basic Questions in Theology*, and *Spirit, Faith, and Church*, *Journal of the American Academy of Religion* 39 (1971): 543-548.

Tripole, Martin R. "Philosophy and Theology: Are They Compatible? A Comparison of Barth, Moltmann and Pannenberg with Rahner," *Thought* 53 (1978): 27-54.

Tupper, E. Frank. "The Christology of Wolfhart Pannenberg," *Exegetical Review* 71 (1974): 59-73.

_____. "The Revival of Apocalyptic in Biblical and Theological Studies," *Exegetical Review* 72 (1975): 279-303.

Turner, Geoffrey. "W. Pannenberg and the Hermeneutical Problem," *Irish Theological Quarterly* 39 (1972): 107-129.

Van Hyssteen, J. W. V. "Systematic Theology and the Philosophy of Science: The Need for Methodological and Theoretical Clarity in Theology," *Journal of Theology for Southern Africa* 34 (1981): 3-16.

Venema, Cornelius P. "History, Human Freedom and the Idea of God in the Theology of Wolfhart Pannenberg," *Calvin Theological Journal* 17 (April 1982): 53-77.

Vignaus, Paul. "Sur la christologie de W. Pannenberg," in *Dieu connu en Jesus Christ*, ed. Henri Marrou. 1973, pp. 119-127.

Wagner, Falk. "Vernünftige Theologie und Theologie der Vernunft," *Kerygma und Dogma* 24 (1978): 262-284.

Walsh, Brian J. "A Critical Review of Pannenberg's *Anthropology in Theological Perspective*," *Christian Scholar's Review* 15 (1986): 247-259.

_____. "Pannenberg's Eschatological Ontology," *Christian Scholar's Review* 11 (1982): 229-249.

Weischedel, W. "Von der Fragwürdigkeit einer philosophischen Theologie," *Evangelische Theologie* 27 (1967): 113-138.

Werbick, J. "Theologie als Wissenschaft (zu Wolfhart Pannenbergs Buch

Wissenschaftstheorie und Theologie)," *Stimmen der Zeit* 99 (1974): 327-338.

West, J. Michael. "The Eclipse of Meaning: Religion and Self-Discovery in Pannenberg's Recent Thought," *Harvard Divinity Bulletin* 14, 3 (1974): 10-12.

Westphal, Merold. "Hegel, Pannenberg, and Hermeneutics," *Man and World* 4 (1971): 276-293.

White, Harvey W. "A Critique of Pannenberg's *Theology and the Philosophy of Science,"* *Studies in Religion* 11, 4 (1982): 419-436.

Wiebe, Donald. "The Failure of Nerve in the Academic Study of Religion," *Studies in Religion* 13 (1984): 401-422.

Wilken, Robert L. "Who Is Wolfhart Pannenberg?" *Dialog* 4 (1965): 140-142.

Wood, Laurence W. "History and Hermeneutics: A Pannenbergian Perspective," *Wesley Theological Journal* 16 (Spring 1981): 7-22.

Yerkes, James. "Hegel and 'the End of Days': Philosophy, Religion and Hope," *Thought* 56 (1981): 353-366.